Early Intervention and the Integration of Handicapped and Nonhandicapped Children

EARLY INTERVENTION AND THE INTEGRATION OF HANDICAPPED AND NONHANDICAPPED CHILDREN

edited by
Michael J. Guralnick, Ph.D.
Director, The Nisonger Center
The Ohio State University

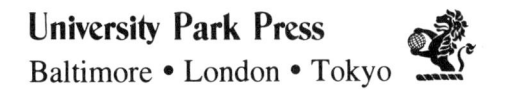

University Park Press
Baltimore • London • Tokyo

UNIVERSITY PARK PRESS
International Publishers in Science and Medicine
233 East Redwood Street
Baltimore, Maryland 21202

Copyright © 1978 by University Park Press

Typeset by The Composing Room of Michigan, Inc.
Manufactured in the United States of America by Universal Lithographers, Inc.,
and The Optic Bindery, Incorporated

All rights, including that of translation into other languages, reserved.
Photomechanical reproduction (photocopy, microcopy) of this book or parts
thereof without special permission of the publisher is prohibited.

Library of Congress Cataloging in Publication Data
Main entry under title:

Early intervention and the integration of handicapped
and nonhandicapped children.

1. Handicapped children—Education—Addresses,
essays, lectures.   I. Guralnick, Michael J.
LC4015.E27   371.9   77-11946
ISBN 0-8391-1165-7

to Dorothy and Al

CONTENTS

Contributors / ix
Preface / xi

RATIONALE AND FOUNDATIONS

A Rationale for the Integration of Handicapped and Nonhandicapped Preschool Children
 Diane D. Bricker, Ph.D. / 3
Peer Interaction and the Processes of Socialization
 Willard W. Hartup, Ed.D. / 27
A Behavioral Approach to the Analysis of Peer Interactions
 Vey Michael Nordquist, Ph.D. / 53
Strategies and Models for Early Childhood Intervention Programs in Integrated Settings
 Nicholas J. Anastasiow, Ph.D. / 85

INTEGRATED PRESCHOOL PROGRAMS: Description, Design, Evaluation, and Research

Integrated Preschools as Educational and Therapeutic Environments: Concepts, Design, and Analysis
 Michael J. Guralnick, Ph.D. / 115
Integrated Programming at the Infant, Toddler, and Preschool Levels
 Tony Apolloni, Ph.D., and Thomas P. Cooke, Ph.D. / 147
Integrating Handicapped Preschool Children Within a Cognitively Oriented Program
 Jean Ispa, Ph.D., and Robert D. Matz, Ph.D. / 167
Integrating the Moderately and Severely Handicapped Preschool Child into a Normal Day Care Setting
 H. D. Bud Fredericks, Ed.D.; Victor Baldwin, Ed.D.; David Grove, Ph.D.; William Moore, Ed.D.; Cheryl Riggs; and Barbara Lyons / 191
Integrating the Preprimary Hearing-Impaired Child: An Examination of the Process, Product, and Rationale
 Winifred H. Northcott, Ph.D. / 207
Open Education and the Integration of Children with Special Needs
 Samuel J. Meisels, Ed.D. / 239
The Marriage of Special and Generic Early Education Services
 Charles Galloway, Ph.D., and Phyllis Chandler / 261

Author Index / 289
Subject Index / 297

CONTRIBUTORS

Nicholas J. Anastasiow, Ph.D.
Director, Institute for Child Study
Indiana University
10th and By-pass 46
Bloomington, Indiana 47401
Tony Apolloni, Ph.D.
Assistant Professor of Special
 Education
Sonoma State College;
Co-Director, Human Services
 Associates
1639 Manzanita Avenue
Santa Rosa, California 95404
Victor Baldwin, Ed.D.
Director, Exceptional Child
 Research Program;
Research Professor, Teaching
 Research Division
Oregon State System of Higher
 Education
Todd Hall
Monmouth, Oregon 97361
Diane D. Bricker, Ph.D.
Associate Professor of Pediatrics and
 Educational Psychology;
Administrator, Debbie Institute
Mailman Center for Child
 Development
University of Miami
P.O. Box 520006 Biscayne Annex
Miami, Florida 33152
Phyllis Chandler
Director, Center for Children
University of Nebraska at Omaha
Box 688, Downtown Station
Omaha, Nebraska 68101
Thomas P. Cooke, Ph.D.
Coordinator of Special Education
Sonoma State College
1801 East Cotati Avenue
Rohnert Park, California 94928;
Co-director, Human Services Associates
H. D. Bud Fredericks, Ed.D.
Associate Director, Exceptional
 Child Research Program;
Research Professor, Teaching
 Research Division
Oregon State System of Higher
 Education
Todd Hall
Monmouth, Oregon 97361
Charles Galloway, Ph.D.
Director, The California Project
1455 Response Road, Suite 138
Sacramento, California 95815
David N. Grove, Ph.D.
Research Professor, Teaching
 Research Division
Oregon State System of Higher
 Education
Todd Hall
Monmouth, Oregon 97361
Michael J. Guralnick, Ph.D.
Director, The Nisonger Center
The Ohio State University
1580 Cannon Drive
Columbus, Ohio 43210
Willard W. Hartup, Ed.D.
Professor of Child Psychology;
Director, Institute of Child
 Development
University of Minnesota
51 East River Road
Minneapolis, Minnesota 55455
Jean M. Ispa, Ph.D.
Research Associate
High/Scope Educational Research
 Foundation
600 North River Street
Ypsilanti, Michigan 48197

Barbara Lyons
Instructor, Teaching Research Division
Oregon State System of Higher Education
Todd Hall
Monmouth, Oregon 97361

Robert D. Matz, Ph.D.
Research Associate
High/Scope Educational Research Foundation
600 North River Street
Ypsilanti, Michigan 48197

Samuel J. Meisels, Ed.D.
Director, Eliot-Pearson Children's School
Department of Child Study
Tufts University
Medford, Massachusetts 02155

William Moore, Ed.D.
Research Professor, Teaching Research Division
Oregon State System of Higher Education
Todd Hall
Monmouth, Oregon 97361

Vey Michael Nordquist, Ph.D.
Associate Professor of Child and Family Studies
University of Tennessee
Knoxville, Tennessee 37916

Winifred H. Northcott, Ph.D.
Associate Professor of Special Education
Mankato State University
Mankato, Minnesota 56001

Cheryl Riggs
Instructor, Teaching Research Division
Oregon State System of Higher Education
Todd Hall
Monmouth, Oregon 97361

PREFACE

This volume represents the collective efforts of professionals seeking to meet the significant challenges posed by programs that integrate handicapped and nonhandicapped preschool children. It is always difficult to establish the optimal time to step back and appraise progress and to clarify rationales in a rapidly developing area, especially in a field such as this, so characterized by exploration and change. Despite this uncertainty, this volume is offered as both an illustration of the processes and strategies employed in understanding and implementing new concepts, models, and designs as well as for the conceptual, programmatic, and empirical information it may contain.

The first section of the book orients the reader to the fundamental issues and rationale regarding integrated programs at the early childhood level.* In addition, certain psychological, developmental, and educational issues, concepts, and findings relevant to the integration process are discussed. In the first chapter, Diane Bricker presents a well reasoned rationale for establishing an integrated approach to early childhood intervention. Three lines of argument are developed to support this position. First, social-ethical arguments are presented, including the possibility of modifying the attitudes of various segments of society toward the handicapped, eliminating the harmful effects associated with the placement of children in segregated environments, and the need for a careful allocation of resources for all children. The second argument discusses the judicial and legislative forces that have provided a clear mandate for exploring integrated programs. Psychological-educational arguments form the third line of support. It is pointed out that, although firm evidence is meager at this time, it is likely that the demands and challenges found in integrated environments and in the opportunities available for observational learning from more advanced peers will benefit the handicapped child. Finally, Dr. Bricker underscores the need for a careful evaluation of the integration process.

In the second chapter, Willard Hartup analyzes and emphasizes the critical yet frequently overlooked impact of peer interactions on the development of a child's basic social and communicative skills. He urges us to consider the utilization of children in the planning of peer socialization processes in integrated early intervention programs. His discussions include the characteristics unique to peer interaction that can promote social learning and the mechanisms of peer influence. In addition, Dr. Hartup describes some recent research comparing the social behavior of preschool children in same- and mixed-age groups. These studies provide a number of significant implications for programs that integrate children at different developmental levels.

---

*Given our current knowledge base, it was decided not to create semantic restrictions for the use of the terms "mainstreaming" and "integration." The reader should tie the terminology in each chapter to the specific program descriptions and activities.

Many programs that integrate handicapped and nonhandicapped children utilize behavioral procedures in one form or another. Vey Michael Nordquist provides us with a review of the behavioral literature focusing on behavioral techniques that have been successfully used to develop and maintain peer interactions. His discussions include the effects of peer and teacher attention, peer modeling, and the role of physical and spatial features of the environment. Dr. Nordquist also alerts us to the fact that the durability and generalizability of behavior changes using these methods remains to be established and that our understanding of the multiple effects of behavioral procedures is very limited. Nevertheless, the behavioral approach is presented as an important means of promoting positive interactions among handicapped and nonhandicapped children.

Effective early childhood intervention programs, whether or not they are integrated, tend to be conducted within an identifiable educational or developmental framework. A program's theoretical base and corresponding educational activities are likely to place limits on its ability to provide an effective integrated program. Nicholas Anastasiow, in the final chapter of this section, places this issue in perspective. He describes four basic types of model preschool programs serving handicapped children—normal developmental, behavioral, cognitive developmental, and cognitive learning—and analyzes each along a variety of dimensions. An in-depth view of each model is then presented by Dr. Anastasiow and analyzed according to its potential for effectively integrating handicapped and nonhandicapped children. Most of these models or variations of them are represented in the programs described in the second section of this book.

This second section contains a more detailed description of individual programs, their design, evaluation, and corresponding research. In its own way, each program is grappling with basic issues and exploring particular areas of interest. The diversity of approaches, the different characteristics of the children in the programs, and the varying emphases and interests of the contributors presented in this section, although perhaps disconcerting to some, probably accurately reflect the processes involved in attempting to achieve conceptual, philosophical, and empirical clarity in this complex area. New problems tend to generate a process approach, whereby systematic observations, probes, and experimental manipulations of variables on a limited scale are carried out within the context of a developing model or program. At this stage, no attempt is made to generalize the outcomes or program successes much beyond the parameters of one's own program. Rather, the primary emphasis is to establish a coherent and feasible model, containing a high degree of logical and face validity, and to begin to identify the critical dimensions and variables that affect the success of integrated programs.

As will be seen in the chapters in this section, success has tended to be defined along different dimensions and at various levels. First, and most significant, an integrated program is considered successful if it has the ability to meet the developmental needs of all children in the setting, without radically departing from the fundamental assumptions and structure of the program's model. In other words, the program is feasible. Measurement usually includes the use of standardized instruments and direct observations of, for example, social play behavior, to reflect the child's growth in key developmental areas. Consideration of a second level of success is evident in efforts to establish the nature of the benefits received by handicapped children that can be directly linked to their involvement with children at different developmental levels. For example, these potential benefits may include documentation that access by handicapped children to more appropriate opportunities for observational learning found in integrated settings has developmental significance, that positive social interactions among children at different developmental levels do occur and that these have a favorable effect on social growth, or that the availability of nonhandicapped children to assist teachers as agents of change is an important educational strategy. In addition, other measures, although less frequently used at this time, include satisfaction of parents, later school adjustment, and immediate and long-term changes in attitudes. The seven chapters in the second section of the book address these and other issues.

In my own chapter, a detailed argument is presented to support the notion that well designed integrated programs provide a significant, independent, positive contribution to the development of the handicapped child. The first portion of the chapter describes an integrated program for a diverse group of children and discusses the principles, concepts, and techniques that guided its design. Next, it reviews a series of experiments describing the role of advanced peers in promoting the social, play, and language development of handicapped children. The final section analyzes the extensive developmental opportunities available to handicapped children that are unique to integrated settings, and summarizes the strategies and guidelines helpful in ensuring productive interactions among children at different developmental levels.

The potential educational value of imitation, in particular the imitation of nonhandicapped children by handicapped children in integrated settings, is a key issue addressed in the chapter by Tony Apolloni and Thomas Cooke. These authors describe an experimental procedure, referred to as "peer imitation training," in which peers are directly trained to imitate one another. The effects of this procedure are systematically evaluated, and both stimulus and response generalization are assessed. In addition, Drs. Apolloni and Cooke present a series of recommendations for both educators and researchers relating to the design of effective educational programs in integrated settings.

Jean Ispa and Robert Matz describe a cognitively oriented program (cognitive developmental) suggesting that the assumptions of the model and corresponding educational activities are appropriate for and can effectively accommodate handicapped children. This proposition is clearly supported in their report of the results of a multidimensional observational study of their integrated classrooms. Their analysis indicated that virtually all children were socially well integrated and that nearly equivalent gains in development were achieved by both the handicapped and nonhandicapped groups.

The next two chapters focus on integration issues for two identifiable populations of children. First, Bud Fredericks and his colleagues address questions relating to the feasibility and value of integrating severely and moderately handicapped children into a normal day care setting. Measuring both social and language behaviors, they demonstrated that handicapped children can derive substantial and often generalizable gains from participation in an integrated setting. Nevertheless, the authors caution that in order to achieve these benefits a systematic arrangement of activities, extensive staff training, and additional supportive services are required.

Next, Winifred Northcott presents a forceful series of arguments to support the value of integrating the preprimary hearing-impaired child. A comprehensive model program offering a wide variety of alternatives through a continuum of services carried out within the public school system is described. This model emphasizes the initial use of the auditory/oral method of communication and underscores the central role of parents at all levels of the educational process. Dr. Northcott also reviews a number of follow-up studies analyzing the later educational placements of hearing-impaired children, their social status in regular classrooms, and their academic progress.

In the chapter that follows, Samuel Meisels describes the rationale, goals, and elements of open structure classrooms and outlines the value of this model in supporting the development of the handicapped child. Dr. Meisels presents a description of an integrated program based on this model, its structural and organizational aspects, the teaching process, and the environmental design. The final section of the chapter contains two case illustrations of individualized programs for handicapped children carried out in the open classroom.

Designing and implementing an integrated program within a laboratory school, research, or model demonstration center presents a somewhat different perspective than that encountered when establishing community-based programs on a relatively wide scale. In the final chapter, Charles Galloway and Phyllis Chandler provide important insights to the development of integrated early education programs within the larger community. They describe the philosophical base and goals of the ENCOR model, the questions raised, the decisions made, and the strategies employed during the course of the model's development and implementation. Also discussed are the various program elements, staffing patterns, desired staff competencies, and the programmatic options available to the children. In the final section of the chapter, Dr. Galloway and Ms. Chandler analyze developmental profiles and direct observation data and discuss a number of conditions that need to be established to ensure the effectiveness of community-wide integrated programs.

I wish to thank the authors who contributed to this volume for their diligent work to meet the schedules of others. Finally, a very special debt of gratitude is owed to Vivian Ottenberg for her invaluable technical assistance and optimism throughout the editing of this book.

Early Intervention and the Integration of Handicapped and Nonhandicapped Children

RATIONALE AND FOUNDATIONS

A RATIONALE FOR THE INTEGRATION OF HANDICAPPED AND NONHANDICAPPED PRESCHOOL CHILDREN

Diane D. Bricker, Ph.D.

Over the course of our history, the prevailing social philosophy of this country has been shifting from providing educational programs for a select group of children to the gradual inclusion of all the nation's young—rich and poor, normal and handicapped. Recent state and federal legislative enactments have been providing impetus for the inclusion of the even more severely impaired by mandating the establishment of educational services for all school-age children. Furthermore, the development of programs for the preschool handicapped child has been gaining momentum since the early 1970s (Haring, 1974). The creation of educational programs to accommodate previously excluded handicapped children has presented the educator with complex problems that have produced significant challenges.

Expansion of public education programs to include preschool handicapped children and more severely impaired children argues for the development and implementation of innovative programs. Intelligent innovation would seem to depend upon the careful evaluation of past educational successes and failures. Without knowledge of previous educational ventures, current efforts might replicate past failures and, in so doing, waste valuable time and effort. Surely, the sensible approach is to glean from the literature information that suggests viable alternatives rather than to implement ideas already demonstrated to be ineffective (Bricker, 1970).

To be sure, an almost infinite number of alternatives or variations on current educational practice is possible; however, because resources are limited, thoughtful selection of the alternatives to be pursued is essential. The systematic and careful integration of handicapped and nonhandicapped preschool children into the same classroom setting is one potentially useful alternative to the current educational practice of segregating disabled children into isolated programs. This chapter presents a rationale for why the examination of an integrated approach to early childhood intervention is worthy of consideration and, therefore, provides a justification for committing resources to such a model. Tentative but hopeful signs are appearing in the literature to suggest that educational benefits can result from the exposure of handicapped children to more normal environments.

The development of the rationale for considering the integration of preschool handicapped and nonhandicapped children in this chapter has been somewhat arbitrarily divided into three areas for argument: social-ethical, legal-legislative, and psychological-educational. The social-ethical arguments are developed from a discussion of the social implications of segregating handicapped children, the most effective use of limited educational resources, and the societal attitudes held toward the disabled individual in our society. The legal-legislative arguments are based on decisions reached in relevant judicial litigation as well as recent state and federal statutes mandating modification of current educational practice. The final set of arguments is categorized as psychological-educational and deals specifically with developmental theory, imitation learning, and a description of the few projects appearing in the literature that have reported success in combining preschool handicapped and nonhandicapped children. The fact that several projects have already implemented this approach apparently with positive results may be the most persuasive argument for the continued experimentation and evaluation of integrating handicapped and nonhandicapped preschool children.

SOCIAL-ETHICAL ARGUMENTS

Education is one of the primary mechanisms for the transfer of social values from generation to generation; therefore, it seems appropriate that social-ethical considerations form the basis for the first arguments for exploring the educational integration of handicapped and nonhandicapped preschool children. Arguments based on social considerations depend heavily upon established social values which may be difficult to articulate and defend from an empirical perspective.

> Human beings first act according to what we later call moral codes, that are describable by sociological laws. They then act from those laws... but these laws invariably change the behavior of those who act from them. Finally, they

change these rules, not on the basis of what their environment is, but on the basis of what they believe is best (Garner and Rosen, 1967, p. 17).

Eschew this state of affairs as one might, the lack of appropriate tools and methodologies in education limits one's ability to provide empirical support for choosing one educational procedure over another (Reese and Lipsitt, 1970). For example, to compare the effects of different intervention strategies, one must control relevant variables (i.e., teacher's training, school setting, peer influence, children's past history, curriculum), a necessary but almost impossible task. The fields of psychology, sociology, and education lack appropriate instruments to examine the longitudinal effects of intervention on all but a few variables (e.g., academic achievement). Procedures to isolate and measure the multitude of childhood variables that interact to produce healthy, productive, adaptive adults still elude the social scientist. Given this set of circumstances, many decisions concerning educational practice must be arrived at through value judgments rather than empirically based judgments.

In considering social-ethical arguments for integration, three major issues emerge: (1) the possibility of altering societal attitudes toward the handicapped child through integration, (2) the deleterious effects on the handicapped child of segregation into separate educational programs, and (3) the efficient allocation of resources for the handicapped and nonhandicapped child through integrated programs. These topics are discussed with the intent of providing part of the rationale for the integration of the preschool handicapped and nonhandicapped child.

Attitudes Toward the Handicapped Child

Attitudes refer to a nebulous construct covering that aspect of human behavior which has a critical influence on our verbal behavior and actions but often eludes our attempts at description and documentation. How parents, peers, and community members respond to the handicapped individual seems largely to be a function of the prevalent attitude adopted by a society toward its atypical or deviant member (Rhodes and Sagor, 1975). Any species, human or otherwise, can produce offspring that are atypical or different and can be defined by the society as deviant. That is, deviancy is determined by societal definition, and the treatment of the "deviant" (in this case the handicapped child) is colored by the predominate societal attitude held toward that particular form of defined deviancy (Bartel and Guskin, 1971). For example, if mental retardation were defined as an acceptable condition in this society, then moves to eliminate (eugenics), exclude (institutionalization), and isolate (special classes) would never have become acceptable forms of treatment (Sarason and Doris, 1969).

Improvements in the attitudes of society toward the handicapped individual have occurred, but as the President's Committee on Mental Retardation (1976) points out "... the task of public enlightenment is far from finished." The careful inclusion of the "different" child in community-based school programs may provide the exposure and experience that will lead to the development of more positive attitudes by the public. Although empirical support of this position is limited and conflicting, Sheare (1974) conducted an investigation which found that "... integration of EMR students into regular classes and social/recreational activities will, in and of itself, result in more positive ratings of EMR children by nonretarded children" (p. 681). If "more positive ratings" can be equated with more positive attitudes, then the integration of handicapped and nonhandicapped children may have the potential for shifting favorable societal attitudes toward the "deviant" child.

Another powerful argument for including handicapped with nonhandicapped children is based on our knowledge about the effects of peer interaction on attitude change. The importance of peer interaction is an accepted phenomenon.

> ... direct reinforcement from peers is a potent form of social influence during childhood. The effects of such social influence are evident in very early childhood (Hartup, 1970, p. 429).

Apolloni and Cooke (1975) extended this position to argue that peer play or interaction may be essential to the normal growth and development of the young child. It seems agreed that peer interaction is both necessary for and has the potential of influencing a child's behavior and attitudes; however, peer interaction can have an influence only when children are given the opportunity to observe and have contact with one another. For normally developing children to gain knowledge about and tolerance for varying handicapping conditions, they probably need the chance for direct interaction. Providing such opportunities at the preschool level would seem appropriate.

Of equal importance to the peer's view of the handicapped child is the child's view of himself as a handicapped person. Conflicting evidence exists regarding a child's self-image based on placement in a regular or special class (Guskin, Bartel, and MacMillan, 1975). The ambiguous results of the effects of integration might be a reflection of ill-prepared and poorly executed integration efforts which left the teachers, the handicapped, and the nonhandicapped uncertain and uneasy. A child's attitude about himself might be enhanced by placement with nonhandicapped children, as long as the placement was predicated on relevant variables such as developmental level rather than chronological age. More vigorous research into this important question is needed.

Another factor to consider is the effect of societal attitudes on the parents of handicapped children.

> Society does not view their (the parents') children as worthy of investment; in fact, it disdains those with certain handicaps. The parent, in turn, feels devalued and often *is* as he proceeds about the business of looking for help for this child (Gorham et al., 1975, pp. 154-155).

The bitterness felt by parents of handicapped children is reflected in the following observation:

> A lack of money is not really the obstacle that keeps children from reaching their potential. The real obstacle may be the average man's unwillingness to spend it on persons who are "different" (Gorham et al., 1975, p. 156).

Surely, perceiving the attitudes of the "average person" as negative may lead parents to develop negative attitudes toward their own child. The opportunity to place a handicapped child in a more typical environment may do much to provide support for a parent both in personal and broad social terms.

One additional target for which integration may have a positive impact on attitude change is the parent of the "normal" child in an integrated classroom. Over a period of four years an experimental early intervention project was conducted at Peabody College (Bricker and Bricker, 1971, 1972, 1973, 1976). In this project handicapped and nonhandicapped preschool children were educated in the same classrooms. When the project began, it was difficult to find parents who were willing to place their normally developing youngsters in a program with retarded toddlers. After a surprisingly successful first year, recruitment of nonhandicapped children for the second year was accomplished with relative ease. By the end of the second year a waiting list became necessary because of requests for placement in the program. It seems a reasonable assumption that the attitudes of some members of the Nashville community toward handicapped children had been changed and perhaps enhanced as a result of the project. In fact, conversations with parents gave the staff the impression that parents of the nonhandicapped children had become advocates for the handicapped children.

Legal, legislative, and social pressures appear to have converged in the 1970s to produce a climate that is now ripe for shifting attitudes about handicapped children and their educational potential. Major changes are underway in terms of education, and the success of such changes may be largely a function of the surrounding attitudes or climate in which they are tried. Educators and concerned parents can offer alternatives, but unless such changes are accompanied by appropriate attitude shifts by the general population, the chances of success will be minimal. Integration may be the kind of educational alternative that may facilitate such necessary attitudinal shifts.

Segregation of the Handicapped Child

The second topic to be discussed under social-ethical arguments concerns the effect of educational isolation on the handicapped child. Historically, to provide appropriate schooling for the handicapped child, professionals, parents, and interested community members made concerted efforts to build separate, distinct programs for the visually impaired, hearing impaired, emotionally disturbed, speech impaired, retarded, and learning-disabled child (Robinson and Robinson, 1976). Until recently, most children with moderate to severe handicapping conditions were segregated into large residential facilities for the blind, deaf, emotionally disturbed, and mentally retarded. In the opinion of many writers, the only successful aspect of the large residential facility has been its ability to exclude its residents from the rest of society. The harm produced by the incarceration of children has been documented in painful detail (Blatt, 1966).

Although the use of self-contained schools and classes seems on the surface more humane, the effect of segregation may be similar although less dramatic. This last statement lacks sufficient objective documentation, and some individuals genuinely believe that placement in special segregated facilities serves the best interest of the handicapped child. The creation of special education programs was based on the assumption that handicapped children need special and therefore *separate* services. It should be emphasized that most educators still believe that handicapped children need special services; it is the separate nature of such services that is being challenged (Dunn, 1968; Lilly, 1970). In fact, recently this challenge has been extended to question whether the more severely handicapped child could not benefit also from exposure to more "normal" environments (Sontag, 1976).

The practice of placing handicapped children in separate programs has raised the related issue of labeling. As Hobbs (1975) has pointed out, labeling individuals is inevitable and only the romantic in our society believes that some form of labeling is not going to exist. Furthermore, the use of labels is not inherently bad. But we must confront the fact that the nature of the label takes on substantial importance, particularly as it influences the child's surrounding environment. Neutral or positive labels appear to be useful, while labels construed by society to be negative (i.e., retarded, disturbed, crippled) may produce undesirable side effects (Edgerton, 1967). Although some investigators have attempted to study the effects of labeling children (Rosenthal and Jacobson, 1968), the results are compromised because of methodological problems (Thorndike, 1968). We seem to be faced with making decisions about whether to use labels based on value-laden considerations once again. MacMillan, Jones, and Aloia (1974) argue that ". . . the burden of proof lies with those who advocate the use of labels to demonstrate that the categorization demonstrably benefits the individual. . ." (p. 241). Arguments can be mustered to defend both sides of the labeling issue; but until substantial evidence can be assembled to support the educational usefulness of labeling children according to their disability, the safest and, therefore, the most ethical practice may be to reduce the use of labels to a minimum.

Caution would appear to be critical particularly when applying labels to the young child. The inability of diagnosticians to predict future performance of the young child based on the child's current repertoire is not encouraging. Even the most sophisticated instrumentation available, the individual intelligence test, is almost useless as a predictor of future IQ when applied to all but the most severely handicapped child under two years of age (McCall, Hogarty, and Hurlburt, 1972). Investigators apparently fare even less well when attempting to predict future social-vocational performance. Thus, we may be faced with a situation of using instruments that are not particularly valid to label and categorize young children. The integration of the young handicapped child with nonhandicapped peers may serve to keep the use of "negative" labels to a minimum by not shunting the child off to a special classroom for children with special problems. The restricted use of potentially debilitating labels may, at least, reduce the probability of interfering with the child's growth even if it does not, in fact, facilitate progress.

A final concern in segregating handicapped children from their normal counterparts has been discussed by Martin (1976):

> Our present thinking about education for handicapped and nonhandicapped children may be based on two false assumptions: A) that handicapped children are a small discrete population, not central to the schools' concerns, and B) that the learning problems they present are unique and not relevant to regular education (p. 5).

Martin's point is that generally one cannot sort children into neat categories of handicapped and nonhandicapped—that children fall along a continuum of development that differs according to the specific skill being considered.

Again it appears valid to raise the ethical issue of segregating children into groups based on one aspect of the child's physiology (e.g., hearing impaired) or behavior (e.g., aggressive). The placement of a child into a program for a specific disability may ignore many other important aspects of the individual that fall entirely within "normal" limits. Who among us can boast of having no deficiencies or disabilities? Had our culture emphasized different values for physiological or behavioral traits many of us might have received the label "abnormal." Many young, handicapped children can function normally along many behavioral dimensions, and placement into separate programs may have the unfortunate result of emphasizing atypical aspects of a child's behavior to the exclusion of his or her strengths. Developmentally integrated programs may provide each child with opportunities to use and expand "normal" aspects of his or her behavioral repertoire while working on the remediation of deficit areas.

Efficient and Effective Allocation of Resources for Both Handicapped and Nonhandicapped Children

The final topic to be discussed in this section on social-ethical arguments is the appropriate and efficient use of resources in the education of the handicapped child. The National Advisory Committee on the Handicapped (Education of the Handicapped Today, 1976) has indicated that this country has eight million children who can be legitimately classified as handicapped. Although there has been a steady increase in the delivery of services to this population, an estimated four million children still are either unserved or receiving inadequate services (Education of the Handicapped Today, 1976). As discussed later, recent legislation and judicial decrees are providing strong impetus for developing programs to serve the previously neglected profoundly handicapped child and the preschool handicapped child.

To meet the educational problems of the handicapped child appropriately, the use of multiple resources appears to be necessary; however, the nation has a specified allocation of resources that must be invested across a wide range of needs generated by a complex society. Educational resources at the local, state, and federal level are limited. Therefore, thoughtful analysis needs to precede the distribution of the materials and personnel that have been allocated for the education of the nation's young.

The thoughtful integration of handicapped and nonhandicapped preschoolers may be one mechanism for more efficient use of our resources to provide children with better educational programs. But such a strategy is the subject of considerable debate. At a recent conference on mainstreaming, Scriven (1976) indicated that we run the risk "... of finding ourselves on that expensive legal pendulum again" (p. 67). That is, without careful programming and evaluation, the rights of more able children may be violated by placing less able children into the same program.

> ... we are valuing the achievement of certain basic skills and a certain degree of social acceptability as a true right for all who can possibly attain them, even if the cost to others is high. We are arguing, implicitly, that the marginal value to the successful student of individualized attention and "honors programs," for example, is much less than it is to the "unsuccessful student" (Scriven, 1976, p. 67).

Scriven's recommendation for careful study of the mixing of handicapped and nonhandicapped children before wholesale implementation deserves attention. Caution must be exercised when implementing new procedures, or else we may find that in the attempt to protect and better educate one group of children the rights of other children have been violated. Should this occur, the nation's most valuable resource, its children, will not have been well used or well served. The essential point in Scriven's argument is not that we should inhibit the development of new procedures but that we must guarantee that mechanisms are established to ensure that no child's rights are violated.

The thoughtful integration of the handicapped and nonhandicapped child may be a strategy that will ultimately assist in changing societal attitudes toward the handicapped child, modifying the handicapped child's self-perceptions, eliminating deleterious effects of segregation, and developing more effective use of the nation's educational resources. Exposure early in life to a handicapped child in an integrated setting may allay many of the fears of peers, parents, and the community in general that form the basis of intolerance and impede progress toward the normalization of the handicapped individual.

LEGAL-LEGISLATIVE ARGUMENTS

Legal and legislative decisions form the basis for a second set of major arguments that make urgent the need for serious investigation of new strategies for the education of handicapped children. Legal mandates which have evolved from court decisions and legislative acts that appear to be producing the most significant pressure for change are: (1) the right of all handicapped children to a free public education, (2) the right of all handicapped children to educational placement in the least restrictive yet productive educational setting, and (3) a guarantee of due process for parents concerning educational decisions relevant to their child through the establishment of specific review procedures.

Court Decisions

The scope of this chapter precludes a lengthy discussion on law and the handicapped individual, but several comprehensive reviews are readily available (Cohen and DeYoung, 1973). However, a brief review of selected court cases that have had a significant impact on the educational rights of the handicapped citizen will provide the necessary background for further discussion.

Two court cases that have set precedents for some of the more pertinent recent judicial decisions were *Hobsen v. Hansen* and *Brown v. the Board of Education*. The decisions resulting from these litigations indicated that separate education, whether in different facilities as in the Brown case or in separate tracks in the same school as in the Hobsen case, is a violation of the constitutional rights of the individual placed in such segregated settings. In *Wyatt v. Stickney* it was ruled that the state must provide adequate treatment for individuals incarcerated in state residential facilities; the decision has indirect implications for the handicapped in that it established the right to treatment. A series of more recent suits have had more direct relevance for the handicapped. *The Pennsylvania Association for Retarded Citizens (PARC) v. the Commonwealth of Pennsylvania* ensured the right to a free public education for a group of previously excluded retarded children. In this agreement, the state acknowledged the right of all children to a free public education, and agreed to provide this education in the least restrictive environment and to guarantee due process procedures for parents. This was a landmark agreement with incalculable impact on the future education of the handicapped. The *Mills v. the District of Columbia* decision closely paralleled the PARC decision but additionally ruled that lack of funds is not an acceptable excuse for excluding handicapped children from the public schools. Thus, through a series of judicial decrees, all handicapped children have been given legal access to a free and equal public education.

Legislative Enactments

According to the National Advisory Committee on the Handicapped (Education of the Handicapped Today, 1976), all but two states have legislative statutes that make public education for the handicapped mandatory; however, the timelines for implementation extend well into the future for many states. Although legislative acts differ across states, the basic intent of these various pieces of legislation is the inclusion of all school-age children, regardless of degree of impairment, into the domain of public education.

The importance of this state legislation is bolstered by the new federal Education for All Handicapped Children Act (Public Law 94-142). This document must be considered landmark legislation for the handicapped child and may be of major significance for the normal youngster as well. A synopsis of Public Law 94-142 has been presented elsewhere by Goodman (1976) and only the most significant aspects of this legislation are highlighted here. First, by fiscal year 1978, all handicapped children between the ages of three and eighteen years are to have access to public education. Second, in order to ensure that every child has an opportunity to an appropriate education, an individual written plan will be developed cooperatively by the school, parents, and the child when possible. Third, handicapped children will be educated in the same setting with nonhandicapped children when possible and always placed in the least restrictive, yet appropriate, environment. Fourth, methods used to evaluate children will take into account the child's cultural background, primary language, and past history. Fifth, a priority of this legislation is to set up a mechanism to locate all eligible children currently not receiving services and to target the development of appropriate public education programs for these youngsters. Sixth, parents will be notified in advance when educational decisions are to be made about their child and will have an opportunity to institute a formal review of decisions which they feel are inappropriate. Seventh, procedures will be developed to ensure that due process has been established. Eighth, because this legislation will have a significant impact on current public school practices, special training will be provided for teachers and professional staff to become conversant with new educational practices and materials. A final point emphasized in the legislation is the need to reduce architectural barriers in public school facilities.

The comprehensive regulations proposed in P.L. 94-142, recent court decisions, and state statutes broadening the handicapped child's access to the educational programs indicate that:

> the basic machinery would seem to be in place for propelling education of the handicapped into a new era. The handicapped person's right to a good education is now guaranteed, and though lamentably often there has been a serious difference between actual practice and what State and Federal laws supposedly require, there is now at least a firm foundation on which to build (Education of the Handicapped Today, 1976, p. 3).

Differences Between Rights and Practice Specifically, what are some of the "lamentable" differences between the handicapped child's guaranteed rights and actual practice? Kirp, Kuriloff, and Buss (1975) have written an extensive analysis of two of the court decisions discussed above, the PARC and Mills suits. Their analysis reveals some of the problems that have surfaced when attempting to implement court decisions and legislative acts. For example, in the PARC decision the state of Pennsylvania agreed to provide an appropriate public school education to all school-age children. In order to accomplish such a directive, children had to be located, teachers hired, classroom facilities established, and, more importantly, relevant individual educational plans devised and implemented. Such massive shifts in a state's educational system understandably can take years to accomplish no matter how firm the court decision and how good the intentions of public school officials. According to Kirp, Kuriloff, and Buss (1975), implementation of the *Mills v. the District of Columbia* decision has been even less successful. The Washington, D.C., school system apparently has difficulty providing adequate schooling for even the nonhandicapped population. Such conditions must hinder the development of programs for the handicapped child, even when public school officials attempt to implement court directives. Analysis of the impact of the *Mills* decision has been difficult because "The court decree made no provision for data keeping or for reporting to the court, the welfare-rights group, plaintiffs' attorneys or the public" (Kirp, Kuriloff, and Buss, 1975, p. 352). Fortunately, the PARC decision provided several mechanisms for monitoring progress which have provided useful information. The Kirp, Kuriloff, and Buss (1975) analysis clearly suggests that the hiatus between judicial decree and subsequent implementation may be significant.

The new federal Education for All Handicapped Children Act has a system for monitoring progress toward established goals in which state officials have the responsibility for monitoring practices at the local level, and the United States Commissioner of Education is, in turn, responsible for monitoring compliance at the state level. Whether such a system will prove workable will depend, in part, on the mechanics of the monitoring system and the dedication of the personnel involved in implementing the system.

Implications for Educational Strategies Now that we have both the judicial and legislative support necessary to educate all our children and to carry out that education in the least restrictive environment possible, what are the specific implications for providing new educational strategies such as the integration of handicapped and nonhandicapped children?

From this writer's perspective, the legislative and litigative acts discussed here provide a basis for strong arguments for exploring the integration of handicapped and nonhandicapped preschoolers. For example, at both the judicial and legislative level there is a mandate for placement of the handicapped child into the most "normal" environment. For many mildly and moderately impaired children this means placement in intervention programs that include normally developing youngsters. For other preschoolers for whom total integration is unfeasible, it may mean that they are routinely integrated into portions of a program that include normally developing children as well. Another argument for integration can be based on the priority for placement of all unserved children into educational programs. The inclusion of these unserved children (estimated to be about one million) into current programs will produce the need for conserving resources. In spite of increasingly generous amounts of money spent by the government on education, resources are limited and must be used most efficiently. The integration of handicapped children into programs with nonhandicapped children may be a possible strategy for using available resources effectively. Of course, as Scriven (1976) has pointed out, if integration leads to lack of productivity by the normal or above average youngster, the resources are not being effectively used and the apparent economic advantage is only an illusion.

Implications of Recent Laws As mentioned above, P.L. 94-142 advocates the enlightened practice of writing individual intervention plans designed to meet the unique needs of each child. In an integrated program, it would seem possible that both handicapped and nonhandicapped children would be the fortunate recipients of sound planning. The second implication centers on due process. The possibility exists that nonhandicapped children are subjected to inappropriate evaluations, settings, and personnel. As parents of handicapped children learn to exercise their rights to question the educational decisions made about their children, perhaps concerned parents of nonhandicapped children will perceive and employ similar strategies to become active participants in decisions about their children. Parental involvement should be welcomed by all public school personnel as an opportunity to build toward increasing accountability (Abeson, Bolick, and Hass, 1975). In summary, any aspect of the court decisions and legislative action discussed above that encourages sound educational practice for a handicapped population has the potential of improving the entire public school system (Kirp, Kuriloff, and Buss, 1975).

This section has attempted to provide a rationale for the integration of handicapped and nonhandicapped children based on legislative and judicial decisions. The inevitable conclusion of these recent actions is that social change with educational implications is upon us:

> We cannot arrest these changes until such time as research catches up, but we might note that research should at least follow on the heels of the changes that are taking place and should thereby provide better information with which to direct future change (Edgerton, Eyman, and Silverstein, 1975, p. 79).

Equally important to note is that change cannot always await systematic verification to mold attitudes toward tolerance and acceptance. Legal or legislative activity alone cannot produce progress if the individuals implementing such suggested changes fail for any reason to facilitate the "intent" of providing equal educational opportunity to all children. Legal mandates provide the groundwork, but continued efforts by parents and educators are needed to ensure that the spirit as well as the letter of the law is followed.

PSYCHOLOGICAL-EDUCATIONAL ARGUMENTS

Psychological-educational considerations provide a final basis for the developing rationale for considering the integration of handicapped and nonhandicapped preschool children. With little empirical evidence available to support, or for that matter oppose, the use of educational or developmental groupings, this educational rationale has been developed from relevant developmental theory, selected literature on imitation learning, and a few educational programs described in the literature that have adopted an integrative strategy.

Developmental Approach to Early Childhood Education

A growing number of individuals are coming to accept Piaget's position that more complex linguistic and cognitive skills are based on the acquisition of simpler sensorimotor responses (Bricker and Bricker, 1976; Miller and Yoder, 1974). Most infants come equipped with reflexes triggered by certain environmental events. As the child's reflexive behavior interacts with the environment, broadly defined, control of the infant's motor responses gradually shifts from involuntary to voluntary activation. As the infant attempts to suck, mouth, grasp, track, locate, touch, or kick objects, the number of action schemes and control over those schemes gradually increase. Simple action schemes, through subsequent environmental interactions, are modified and develop into more complex response forms. The interaction between existing schemes or action patterns in the child's repertoire and greater environmental demands leads to progressively more mature behavior.

In such a theory of development two key concepts need elaboration for the purpose of this chapter. First, change in the repertoire of the young child is predicated on action; and second, for growth, environmental demands must gradually increase. If the infant's repertoire is to change, behavior must be produced that has the potential of being modified by the environment. For example, the initial grasp response produced by the infant appears to be crude and the contact made with objects occurs almost by chance. As the infant exercises the grasping scheme, the hand and arm movements become more coordinated and better directed toward making contact with the environment. Through further interaction between the infant and the environment, the grasping scheme develops into an effective tool for retrieving and examining desired objects. For the young child's sensorimotor schemes to develop, it seems essential that the child be actively engaged in exploring his environment and that the environment gradually exert more complex demands on the child's repertoire (Bricker et al., 1976).

If interaction with a progressively more demanding environment is important for the "normal" child, it is equally essential for the impaired child. Unfortunately, the young impaired child may not be as actively involved with the environment for a variety of reasons. First, a motor disability may exist that precludes or interferes with the development of some basic action schemes, or the child may have a sensory deficit that reduces environmental stimulation. Second, many retarded infants appear relatively lethargic or unresponsive. Without encouragement these infants may not explore their environment. Third, some handicapped children are maintained in relatively isolated settings. Parents may be reluctant to take the child out or have others into their home. Exposure to other children and adults and to different environments may be severely restricted and, therefore, the child's opportunity to view and explore other settings or individuals is limited. Such circumstances may have the effect of depressing already lagging developmental growth.

Many parents are greatly disturbed by the discovery that their baby is handicapped. The emotional responses generated may further serve to interfere with the child's already delayed or atypical development. Some parents compensate for their child's deficit by responding for the child, which in fact gives the child less opportunity to exercise schemes and receive environmental feedback. Many times we confront parents who carry their handicapped child who can walk, feed the child who is capable of self-feeding, activate toys the child should be learning to manipulate, permit inappropriate social responses that are in no way tied to the handicap, and generally are so solicitous that the youngster has little opportunity to act on his or her environment. In such circumstances, one can hypothesize that the result will be a child with little motivation for becoming independent. Conditions that inhibit the acquisition of action schemes in the young child should never be allowed to persist.

Integrating handicapped and nonhandicapped children has the potential to create a more demanding environment for the handicapped child, an environment that may assist in the continued development of the child's behavioral repertoire. It is possible that when young impaired and normal preschoolers are grouped together, teachers and parents may develop more realistic expectations about what the handicapped child should be attempting to do. Furthermore, such an environment would be "naturally" more demanding simply because of the presence of the normally developing child. Not only may the physical environment be filled with more interesting objects and persons, but the nonhandicapped peers may expect and encourage behavior that would produce significant changes in the handicapped child's repertoire. Hypotheses such as these are exciting, but empirical verification prior to broad implementation is essential.

Imitation Learning

An interpretation of the literature on imitation learning by children suggests an additional reason for the integration of handicapped and nonhandicapped preschoolers. As a learning mechanism, or as a developing strategy, imitation is not fully understood; nonetheless, the effects produced by observational learning have been clearly documented (Parton, 1976). Observations of a model have produced behavioral changes across a widely disparate range, from reducing overt fear responses (Bandura, Grusec, and Menlove, 1967) to increasing appropriate behavior (Guess et al., 1968) and, perhaps more importantly, learning to apply "rules or rule structures" (Zimmerman and Rosenthal, 1974).

Imitation has been defined as, ". . . any response, molecular or molar, which resembles previously observed behavior and occurs as a result of that prior observation" (Parton, 1976, p. 14). In discussing imitation learning, Parton (1976) makes an important distinction between learning *to* imitate (i.e., how one acquires the capacity to duplicate a specific behavior pattern previously seen or heard) and learning *by* imitation (i.e., duplicating a model's performance by the production of similar behavior through the use of behavior already in the child's repertoire). It is this latter mechanism, learning by imitation, that concerns us when discussing the possible benefits of including handicapped children in programs with "normally" developing youngsters.

Little doubt exists that young children can learn to produce a behavior by observing the actions of other individuals; however, this relatively straightforward statement must be qualified:

> Exposing a person to a complex sequence of stimulation is no guarantee that he will attend to the entire range of cues, that he will necessarily select from a total stimulus complex only the most relevant stimuli, or that he will even perceive accurately the cues to which his attention is directed (Bandura, 1971, p. 79).

Modeling a desired response does not mean that the child will necessarily imitate the response, even if the modeler has the child's attention. As

Bandura (1971) observed, a multitude of variables can affect the child's ability or willingness to reproduce a modeled behavior. For example, a young child's interest in imitating a response can be affected by the novelty of the response and by the child's past history of reinforcement for imitation. Parton (1976) has reported that imitation in young children can be facilitated by novelty and suggests that more attention be given to novelty as an important factor in eliciting imitative responses.

Variables surrounding the model can also affect a child's willingness to imitate. For example, the observed competency of a model affected the amount of imitative behavior produced by older school children (Strichart, 1974). Positive identification with the model, through a past history of associated reinforcement, may enhance the young child's imitation of the model's responses (Gewirtz and Stingle, 1968). Bandura (1971) has demonstrated that the consequences a model receives can affect a child's willingness to engage in the observed behavior; and, of course, the consequences to the imitator who produces a modeled response can affect the production of imitative behavior. A body of behavioral literature exists demonstrating the functional relationship between the production of imitative responses and the application of extrinsic reinforcement. In addition, evidence is gathering that production of a response similar to observed behavior may in itself have reinforcing properties (Fouts, Waldner, and Watson, 1976).

It seems clear that children can learn by a mechanism called imitation, but the willingness to imitate is affected by a range of motivational, discrimination, and reinforcement variables. It may be important that the peer model be perceived as a competent individual who engages in specific responses that yield positive consequences. Furthermore, several investigators have found that significantly more imitation occurs under conditions of active participation rather than passive observation (Bandura, Grusec, and Menlove, 1967; Guralnick, 1976).

Based on the above review of imitation learning, the integration of handicapped and nonhandicapped children would seem to be a potentially effective educational alternative for several reasons. First, children can acquire new responses from observing and modeling others' behavior; however, the opportunity for watching and imitating more complex behavior must be available. Isolation of the young, handicapped child from nonhandicapped peers may reduce an important avenue of stimulation and subsequent learning. Second, active participation appears to enhance imitation learning, a finding which argues for programs that provide contact among handicapped preschoolers and their "normal" peers. Third, there are indications that children tend to selectively model. That is, children will imitate the behavior of individuals who can perform responses more effectively (Strichart, 1974). These findings argue for the exposure of handicapped children to competent models rather than to restrict their experiences to only other "different" individuals. In addition, such results should reduce the fear that nonhandicapped children will imitate simpler responses or atypical behavioral patterns produced by a handicapped child.

Merely placing children together in a classroom will probably not yield the desired outcomes. As emphasized above, imitative behavior depends on many variables. Arranging the environment to elicit imitation of young children by their handicapped peers requires systematic planning and implementation.

Integrated Approaches

Included in this section is a brief review of a few projects that have appeared in the literature describing integrated approaches to the education of the handicapped child.

Bricker and Bricker (1971, 1972, 1973, 1976) initiated an early intervention project in the 1970s that integrated developmentally retarded toddlers with normally developing children. These investigators, using two mechanisms, attempted to evaluate the effect of the retarded child on his normal classmates. First, despite difficulties, discussed in detail elsewhere (Filler et al., 1975), pre-post standardized intelligence measures were used. In general, the data indicated that the "normal" child's development, as measured by such instruments, was progressing as expected or better with no regression effects noted (Bricker and Bricker, 1971, 1972). Thus, apparently the developmental progress of the nonhandicapped child need not be adversely affected by developmental integration. The second method used to evaluate the effect of the retarded child on the "normal" youngster was the parental evaluation:

> The parents of all nine non-delayed children in the first year (of the project) and 10 out of 12 were non-delayed children in the second year were willing to re-enter their children in the program. None of the parents in the first year felt their non-delayed child had suffered any negative effect from interacting with less capable children, while 2 out of 12 during the second year said *perhaps* their child had picked up some undesired responses from non-delayed children (Bricker and Bricker, 1972, pp. 6-7).

Although such data are tentative and open to criticism in terms of objectivity, they should encourage further examination of nontraditional educational groupings.

Kennedy et al. (1976) have reported that, "The integration of selected hearing impaired children in regular classes with normal hearing peers . . . is one of the major trends in comprehensive special education programming in the United States today'' (p. 71). The University of Minnesota, State Department of Education, and Minneapolis Public Schools have jointly sponsored a demonstration project for hearing-impaired children birth through six years. Three notable features of this project are: (1) the emphasis on early detection and intervention, (2) inclusion of the parents, and (3) integration into regular nursery programs by age three whenever possible. As the children enrolled in this project have reached school age, they have been integrated into regular public school classes. Investigation of a selected sample of these hearing-impaired youngsters has revealed that their social acceptance by peers is not significantly different, in general, from their hearing peers (Kennedy et al., 1976).

Allen, Benning, and Drummond (1972) have reported on a program developed at the Experimental Education Unit, University of Washington, which included eight normal children and eight handicapped children with varying problems. The writers reported that simple integration of a particular handicapped child with normal peers did not eliminate all of the child's maladaptive behaviors, but in combination with other systematic manipulations it did produce a significant decrease in undesired behaviors. The importance of this project is that it provides some tentative data suggesting that behavioral differences which may exist in the handicapped child (in this case, extremely disruptive behavior, such as physical attacks and throwing toys) can be modified within an integrated setting without consuming an undue amount of the teacher's time and "with no deleterious side effects" to the normal child (Allen, Benning, and Drummond, 1972).

Guralnick (1976) has reported some interesting findings on the use of nonhandicapped preschoolers as intervention agents. In one case, nonhandicapped preschoolers were given instructions to selectively attend to and encourage the appropriate play behavior of a handicapped child. In a second instance, a nonhandicapped preschooler was reinforced for modeling appropriate verbal behavior for a mildly handicapped child. In both cases the handicapped child's performance was affected by contingencies delivered to or by the nonhandicapped peer. This type of objective information has two implications. First, preschool children can be assisted in becoming effective tutors for less competent children, suggesting the potential educational benefit for the handicapped child. Second, in the process of teaching, the nonhandicapped child may acquire more knowledge about a specific area. Effective teaching appears to be predicated on grasping a topic well enough for the transmittal of information to others. In becoming a tutor for the less competent child, the more competent child's repertoire may be greatly enhanced.

The integration of preschool handicapped and nonhandicapped children in the same program, although not a novel idea, has only recently been demanding widespread attention as a potentially viable educational alternative. Although the supporting evidence discussed in this section is either of an indirect nature (i.e., developmental theory and imitation learning) or meager where actual implementation is concerned, the pilot work indicating the necessity for further and more exacting exploration has been established.

In the preceding section, arguments for integrating handicapped and nonhandicapped preschool children have been developed from a psychological-educational perspective. Specifically, it was suggested that educational or developmental progress is probably maximized when the environment places slowly increasing demands upon the child. In a sense, this portion of the rationale has emphasized locating children in situations which elicit appropriate responses and/or provide the child opportunity to "learn" more complex behavior. The job before us is to develop and implement challenging educational environments for all children. The educational integration of the handicapped and nonhandicapped preschooler may be a viable approach to creating one such challenging environment.

SUMMARY

The purpose of this chapter has been to develop a rationale to argue for the further exploration of the educational integration of handicapped and nonhandicapped preschool children. As discussed earlier, the dichotomizing of children into tidy groups such as handicapped and nonhandicapped often means that much of a child's behavioral repertoire is being overlooked. When a child is labeled handicapped, it often seems that the disability is being focused upon to the exclusion of the child's many other behavioral attributes. Labeling and classification of the infant and young child as handicapped are particularly tenuous. Our ability to predict future performance based on the assessed behavioral repertoire of the young child is hampered by environmental expectations, by lack of appropriate evaluation procedures, and by not fully understanding the longitudinal effects of certain disabling conditions. Extreme caution should be exercised in the premature labeling of the young child as handicapped and the placement of the child in intervention programs exclusively for exceptional children.

In developing the rationale for integrating preschoolers with diverse behavioral repertoires, social-ethical, legal-legislative, and psychological-educational arguments were presented and examined. As pointed out in each of these discussions, the rationale rests largely on societal values, legal decisions, legislative enactments, and educational theory rather than empirical support.

The specific social-ethical arguments encompassed the impact of the predominate negative societal view of the handicapped child, how isolation and segregation of the handicapped may maintain a negative attitude, and finally how the inclusion of the young handicapped child into regular programs may assist in modifying attitudes as well as better using limited educational resources. The arguments falling under the rubric of legal-legislative focused on a review of relevant court decisions and legislative enactments that have had a significant effect on the educational placement of the handicapped child. The psychological-educational arguments were based on a developmental approach to early childhood education that emphasizes the importance of interaction with an increasingly demanding environment, the clear indication that young children can learn through the imitation of others, and the apparent success of several intervention programs that have integrated handicapped and nonhandicapped children.

Of the many reasons presented for integrating handicapped and nonhandicapped preschool children, perhaps the most persuasive are the legal and legislative mandates to educate children in the most normal-like environment. The message of such mandates may be that the integration of handicapped children into programs with nonhandicapped children is not an option but a necessity. Exposing the handicapped child to "normal" peers early in life may be one of the best strategies for maximizing the handicapped youngster's potential for maintaining unrestricted contact with his community.

The intent of this chapter has not been to encourage ill-prepared, wholesale implementation of combining handicapped and nonhandicapped preschool children. Rather, the purpose has been to argue for further examination of the approach as a viable educational alternative. Innovation and change appear necessary, given the lack of success to date in the education of the handicapped child. An aim of this chapter has also been to generate support for the development of well articulated projects that will objectively study the combining of handicapped and nonhandicapped preschool children. Widespread implementation without evaluation is not being advocated. The integration of children should be based on educational or developmental groupings rather than artificial homogenous groupings derived from variables such as age, etiology, or cultural background. Sensible educational or developmental grouping across broad populations of children may ultimately prove to be a wise use of educational resources for both the handicapped and nonhandicapped child. However, we will never know unless the study of such an approach is undertaken.

ACKNOWLEDGMENTS

The author is deeply indebted to Jeff Seibert, Ph.D. and Richard Iacino, M.A., for their thoughtful analysis of and subsequent assistance in clarifying the issues presented in this chapter.

REFERENCES CITED

Abeson, A., Bolick, N., and Hass, K. 1975. A primer on due process: Education decisions for handicapped children. Exceptional Children, 42, 68-76.

Allen, K. E., Benning, P. M., and Drummond, W. T. 1972. Integration of normal and handicapped children in a behavior modification preschool: A case study. In G. Semb (Ed.), Behavior Analysis and Education. Lawrence, Kan.: University of Kansas Support and Development Center.

Apolloni, T., and Cooke, T. P. 1975. Peer behavior conceptualized as a variable influencing infant and toddler development. American Journal of Orthopsychiatry, 45, 4-17.

Bandura, A. 1971. Influence of model's reinforcement contingencies on the acquisition of imitative responses. In E. McGinnies and C. B. Ferster (Eds.), The Reinforcement of Social Behavior. Boston: Houghton Mifflin.

Bandura, A., Grusec, J., and Menlove, F. 1967. Vicarious extinction of avoidance behavior. Journal of Personality and Social Psychology, 5, 16-23.

Bartel, N. R., and Guskin, S. L. 1971. A handicap as a social phenomenon. In W. M. Cruickshank (Ed.), Psychology of Exceptional Children and Youth. Englewood Cliffs, N.J.: Prentice-Hall.

Blatt, B. 1966. Christmas in Purgatory. Boston: Allyn & Bacon.

Bricker, D. D., and Bricker, W. A. 1971. Toddler research and intervention project report: Year I. IMRID Behavioral Science Monograph 20. Nashville, Tenn.: Institute on Mental Retardation and Intellectual Development, George Peabody College.

Bricker, D. D., and Bricker, W. A. 1972. Toddler research and intervention project report: Year II. IMRID Behavioral Science Monograph 21. Nashville, Tenn.: Institute on Mental Retardation and Intellectual Development, George Peabody College.

Bricker, D. D., and Bricker, W. A. 1973. Infant, toddler and preschool research and intervention project report: Year III. IMRID Behavioral Science Monograph 23. Nashville, Tenn.: Institute on Mental Retardation and Intellectual Development, George Peabody College.

Bricker, D., Bricker, W., Iacino, R., and Dennison, L. 1976. Intervention strategies for the severely and profoundly handicapped child. In N. Haring and L. Brown (Eds.), Teaching Severely/Profoundly Handicapped Individuals. New York: Grune & Stratton.

Bricker, W. A. 1970. Identifying and modifying behavioral deficits. American Journal of Mental Deficiency, 75, 16-21.

Bricker, W. A., and Bricker, D. D. 1976. The infant, toddler, and preschool research and intervention project. In T. D. Tjossem (Ed.), Intervention Strategies for High Risk Infants and Young Children. Baltimore: University Park Press.

Cohen, J. S., and DeYoung, H. 1973. The role of litigation in the improvement of programming for the handicapped. In L. Mann and D. Sabatino (Eds.), The First Review of Special Education. Philadelphia: JSE Press.

Dunn, L. M. 1968. Special education for the mildly retarded—Is much of it justifiable? Exceptional Children, 35, 5-22.

Edgerton, R. B. 1967. The Cloak of Competence: Stigma in the Lives of the Retarded. Berkeley: University of California Press.

Edgerton, R. B., Eyman, R. K., and Silverstein, A. B. 1975. Mental retardation system. In N. Hobbs (Ed.), Issues in the Classification of Children (Vol. I). San Francisco: Jossey-Bass.

Education of the Handicapped Today. 1976 (June). Washington, D.C.: U.S. Department of Health, Education, and Welfare, U.S. Government Printing Office. (Reprinted from the 1976 annual report of the National Advisory Committee on the Handicapped.)

Filler, J. W., Robinson, C. C., Smith, R. A., Vincent-Smith, L., Bricker, D. D., and Bricker, W. A. 1975. Mental retardation. In N. Hobbs (Ed.), Issues in the Classification of Children (Vol. I). San Francisco: Jossey-Bass.

Fouts, G. T., Waldner, D. N., and Watson, M. W. 1976. Effects of being imitated and counter-imitated on the behavior of preschool children. Child Development, 47, 172-177.

Garner, R. T., and Rosen, B. 1967. Moral Philosophy: A Systematic Introduction to Normative Ethics and Meta-ethics. New York: Macmillan.

Gewirtz, J. L., and Stingle, K. G. 1968. Learning of generalized imitation as the basis for identification. Psychological Review, 75, 374-397.

Goodman, L. V. 1976 (July). A bill of rights for the handicapped. In: American Education. Washington, D.C.: U.S. Department of Health, Education, and Welfare, U.S. Government Printing Office.

Gorham, K. A., DesJardins, C., Page, R., Pettis, E., and Scheiber, B. 1975. Effect on parents. In N. Hobbs (Ed.), Issues in the Classification of Children (Vol. II). San Francisco: Jossey-Bass.

Guess, D., Sailor, W., Rutherford, G., and Baer, D. M. 1968. An experimental analysis of linguistic development: The productive use of the plural morpheme. Journal of Applied Behavior Analysis, 1, 297-306.

Guralnick, M. J. 1976. The value of integrating handicapped and nonhandicapped preschool children. American Journal of Orthopsychiatry, 46, 236-245.

Guskin, S. L., Bartel, N. R., and MacMillan, D. L. 1975. Perspective of the labeled child. In N. Hobbs (Ed.), Issues in the Classification of Children (Vol. II). San Francisco: Jossey-Bass.

Haring, N. G. 1974. Perspectives in special education. In N. G. Haring (Ed.), Behavior of Exceptional Children: An Introduction to Special Education. Columbus, Ohio: Charles E. Merrill.

Hartup, W. W. 1970. Peer interaction and social organization. In P. H. Mussen (Ed.), Carmichael's Manual of Child Psychology (Vol. II). New York: John Wiley & Sons.

Hobbs, N. 1975. The Futures of Children. San Francisco: Jossey-Bass.

Kennedy, P., Northcott, W., McCauley, R., and Williams, S. 1976. Longitudinal sociometric and cross-sectional data on mainstreaming hearing impaired children: Implications for preschool programming. The Volta Review, 78, 71-81.

Kirp, D. L., Kuriloff, P. J., and Buss, W. G. 1975. Legal mandates and organizational change. In N. Hobbs (Ed.), Issues in the Classification of Children (Vol. II). San Francisco: Jossey-Bass.

Lilly, M. S. 1970. Special education: A teapot in a tempest. Exceptional Children, 37, 43-49.

MacMillan, D. L., Jones, R. L., and Aloia, G. F. 1974. The mentally retarded label: Libelous or legendary? American Journal of Mental Deficiency, 79, 241-261.

McCall, R. B., Hogarty, P. S., and Hurlburt, N. 1972. Transitions in infant sensorimotor development and the prediction of childhood IQ. American Psychologist, 27, 728-748.

Martin, E. 1976. Integration of the handicapped child into regular schools. Proceedings from July, 1975, Dean's Projects Conference. Minnesota Education, 2, 5-8.

Miller, J. F., and Yoder, D. E. 1974. An ontogenetic language teaching strategy for retarded children. In R. L. Schiefelbusch and L. L. Lloyd (Eds.), Language Perspectives—Acquisition, Retardation, and Intervention. Baltimore: University Park Press.

Parton, D. A. 1976. Learning to imitate in infancy. Child Development, 47, 14-31.

President's Committee on Mental Retardation. 1976 (March). Mental Retardation: Century of Decision (DHEW Publication (OHD) 76-21013). Washington, D.C.: President's Committee on Mental Retardation.

Reese, H. W., and Lipsitt, L. P. 1970. Experimental Child Psychology. New York: Academic Press.

Rhodes, W. C., and Sagor, M. 1975. Community perspectives. In N. Hobbs (Ed.), Issues in the Classification of Children (Vol. I). San Francisco: Jossey-Bass.

Robinson, N. M., and Robinson, H. B. 1976. The Mentally Retarded Child: A Psychological Approach. New York: McGraw-Hill.

Rosenthal, R., and Jacobson, L. 1968. Pygmalion in the Classroom: Teacher Expectations and Pupil's Intellectual Development. New York: Holt, Rinehart and Winston.

Sarason, S. B., and Doris, J. 1969. Psychological Problems in Mental Deficiency. New York: Harper & Row.

Scriven, M. 1976. Some issues in the logic and ethics of mainstreaming. Proceedings from July, 1975, Dean's Projects Conference. Minnesota Education, 2, 61-68.

Sheare, J. B. 1974. Social acceptance of EMR adolescents in integrated programs. American Journal of Mental Deficiency, 78, 678-682.

Sontag, E. 1976. Zero exclusion: No longer rhetoric. Apropos, spring-summer. (Apropos is a publication of the National Center on Educational Media and Materials for the Handicapped at Ohio State University.)

Strichart, S. S. 1974. Effects of competence and nurturance on imitation of nonretarded peers by retarded adolescents. American Journal of Mental Deficiency, 78, 665-674.

Thorndike, R. L. 1968. Review of Rosenthal, R., and Jacobson, L., Pygmalion in the Classroom. American Educational Research Journal, 5, 708-711.

Zimmerman, B. J., and Rosenthal, T. L. 1974. Observational learning of rule-governed behavior by children. Psychological Bulletin, 81, 29-42.

PEER INTERACTION AND THE PROCESSES OF SOCIALIZATION

Willard W. Hartup, Ed.D.

While the psychological and pediatric literatures have long stressed the importance of parent-child relations to the development of social and intellectual competencies in children, much less attention has been given to peer relations. No one has ever doubted that peer interactions are common events (we all remember something about the role played by other children in our own growing up), but few scientists and few teachers have given much thought to the functions of peer interaction in human development. In contrast, the individual who wrote the following letter[1] recognizes the significance of early social experience as well as the relation between peer interaction and the development of social competence.

> Dear Dr. ———:
> I read the report in the Oct. 30 issue of ———— about your study of only children. I am an only child, now 57 years old and I want to tell you some things about my life. Not only was I an only child but I grew up in the country where there were no nearby children to play with. My mother did not want children around. She used to say, 'I don't want my kid to bother anybody and I don't want nobody's kids bothering me.'
> ... From the first year of school I was teased and made fun of. For example, in about third or fourth grade I dreaded to get on the school bus to go to school because the other children on the bus called me 'Mommy's baby.' In about the second grade I heard the boys use a vulgar word. I asked what it meant and they made fun of me. So I learned a lesson—don't ask questions. This can lead to a lot of confusion to hear talk one doesn't understand and not be able to learn what it means...

Preparation of this chapter was supported by Grant 5 P01 HD05027, from the National Institute of Child Health and Human Development.

[1]Used by permission of the letter-writer and the recipient (Prof. Shirley G. Moore).

I never went out with a girl while I was in school—in fact I hardly talked to them. In our school the boys and girls did not play together. Boys were sent to one part of the playground and girls to another. So, I didn't learn anything about girls. When we got into high school and the boys and girls started dating I could only listen to their stories about their experiences.

I could tell you a lot more but the important thing is I have never married or had any children. I have not been very successful in an occupation or vocation. I believe my troubles are not all due to being an only child... but I do believe you are right in recommending playmates for preschool children and I will add playmates for the school agers and not have them strictly supervised by adults. I believe I confirm the experiments with monkeys in being overly timid sometimes and overly aggressive sometimes. Parents of only children should make special efforts to provide playmates for [their children].

Sincerely yours,

Research confirms nearly every conclusion reached by this letter writer. Current evidence shows that, without an opportunity to interact with other children, children have difficulty in learning effective communication skills, modulating aggressive feelings, accommodating to social demands for appropriate sexual behavior, and forming a coherent set of moral values. Peer relations are not luxuries in human development; they are necessities. Peers do not act as subversive agents of the counterculture who entice the child into delinquency and other antisocial activities. Such notions are fodder for television dramatists and newspaper writers, but the facts are otherwise. The peer culture reinforces the values of the core culture more often than not, and works to extend and facilitate the socialization efforts of home and school rather than to contradict them. In fact, a vast and untapped potential exists in peer relations that is generally unknown or ignored by professionals who work with children.

In 1951, Anna Freud and Sophie Dann published an interesting series of observations on six three-year-old German-Jewish children who had come to Britain and into their care in August 1945. Earlier that summer, these children—three boys and three girls—had been found living by themselves in a "motherless" ward in a concentration camp in Moravia. Various scraps of information revealed the following. Each of the children had been in concentration camps since before his/her first birthday. The mothers of each had been killed within a short period of the confinement, and the children had mostly been passed from camp to camp until they ended up at Theresienstadt. Their care, in terms of food and facilities, was impoverished but not extreme. Socially, however, the children had essentially reared themselves. Adults had not cared for them other than minimally. One may thus regard these three-year-olds as "peer-reared."

After being discovered, the children were removed to a relocation center in a nearby castle and fed lavishly for several weeks until they were flown by bomber to a children's facility in England. The significance of this "natural" experiment is recorded in the following three excerpts from the report: First, the children's behavior toward adults was bizarre. Freud and Dann write that the children ". . . showed no pleasure in the arrangements which had been made for them and behaved in a wild, restless, and noisy manner. . . . They destroyed all the toys and damaged the furniture. . . . Toward the staff they behaved either with cold indifference or with active hostility. . . . At times they ignored the adults completely" (p. 130). Second, the children showed a high degree of mutual attachment. ". . . [P]ositive feelings were centered exclusively in their own group. . . . They cared greatly for each other and not at all for anybody or anything else. They had no other wish than to be together and became upset when they were separated. When separated, a child would constantly ask for the other children, while the group would fret for the missing member" (p. 131). Last, the most important observation from this study: "They were neither deficient, delinquent, nor psychotic. They had found an alternative placement for their [attachments] and, on the strength of this, had mastered some of their anxieties, and developed social attitudes. That they were able to acquire a new language in the midst of their upheavals, bears witness to a basically unharmed contact with their environment" (p. 168). In spite of the horrendous deprivations experienced by these children, peer-rearing (and the accompanying events) had kept their social repertoires intact, preserving a large measure of what may be called "social competence." Now, thirty years later, Sophie Dann reports (personal communication) that these children are leading happy lives as adults—by and large with good social adjustment. The power of peer interaction to contribute positively to child development is somewhat obscured in this study because of the many unusual events that accompanied the "peer-rearing," but the suggestive evidence is strong.

PEER RELATIONS AND CHILD DEVELOPMENT

In the absence of sustained and successful encounters with age-mates, children are developmentally "at risk" in several respects. Longitudinal studies show that nonsociable children, both boys and girls, manifest greater discomfort, anxiety, and less willingness to engage the environment than more sociable individuals. Submissiveness and high variability in self-esteem are characteristic of nonsociable children (Bronson, 1966). So are anxiety and inappropriate aggression.

Laboratory studies in which rhesus monkeys have been deprived of peer contact for varying lengths of time confirm such correlational results. Wariness and hyperaggressiveness are characteristic of animals who have not had social contact with age-mates through the first four to eight months of life (Harlow, 1969). Observations conducted in the field also demonstrate that effective socialization requires peer interaction, particularly rough-and-tumble play. Such activity is ubiquitous in the early development of all primates, including man, and seems to be necessary in order for the animal to acquire a repertoire of effective aggressive behaviors and mechanisms for coping with the emotional concomitants of aggressive interaction.

Cross-cultural observations confirm that adults seldom claim exclusive responsibility for the child's socialization. It is apparent from recent anthropological work (Whiting and Whiting, 1975) that social interaction among children is very different from interaction with other individuals (e.g., parents or infants). Most important, these differences are the same across cultures. "Aggressiveness," "sociable behavior," and "prosocial activity" held more highly rank-ordered positions in peer interaction than in adult-child interaction in the six cultures included in this study. "Dependency," "nurturance," and "intimacy," on the other hand, occupied the lowest rank-ordered positions in the six cultures. Nowhere, then, does socialization for aggression occur primarily within the family (as some of our earlier theories would have us believe), and prosocial activity also seems to be derived from peer interaction rather than from parent-child interaction. While it may be understandable that aggression occurs among peers rather than in social behavior with adults (adults are both larger and vested with more authority than peers), the fact remains that peers were the first- or second-ranked targets for aggression in all of these societies. Recent data on American children confirm that cooperative behaviors are more common among preschool children rated as sociable than children rated as nonsociable (Getz, 1977), implying that peer relations contribute importantly to the acquisition of a repertoire of effective positive social skills as well as to a repertoire of controlling mechanisms over negative social behaviors.

The child's experiences with other children also bear on so-called social intelligence. Children who are able to "put themselves in someone else's shoes" are more sociable and more competent in their social interactions than are children who are less capable role-takers (Gottman, Gonso, and Rasmussen, 1975). And children who are leaders show generally advanced levels of social understanding and responsibility (Gold, 1962).

The notion that peer interaction contributes to moral development is a cornerstone of Piaget's (1932) theorizing concerning the socialization of moral judgment. A limited amount of supportive evidence exists for this theory. Keasey (1971), who studied one hundred forty-four elementary school children, found that those who belonged to relatively many social organizations had higher moral judgment scores than those who belonged to fewer groups. Those with the higher moral judgment scores were also rated (both by teachers and other children) as more popular than those with lower levels of moral judgment. Owing to their correlational nature, these data do not conclusively prove that advances in moral judgment derive from peer relations. Membership in clubs may facilitate changes in the nature of the child's moral judgments, but high levels of moral reasoning may also facilitate the child's entrance into the peer culture and even be a prerequisite to membership in it. And, of course, the relation between popularity and moral judgment may exist because both variables are related to some third variable such as general intelligence. Even so, the evidence indicates that peer interaction and moral development are linked, and the existence of this linkage is consistent with the hypothesis that child-child relations make significant contributions to the development of moral values.

Longer term studies show that inadequate peer relations are prognostic indicators of social and emotional trouble. Children who are "loners" are more likely to be delinquent, to be school drop-outs as adolescents, and to experience adjustment difficulties as adults than children who are well accepted (Roff, Sells, and Golden, 1972). Other studies (Rolf, 1972) show that risk for psychopathology is negatively related to peer acceptance as measured by sociometric interviews with both teachers and children.

In summary, peer relations occupy a central position in child development. Adequate peer relations contribute to the acquisition of basic social and communicative skills in a manner that interactions with adults either cannot or will not produce. The centrality of peer interaction in childhood socialization needs to be better recognized by both research workers and practitioners.

PEERS AS SOCIALIZING AGENTS

Some investigators (e.g., Lee, 1975) have suggested that cognitive "schemes" based on social objects are more difficult for the child to construct than schemes based on nonsocial objects. This difficulty stems from the complexity and variability of social objects (persons) as contrasted to nonsocial objects. Peer relations, then, must be extraordinarily difficult for the child to schematize because the behavior of children toward other children is even more variable than the behavior of adults.

Research indicates that, with increasing age, children's conceptions of interpersonal relations become more complex and more varied. The number of categories used to describe other individuals, the flexibility and precision with which such categories are used, and the level of interpretive analysis all increase from early childhood through adolescence (Livesley and Bromley, 1973). Some writers, such as Selman (1976), argue that the understanding of interpersonal relations emerges in a stage-like progression. An invariant series of shifts is thought to occur, beginning with the naive, egocentric conceptualizations of the young child and extending to the sophisticated interpersonal understanding of the adult, who recognizes the mutuality that exists in human relations across a broad range of situations.

Such conceptual advances by the child are believed to be enhanced by contacts with other children, if not to be direct outcomes of them. Why? Because peer interaction is uniquely adapted to the requirements of the child's social/cognitive development. Peer experience is *equalitarian* experience, providing the child with the give-and-take that is essential to aggressive socialization, to the acquisition of communications skills, and to the development of a mature moral orientation. Such reciprocity is not commonly a feature of the child's interactions with adults; the family and the classroom are authoritarian social systems. Peer relations, on the other hand, are organized in an equalitarian mode and possess many features (including the equivalent abilities of the participants) that foster give-and-take learning.

Some events, including play, occur in peer interaction and only rarely occur in adult-child interaction. Mothers and fathers do not play with their children for more than short periods of time, usually acting as play supervisors rather than participants. Even when parents and children "play," the parents must engage in role-playing—they must participate with a cognitive and affective involvement that is different from the child's. Also, it is not clear that play represents adaptive behavior for adults. The mature members of our species must invest enormous time and effort in activities aimed at ensuring the child's survival—activities that exclude extended opportunities for rough-and-tumble interaction with children. Adult responsibilities also require a mature and reality-oriented cognitive apparatus that is capable of both operational and logical functions, and that does not "slip back" into the assimilative modes of earlier stages in intellectual development.

Children, however, need to play. Most experts agree that such activity contributes to intellectual development, the acquisition of social skills, and the regulation of various kinds of affect (Bruner, Jolly, and Sylva, 1976).

Everyday experience demonstrates that play is a distinctive feature of child-child interaction, and the presence of another child is among its most common elicitors. Peer interaction, then, seems better adapted to children's play than adult-child interaction.

Social activity with other children (including play) is not subject to the same constraints that govern social activity with adults. Parent-child interaction is based on a specific attachment between the child and the adult, an attachment that exists to protect and sustain the child through the years when survival is impossible without assistance (Bowlby, 1969). These attachments, which persist throughout childhood and adolescence, cannot be maintained within an atmosphere in which certain events, such as aggression and sexual behavior, occur. Parents cannot function as parents when children do not contain their rage, and, at the same time, children cannot maintain their attachments to their parents while enduring unbridled abuse. Both aggression and sex are antithetical to the maintenance of the attachments upon which the family is founded. Children need some other arena in which to learn how to aggress against others without sustaining permanent damage to themselves, how to handle aggressive affect, and how to handle sexual arousal. Less constrained conditions exist in peer interaction.

In summary, peer interaction provides the child with social situations that are constrained in different ways from adult-child interaction. Peer relations possess unique equalitarian features that facilitate social learning. The outcomes of peer socialization include advances in both social competence and social behavior.

SAME- AND MIXED-AGE PEER INTERACTION

Implicit in the research literature is the notion that a child's "peers" are children of more or less the same age. Since chronological age is a rough indicator of a child's abilities, peer status connotes equivalence in motor skills, intellectual capacities, and social status. That is, children are called "peers" when they interact at comparable levels of behavioral complexity (Lewis and Rosenblum, 1975).

But wide individual differences exist among children of the same age. Two children of identical ages may or may not be peer-like according to the setting and the maturity of their actions within it. Similarly, two children of different ages may interact in a completely peer-like fashion, providing they relate to the situation and to each other at comparable levels of behavioral maturity.

Socialization involves considerable contact among children at similar developmental levels. Most Western cultures are age-graded (consider institutions such as schools, recreation programs, clubs, camps, and sports teams). It is easy, therefore, to assume that age-mates have greater significance as socializing agents than non-age-mates.

In point of fact, children's societies include individuals of a variety of ages. Barker and Wright (1955) found that about sixty-five percent of children's interactions in a small midwestern town involved children who differed in age by *more* than twelve months. Konner (1975) has shown that children's socialization actually evolved under conditions favoring the selection of a mixed-age group, partly because human populations in hunter-gatherer societies (from which modern man evolved) are not sufficiently concentrated to supply large numbers of age-mates, but also because unique benefits appear to accrue to the child from contact with children of various ages. American teachers, administrators, and psychologists may consider the same-age situation to be best suited to the child's needs, but peer interaction under such conditions was relatively rare—even in schools—before the beginning of the twentieth century (Allen, 1976). Even now, same-age socialization is uncommon in many of the world's cultures.

To illustrate concretely the manner in which cross-age peer interaction differs from same-age interaction, a study can be cited that was completed more than ten years ago (Ferguson, 1965). Boys and girls, initially strangers, were chosen from second and fifth grade classrooms and were paired as follows: fifth graders with fifth graders, fifth graders with second graders, second graders with fifth graders, and second graders with second graders. One member of each pair served as "learner" in this experiment and the other served as "teacher." Learners were asked to select marbles from a bin and drop them through holes into a second bin. Baseline levels were established at the beginning of the session during which the teacher silently watched the learner. The teacher was then covertly signaled by the experimenter to say "good" or "fine" to the learner on a twenty-second interval schedule during the remainder of the six-minute session.

Although the older children worked harder at this task than the younger children, the difference between baseline and rewarded performance showed an interesting effect. Children whose teachers were not age-mates increased their rates of marble-dropping during the session more than did those subjects whose teachers were age-mates. The performance of the latter children remained steady during this period at levels only slightly above the baseline rate. Here, then, is evidence that the outcomes of cross-age interaction are not the same as the outcomes of same-age interaction.

Work with nonhuman primates also shows that mixed-age and same-age interaction have different outcomes. In 1972, Suomi and Harlow used a mixed-age procedure for ameliorating the effects of social isolation in young rhesus monkeys. Over the years, Harlow and his colleagues have tried many different methods for restoring normal social activity in the withdrawn, depressed animals that are produced by periods of social and sensory isolation. Interactions with adult animals or with animals of the juveniles' own ages have failed to restore social competence in such isolates. It has seemed that the early deprivation leaves irreversible scars—scars that persist into the animal's adulthood and leave it vulnerable to reproductive and parenting malfunctions.

But, using four experimental animals that had spent their first six months in total isolation, these investigators tried a new kind of intervention. It consisted of successive exposures to a normal infant monkey who was only three months old—three months younger than the subject. The results were dramatic. First, self-stimulation, huddling, and other behaviors that are stereotypic of the isolated animal declined. Second, locomotion and exploration increased. And, third, social contacts and social play began to emerge. The initial overtures were made by the therapist monkeys who would approach the isolate infant and cling to it. Then (unlike instances in which age-mates were used as therapists), the isolates reciprocated and play behavior emerged. Once these interaction patterns were established, the isolates themselves initiated play bouts with increasing frequency. Replication work (Novak and Harlow, 1975) has been published involving other animals whose isolation extended over twelve months, the effects of which were even more severe than the effects of shorter isolation.

Previous work in this series of studies suggested to some investigators that without early social experience certain social competencies never develop. The data suggested a "critical period" in primate development in which social interaction must occur in order for social behavior to emerge normally. Now, it appears that this is a "sensitive" rather than a "critical" period. The social pathology induced by early isolation *can* be reversed through a carefully managed program of play with peers who are younger than the subject.

Observations of Same- and Mixed-age Groups

Just how does children's interaction with age-mates differ from their interaction with children who are not their same age? To answer this question, observations of pairs of nursery school children were conducted

(Lougee, Grueneich, and Hartup, in press) who differed by: (1) not more than two months, or (2) an average of sixteen months in chronological age. Play behavior was observed on two occasions, and social activity was subsequently tabulated from videotape recordings. First, striking differences were observed in the sociability of the same-age and mixed-age pairs. Sociability was intermediate, in terms of the number of social contacts, in mixed-age pairs compared to same-age pairs of younger children and same-age pairs of older children. Second, and most important, the sociability of individual children differed in the two types of social situations: Three-year-olds were *more* active socially when associating with a five-year-old than when associating with another three-year-old; and five-year-olds were *less* sociable with a three-year-old than with another five-year-old. Shatz and Gelman (1973) showed that verbal communication is also adjusted in same- and mixed-age conditions. When talking to other four-year-olds, four-year-old children used longer and more complex utterances than when talking to two-year-olds. Thus, a large capacity exists, even among very young children, for making subtle accommodations in social behavior to the needs and demands of other children. Preschool children are not as egocentric and socially naive as the literature would have them be. And the salience of the age variable in these peer interactions is evident in another way: Age-related comments occur with a much higher frequency (fifty-four percent) in same-age pairs than in mixed-age pairs (seventeen percent). When preschool children are not certain about the developmental status of another child, they find out!

Is age-mixture related to patterns of social behavior in larger groups? Does social activity in multi-age classrooms differ from social behavior in same-age classrooms? Do mixed-age situations provide a different socialization context from same-age situations? In spite of great interest in recent years in multi-age school situations, little is known about social activity in them. School personnel have been more interested in the implications of such classroom structures for cognitive development than for social development, so that relatively little published work exists in this area. The most recent studies, however, have involved preschool children.

Goldman (1976) completed an investigation in which the amount of time spent in various forms of social participation was compared between homogeneous and heterogeneous classrooms. The social relations existing among the children within the heterogeneous classrooms were also studied. Observations involved three classes of three-year-olds, three classes of four-year-olds, and three mixed-age classes that included both three- and four-year-olds. Each class was observed during ten periods of free play in which encounters between each child and every other child were recorded.

For both three- and four-year-olds, social participation in mixed-age classes differed from social behavior in same-age classes. The three-year-olds in the mixed-age situations spent more time in positive interaction and in solitary play, and less time in parallel play and teacher-directed activities. The four-year-olds in mixed-age classrooms also spent more time in solitary play and less time in parallel activity and teacher-directed work. Rubin, Maioni, and Hornung (1976) reported that solitary play is more "mature" than parallel play, contrary to earlier interpretations (Parten, 1932). Thus, preschool children in mixed-age conditions (*both* three- and four-year-olds) displayed more "mature" social activity than children in same-age classrooms.

Within the mixed-age classes in Goldman's (1976) study, there were no significant differences between the three- and four-year-olds in the amount of time spent in the various categories of social play. Other work, however, shows that social encounters within mixed-age classes are more frequent among same-age children than among different-age children (Lougee, Mason, and Hartup, in preparation).

Same- and cross-age interaction in problem-solving situations was examined by Graziano et al. (1976). Task performance was studied under two instructional conditions (group or individual reward) in four types of three-person enclaves: (1) all first graders, (2) two first graders and one third grader, (3) two third graders and one first grader, and (4) all third graders (the children in each triad were from different classrooms). The strategies employed in problem solving and the group's performance did not vary as a function of group composition. Children in the mixed-age groups talked with one another less than children in same-age groups, and performance was generally better in the group reward (cooperative) condition than in the individual reward (competition) condition; but the groups' overall performance was not different in same- and mixed-age circumstances. Individual members, however, behaved differently in the various triadic arrangements. Singleton third graders had particularly high performance scores, showing more initiative and a greater willingness to assume strategic roles than children in triads composed entirely of third graders. These differences were not found for the first graders. Thus, differentiation of individual performance varied according to both the composition of the triad and the children's ages.

Mixed-age Interaction and Social Development

Studies like those discussed above show that unique social learning opportunities exist in mixed-age interaction. The literature remains sparse, however, and the implications of the new results are not well understood. Does the finding that both three-year-olds and four-year-olds show more positive interaction in mixed-age classrooms than in same-age classrooms mean that heterogeneous classes *facilitate* social development? When social interaction in dyads of preschool children increases in mixed-age interaction among three-year-olds and decreases among five-year-olds, does this mean that the mixed-age situation *facilitates* social development among the younger children but *retards* socialization among the older ones? Interpretive evidence is greatly needed. Acceleration in amount of social activity is not necessarily a positive contribution to socialization, and deceleration is not necessarily a negative contribution. Differences between same-age and mixed-age social behavior may reflect a social "accommodation" rather than a reorganization of social competencies. After all, moment-to-moment accommodations are essential elements in social relations. Mixed-age situations may contribute more to the child's socialization through the "fine-tuning" of social behavior than the opportunity it provides for exposure to new social skills.

MECHANISMS OF PEER INFLUENCE

Social learning in peer interaction involves the same psychological processes as social learning in other contexts. Rewards and punishments, modeling, and social pressures occur in peer interaction in the same way that they occur in adult-child interaction. Oftentimes, peer pressures are exerted unintentionally rather than intentionally, and, as mentioned, a high degree of reciprocity characterizes them. Indeed, it can be argued that the value of peer experience in child development derives from this very reciprocity and informality (Hartup, 1977). Greater attention, however, should probably be paid to the potential for formal learning that exists within peer interaction, particularly in schools, religious organizations, and neighborhood activities. To restructure children's societies along authoritarian lines might be dangerous in long-term excess, but as long as peer interaction can be kept reasonably informal, there is no reason to avoid exploiting the peer culture in the process of socializing our children.

Peer Reinforcement

Peer interaction is not a random process. Even among one-year-old babies, social approaches are more likely to produce reactions from the recipient than no response. Observational studies show that babies who respond contingently to the overtures of other babies tend to be sought out more frequently than babies who do not (Lee, 1973), and, by the preschool years, there is a correlation of .79 between the frequency with which a child gives and receives positive social overtures (Charlesworth and Hartup, 1967). Positive peer interaction increases from age three onward, both in large groups (Charlesworth and Hartup, 1967; Parten, 1932; Rubin, Maioni, and Hornung, 1976) and in one-to-one situations (Lougee, Grueneich, and Hartup, in press). Hence, the development of peer relations is marked by a greater and greater density of events that are potentially reinforcing.

Instances of four kinds of generalized positive reinforcers were observed by Charlesworth and Hartup (1967): (1) giving positive attention and approval, (2) affection and personal acceptance, (3) submission, and (4) tangible objects. Individual differences in the rates with which such reinforcers were exchanged were only moderately stable (test-retest reliabilities over several months approximated .50), and situational variance was notable (rates varied considerably from classroom to classroom). But positive exchanges greatly outnumbered negative ones in all classrooms, and the rates of such exchanges were markedly higher among older children than among younger ones.

These interactive events are related to the accelerations and decelerations that occur over time in social interaction. For example, most children believe that one should act more positively toward same-sex individuals than toward opposite-sex individuals, and observation reveals that generalized reinforcers are, in fact, exchanged more frequently among children of the same sex than children of the opposite sex (Fagot and Patterson, 1969). Three-year-old boys rewarded one another about five times as frequently as they rewarded girls, and girls were observed to reward one another about seven times as frequently as they rewarded boys. Most of these reinforcements were for sex-appropriate behavior. Criticism was observed (mostly among the boys) and was focused on inappropriate sex behavior.

It is difficult to believe that these events are not related to the parallel observation that children of both sexes show increasingly appropriate sex-role behavior during the preschool years (Hartup and Zook, 1960) and increasing avoidance of inappropriate sex-role activity (Hartup, Moore, and Sager, 1963). The linkage between peer interaction and accelerations in sex-role activity has not been demonstrated within the same study, although research workers are currently engaged with this issue (Seegmiller, personal communication).

Patterson and his associates (Patterson, Littman, and Bricker, 1967) showed that reinforcement for aggression is provided within peer interaction. Nursery school children's responses to peer aggression were observed in two classrooms and were coded as *passive, cries, defensive reactions, telling the teacher, recovering property,* and *retaliation.* The most common reactions to acts of aggression in these classrooms were crying, passivity, and defensive behaviors. When the victim behaved in such ways, a second aggressive response was likely to follow and to be directed at the same victim. This escalation of aggressive activity as a function of the victim's reaction is consistent with an interpretation that the aggressive behavior was "reinforced." Counteraggression (an instance in which aggression leads to counterattack) was likely to be followed by a change in response, a change in choice of victim, or both. Such decelerations describe a process of negative reinforcement. Reinforcement processes were also revealed in the long-term histories of several children in this study who were initially nonaggressive and who were victimized by their more aggressive classmates. If these children counterattacked when they themselves were attacked and, if the counterattack was successful (i.e., produced tears or retreat by the attacker), the child became more aggressive as time passed. Children who were not victimized or who counterattacked unsuccessfully showed no increase in aggressive behavior.

Such changes may be observed in other social behaviors besides aggression. Kopfstein (1972) recorded free play interactions in two small groups of retarded children whose median age was twelve years, four months and whose median IQ was 47.5. Both aggression and prosocial activity (e.g., conversation, suggestions) were observed. When an aversive reaction occurred to these behaviors, aggression tended to be repeated but prosocial activity was not repeated. Thus, not all accelerations and decelerations in peer interaction are synonymous with reinforcement effects; some behavioral changes appear to be elicitation effects only. Nevertheless, peer interaction clearly contains elements related to behavior maintenance and change, and these elements extend across behavior classes ranging from sex-role activity to prosocial overtures.

The effectiveness of peer reinforcement has been documented in several studies in which the social exchange was controlled by the experimenter rather than by the children themselves. Wahler (1967) established baseline rates for a number of different response classes (e.g., speech, cooperation, dramatic play) among five preschool children. Response classes associated with high rates of peer reinforcement were identified for three children and with low rates of peer reinforcement for two children. For the "high-rate" children, the experimenter explained to a small peer group that he wanted them to ignore the subject when the targeted behavior occurred but to respond to all other classes of behavior. The "low rate" subjects were treated similarly, except that their peers were asked to increase the frequency with which they attended to the subject contingent upon the occurrence of the target behavior. Extinction periods were included in the experimental design for each of the children.

The results were concordant across the five subjects: (1) the instructions were effective in producing selective attention by the children's playmates; and (2) behavior changed in the selected response classes during the experimental phase for each subject, and reversal of this change produced a shift toward the rate of responding that had prevailed during the baseline period. Subsequently, Solomon and Wahler (1973) found that selective use of peer rewards could be used to reduce disruptive activity in a sixth-grade classroom. Relatively few studies of this type have appeared in the literature, but these investigations demonstrate both the efficacy of peer reinforcement and the feasibility of programming its use.

Long-term experience with peer reinforcement alters the impact of a wide range of peer influences. For example, there is an interaction between the peer reinforcement experience and the efficacy of peer modeling. Hartup and Coates (1967) found that children who had histories of positive interaction with their peers imitated rewarding models more readily than models with whom no rewarding experience had been shared. On the other hand, children who had had little positive reinforcement imitated nonrewarding models more readily than rewarding ones. Seemingly, children must experience some minimal level of interaction with other children in order for peer imitation to acquire incentive value.

The relationship existing between two children also determines the incentive value of peer rewards. Rewards such as praise, when given by one preschool child to another, are more effective when given by a disliked peer than when given by a friend (Hartup, 1964). Peer reinforcement also changes the degree of attraction between two children. One investigator (Karen, 1965) found that friendship nominations fluctuated in direct relation to the number of pennies and candies that were shared by the children. Here again is evidence of reciprocity in peer relations: Friendship status determines the value of peer reinforcement, but, at the same time, the exchange of rewards among children determines the friendship relations existing among them.

Peer Modeling

As models, peers affect many different aspects of the child's life. Such social learning is salient in early childhood as well as middle childhood and adolescence, although no one has surveyed the extent to which children mimic one another in everyday life. Seemingly, most exposure to peer modeling occurs under informal conditions rather than formal circumstances, and most are constructive. The effects of peer modeling may not always be benign, but there is no reason to believe that peer models work at cross purposes to modeling based on adults.

Existing evidence shows that peer models possess strong and diverse potential for affecting the course of the child's development. Alterations in social and emotional behavior may be brought about in this manner, as well as alterations in problem-solving behaviors and cognitive style. In one study, Bandura, Grusec, and Menlove (1967) selected children between the ages of three and five who were identified as being afraid of dogs and exposed them to one of the following situations: (1) a "fearless" four-year-old model who demonstrated progressively direct approach responses to a dog, (2) a dog with no model present, and (3) a play period with neither the model nor the dog present. On both immediate and delayed posttests, subjects who observed the model interact with the dog showed a reduction in avoidance behavior. These children were less avoidant than were the children assigned to the other two groups. Film exposure to nonavoidant models has also proved successful in behavior modification (Bandura and Menlove, 1968).

Other work shows that peer models can be used to increase children's sociability. Severely withdrawn nursery school children were selected (O'Connor, 1969), and one experimental group was shown a movie about peer interaction in a nursery school in which the interaction began quietly (with the sharing of toys) and then increased both in tempo of social interaction and the number of children involved. A control group saw a film of equal length about dolphins. Evaluation of the outcomes of this experiment took place after the children had returned to their classrooms. Increases were noted among the children who viewed the peer interaction, but no increases occurred among the children who had watched the dolphins.

Peer modeling serves to extend the efforts of the core culture in sex-role socialization. Kobasigawa (1968) exposed young children to situations in which other children were observed: (1) playing with toys that were considered inappropriate for the subject's sex, (2) playing with neutral toys, or (3) resisting verbally the temptation to play with inappropriate toys. Results showed that exposure to models who played with the inappropriate toys had a disinhibitory effect on the observer, although boys disinhibited such behavior only when the peer model was a boy. Observation of models who inhibited inappropriate sex-role behavior enhanced the observers' own control over inappropriate behavior; and observation of models who engaged in alternative activity with the neutral toys also reduced the subject's interaction with the inappropriate toys.

Problem-solving behavior can also be altered by observation of peer models. Miller and Dollard (1941) showed that the solution of two-choice discrimination problems could be learned in this way, and Walters, Parke, and Cane (1965) showed the same to be true on a memory task. Other studies have indicated that conceptual tempo, as measured in problem-solving situations, is susceptible to modeling influences. Debus (1970) exposed third-grade children who were identified as "impulsive" problem-solvers to sixth-grade models who were identified as "reflective." Posttest results showed that the latency of responding was increased as a consequence of the subject's exposure to the peer model.

Finally, the efficacy of peer modeling has been demonstrated in special learning situations. Talkington, Hall, and Altman (1973) employed peer models to teach basic receptive command skills to severely retarded institutionalized children. Some subjects observed a model respond to a command given by the experimenter; others watched the command given without being provided with an opportunity to observe the model; a control group received no training. Change scores were significantly greater in the modeling group than in either of the other groups, although the directly trained group outperformed the control group. Guralnick (1976) has reported results from a study in which a handicapped child observed certain speech forms in the language behavior of a nonhandicapped peer and was subsequently reinforced for them. Usage of such forms by the handicapped child was increased.

Conditions Affecting Peer Imitation Situational conditions impinge on these modeling effects. Peer imitation in problem-solving situations increases when the subject observes the model receive a reward, but feedback supplied to the model must be clearly "rewarding" in order for this to happen. Geshuri (1972) found that correct responses in a problem-solving situation occurred more frequently among children who observed a peer model receive clear-cut approval but not among children who saw the model receive less relevant information. A clear rationale has also been found to enhance the modeling of sharing under reward as compared to no-reward conditions (Elliott and Vasta, 1970). Punishment of the model for nonsharing has a similar effect; that is, observation of such models increases sharing behavior (Morris, Marshall, and Miller, 1973). But observation of a peer model being punished also inhibits *all* antisocial activity and increases the extent to which the subject adheres to generalized "good boy" norms.

Several studies (e.g., Bandura, Ross, and Ross, 1963) show that imitation occurs most readily when the subject and the model are of the same sex. As Rosekrans reported (1967), it also seems to be the case that perceived similarity on various dimensions of personality and social status enhances peer imitation. Friendly relations between model and observer (Grosser, Polansky, and Lippitt, 1951) and the opportunity to share emotional experiences (Aronfreed, 1968) also increase imitation in some situations. Variables such as the competence of the model and the status of the model affect children's imitation of adults, and there is no reason to assume that they would not also be involved in imitation of peers. The age difference between subject and model is relevant, too. In one study, young children imitated older children (or children perceived to be older) more often than they imitated children close to the subjects' own age (Peifer, 1971).

Effects of Being Imitated Being imitated affects children, and these effects should not be overlooked. In many formalized tutoring situations (see below), children who have had tutoring experience report increased feelings of self-satisfaction and responsibility. Allen and Devin-Sheehan (1974) actually studied the effects on sixth-grade tutors of being imitated by younger tutees. Female tutors reported increased liking for their tutees (who were same-sex) the more frequently they were imitated. Male tutors, on the other hand, liked their tutees less well when there was a large amount of imitation. Thelen and Kirkland (1976) have studied the effects of being imitated on the child's tendency to reciprocate, that is, his tendency to imitate someone who has imitated him. Some subjects in this investigation were imitated by children a year older than themselves (the experimenters' confederates) while others were imitated by children a year younger (also confederates). Comparisons were then made in the amount of imitation that was reciprocal versus the amount of imitation directed at a nonimitating peer. Reciprocal imitation was more frequent than nonreciprocal imitation of children when the confederates were older children. Also, more subjects who interacted with older confederates chose the imitator over the nonimitator on measures of interpersonal attraction. But no differences were obtained in the subjects' behavior toward imitators and nonimitators who were younger than the subjects themselves. Status, as defined by the age difference between the imitator and the imitated, is thus a highly salient variable in determining the individual's response to being copied. Little more is known about the reinforcement value of being imitated, but clearly such experience affects children's social behavior within the context of peer relations.

Few cultures institutionalize children's exposure to each other as models even though utilization of such social learning opportunities would add appreciably to available educational resources. Children themselves are an educational resource that most teachers neither appreciate nor exploit, and modeling is clearly one of the processes contained in peer interaction that needs more extensive use.

Peer Tutoring

Considerable interest has been expressed in peer tutoring, the more or less formal utilization of children as teachers in schools and other agencies. The use of tutoring as an educational device has a long history in educational work (Allen, 1976), but it has gained new popularity during recent years. Tutoring is thought to have three main outcomes. First, it utilizes the potential existing in peer interaction for constructive educational ends. Second, the tutoring situation is thought to benefit both tutor (the teacher) and tutee (the child being taught). In most instances, tutoring programs are designed to assist both. Third, peer tutoring provides valuable assistance to overworked teachers.

Ample evidence shows that children can teach things to other children in more-or-less formal situations (Allen, 1976). The tutoring relationship is a complicated one, however, and few generalizations can be made about it. Among more commonly reported results are that: (1) children prefer to teach children younger than themselves and to be taught by children who are older; (2) children prefer same-sex situations to opposite-sex situations; and (3) tutors do not like to participate in the evaluation of their tutees. Particularly if it will determine something that really matters to the tutee, evaluation is anathema. Children's attitudes about tutoring and its effectiveness are also related to the task, the competence of both tutor and tutee (consequences are different when programs involve learners who are failures and learners who are not failures), the intrinsic and extrinsic motivation of both parties, and other conditions (Allen and Feldman, 1976).

The benefits to the tutor in this type of peer interaction are numerous. The teacher role carries with it such attractive elements as status, attention from adults, and deference from other children. Assuming that the tutoring experience includes an identification with the teacher role, such experiences can enhance self-esteem and change attitudes toward authority figures, the school, and society. Tutoring also provides role-taking opportunities, enhances perspective-taking, assists in the acquisition of helping competencies, and leads to more positive attitudes about nurturance and sympathetic behavior.

The tutee's benefits are usually conceptualized in terms of cognitive learning: increases in reading level, mathematical competencies, or whichever ability the tutoring has been focused upon. The effectiveness of tutoring derives from several factors, most notably the individualized nature of the instruction. But peer tutoring involves a reciprocity not found in other tutorial situations, and in that reciprocity must lie some of its unique potential for the tutee.

Research workers have discovered that close and continuing attention must be paid to the "maintenance system" that accompanies the tutoring. Little can be expected from putting two children in a room with instructions to "teach" or to "learn." Possibilities of both mayhem and exploitation exist in the tutoring situation. Not only does the tutor need supervision with respect to the process of teaching, but the whole institutional system must be geared to motivate the tutor-tutee relationship.

One investigation (Allen and Feldman, 1973) illustrates the complexities of peer instruction. Low-achieving children taught younger children who, themselves, were average achievers. On various days, the tutor either engaged in the tutoring or spent an equivalent amount of time studying alone. Similar controls were exercised over the tutees: They were taught on certain days and studied alone on other days. Performance was assessed regularly. For the tutors, studying alone was more efficient during the early stages of the experiment, but, later, tutoring resulted in better learning than solitary activity. Reverse results were obtained for the learners: At the beginning of the experiment, they learned more during the tutoring sessions than by studying alone, but by the second week their performance was somewhat better when they studied alone. The results of this study illustrate two things: (1) the complexities of the tutoring experience, and (2) the changes in tutoring effectiveness that result for both tutor and tutee with the passage of time.

Certain cautions need to be stated with respect to peer tutoring. Wholesale use of formalized peer relations is probably unwise. Peer interaction contributes to children's socialization by means of the give-and-take that occurs between individuals of similar developmental status. The equalitarian nature of peer interaction is its *raison d'etre*. For peer relations to evolve into formal, authoritarian structures (á la *The Lord of the Flies*) would be counterproductive, at least with respect to the socialization objectives sought in most contemporary Western societies. To engineer a major change in modes of peer interaction without better evidence concerning the consequences of such change would be to place our entire society at risk.

PEER RELATIONS AND GROUP TENSIONS

Mainstreaming, the integration of handicapped children and their nonhandicapped peers, is an attempt at social engineering as well as an educational tactic. Most classroom learning is *social* learning, and experimentation with the composition of classrooms is *social* experimentation. Mainstreaming is an attempt to find the most desirable social context for the education of both handicapped and nonhandicapped children.

Students of mainstreaming learned many years ago that interaction between handicapped and nonhandicapped children *by itself* does not provide the sort of social context that facilitates either social or cognitive learning (Guralnick, 1976). Social interaction between the handicapped and nonhandicapped members of such classes is constrained and differs both quantitatively and qualitatively from interaction among nonhandicapped children (Hibbs, 1975). Differences in self-esteem are evident, and social isolation of the handicapped child is a common occurrence.

In fact, this situation is not very different from any social situation in which the participants have not previously enjoyed harmonious relations with one another. Many years ago, the Sherifs (e.g., Sherif et al., 1961) discovered that members of different membership groups, when exposed to competitive situations, show hostility, conflict, and alienation from one another. Group contact, alone, was demonstrated to be very unreliable as a means of reducing the hostility and alienation. These experiments revealed, however, the sort of condition that would increase solidarity, positive social interaction, and constructive outcomes in peer interaction, namely, cooperative activity in the service of a so-called superordinate goal.

Enrollment in the same classroom and daily exposure to the same teacher(s) do not constitute superordinate goals for handicapped and nonhandicapped children. Preschool activities sometimes carry sufficient generalized incentive value to classify them as superordinate, but most do not. And, for older children, classroom structures often involve competition for scarce resources (e.g., grades or praise) or the uneven distribution of them. Classrooms rarely possess the cohesion of highly cooperative societies. In fact, they lack the ingredients essential for reducing within-groups tensions—shared goals of high incentive value *to everyone* and opportunities *for everyone* to participate in reaching these goals. The Sherif studies are clear: Intergroup contact must involve mutually shared norms and cooperative activity in order for reduction in tensions and productive social intercourse to occur. This elemental lesson is seldom mentioned in the literature on mainstreaming, and yet it is one of the most relevant principles to be found in the entire social psychology of childhood.

CONCLUSION

Peer interaction contains numerous elements through which it contributes to the socialization of the child. Such contributions are unique in that aggressive socialization, sex-role learning, and moral development would be seriously impeded if children did not have contact with other children during their formative years. Peer relations contribute to socialization synergistically (i.e., in an additive manner) with adult-child relations. Usually, family and school values tend to reinforce values emanating from the peer culture and vice versa. Discord sometimes occurs, but most children experience greater concordance in their social relations than discordance.

Programming of peer interaction in the interests of childhood socialization is a complex process, entailing many management decisions. But practitioners are not without guidelines in this endeavor. Many good guesses and points of departure can be found in the literature dealing with children as both formal and informal socializing agents. The utilization of children as agents in their own socialization should be a key consideration in planning many different kinds of early intervention activities, particularly those activities that involve the integration of handicapped and nonhandicapped children.

REFERENCES CITED

Allen, V. L. (Ed.). 1976. Children as Teachers. New York: Academic Press.

Allen, V. L., and Devin-Sheehan, L. D. 1974. The tutor as a role model: Effects of imitation and liking on student tutors. Technical report 304. Madison, Wis.: Wisconsin Research and Development Center for Cognitive Learning.

Allen, V. L., and Feldman, R. S. 1973. Learning through tutoring: Low-achieving children as tutors. Journal of Experimental Education, 42, 1-5.

Allen, V. L., and Feldman, R. S. 1976. Studies on the role of tutor. In V. L. Allen (Ed.), Children as Teachers. New York: Academic Press.

Aronfreed, J. 1968. Conduct and Conscience: The Socialization of Internalized Control over Behavior. New York: Academic Press.

Bandura, A., Grusec, J. E., and Menlove, F. L. 1967. Vicarious extinction of avoidance behavior. Journal of Personality and Social Psychology, 5, 16-23.

Bandura, A., and Menlove, F. L. 1968. Factors determining vicarious extinction of avoidance behavior through symbolic modeling. Journal of Personality and Social Psychology, 8, 99-108.

Bandura, A., Ross, D., and Ross, S. A. 1963. Imitation of film-mediated aggressive models. Journal of Abnormal and Social Psychology, 66, 3-11.

Barker, R. G., and Wright, H. F. 1955. Midwest and Its Children. New York: Harper & Row.

Bowlby, J. 1969. Attachment and Loss. Vol. 1. New York: Basic Books.

Bronson, W. C. 1966. Central orientations: A study of behavior organization from childhood to adolescence. Child Development, 37, 125-155.

Bruner, J. S., Jolly, A., and Sylva, K. 1976. Play—Its Role in Development and Evolution. New York: Basic Books.

Charlesworth, R., and Hartup, W. W. 1967. Positive social reinforcement in the nursery school peer group. Child Development, 38, 993-1002.

Debus, R. L. 1970. Effects of brief observation of model behavior on conceptual tempo of impulsive children. Developmental Psychology, 2, 22-32.

Elliott, R., and Vasta, R. 1970. The modeling of sharing: Effects associated with vicarious reinforcement, symbolization, age, and generalization. Journal of Experimental Child Psychology, 10, 8-15.

Fagot, B. I., and Patterson, G. R. 1969. An in vivo analysis of reinforcing contingencies for sex-role behaviors in the preschool child. Developmental Psychology, 1, 563-568.

Ferguson, N. 1965. Peers as social agents. Unpublished masters thesis, University of Minnesota.

Freud, A., and Dann, S. 1951. An experiment in group upbringing. Psychoanalytic Study of the Child, 6, 127-168.

Geshuri, Y. 1972. Observational learning: Effects of observed reward and response patterns. Journal of Educational Psychology, 63, 374-380.

Getz, S. 1977. Components and characteristics of early spontaneous cooperative play among preschool children. Unpublished doctoral dissertation, University of Minnesota.

Gold, H. A. 1962. The importance of ideology in sociometric evaluation of leadership. Group Psychotherapy, 15, 224-230.

Goldman, J. A. 1976. The social participation of preschool children in same-age versus mixed-age groupings. Unpublished doctoral dissertation, University of Wisconsin.

Gottman, J., Gonso, J., and Rasmussen, B. 1975. Social interaction, social competence, and friendship in children. Child Development, 45, 709-718.

Graziano, W., French, D., Brownell, C. A., and Hartup, W. W. 1976. Peer interaction in same- and mixed-age triads in relation to chronological age and incentive condition. Child Development, 47, 707-714.

Grosser, D., Polansky, N., and Lippitt, R. 1951. A laboratory study of behavioral contagion. Human Relations, 4, 115-142.

Guralnick, M. J. 1976. The value of integrating handicapped and nonhandicapped preschool children. American Journal of Orthopsychiatry, 46, 236-245.

Harlow, H. F. 1969. Age-mate or peer affectional system. In D. S. Lehrman, R. A. Hinde, and E. Shaw (Eds.), Advances in the Study of Behavior (Vol. 2). New York: Academic Press.

Hartup, W. W. 1964. Friendship status and the effectiveness of peers as reinforcing agents. Journal of Experimental Child Psychology, 1, 154-162.

Hartup, W. W. 1977. Adolescent peer relations: A look to the future. In J. P. Hill and F. J. Monks (Eds.), Adolescence and Youth in Prospect. Guildford, England: IPC Science and Technology Press.

Hartup, W. W., and Coates, B. 1967. Imitation of peers as a function of reinforcement from the peer group and rewardingness of the model. Child Development, 38, 1003-1016.

Hartup, W. W., Moore, S. G., and Sager, G. O. 1963. Avoidance of inappropriate sex-typing in young children. Journal of Consulting Psychology, 27, 467-473.

Hartup, W. W., and Zook, E. 1960. Sex-role preferences in three- and four-year-old children. Journal of Consulting Psychology, 24, 420-426.

Hibbs, B. 1975. Effects of cooperative and individualized goal structures on reading achievement, social skills, and social status of learning disabled and normal progress elementary school pupils. Unpublished doctoral dissertation, University of Minnesota.

Karen, R. L. 1965. Operant conditioning and social preference. Unpublished doctoral dissertation, Arizona State University.

Keasey, C. B. 1971. Social participation as a factor in the moral development of preadolescents. Developmental Psychology, 5, 216–220.

Kobasigawa, A. 1968. Inhibitory and disinhibitory effects of models on sex-inappropriate behavior in children. Psychologia, 11, 86–96.

Konner, M. 1975. Relations among infants and juveniles in comparative perspective. In M. Lewis and L. A. Rosenblum (Eds.), Friendship and Peer Relations. New York: John Wiley & Sons.

Kopfstein, D. 1972. Effects of accelerating and decelerating consequences on the social behavior of trainable retarded children. Child Development, 43, 800–809.

Lee, L. C. 1973. Social encounters of infants: The beginnings of popularity. Paper presented at the biennial meeting of the International Society for the Study of Behavioral Development, Ann Arbor, Mich.

Lee, L. C. 1975. Toward a cognitive theory of interpersonal development: Importance of peers. In M. Lewis and L. A. Rosenblum (Eds.), Friendship and Peer Relations. New York: John Wiley & Sons.

Lewis, M., and Rosenblum, L. A. (Eds.). 1975. Friendship and Peer Relations. New York: John Wiley & Sons.

Livesley, W. J., and Bromley, D. B. 1973. Person Perception in Childhood and Adolescence. New York: John Wiley & Sons.

Lougee, M. D., Grueneich, R., and Hartup, W. W. Social interaction in same- and mixed-age dyads of preschool children. Child Development. In press.

Lougee, M. D., Mason, M., and Hartup, W. W. Social interaction in mixed-age nursery school classes. In preparation.

Miller, N. E., and Dollard, J. 1941. Social Learning and Imitation. New Haven, Conn.: Yale University Press.

Morris, W. N., Marshall, H. M., and Miller, R. S. 1973. The effect of vicarious punishment on prosocial behavior in children. Journal of Experimental Child Psychology, 15, 222–236.

Novak, M. A., and Harlow, H. F. 1975. Social recovery of monkeys isolated for the first year of life. 1. Rehabilitation and therapy. Developmental Psychology, 11, 453–465.

O'Connor, R. 1969. Modification of social withdrawal through symbolic modeling. Journal of Applied Behavior Analysis, 2, 15–22.

Parten, M. B. 1932. Social participation among preschool children. Journal of Abnormal and Social Psychology, 27, 243–269.

Patterson, G. R., Littman, R. A., and Bricker, W. 1967. Assertive behavior in children: A step toward a theory of aggression. Monographs of the Society for Research in Child Development, 32(113).

Peifer, M. R. 1971. The effects of varying age-grade status of models on the imitative behavior of six-year-old boys. Unpublished doctoral dissertation, University of Delaware.

Piaget, J. 1932. The Moral Judgment of the Child. Glencoe, Ill.: Free Press.

Roff, M., Sells, S. B., and Golden, M. M. 1972. Social Adjustment and Personality Development in Children. Minneapolis: University of Minnesota Press.

Rolf, J. E. 1972. The social and academic competence of children vulnerable to schizophrenia and other behavior pathologies. Journal of Abnormal Psychology, 80, 225–243.

Rosekrans, M. A. 1967. Imitation in children as a function of perceived similarity to a social model and vicarious reinforcement. Journal of Personality and Social Psychology, 7, 307–315.

Rubin, K. H., Maioni, T. L., and Hornung, M. 1976. Free play behaviors in middle- and lower-class preschoolers: Parten and Piaget revisited. Child Development, 47, 414–419.

Selman, R. L. 1976. Toward a structural analysis of developing interpersonal relations concepts: Research with normal and disturbed preadolescent boys. In A. D. Pick (Ed.), Minnesota Symposia on Child Psychology (Vol. 10). Minneapolis: University of Minnesota Press.

Shatz, M., and Gelman, R. 1973. The development of communication skills: Modification in the speech of young children as a function of listener. Monographs of the Society for Research in Child Development, 38(152).

Sherif, M., Harvey, O. J., White, B. J., Hood, W. R., and Sherif, C. W. 1961. Intergroup Conflict and Cooperation: The Robbers Cave Experiment. Norman: University of Oklahoma Press.

Solomon, R. G., and Wahler, R. 1973. Peer reinforcement control of classroom problem behavior. Journal of Applied Behavior Analysis, 6, 49–56.

Suomi, S. J., and Harlow, H. F. 1972. Social rehabilitation in isolate-reared monkeys. Developmental Psychology, 6, 487–496.

Talkington, L. W., Hall, S. M., and Altman, R. 1973. Use of a peer modeling procedure with severely retarded subjects on a basic communication response skill. Training School Bulletin, 69, 145–149.

Thelen, M. H., and Kirkland, K. D. 1976. On status and being imitated: Effects on reciprocal imitation and attraction. Journal of Personality and Social Psychology, 33, 691–697.

Wahler, R. G. 1967. Child-child interactions in free-field settings: Some experimental analyses. Journal of Experimental Child Psychology, 5, 278–293.

Walters, R. H., Parke, R. D., and Cane, V. A. 1965. Timing of punishment and the observation of consequences to others as determinants of response inhibition. Journal of Experimental Child Psychology, 2, 10–30.

Whiting, B. B., and Whiting, J. W. M. 1975. Children of Six Cultures: A Psychocultural Analysis. Cambridge, Mass.: Harvard University Press.

A BEHAVIORAL APPROACH TO THE ANALYSIS OF PEER INTERACTIONS

Vey Michael Nordquist, Ph.D.

Behavioral scientists of almost every theoretical persuasion currently agree that normal human development depends in part upon peer interactions that occur during early childhood. The importance that scientists place on this area of development is attested to by the large number of studies that have been conducted on early peer interactions since the late 1920s and 1930s as well as the current renewal of interest (see Lewis and Rosenblum, 1975). Several detailed reviews of this research can be found in the first three editions of the *Manual of Child Psychology* (Carmichael, 1946, 1954, 1970); volumes 1, 2, and 5 of the *Review of Child Development Research* (Hoffman and Hoffman, 1964, 1966; Hetherington, 1975); the *Handbook of Research Methods in Child Development* (Mussen, 1960); and the Lewis and Rosenblum (1975) volume.

Many researchers in this area searched for conditions that would optimally enhance early peer interactions. These investigators conducted their research in nursery schools, kindergartens, and day care centers, with the hope that their findings would be particularly useful to early education teachers. Their strategy was to document the development of normal peer interactions. For example, Parten (1932) showed that nursery school children participated more frequently in parallel, associative, and cooperative activities and less frequently in idleness, solitary play, and onlooker activities during the years from two to five. Other investigators reported similar age-behavior relationships for initiation of social contacts (Beaver, 1932), aggressive behavior (Jersild and Markey, 1935), quarrels (Dawe, 1934; Green, 1933a, b), cooperation (Murphy, 1937), and competition and rivalry (Leuba, 1933). Anderson (1937) reviewed this literature and traced the evidence showing that peer interactions become more pronounced as children advance through their early childhood years. Soon, chronological age functioned for many child development scientists as the central variable in the study of peer interactions, and teachers were expected to learn about child behaviors that occurred between the ages of two to six.

Today, chronological age is still a central variable in the study of early peer interactions, as the above reviews will demonstrate, and teachers are still being told that the development of these behaviors depends primarily upon age. For example, Swift (1964) advised teachers that two-year-old children are generally not "ready" to participate actively in interactions with other children because the majority of their behavior is characterized by onlooker activities and solitary play. On the other hand, three-year-old children are excellent candidates for early education because they are just "... beginning to spend a greater portion of their time in more active social interaction..." (p. 272). Thus, the preveiling belief among many teachers is that peer interactions depend more upon a child's age and less upon the teaching procedures, activities, physical space, or equipment that constitute early education settings.

Some scientists have noted that chronological age is actually a residual variable that provides nothing more than "... an index of the occasions and limits for the process of environmental impact..." on child behavior (Gewirtz, 1971, p. 112). According to this behavioral view, age itself is never a major variable responsible for the development of peer interactions. Rather, it is an indication of the types of learning conditions children are presented with in natural settings, conditions that are seldom optimally efficient in facilitating behavioral development. Accordingly, child development scientists may be equating changes in peer interactions with the relatively inefficient learning conditions in early education settings. By paying routine attention to age-related changes, they risk overlooking functional relationships between environmental variables and child behavior. As described later in the chapter, behavioral scientists have gathered considerable empirical evidence to support this latter view of peer interactions.

Chronological age is not the only residual variable that has captured the interest of child development scientists. They have also investigated variables such as birth-order, socioeconomic level, sex, intelligence, and personality factors. Unfortunately, the current use of information provided by the analyses of these variables has often obscured rather than facilitated the discovery of conditions that relate to peer interactions. As a result, early education teachers cannot turn to the child development literature for information about teaching procedures that promote appropriate child-child relationships. With few exceptions, this literature advises teachers about peer interactions they can *expect;* it rarely advises them about peer interactions they can *develop.*

If early education teachers want to influence young children's development, they need to know about procedures that promote peer interactions. This knowledge is especially important for teachers who work with handicapped and nonhandicapped children in integrated early education settings. In order for handicapped children to receive many of the benefits of integrated programming, they must interact routinely with nonhandicapped children. However, teachers who "expect" handicapped and nonhandicapped children to interact with one another are likely to be disappointed (Devoney, Guralnick, and Rubin, 1974; Guralnick, 1976; Snyder, Apolloni, and Cooke, 1977). What can early education teachers do to encourage these interactions? If the child development literature does not provide useful information, where can early education teachers seek information about teaching procedures that develop and maintain early peer interactions? One possibility is the behavioral literature.

BEHAVIOR ANALYSIS OF PEER INTERACTIONS

During the last decade and a half, a number of behavioral scientists have searched for procedures that develop and maintain peer interactions. Guided largely by the principles of operant conditioning theory (Bijou and Baer, 1961; Skinner, 1953), they speculated that children often interact with one another because of reinforcing consequences provided by the social environment. Furthermore, they specified some experimental procedures that would permit them to detect social consequences that are functionally related to (controlled) peer interactions (Baer, Wolf, and Risley, 1968). They reasoned that if the operant conditioning view of child behavior was valid, that is, that child-child relationships are developed and maintained by social reinforcers, then it followed that detecting and changing these reinforcement contingencies would result in the modification of peer interactions. Making social reinforcers contingent on these behaviors should increase their frequency of occurrence; removing contingencies for these behaviors should decrease their frequency of occurrence.

Recently, a few behavioral scientists have shown an interest in early education events whose effects cannot be understood in terms of a strict application of operant conditioning principles. These events include the impact of certain physical, spatial, and organizational features of early education settings (e.g., Doke and Risley, 1972; Quilitch and Risley, 1973; Risley, 1975; Twardosz, Cataldo, and Risley, 1974), but very little is known about their range and precise effects on peer interactions. Nevertheless, to date, behavior analysis still represents for most scientists a method of documenting the various effects of reinforcement contingencies on young children's behaviors. Thus, the applied implications of this view for early education teachers depend almost entirely upon a reinforcement interpretation of peer interactions; that is, to the extent that teachers can control the social reinforcement contingencies in early education settings, they can develop, maintain, or modify peer interactions.

In general, the behavior analysis approach to the study of peer interactions includes the following aspects:

1. The analysis of peer interactions as they occur in *natural settings*
2. The use of *teachers* and/or *peers* as the primary agents responsible for developing peer interactions
3. The training of teachers or peers to apply *operant conditioning procedures* (one corollary to this activity is that the procedures are to be used to *develop* or *modify* current peer interactions and that these procedures are to be *retained* by teachers and peers for use in the event of future problems)
4. The maintenance of peer interactions through teacher and/or peer *reinforcement contingencies*

Utilizing this approach, behavioral scientists have identified to date only a small number of procedures that develop and maintain peer interactions. But these procedures are powerful in the sense that they can produce large changes in peer interactions. They are also general in the sense that they can produce changes in several types of peer interactions, and they are reliable in the sense that they can repeatedly produce the same interactions. Consequently, teachers in integrated early education programs are likely to find them useful when faced with the task of developing and maintaining interactions between handicapped and nonhandicapped children.

Teacher Attention Procedures
That Develop and Maintain Peer Interactions

Without exception, early childhood educators consider the promotion of appropriate peer interactions one of their primary functions. They even agree generally on the interaction characteristics that parents, teachers, and peers find most acceptable (Moore, 1967). However, they do not agree on precisely what conditions develop and maintain these interactions in early education settings. Consequently, it is not clear what teachers should do when a child begins to interact inappropriately with his or her peers. For example, Harris, Wolf, and Baer (1967) noted that ''... there is considerable variation and vagueness in the procedures recommended, particularly those dealing with such problem behaviors as the child's hitting people, breaking valuable things, or withdrawing from people and things" (p. 13). Thus, Read (1955) recommended talking to the child, accepting his or her feelings, and redirecting the child into activities that provide a more appropriate means of emotional expression. Taylor (1954) counseled teachers to accept both appropriate and inappropriate behaviors and to provide "nonemotional" forms of punishment. Swift (1964) advised teachers to deal with these problems by helping the child increase his or her "... social perceptiveness through discussion of incidents that occur in the classroom" (p. 278), and recently, Read (1971) presented virtually the same recommendations that she offered in 1955.

Early education teachers usually feel that some combination of the above procedures will help promote appropriate peer interactions. However, they will admit that these procedures do not work with every child, and when they do work it is usually not clear which procedures and priniples were operative (Harris, Wolf, and Baer, 1967). Yet, careful inspection of these procedures reveals one interesting commonality: they require that the teacher attend to the child.

If the operant conditioning view of peer interactions is valid, we might expect to learn that adult attention is the most primitive and pervasive form of social reinforcement that affects early peer interactions (Bijou and Baer, 1965). Thus, teachers run the risk of unintentionally increasing the frequency of inappropriate interactions, simply by providing attention whenever these interactions occur (Baer and Wolf, 1969). Indeed, the results of several behavioral studies indicate that this is often the case.

Peer Aggression A child who is aggressive toward peers usually generates immediate activity. Patterson, Littman, and Bricker (1967) noted that aggressive behaviors such as hitting, kicking, pushing, yelling, throwing objects, taking play materials from other children, and so forth, are coercive in the sense that they "demand" certain responses from teachers and peers. Consequently, with respect to teacher behavior, a systematic distribution of their attentional responses must be made so as not to inadvertently increase the frequency of child aggression toward peers.

Hart et al. (1968) reported that teachers could reduce the frequency of aggressive (though nonviolent) behaviors of a five-year-old child by ignoring them and making their attention contingent upon the child's cooperative play with peers. Furthermore, they found that abundant amounts of noncontingent teacher attention had no effect on the frequency of cooperative play. Abundant teacher attention did not maintain the child's newly developed play skills during periods when contingent reinforcement for play was discontinued. The Hart et al. (1968) procedures have been replicated by several other investigators with similar results (e.g., Allen, Turner, and Everett, 1970; Strain, Shores, and Kerr, 1976; Strain and Timm, 1974). The general conclusion that can be drawn from these studies is that early education teachers are more likely to develop appropriate peer interactions when their attention is dispensed on a contingent basis.

In several of the above studies the subject children did not represent a serious threat to the safety of their peers. For example, in Hart et al. (1968), the subject child taunted her peers, expressed foul language toward them, or produced rambling accounts of violent accidents; these are unpleasant behaviors certainly, but hardly threatening. In Strain, Shores, and Kerr (1976), two subject children were oppositional and frequently produced tantrums, but they were not assaultive. Strain and Timm (1974) worked with subject children who presented similar behavior problems. Thus, it might be argued that teachers would probably find it easier to ignore "low risk" behaviors such as these, but would be reluctant to ignore aggressive behaviors that might result in injury to a peer. Fortunately, there are at least two procedures that deal effectively with this problem.

Allen, Turner, and Everett (1970) selected a four-and-one-half-year-old subject child who was described by his teachers as excessively disruptive, hyperactive, noncompliant, and aggressive. The child's problems warranted placement in a remedial classroom where trained teachers redirected his disruptive behaviors, provided attention and comfort during tantrums, physically restrained him when he assaulted other children, and helped him verbalize his feelings. Observations of the boy's inappropriate behaviors during several baseline sessions revealed essentially no changes in their high rates. However, these rates dropped to zero when the teachers ignored his tantrums, classroom disruptions, noncompliance, and peer aggression. Of particular interest is the strategy the teachers used when the child hit or kicked his peers, spit at them, or took their play materials. When these behaviors occurred, the nearest teacher immediately attended to the assaulted peer and turned her back to the subject child. With this simple procedure, the teachers reduced the risk of peer injury and also ignored the subject child's aggressive behavior. Of course, when the child interacted appropriately with his peers, the teachers provided attention and verbal approval. Unfortunately, during the intervention period the child began to produce new disruptive behaviors. At lunch time he would throw his food on the floor and smear it with his hands and feet. Initially, the teachers required the child to help them clean the floor with a sponge, but this procedure had no effect on food throwing and smearing. However, these behaviors finally disappeared when the teachers ignored them.

Although the procedures of Allen, Turner, and Everett (1970) have been replicated with virtually the same results (i.e., Pinkston et al., 1973), this strategy does require teachers to spend a considerable amount of time attending to an assaulted peer. Consequently, some investigators have experimentally assessed the effects of a second procedure for dealing with the assaultive child. Specifically, this procedure still requires a teacher to attend to appropriate interactions, but it also isolates the child from reinforcement whenever he or she is aggressive (Burmeister, 1973; Sibley, Abbott, and Cooper, 1969; Wahler and Nordquist, 1973). This strategy is extremely effective and may be necessary in cases where an extinction procedure is ineffective (Wahler, 1969).

Peer Withdrawal Like the aggressive child, the socially withdrawn child possesses behaviors that often attract teacher attention. Consider, for example, a child who rarely interacts with peers, who plays alone most of the time, who does not talk very often, and who rarely laughs or smiles. It is hard to imagine any teacher totally ignoring such a child. Yet, the teacher may inadvertently strengthen these behaviors by attending to them.

Allen et al. (1964) suspected that teacher attention was maintaining the withdrawn behaviors of a four-year-old preschool child. After obtaining several baseline counts of these behaviors, the investigators instructed the child's teachers to ignore them and attend to the child only when she approached or played with other children. As predicted, the child quickly began to interact with her peers. To demonstrate causality, the baseline and intervention procedures were replicated and produced the expected results. Moreover, anecdotal information revealed that the child did not complain to her teachers about imaginary bumps and abrasions on her body during the intervention periods, and she also began to talk in a more articulate manner. Apparently, these collateral behavior changes occurred even though the child's teachers did not try to develop them.

Shortly after Allen et al. (1964) published their findings, a number of other investigators conducted experimental assessments of the effects of teacher attention on withdrawn children and reported similar results (e.g., Cooper et al., 1966; Foxwell et al., 1966; Johnston et al., 1966). However, one set of investigators (Buell et al., 1968) analyzed the problem from a somewhat different perspective. These investigators not only monitored child behaviors that were designated for behavior change, but they monitored other child behaviors as well. Their subject was a three-year-old, socially withdrawn child who rarely talked to teachers, used other children's names, touched other children, played with other children, or used outdoor play equipment, either alone or with other children. However, the child often touched her teachers, produced baby talk, and engaged in parallel play. Buell et al. (1968) reasoned that they might observe changes in one or more of the above behaviors if they could induce the child to use the outdoor play equipment. Accordingly, the teachers were instructed to prompt the child to use the equipment and attend to her at these times. As expected, the child began to use the outdoor play equipment, but she also began to touch other children, talk to them, and play with them, even though the teachers did not systematically vary their attention to any of these behaviors. When the teachers eventually discontinued attending to equipment-use, the frequency of equipment-use decreased. However, the other social behaviors did not decrease. Evidently, these behaviors were not functionally related to equipment-use because they did not covary with its baseline and intervention rates.

Unfortunately, the study was not designed to analyze the variables that might have caused them to change, but some behavioral scientists (e.g., Baer and Wolf, 1969) have speculated that the child was thrown into numerous social contingencies with her peers when she began to use the play equipment. Thus, peer reinforcement contingencies may have "trapped" child behaviors that were important for developing and maintaining peer interactions. Consistent with this interpretation, the child's teacher-oriented behaviors did not vary systematically with the procedural changes, and parallel play, though greatly variable throughout the study, was essentially unaffected by the procedures. Nevertheless, this study established that teachers who systematically attend to certain child behaviors may unknowingly alter other behaviors not designated for behavior change.

Anecdotal (Allen et al., 1964) and experimental (Buell et al., 1968) accounts of the general effects of teacher attention contingencies indicated that withdrawn children might develop new behaviors once they begin to interact with their peers. In particular, the anectodal information presented by Allen et al. (1964) suggested that peer play and language might be functionally related. To examine this possibility, Nordquist and Bradley (1973) conducted an experimental analysis of a severely withdrawn, nonverbal preschool child. Several baseline sessions revealed that the child never played with or spoke to her peers. She always played alone and was accompanied by at least one teacher eighty percent of the time. The child's behaviors changed dramatically, however, when play with a confederate peer (i.e., a classmate who assisted the teacher by initiating play with the withdrawn child) was attended to by the teachers. The child not only began to play frequently with the confederate peer, but she also began to play with several other peers. Replications of the baseline and intervention procedures demonstrated that contingent teacher attention was responsible for these changes. In addition, the child began to talk to her peers approximately sixty percent of the time that she played with them. However, an analysis of the teacher attention contingencies failed to reveal systematic variations across the baseline and intervention sessions that might have accounted for the changes in language interactions. Thus, the child's newly developed language skills could not be attributed to differential teacher attention. Still, it was possible that peer modeling and/or peer reinforcement contingencies were responsible for its development, but unfortunately this possibility could not be assessed experimentally.

The preceding studies provide considerable empirical support for the reinforcing effects of teacher attention on aggressive and socially withdrawn children. This support is generally consistent with the operant conditioning view of child behavior, although variations in nontargeted behaviors may have important theoretical and applied implications (discussed in a later section). Thus, early education teachers can often promote the development and maintenance of appropriate peer interactions by attending to these behaviors. With respect to teachers in integrated programs, they might be advised to prompt and reinforce interactions between handicapped and nonhandicapped children in much the same way that Buell et al. (1968) or Nordquist and Bradley (1973) prompted and reinforced socially withdrawn children. The use of a confederate peer to prompt interactions may be a particularly useful strategy for teachers in programs that integrate handicapped and nonhandicapped children.

Peer Attention Procedures
That Develop and Maintain Peer Interactions

In several of the preceding studies it was assumed that newly developed peer interactions were maintained by numerous peer contingencies. There is considerable correlational (e.g., Charlesworth and Hartup, 1967; Hartup, Glazer, and Charlesworth, 1967; Kohn, 1966; Marshall and McCandless, 1957; Patterson, Littman, and Bricker, 1967) and laboratory/experimental evidence (e.g., Hartup 1964; Horowitz, 1962; Patterson and Anderson, 1964; Tikten and Hartup, 1965) to support this assumption. For example, Patterson, Littman, and Bricker (1967) searched for peer responses that correlated significantly with the aggressive behaviors of several preschool children. Peer responses were categorized as either "passive," "cries," "defensive postures," "telling the teacher," "recovering property," or "retaliation." It was found that bodily attack and attacking with objects were followed by either passivity, cries, or defensive postures between seventy-five percent and ninety-seven percent of the time. This suggested that peer responses play an important role in the maintenance of aggressive child behaviors. Moreover, these authors predicted that: (1) peers who reinforced aggressive acts were likely to be the recurrent victims of the aggressive child; (2) peers who counteraggressed were less likely to be attacked in the future, or if they were attacked the form of attack would be different; and (3) a child who successfully counterattacked was more likely to be aggressive in the future as compared to a child whose counterattacks were unsuccessful or who was never victimized. As expected, all of the above predictions were confirmed, indicating that peers may contribute to the development and/or modification as well as the maintenance of aggressive child behaviors in early education settings.

Although correlational studies suggest that peer reinforcement contingencies develop and maintain some types of peer interactions, they do not establish the precise effects of these contingencies on interactions that occur in early education settings. Consequently, Wahler (1967) conducted an experimental analysis of the effects of high and low rates of peer attention on several child social behaviors. Working in a nursery school setting, Wahler selected three subject children who produced social behaviors that received high baseline rates of peer attention and two other subject children who produced behaviors that received unusually low baseline rates of peer attention. To determine the effect of peer attention on these behaviors, the high-rate peers were instructed to continue playing with the subject children (i.e., attend to them) except when they produced the social behaviors designated for extinction. When these behaviors occurred, the peers were told to ignore them. On the other hand, the low-rate peers were told to play with the other two subject children only when they produced the social behaviors designated for reinforcement. As expected, social behaviors that were ignored by the peers decreased substantially while those that peers attended to increased. These changes were subsequently reversed and then recovered when the baseline and intervention procedures were replicated. With this demonstration, Wahler (1967) provided experimental evidence of the precise reinforcing effects of peer attention on social interactions in an early education setting.

Since Wahler published his findings, several behavioral scientists have examined the effects of peer attention on the social and academic behaviors of preadolescent and adolescent problem children (e.g., Bailey et al., 1971; Greenwood, Sloane, and Baskin, 1974; Harris and Sherman, 1973; Solomon and Wahler, 1973). However, Wahler's study has not been replicated, perhaps because investigators generally feel that it is difficult to experimentally control the behaviors of young children in early education settings. In fact, only one additional study that looked exclusively at the reinforcement effects of peer attention on interaction responses (i.e.,

Johnston and Johnston, 1972) has appeared in the behavioral literature. This study was comprised of a series of three experiments performed in a kindergarten setting with small groups of children who exhibited various degrees of articulation problems. Experimental assessments of three procedures for producing control over correct and incorrect consonant sound articulation rates were conducted, initially in a training setting, and then in a free play (generalization) setting. In the first experiment, a teacher reinforced correct consonant sounds with attention and tokens. In the second experiment the subject children had to record each correct consonant sound to receive teacher approval and tokens. In both experiments the procedures produced increases in the rates of correct consonant sounds in the training setting. However, neither procedure produced any degree of stimulus generalization to the free play setting, even though this setting comprised the same physical space, peers, and teachers as the training setting. This suggested that simply maintaining the presence of these stimuli was not sufficient to obtain even a moderate degree of generalization. However, when two children were taught to differentially attend to one another's correct and incorrect consonant sounds, the number of these responses increased and decreased respectively in both the training and generalization settings. Eventually it was established that the children became discriminative stimuli for one another, setting the occasion for appropriate articulation. Thus, peer attention produced a high degree of stimulus control over one component of a behavior (speech) that is generally considered essential for the development and maintenance of peer interactions.

The preceding studies provide limited but convincing evidence that child behaviors are more likely to occur when they precede peer attention. Peer attention, like teacher attention, often functions as a powerful social reinforcer for the development and maintenance of peer interactions; consequently, its effects can be understood in terms of operant conditioning principles. Moreover, in some instances, peers may be more effective generalization-facilitating agents than teachers. This possibility has important implications for integrated early education programs and is discussed later in some detail.

Peer Modeling Procedures
That Develop and Maintain Peer Interactions

Significant behavior change involves developing a similarity between a subject child's behavior and the behavior of other children who are functioning appropriately. This similarity can often be developed by having a teacher or peer "model" the desired behavior. If the subject child produces a close approximation to the model's behavior, it is said that the subject child acquired the behavior "through imitation" (Risley and Baer, 1973). If a child cannot imitate, it is virtually certain that his or her social interactions will be markedly impaired because the development of social interactions depends to a great extent upon learning through imitation. Consequently, considerable attention has been given to establishing the specific operant conditioning principles that govern the imitation process (e.g., Baer and Sherman, 1964; Brigham and Sherman, 1968; Burgess, Burgess, and Esveldt, 1970; Peterson, 1968; Peterson and Whitehurst, 1971) as well as describing operant teaching procedures that develop and maintain imitative behaviors in young children (e.g., Baer and Sherman, 1970; Risley and Baer, 1973; Sherman and Baer, 1969, Sherman and Bushell, 1975). However, few behavioral scientists have examined the effects of peer models on children's social interactions.

Although behavioral scientists generally assume that children serve important modeling functions for one another's behavior in natural settings (Hartup, 1970), there is little experimental evidence to support this assumption. With respect to children with limited imitative repertoires (e.g., young handicapped children), recent evidence suggests that imitation of peer models can be increased through systematic programming (Guralnick, 1976; Snyder, Apolloni, and Cooke, 1977). Consequently, behavioral scientists have recently begun to conduct experimental assessments of the effects of advanced peers as models for handicapped children.

Guralnick (1976) reported that the play behaviors and positive verbalizations of two retarded children did not increase during periods when they observed peer models engaged in these behaviors. However, when nonhandicapped peers were trained to attend selectively to the subject children's appropriate behaviors, play and positive verbalizations increased considerably. In a second experiment, the inappropriate language behaviors of a handicapped preschool child were modified by having the subject child observe a trained peer use appropriate language forms. When the peer model was reinforced by the experimenter for appropriate form usage in the presence of the subject child, the latter soon began producing the same appropriate forms. By simply attending to reinforced language responses in a more advanced peer, an increase in the use of these same responses was produced in the subject child. Thus, this study provided experimental support for what other investigators (e.g., Apolloni, Cooke, and Cooke, 1975; Devoney, Guralnick, and Rubin, 1974) had already suspected; namely, that peer modeling alone is not sufficient to develop imitative responding in some handicapped children.

Although peer modeling of interaction responses cannot be counted on to develop imitative responding in handicapped children, it may affect the interactions of socially withdrawn children if peers can be trained to systematically model appropriate interactions. For example, O'Connor (1969) reported that several socially withdrawn children played more often with their peers shortly after they viewed a film that depicted a number of peer models playing happily together. Children assigned to a control group viewed an unrelated film and did not play with their peers more often after viewing its content. Since the socially withdrawn children in this study had numerous opportunities to observe natural peer play behaviors prior to viewing the films, one must conclude that the peer modeling conditions commonly found in early education settings may not be sufficient to develop interaction responses.

Extending this analysis to children with other handicapping conditions, and based on related discussions (Guralnick, 1976; Snyder, Apolloni, and Cooke, 1977), it appears that teachers may have to alter environmental conditions before handicapped and nonhandicapped children will interact with one another. Perhaps one way to proceed would be to "package" and then apply all of the variables described above. That is, a small number of nonhandicapped children might be trained to model and reinforce interaction responses in handicapped children. Then, teachers could strengthen these behaviors by attending to them. As the preceding studies show, these procedures should produce substantial increases in interactions between handicapped and nonhandicapped children. Furthermore, by including peers in the training process, one might expect that handicapped children would eventually interact with nonhandicapped children who were not included in the training process (Johnston and Johnston, 1972). Both of these possibilities will be explored momentarily.

Physical and Spatial Events
That Develop and Maintain Peer Interactions

In all but one of the preceding studies the research strategy involved the manipulation of social reinforcement contingencies. However, teachers are often advised that certain physical and spatial features of early education settings promote children's physical and social development (Read, 1971). This emphasis upon physical and spatial events can be traced to several studies that appeared in the early peer interaction literature. For example, several studies related space allotments to aggressive interactions in nursery school settings (Green, 1933a; Jersild and Markey, 1935; Murphy, 1937). In general, these studies suggested that aggressive interactions were more likely to occur when play space was restricted. Conflicts among children were also related to certain types of play equipment. For example, Green (1933b) reported that preschool children were likely to quarrel with one another when playing with sand. On the other hand, children were not as likely to quarrel with one another if they were swinging, climbing on a jungle gym, or riding a rocking horse. In a similar study Murphy (1937) reported that fewer quarrels occurred when preschool children were using swings, tricycles, and wagons. Other equipment such as blocks (Markey, 1935) and clay (Updegraff and Herbst, 1933) have also been related to a low number of conflicts in preschool children.

Johnson (1935), rather than looking at specific types of equipment, examined the effects of the amount of available play equipment on behaviors such as teasing, crying, and hitting. He reported that when relatively few pieces of equipment were available for children's play, the children engaged in considerably more of the above behaviors than when a lot of equipment was available. In an interesting study conducted twenty years later, Body (1955) reported similar findings, but additionally found that the number of conflicts among preschool children was also associated with the temperature of the play environment. That is, children who played in a hot, unshaded area were more likely to quarrel with one another than children who played in a cool, shaded area.

The above studies suggested that children's interactions may be affected by the physical and spatial characteristics of early education settings. Unfortunately, none of these studies provided functional analyses of the effects of equipment or space. However, in a recent study, Quilitch and Risley (1973) did conduct a functional analysis and found that young children who attended a community recreation center would play alone or together depending upon the toys that were available in the center. Systematic variations of the presence and absence of six "social" toys and six "isolate" toys revealed that the children played with one another seventy-eight percent of the time when "social" toys such as checkers or playing cards were present, but only sixteen percent of the time when "isolate" toys such as puzzles, tinker toys, or Playdoh were present.

This study suggests that some play materials are functionally related to certain types of peer interactions. It will be recalled that climbing equipment was also found to produce increases in peer interactions (Buell et al., 1968; Cooper et al., 1966; Johnston et al., 1966), but climbing behaviors in these studies were under the control of social reinforcement contingencies. In Quilitch and Risley's (1973) study, reinforcement contingencies were not manipulated. This suggests that the physical and spatial features of early education settings limit the range and alter the probabilities of peer interactions and may be an important means of developing and maintaining peer interactions. However, the available research is too limited to draw any firm conclusions concerning its implications for teachers in integrated programs.

Summary

For nearly five decades residual variables such as age, birth order, sex, socioeconomic level, and personality factors have captured the interest of child development scientists. Seeking to discover conditions that related to the development of peer interactions, they hoped to find information that would be useful to early education teachers. Unfortunately, residual variables cannot be manipulated by early education teachers. Moreover, behavioral scientists have noted that residual variables are better understood as indexes of the relatively inefficient learning conditions that are often present in early education settings. By paying routine attention to these variables, child development scientists have created a research literature that rarely advises early education teachers about peer interactions they can *develop*. Rather, this literature usually advises them about peer interactions they should *expect*.

Recently, behavioral scientists have searched for procedures in early education settings that develop and maintain peer interactions. Guided largely by the principles of operant conditioning theory, they discovered that (1) teacher attention, (2) peer attention, (3) peer modeling, and (4) physical and spatial features were often related to peer interactions. Unlike residual variables, these events could be manipulated by early education teachers to develop and maintain peer interactions.

Now, teachers who work exclusively with nonhandicapped children may not have much need for the above procedures because nonhandicapped children usually possess well developed interaction skills by the time they begin their early education. However, teachers who are faced with the task of integrating handicapped and nonhandicapped children into early education settings are likely to find all of these procedures very useful. Thus, teachers who seek procedures that produce effects on peer interactions that are powerful, general, and reliable should find the behavioral literature especially helpful.

BEHAVIOR ANALYSIS OF PEER INTERACTIONS: SOME FURTHER CONSIDERATIONS

Although the behavioral literature provides very useful information about early education procedures that develop and maintain peer interactions, at the same time it fails to answer several questions that relate to the problem of generalization. Answers to these questions could have important theoretical and applied implications. Consequently, each question warrants careful consideration.

The Durability Question

One of the most important questions to ask about any procedure concerns its ability to produce effects that generalize over time. Granted that the above procedures can often produce desirable changes in peer interactions, can they also produce changes that are durable? With very few exceptions (i.e., Allen et al., 1964; Pinkston et al., 1973) behavioral scientists have failed to seek an answer to this question. Moreover, the little information that is available is not very enlightening because it is based on short-term follow-up data.

Perhaps the durability question would not be so disconcerting if it could be shown that the above procedures produce durable changes in other child behaviors. With this type of support, it might be expected that similar effects would be found eventually for peer interactions. Unfortunately, the prevailing evidence indicates that these procedures do not produce effects that are maintained over time (O'Leary and Kent, 1973). Thus, the assumption that peer interaction changes will be maintained by teacher and/or peer reinforcement contingencies is as yet unsupported.

The Setting Generality Question

There is little question that the above procedures offer early education teachers new and effective ways of developing appropriate peer interactions. Viewing peer interactions as behaviors primarily under the control of reinforcement contingencies has proved useful in terms of theory validation as well as technological development. However, to be effective, a procedure must often do more than produce a durable behavior change. Sometimes it must produce a change that will generalize beyond the early education setting, or more commonly, from one activity to another in the same early education setting. For example, children who do not interact appropriately in early education settings are also unlikely to interact appropriately in home or neighborhood settings (Wahler, 1976). Since it is usually impossible for a teacher to exert direct reinforcement control over peer interactions that occur outside of the early education setting, it would seem desirable to develop peer interactions that will generalize to noneducational settings. Or perhaps the teacher is concerned about training children to produce interactions in a variety of activities. Accordingly, the children might be taught initially to produce certain interactions in a training activity. The hope would be that they would eventually produce the same interactions in nontraining activities. In either case, behavioral scientists must provide believable demonstrations that newly developed interaction responses extend beyond the initial training setting. With the exception of Johnston and Johnston (1972), these demonstrations have not been forthcoming.

The Behavior Covariation Question

Children's interactions assume many forms. If early education teachers had to develop every new interaction, the effort would be considerable. It would be more desirable to develop a few interactions and concurrently obtain changes in other interactions. This type of generalization has been shown to occur (e.g., Buell et al., 1968; Nordquist and Bradley, 1973), but unfortunately it has also been associated with the development of undesirable behaviors (Sibley et al., 1969). Currently, known as "behavior covariation," this phenomenon was repeatedly alluded to in the preceding literature review. For example, Allen et al. (1964) reported covariations between play behaviors, complaints about imaginary bumps and abrasions, and speech articulation. When teachers increased play behaviors in a socially withdrawn child, her complaints disappeared and she began to talk in a more articulate manner. Buell et al. (1968) reported that several social behaviors increased when a withdrawn child was taught to use play equipment, and Nordquist and Bradley (1973) found that an isolate child began to talk to peers more often when teachers reinforced play with a confederate peer. On the other hand, Sibley et al. (1969) found that an aggressive preschool child developed new inappropriate behaviors when his aggressive interactions with peers decreased. The general conclusion to be drawn from these studies is that other child behaviors are likely to be altered when teachers produce changes in peer interactions.

The behavior covariation phenomenon should be familiar to most behavioral scientists. The concept was originally formulated by Baer and Sherman (1964) and was known by the term "response class." These investigators found that imitative responses are often developed and maintained in the absence of reinforcement when other imitative responses are periodically reinforced. Imitative behaviors become members of the same response class by virtue of their functional links with one another such that when one member of the class of imitative behaviors is changed, the other members also change. Thus, the concept of response class was entirely descriptive; it said nothing about the conditions that were responsible for its development.

Eventually, behavioral scientists working in the fields of clinical and educational psychology began to search for response-response relationships. They hoped to discover covariations that would make it possible to control deviant child behaviors that were typically inaccessible to operant conditioning procedures. For example, Wahler et al. (1970) controlled the stuttered speech of two preadolescent boys by reducing their oppositional and hyperactive behaviors. Nordquist (1971) eliminated nocturnal enuresis in a five-year-old boy by bringing his oppositional behavior under parental reinforcement control. Sajwaj, Twardosz, and Burke (1972) reduced a retarded boy's excessive conversation with teachers and observed a concomitant increase in his social behaviors. Unfortunately, decreases in academic behaviors and increases in classroom disruptions accompanied the reductions in excessive conversation. Wahler and Nordquist (1973) increased the imitative responding of two preschool children by training a parent and teacher to decrease oppositional behavior in home and school settings. Finally, Wahler (1975) reported several behavioral covariations in predelinquent children that occurred within and across home and school settings.

Clinical and educational studies of the behavior covariation phenomenon have important implications for early education specialists. It will be recalled that behaviors which covaried with peer interactions were assumed to be under the reinforcement control of numerous peer contingencies (e.g., Baer and Wolf, 1969). However, this "trapping" assumption has not been subjected to careful experimental analysis. Furthermore, the clinical and educational studies repeatedly demonstrated that behavior covariations often occurred in the absence of corresponding shifts in reinforcement contingencies. Consequently, it was difficult to see how these changes could be accounted for in terms of operant conditioning principles.

When the durability, setting generality, and behavior covariation questions are considered together, they represent a formidable challenge to the operant conditioning view of peer interactions. Answers to these questions will not come easily. At the very least they will require an analytic strategy that seeks repeated measures of several behaviors in more than one setting. As Wahler et al. (1977) recently noted, this strategy should "... carry no assumptions concerning *why* or *how* child and caretaker behaviors are interrelated. Rather, the analytic strategy argues for the broadest possible scope of measurement—a scope constrained only by the usual psychometric requirements of reliability" (p. 17). The unit of analysis should not be limited to behavior-contingency relationships, but should be extended to include other stimuli in early education settings (e.g., physical and spatial stimuli) that may relate to peer interactions. The hope, of course, will be the development of a more complete description of the ways that children interact in early education environments.

Recently, this strategy was adopted in the behavioral analysis of an autistic child enrolled in an integrated early education program. The description below provides an example of behavioral procedures, their effects, and their practical and theoretical implications for improving peer interactions in integrated settings.

BEHAVIORAL ANALYSIS OF AN AUTISTIC CHILD IN AN INTEGRATED PRESCHOOL PROGRAM

Autism is an extremely debilitating childhood disorder that usually requires institutional care. Operant conditioning procedures are often effective when applied to autistic children in institutional settings, but generalization from the institution to community settings is unlikely unless community people are trained to apply operant conditioning procedures (Lovaas et al., 1973).

One alternative to institutional care is behavioral community care (Nordquist, 1974; Nordquist and Wahler, 1973). A behavioral community approach obviates the generalization problems inherent in institutional programs, but it also raises new problems related to the application of operant conditioning procedures by nonprofessionals (i.e., parents, teachers, and peers). One of these problems concerns the general effects of operant procedures. That is, the preceding response covariation literature indicated that a number of different child behaviors may be altered when parents, teachers, or peers apply operant conditioning procedures in home and school settings. Recently, Koegel and Rincover (1974) reported that self-stimulation and play behaviors covaried in two autistic children. When self-stimulatory behaviors decreased, their play behaviors increased in the absence of corresponding shifts in contingent reinforcement. This finding suggests that very deviant child behaviors may be functionally linked to more appropriate child behaviors such that reductions in the former would covary with increases in the latter. Moreover, it may be possible to control covariations in some activities by controlling one or more behaviors in another activity.

The research presented below was designed to investigate both of these possibilities in the context of promoting appropriate imitative and peer interactions of an autistic child.

Producing Behavioral Changes

The child participating in this investigation was a four-year-old autistic-like boy who was enrolled in an experimental mainstreaming program at the

University of Tennessee Nursery School. A complete description of his family and presenting problems has been described elsewhere (Nordquist, 1974). The present experiment was conducted toward the end of the boy's second year in the mainstreaming program. At that time, many of his initial problem behaviors had improved considerably.

Recording and Activities The data were obtained by means of behavioral checklists, one used by the boy's mother and teacher, the other used by student observers. Behaviors scored during the imitation training activity (see paragraph below) were recorded by the mother and teacher. Behaviors scored during the free play activity (see paragraph below) were recorded by the students from videotapes. A complete description of the checklists and the videotape system can be found in Nordquist (1974).

The experiment was conducted during two nursery school activities: (1) imitation training and (2) free play. During imitation training, the teacher (or mother) stayed in close proximity to the child. The child was free to move about the nursery school, but once he began to show an interest in a play material or activity, the adult commenced imitation training (see "Procedures" section below). Imitation training was conducted at any time during the two-and-one-half-hour daily school period, except during the fifteen-minute indoor and outdoor free play activities. During the play activities the child was also free to do what he wanted, but imitation training was not conducted at these times.

Behavior Definitions, Observation, and Reliability The child's teacher (or mother) was responsible for recording the number of correct imitative responses that occurred during the daily imitation training activity. A correct imitative response was scored whenever the child reproduced an unprompted nonverbal behavior that was modeled by the adult. Some of these behaviors included: (1) clapping hands, (2) waving good-bye, (3) shaking the head "yes" or "no," (4) washing face with hands, (5) brushing teeth with a toothbrush, and (6) pointing a finger to various body parts. Descriptions of all thirty-six nonverbal behaviors can be found in Nordquist (1974). Imitation frequency data were converted to percentages by dividing the total number of daily imitation trials into the number of correct imitation responses.

Two students trained in naturalistic methods of observation and recording scored two fifteen-minute videotapes per week of several child, peer, and adult behaviors that occurred during the free play activity. The videotapes were divided into ten-second time intervals by a prerecorded audiotape signal. Whenever a child, peer, or adult behavior occurred during an interval, a coded check was entered on the checklist. Each interval represented one potential unit of child, peer, or adult behavior. Thus, no more than ninety units of a behavior could be scored during a single fifteen-minute play activity. To convert the frequency data to percentage, the total possible number of intervals that could be scored for a behavior (i.e., ninety) was divided into the number of intervals actually scored. The child, peer, and adult behaviors included:

1. Rituals and self-stimulation (R&S)—This category was scored whenever the child repeatedly jumped up and down, flapped his arms or hands, contorted his fingers, turned in circles, or manipulated a play material inappropriately.
2. Crying and whining (C&W)—These behaviors included high-pitched sounds similar to those of a police siren, yelling, screaming, and crying.
3. Peer interaction (PI)—Any sustained contact (at least ten seconds or more) with a nonconfederate peer during free play that was not prompted by an adult.
4. Peer approach (AP)—Any physical, verbal, or visual contact initiated by the child toward a nonconfederate peer that was not preceded by at least ten seconds of PI.
5. Spontaneous peer imitation (SPI)—Any child behavior not prompted by an adult or confederate peer which was topographically similar to the behavior of a nonconfederate peer in close proximity and the onset of which corresponded temporally (i.e., within twenty seconds) to the commencement of the nonconfederate peer's behavior.
6. Adult attention (A)—Any instance of visual, physical, or verbal contact between an adult and the child during the free play activity that occurred shortly after (twenty seconds) any of the above child behaviors.
7. Peer attention (PA)—any instance of visual, physical, or verbal contact between a nonconfederate peer and the child during the free play activity that occurred shortly after (twenty seconds) any of the above child behaviors.

Reliability checks were periodically conducted throughout the entire experiment on both the imitative training and free play data. Interobserver agreement percentages were computed by counting the number of agreements (between teacher and mother or the two student observers) and then dividing that figure by the sum of agreements and disagreements. Agreement percentages for nonverbal imitation always exceeded ninety percent. Agreement percentages for the other child, peer, and adult behaviors always exceeded eighty percent.

Procedures: Adult Training and the Use of Nonhandicapped Peers

The teacher and mother were trained to model, prompt, and reinforce nonverbal imitation (Nordquist, 1974). If the child began to show an interest in a play material or activity, the adult would quickly place herself between the boy and the material or activity and model one of the nonverbal behaviors. If the boy did not imitate the adult, the behavior was prompted and then reinforced with verbal approval and access to the material or activity. For example, if the boy wanted to use a swing, the adult placed herself between the boy and the swing set. Then she instructed him to look at her. When he attended, she said, "____, do this. Wave good-bye." If he did not imitate, the adult quickly took his arm and moved it in the desired manner. Then she approved and placed him on the swing. Over several imitation trials adult prompts were gradually faded until the boy imitated without assistance.

Imitation training in the nursery school was conducted primarily by the teacher. The mother conducted the same training in the home setting. Within a few weeks, the boy was reliably imitating all thirty-six nonverbal behaviors. At this point, two confederate peers were trained to model and reinforce the same nonverbal behaviors during the imitation training activity. This was accomplished by having the adults model and role play the training procedures. Now, when the boy wanted to swing, the teacher would signal the nearest peer confederate to intercept him, model, and reinforce imitation. The adult was instructed to attend only to the peer, provide assistance if necessary, and verbally approve the peer's behavior.

During the free play activity, the adults were told to interact with the children whenever they wished. However, they were asked not to provide extraordinary attention to the subject child. The peer confederates were told not to model and reinforce the nonverbal behaviors during the free play activity. Otherwise, they were free to play as they pleased. None of the participants in the experiment were informed about the expected outcome.

Results of Intervention

The imitation training and spontaneous imitation data are presented in Figure 1. These data reveal that the adults and confederate peers were equally successful in maintaining a high percentage of imitative responding during the training activity. They also reveal that during the two periods of adult imitation training, the boy's percentage of spontaneous peer imitation during free play was low. However, spontaneous imitation increased during the two periods when the peer confederates conducted imitation training. These results suggest that peers may be better generalization-facilitating agents than adults. They also suggest that autistic children

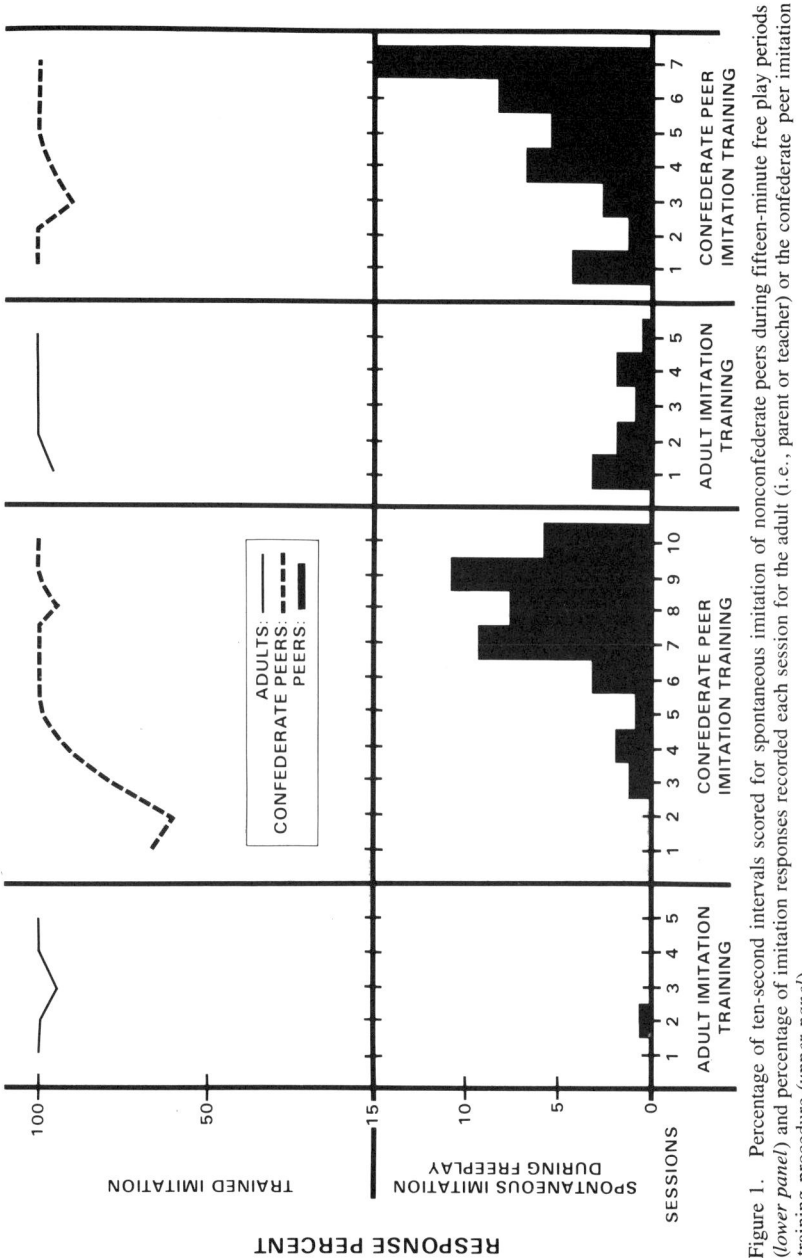

Figure 1. Percentage of ten-second intervals scored for spontaneous imitation of nonconfederate peers during fifteen-minute free play periods (*lower panel*) and percentage of imitation responses recorded each session for the adult (i.e., parent or teacher) or the confederate peer imitation training procedure (*upper panel*).

might begin to imitate more complex and socially appropriate play behaviors when they are reinforced for imitating several simple, nonsocial motor behaviors.

Although peer imitation training was associated with very beneficial maintenance and generalization effects, it is also correlated with undesirable changes that covaried directly with spontaneous peer imitation (SPI). Specifically, rituals and self-stimulation (R&S) increased from an average of about ten percent during the adult imitation training periods to nearly twenty-five percent during the peer imitation training periods. Moreover, sustained peer interactions (PI) decreased from an average of about eight percent during the adult imitation training periods to four percent during the peer imitation training periods. The peer attention (PA) data did not vary systematically across the adult and peer imitation training periods for either R&S or PI. That is, the boy's peers did not attend proportionately more to R&S and less to PI when the confederate peers conducted the imitation training. However, peers did appear to attend more often to SPI during the peer imitation training periods. Thus, increases in R&S and decreases in PI that covaried with reinforced increases in SPI could not be attributed to corresponding shifts in PA reinforcement. Consequently, a search was conducted for shifts in adult attention (A) contingencies that might have explained the covariations. This search revealed that adults did not systematically vary their attention to SPI, R&S, or PI across the adult and peer imitation training periods. Finally, the C&W and AP data revealed that these behaviors remained essentially unchanged during the adult and peer imitation training periods.

Discussion and Implications

An autistic child was initially taught to imitate the nonverbal behaviors of two adult models and then to imitate two confederate peers who modeled the same behaviors. When adults conducted the imitation training, the child rarely imitated the free play behaviors of nonconfederate peers. However, he frequently imitated nonconfederate peers when confederate peers conducted the nonverbal imitation training. This finding supports that of Johnston and Johnston (1972), who reported that peers were more effective generalization-facilitating agents than adults.

Increases in spontaneous imitation correlated with increases in contingent peer attention. Thus, generalized imitation was very likely maintained by peer reinforcement. However, when the child imitated nonconfederate peers during the free-play period, he also engaged in more ritualistic and self-stimulatory behaviors and interacted less with nonconfederate peers.

Neither of these changes could be attributed to corresponding shifts in adult or peer reinforcement contingencies. These findings suggest that desirable changes in appropriate child behaviors in intervention programs may sometimes be accompanied by undesirable changes in deviant child behaviors (Sajwaj et al, 1972), and they raise the possibility that handicapped children may be adversely affected in some ways when brought into contact with nonhandicapped children. These results do not lend themselves to simple explanations, but a full understanding of these complex processes will have considerable practical and theoretical significance.

CONCLUSIONS

The child development literature rarely provides descriptions of teaching procedures that develop and maintain peer interactions in early education settings. Such descriptions are commonly found, however, in the behavioral literature. Behavioral scientists have repeatedly demonstrated that teaching procedures derived from operant conditioning principles often produce socially important changes in peer interactions. Since one of the central objectives of integrated early education programs is the promotion of appropriate interactions between handicapped and nonhandicapped children, teachers in integrated programs should find these procedures very useful.

Although it is important to show that a procedure can produce changes in peer interactions, it is also important to show that the changes are durable; that is, that they can be maintained over a long period of time. Sometimes it is necessary to show that a procedure can produce changes that transfer to other activities in the same setting or to different settings, and it is certainly important to show how a procedure affects other child behaviors to which it has not been applied. Very few of these demonstrations have been forthcoming from behavioral scientists in the field of early childhood education. However, behavioral scientists in the fields of clinical and educational psychology have conducted several experimental analyses of the durability, setting generality, and behavior covariation effects of operant conditioning procedures. Their results have not been encouraging. Operant procedures have not been shown to produce durable behavior changes or changes that transfer readily from one setting to another. Moreover, it is extremely difficult to predict the precise general effects of operant conditioning procedures. Although it is very likely that other child behaviors will be altered when changes are produced in peer interactions, it is currently impossible to predict *which* behaviors will be altered or *how* they will be altered. Thus, although the immediate and direct effects of operant conditioning procedures on peer interactions are well known, their long-term, general effects are virtually unknown.

In recommending what behavioral scientists should do if research on peer interactions is to progress, it should not be implied that what is now being done successfully should be discarded. A research focus that examines ongoing behavior-environment relationships and that utilizes parents, teachers, and peers as the primary behavior change agents is still essential. But perhaps the methodological strategy of behavior analysis should be expanded to include the measurement of multiple behaviors in several settings over longer periods of time. A method of naturalistic observation and computer-based data processing has already been developed which might serve as a model for behavioral scientists (i.e., Wahler, House, and Stanbaugh, 1975). In addition to adopting a multiple-measurement perspective, behavioral scientists might also adopt a purely analytical view of child behavior, a view that bears no allegiance to any particular theory or is derived from any assumptions concerning the interrelationships between child behavior and environmental events.

Guided by this view, behavioral scientists might begin to assess the specific and general effects of physical and spatial stimuli on peer interactions. This area of research may be particularly important for integrated programs because the presence or absence of equipment or the arrangement of the environment could profoundly affect the ways that handicapped and nonhandicapped children interact with one another. Moreover, peers may be powerful generalization-facilitating agents and their inclusion in the behavior change process might have important implications for the durability and setting generality effects of integrated programming. However, a peer may not have to participate directly in the training process in order to produce generalization to nontraining settings. It may only be necessary that peers be prominently present while adults conduct the training. Their number and sex may also be important, and perhaps teachers could enhance generalization effects by reinforcing peers when they are conducting training. All of these questions warrant further consideration.

There is little question that the behavior-covariation phenomenon requires the immediate attention of behavioral scientists, particularly those who are concerned about the effects of integrated programs on both handicapped and nonhandicapped children. Most scientists and educators assume that handicapped children will benefit from procedures that increase interactions with nonhandicapped children. Unfortunately, this assumption has not been subjected to repeated experimental analysis. Indeed, the results of the autistic child's interactions discussed above raise the possibility that some handicapped children may be adversely as well as positively affected by techniques that are designed to promote social development and that include the use of nonhandicapped peers. Given our current understanding of the behavior-covariation phenomenon, there is also no reason to believe that the behaviors of nonhandicapped children will not be altered in ways that are not in their best interests. Consequently, it would seem that the most reasonable and, it is hoped, the most useful course to follow is to measure the general effects of various procedures on several children in more than one setting. Although it will be time consuming and expensive, behavioral scientists must proceed along these lines if they wish to advise parents and teachers about all of the possible effects of integrated early education programs.

ACKNOWLEDGMENTS

I wish to express my appreciation to Dr. Brent Miller, Dr. Robert Wahler, and especially to Dr. Sandra Twardosz for their helpful editorial comments, and to Debbie Koshansky, Mary Comin, and Susan Buckner, who assisted with the literature search.

REFERENCES CITED

Allen, K. E., Hart, B. M., Buell, J. S., Harris, F. R., and Wolf, M. M. 1964. Effects of social reinforcement on isolate behavior of a nursery school child. Child Development, 35, 511-518.
Allen, K. E., Turner, K. I., and Everett, P. M. 1970. A behavior modification classroom for Head Start children with problem behaviors. Exceptional Children, 37, 119-127.
Anderson, J. E. 1937. The development of social behavior. American Journal of Sociology, 44, 839-857.
Apolloni, T., Cooke, S., and Cooke, T. P. 1975. Establishing a non-retarded peer as a behavioral model for retarded toddlers. Unpublished manuscript, George Peabody College.
Baer, D. M., and Sherman, J. A. 1964. Reinforcement control of generalized imitation in young children. Journal of Experimental Child Psychology, 1, 37-49.
Baer, D. M., and Sherman, J. A. 1970. The modification of child behavior: Application to therapy and education. In H. Reese and L. Lipsett (Eds.), Experimental Child Psychology. New York: Academic Press.
Baer, D. M., and Wolf, M. M. 1969. The reinforcement contingency in preschool and remedial education. In R. D. Hess and R. M. Baer (Eds.), Early Education: Current Theory, Research, and Practice. Chicago: Aldine.
Baer, D. M., Wolf, M. M., and Risley, T. R. 1968. Some current dimensions of applied behavior analysis. Journal of Applied Behavior Analysis, 1, 91-97.

Bailey, J. S., Timbers, G. D., Phillips, E. L., and Wolf, M. M. 1971. Modification of articulation errors of pre-delinquents by their peers. Journal of Applied Behavior Analysis, 4, 47-63.

Beaver, A. P. 1932. The initiation of social contacts by preschool children. Monograph of the Society for Research in Child Development, 7.

Bijou, S. W., and Baer, D. M. 1961. Child Development: A Systematic and Empirical Theory (Vol. 1). New York: Appleton-Century-Crofts.

Bijou, S. W., and Baer, D. M. 1965. Child Development (Vol. 2). New York: Appleton-Century-Crofts.

Body, M. K. 1955. Patterns of aggression in nursery school. Child Development, 26, 3-11.

Brigham, T. A., and Sherman, J. A. 1968. An experimental analysis of verbal imitation in preschool children. Journal of Applied Behavior Analysis, 1, 151-158.

Buell, J., Stoddard, P., Harris, F. R., and Baer, D. M. 1968. Collateral social development accompanying reinforcement of outdoor play in a preschool child. Journal of Applied Behavior Analysis, 1, 167-174.

Burgess, R. L., Burgess, J. M., and Esveldt, K. C. 1970. An analysis of generalized imitation. Journal of Applied Behavior Analysis, 3, 39-46.

Burmeister, E. 1973. Compliance-imitation covariations in a non-imitative child. Unpublished master's thesis, The University of Tennessee.

Carmichael, L. (Ed.). 1946. Manual of Child Psychology. New York: John Wiley & Sons.

Carmichael, L. (Ed.). 1954. Manual of Child Psychology (2nd ed.). New York: John Wiley & Sons.

Carmichael, L. (Ed.). 1970. Manual of Child Psychology (3rd ed.). New York: John Wiley & Sons.

Charlesworth, R., and Hartup, W. W. 1967. Positive social reinforcement in the nursery school peer group. Child Development, 38, 993-1002.

Cooper, M. L., Lee, C. J., Bierlein, M. W., Wolf, M. M., and Baer, D. M. 1966. The development of motor skill and consequent social interaction in a withdrawn nursery school child by social reinforcement procedures. Unpublished manuscript, University of Kansas.

Dawe, H. C. 1934. An analysis of two hundred quarrels of preschool children. Child Development, 5, 139-157.

Devoney, C., Guralnick, M. J., and Rubin, H. 1974. Integrating handicapped and non-handicapped preschool children: Effects on social play. Childhood Education, 50, 360-364.

Doke, L. A., and Risley, T. R. 1972. The organization of day-care environments: Required vs. optional activities. Journal of Applied Behavior Analysis, 5, 405-420.

Foxwell, H. R., Thompson, C. L., Coats, B. A., Baer, D. M., and Wolf, M. M. 1966. The development of social responsiveness to other children in a nursery school child through experimental use of social reinforcement. Unpublished manuscript, University of Kansas.

Gewirtz, J. L. 1971. Mechanisms of social learning: Some roles of stimulation and behavior in early human development. In D. A. Goslin (Ed.), Handbook of Socialization Theory and Research. Chicago: Rand McNally.

Green, E. H. 1933a. Friendship and quarrels among preschool children. Child Development, 4, 237-252.
Green, E. H. 1933b. Group play and quarreling among preschool children. Child Development, 4, 302-307.
Greenwood, C. R., Sloane, H. N., and Baskin, A. 1974. Training elementary aged peer-behavior managers to control small group programmed mathematics. Journal of Applied Behavior Analysis, 7, 103-114.
Guralnick, M. J. 1976. The value of integrating handicapped and nonhandicapped preschool children. American Journal of Orthopsychiatry, 46, 236-245.
Harris, F. R., Wolf, M. M., and Baer, D. M. 1967. Effects of adult social reinforcement on child behavior. In W. W. Hartup and N. L. Smothergill (Eds.), The Young Child: Reviews of Research. Washington, D.C.: National Association for the Education of Young Children.
Harris, V. W., and Sherman, J. A. 1973. Effects of peer tutoring and consequences on the math performance of elementary classroom students. Journal of Applied Behavior Analysis, 6, 587-597.
Hart, B. M., Reynolds, N. J., Baer, D. M., Brawley, E. R., and Harris, F. R. 1968. Effect of contingent and non-contingent social reinforcement on the cooperative play of a preschool child. Journal of Applied Behavior Analysis, 1, 73-76.
Hartup, W. W. 1964. Friendship status and the effectiveness of peers as reinforcing agents. Journal of Experimental Child Psychology, 1, 1954-1962.
Hartup, W. W. 1970. Peer interaction and social organization. In P. Mussen (Ed.), Carmichael's manual of child psychology (Vol. II). New York: John Wiley & Sons.
Hartup, W. W., Glazer, J., and Charlesworth, R. 1967. Peer reinforcement and sociometric status. Child Development, 38, 1017-1024.
Hetherington, E. M. 1975. Review of Child Development Research (Vol. 5). Chicago: University of Chicago Press.
Hoffman, M. L., and Hoffman, L. W. 1964. Review of Child Development Research (Vol. 1). New York: Russell Sage Foundation.
Hoffman, M. L., and Hoffman, L. W. 1966. Review of Child Development Research (Vol. 2). New York: Russell Sage Foundation.
Horowitz, F. 1962. Incentive value of social stimuli for preschool children. Child Development, 33, 111-116.
Jersild, A. T., and Markey, F. V. 1935. Conflicts between preschool children. Monographs of the Society for Research in Child Development, 21.
Johnson, M. W. 1935. The effect on behavior of variation in amount of play equipment. Child Development, 6, 56-68.
Johnston, J. M., and Johnston, G. T. 1972. Modification of consonant speech-sound articulation in young children. Journal of Applied Behavior Analysis, 5, 233-246.
Johnston, M. K., Kelley, C. S., Harris, F. R., and Wolf, M. M. 1966. An application of reinforcement principles to development of motor skills of a young child. Child Development, 37, 379-387.
Koegel, R. L., and Rincover, A. 1974. Treatment of psychotic children in a classroom environment: I. Learning in a large group. Journal of Applied Behavior Analysis, 7, 45-59.

Kohn, M. 1966. The child as a determinant of his peers' approach to him. Journal of Genetic Psychology, 109, 91-100.

Leuba, C. 1933. An experimental study of rivalry in young children. Journal of Comprehensive Psychology, 16, 367-378.

Lewis, M., and Rosenblum, L. A. (Eds.). 1975. Friendship and Peer Relations. New York: John Wiley & Sons.

Lovaas, O. I., Koegel, R., Simmons, J. Q., and Long, J. S. 1973. Some generalization and follow-up measures on autistic children in behavior therapy. Journal of Applied Behavior Analysis, 6, 131-166.

Markey, F. V. 1935. Imaginative behavior of preschool children. Monographs of the Society for Research in Child Development, 18.

Marshall, H. R., and McCandless, B. 1957. A study in predication of social behavior of preschool children. Child Development, 28, 149-159.

Moore, S. G. 1967. Correlates of peer acceptance in nursery school children. In W. W. Hartup and N. L. Smothergill (Eds.), The Young Child: Reviews of Research. Washington, D.C.: National Association for the Education of Young Children.

Murphy, L. B. 1937. Social Behavior and Child Personality. New York: Columbia University Press.

Mussen, P. H. 1960. Handbook of Research Methods in Child Development. New York: John Wiley & Sons.

Nordquist, V. M. 1971. The modification of a child's enuresis: Some response-response relationships. Journal of Applied Behavior Analysis, 3, 241-247.

Nordquist, V. M., and Bradley, B. 1973. Speech acquisition in a nonverbal isolate child. Journal of Experimental Child Psychology, 15, 149-160.

Nordquist, V. M. 1974. Naturalistic treatment of childhood autism. Final Progress Report, #MH 21100-01, 1 R03. Washington, D.C.: National Institute of Mental Health.

Nordquist, V. M., and Wahler, R. G. 1973. Naturalistic treatment of an autistic child. Journal of Applied Behavior Analysis, 6, 79-87.

O'Connor, R. 1969. Modification of social withdrawal through symbolic modeling. Journal of Applied Behavior Analysis, 2, 15-22.

O'Leary, K. D., and Kent, R. 1973. Behavior and modification for social action: Research tactics and problems. In L. A. Hamerlynck, L. C. Handy, and E. J. Mash (Eds.), Behavior Change: Methodology, Concepts, and Practice. Champaign, Ill.: Research Press.

Parten, M. B. 1932. Social participation among preschool children. Journal of Abnormal Social Psychology, 27, 243-269.

Patterson, G. R., and Anderson, D. 1964. Peers as social reinforcers. Child Development, 35, 951-960.

Patterson, G. R., Littman, R. A., and Bricker, W. 1967. Assertive behavior in children: A step toward a theory of aggression. Monographs of the Society for Research in Child Development, 32, (113).

Peterson, R. F. 1968. Some experiments on the organization of a class of imitative behaviors. Journal of Applied Behavior Analysis, 1, 225-235.

Peterson, R. F., and Whitehurst, G. J. 1971. A variable influencing the performance of generalized imitative behaviors. Journal of Applied Behavior Analysis, 4, 1-9.

Pinkston, E. M., Reese, N. M., LeBlanc, J. M., and Baer, D. M. 1973. Independent control of a preschool child's aggression and peer interaction by contingent teacher attention. Journal of Applied Behavior Analysis, 6, 115-124.
Quilitch, H. R., and Risley, T. R. 1973. The effects of play materials on social play. Journal of Applied Behavior Analysis, 6, 573-578.
Read, K. H. 1955. The Nursery School (2nd ed.). Philadelphia: W. B. Saunders.
Read, K. H. 1971. The Nursery School (5th ed.). Philadelphia: W. B. Saunders.
Risley, T. R. 1975. Day care as a strategy in social intervention. In E. Ramp and G. Semb (Eds.), Behavior Analysis: Areas of Research and Application. Englewood Cliffs, N.J.: Prentice-Hall.
Risley, T. R., and Baer, D. M. 1973. Operant behavior modification: The deliberate development of behavior. In B. M. Caldwell and H. N. Ricciuti (Eds.), Review of Child Development Research. Chicago: University of Chicago Press.
Sajwaj, T., Twardosz, S., and Burke, M. 1972. Side effects of extinction procedures in a remedial preschool. Journal of Applied Behavior Analysis, 5, 163-175.
Sherman, J. A., and Baer, D. M. 1969. Appraisal of operant therapy techniques with children and adults. In C. M. Franks (Ed.), Assessment and Status of the Behavior Therapies. New York: McGraw-Hill.
Sherman, J. A., and Bushell, D. 1975. Behavior modification as an educational technique. In F. D. Horowitz (Ed.), Review of Child Development Research. Chicago: University of Chicago Press.
Sibley, S. A., Abbott, M. S., and Cooper, B. P. 1969. Modification of the classroom behavior of a disadvantaged kindergarten boy by social reinforcement and isolation. Journal of Experimental Child Psychology, 7, 203-219.
Skinner, B. F. 1953. Science and Human Behavior. New York: Macmillan.
Snyder, L., Apolloni, T., and Cooke, T. P. 1977. Integrated settings at the early childhood level: The role of non-retarded peers. Exceptional Children, 43, 262-266.
Solomon, R. W., and Wahler, R. G. 1973. Peer reinforcement control of classroom problem behavior. Journal of Applied Behavior Analysis, 6, 49-56.
Strain, P. S., Shores, R. E., and Kerr, M. M. 1976. An experimental analysis of "spillover" effects on the social interaction of behaviorally handicapped preschool children. Journal of Applied Behavior Analysis, 9, 31-40.
Strain, P. S., and Timm, M. A. 1974. An experimental analysis of social interaction between a behaviorally disordered child and her classroom peers. Journal of Applied Behavior Analysis, 1, 583-590.
Swift, J. W. 1964. Effects of early group experience: The nursery school and day nursery. In. M. L. Hoffman and L. W. Hoffman (Eds.), Review of child development research. New York: Russell Sage Foundation.
Taylor, K. W. 1954. Parent Cooperative Nursery Schools. New York: Teachers College, Columbia University.
Tikten, S., and Hartup, W. W. 1965. Sociometric status and the reinforcing effectiveness of children's peers. Journal of Experimental Child Psychology, 2, 306-315.
Twardosz, S., Cataldo, M. F., and Risley, T. R. 1974. Open environment design for infant and toddler day care. Journal of Applied Behavior Analysis, 7, 529-546.

Updegraff, R., and Herbst, E. K. 1933. An experimental study of the social behavior stimulated in young children by certain play materials. Journal of Genetic Psychology, 42, 372-391.

Wahler, R. G. 1967. Child-child interactions in free field settings: Some experimental analyses. Journal of Experimental Child Psychology, 5, 278-293.

Wahler, R. G. 1969. Oppositional children: A quest for parental reinforcement control. Journal of Applied Behavior Analysis, 2, 159-170.

Wahler, R. G. 1975. Some structural aspects of deviant child behavior. Journal of Applied Behavior Analysis, 8, 27-42.

Wahler, R. G. 1976. Helping procedures for violent children: Contributions of behavioral ecology and technology. Knoxville: Child Behavior Institute, University of Tennessee.

Wahler, R. G, Berlund, R. M., Coe, T. D., and Leske, G. 1977. Social systems analysis: Implementing an alternative behavioral model. In A. Rogers-Warren and S. Warren (Eds.), Ecological Perspectives in Behavior Analysis. Baltimore: University Park Press.

Wahler, R. G., House, A. E., and Stanbaugh, E. E. 1975. Ecological Assessment of Child Problem Behavior: A Clinical Package for Home, School and Institutional Settings. New York: Pergamon Press.

Wahler, R. G, and Nordquist, V. M. 1973. Adult discipline as a factor in childhood imitation. Journal of Abnormal Child Psychology, 1, 40-56.

Wahler, R. G., Sperling, K., Thomas, M., Teeter, N., and Luper, H. 1970. The modification of childhood stuttering: Some response-response relationships. Journal of Experimental Child Psychology, 9, 411-428.

STRATEGIES AND MODELS FOR EARLY CHILDHOOD INTERVENTION PROGRAMS IN INTEGRATED SETTINGS

Nicholas J. Anastasiow, Ph.D.

This chapter describes and analyzes four basic preschool model programs: *behavioral, normal developmental, cognitive developmental,* and *cognitive learning.* An attempt is made to demonstrate how the preschool handicapped model programs have become the more highly developed of preschool models available for analysis. Arguments are presented to support this position by offering evidence that the so-called normal preschool centers were not fully developed and therefore not easily replicable model centers, and that a great deal of folklore evidence exists among the public as well as in the professional domain as to what preschool education is about. In so presenting this analysis it is first necessary to take a critical look at public education to determine what the public school deems as success. The next section therefore briefly overviews the state of preschool education during the period when two major social movements were initiated. The first was the establishment of intervention programs for poverty-level children. These programs included government programs such as Head Start in 1965, planned variation Head Start and Follow Through classes of 1968 (Klein, 1976), and foundation-supported programs such as the Ford Foundation Education Improvement Projects in 1962. The second was the Early Childhood Assistance Act of the Bureau of Education for the Handicapped of 1968. It is my contention that at the time these programs were initiated the preschool programs for the poor and for the handicapped both faced major problems. It was assumed by both the handicapped and poverty programs that well developed preschool models for normal middle-class children existed, with curriculum and teaching strategies based on learning theory and child development readily available. There were, in fact, none. Thus, the models of preschool described in this chapter, except the normal developmental model, have been developed to serve the need of the poverty child or the handicapped child. A case is established to demonstrate the impact of these programs, and the strengths and weaknesses of each model's ability to productively integrate handicapped and nonhandicapped preschool children are discussed.

WAR ON POVERTY MODELS

Theoretical Origins

The first major modern revival in preschool education was the funding of Head Start and other poverty-related programs. The history of the program has been written elsewhere (Greenberg, 1969), but for our purposes it is important to note that these innovators were faced with the fact that they had to begin at the beginning, for there were no well developed models for preschool education available to them when they began their programs. A few centers became highly visible within a short time, such as Weikart's Perry Preschool Project (Weikart, 1976); the Hodges, McCandless, Spicker Program (1967); the Karnes Ameliorative Program (1969); and the Bereiter and Engelmann (1966) program. In each of these cases, the project directors had to construct a model out of bits and pieces of what was available in the scattered literature. The major preschools that did exist were in university settings. There were some parent cooperatives and private day care baby-sitting arrangements, which to most professionals were not legitimate preschools. The university preschools, in some cases, had long histories, but served largely as models for their teachers in training, not as models for establishing preschools. The major writings concerning the goals of these university programs appeared during the 1920s and 1930s and were long out of print. There were some general pamphlets available, but nothing on how to establish a complete program. In the main, early childhood educators talked to each other and did not produce sets of curriculum. I believe the rash of poor to fair quality books on early childhood education produced during the early 1970s was a response to the needs first perceived in the 1960s.

The directors of the poverty programs had to experiment with ideas and techniques. They were not, in many cases, the typical early childhood educators of the past. Many were psychologists, and as psychologists they turned to psychology for their insights and ideas of how to proceed. In the process, some renewed their interest in the writings of Dewey and Bandura and Gagné; others turned toward peers such as Bijou and Baer. Some—along with the American science educators who brought him to America—rediscovered Piaget, while others turned the technology of Skinner into a theory. Behaviorism and behavioral techniques first hit their vogue in 1960 and appeared to be attractive new strategies (Eysenck, 1960). Still fewer turned to the older literature of progressive education for their approach. It is interesting to note that there was no educator of the stature of Dewey who served as the major spokesman for education during this period. In the process, these innovators had to make assumptions about child development, and all of them derived premises about the elementary schools and about teaching and learning. The directors of programs for poverty children knew that public schools were mainly effective with middle-class white children and other groups of children who shared middle-class goals. These children had been socialized by their families to accept the rules of schooling and were willing to become further socialized upon entry into school. The attempt to give children a "head start" was based on the assumption that the schools would accept children of varying values and skills. Clearly the public schools did not and do not accept children of widely different skills unless ordered by the courts to do so. As we know now from Mercer's work (1973), children whose families held different values and/or were of different racial or ethnic backgrounds were placed, in large numbers, in special classes. At this point, I will pause to briefly describe my perception of the goals of the majority of elementary schools so that the preschool model may be seen in contrast.

Closed Structure of Public Schools

When Tevye sang out "Tradition" in the musical *Fiddler on the Roof*, it was in defense of tradition in the face of its gradual disintegration around him. In some sense, the tradition which has long ruled the public schools is showing cracks in its structure (at least to the extent that schools are abiding by the rulings in civil court cases) by allowing children who are impaired into classrooms with children who are not. We should consider carefully, however, what we are getting by placing impaired children in the regular classroom, which may be more restrictive and thereby less facilitating than the former special class. The reality of teaching in the public schools is that it is a "special but shadowed" profession (Lortie, 1975) with lofty goals and little that is codified or regularized.

Changes in the schools are slow to occur, and slower yet are the changes in teaching strategies and arrangements upon which instruction is organized. As Lortie (1975, p. 23) in his brilliant book states:

Basic teaching techniques have also been extremely slow to change. The principal modes of instruction (lecturing, recitation, demonstration, seat work, small group instruction, etc.) were known and used years ago; and they continue to dominate despite the increased range of possibilities.

Further, Lortie notes that teaching and schools lean toward continuity rather than change. The major mode for learning how to teach is through imitation of in-service teachers by those in training, a condition that, across individuals, generalizes into a containing tradition (Lortie, 1975, p. 63). There has been little concern by the teaching profession toward building a shared technical culture. The newcomer is rarely introduced to analytical and evaluative techniques that will renew or improve instructions. As Lortie (1975), Broudy (1972), and Smith, Cohen, and Pearl (1969) have highlighted in their work, teachers in training tend to diminish the effectiveness of their training by downgrading their course work as being too easy or too abstract (Lortie's term is "too thin and too theoretical"), except for student teaching. By "too theoretical" teachers usually mean impossible goals. Having thirty children in one classroom with a mandate to teach fifteen subjects on an individual basis is an impossible situation for one teacher. I recently used, with a physician who had commented that he felt teachers' jobs were relatively easy, the analogy that teaching in regular schools is comparable to having a physician face a ward of thirty needy youngsters and be permitted to make only one diagnosis and use only one drug.

A teacher is in a similar position of having one treatment, the mandatory text. While teachers may know that each case must be treated individually, that learning begins at the child's current level of accomplishment, and that instruction based anywhere else is too easy or too difficult, there is little evidence that teachers act upon this knowledge. The goal of individualizing instruction has had strong support at the theoretical level, yet at the same time it has had little widespread application (Lord, 1971). The dominant curriculum of the schools is the socialization and reinforcement of the acquisition of personal behaviors which include: perseverance, dependability, consistency, tactfulness, punctuality, and other middle-class values that are essentially social (Bowles and Gintis, 1976). In these areas the school has been eminently successful with middle- and working-class children. In spite of widespread criticism, the schools also have been very successful in teaching the basic skills of reading, writing, and math to the middle-class child. Where the schools have been less successful, according to the reformers, is in producing creativity, independence, and inquiry. Bowles and Gintis (1976) observed that the failure may not be the inability of the schools to develop these capacities but the pressure of the culture through school boards to actively discourage their development in school.

The children who prosper in public schools are those who are ready to comply with the grade-by-grade pace of the regular classroom. Regular education breaks down when children who are different from the norm are enrolled in the class.

DIMENSIONS OF PRESCHOOL HANDICAPPED MODELS

The Handicapped Children's Early Education Program (HCEEP) of the Bureau of Education for the Handicapped has done much to stimulate the growth of preschool handicapped models (DeWeerd, 1974). Many directors who first launched HCEEP preschool handicapped programs eight years ago experienced a shock similar to that of directors of poverty programs. When they started to build a total educational program in which impaired children would receive treatment plus a full curriculum, they found that there was a paucity of curriculum guides or developmental, diagnostic, evaluative, or screening instruments and practically no books or writings on how to establish a preschool program for handicapped children. In reaction, they turned to the preschool poverty programs for guidance. Much of the resulting confusion was reflected in some of the proposals submitted to the Bureau, which claimed that their model classroom programs were to be built upon Piaget, Bereiter and Engelmann, Weikart, and Karnes, without recognition that there were serious differences among some of the programs of these people. Probably the proposal writers lumped these diverse programs together out of desperation.

What have developed over the past eight years are some very unique programs that can be roughly grouped into four types. The first type, which I call the *normal developmental model,* is the only one to be derived from the regular existing preschools for normal children. The other three have been developed by personnel who began in programs for poverty children or impaired children. The second, the *behavioral model,* is based largely on the experimental analysis of behavior. The *cognitive developmental model,* the third type, translates Piagetian development principles into strategies for classroom programs. The fourth type is the *cognitive learning model,* which combines Piagetian and/or cognitive theory with the experimental analysis of behavior. We will begin with some statements regarding the commonalities and major differences of the four models, followed by a discussion of each model individually.

Developmental Perspective

A developmental perspective provides the framework for all the models in that the attention of the educator/trainer/guide is directed toward diagnosing and selecting experiences to match the child's stage of development.

However, critics who use developmental theory as the basis for all education point out that developmental theories such as Piaget's do not provide the educator with the specifics of what to do on a given day (Feldman, 1976). Thus, the developmental perspective provides only a broad base or undergirding for the models. There are major differences, however, in the developmental perspectives of the models varying from behavioral-learning theories to those of a psychodynamic orientation.

Table 1 presents a brief description of some of the major developmental theories. There are two major ways of perceiving development. Some behaviorists perceive development as a result of learning, and the term "development" itself can be replaced by the term "behavior-changing process" (Baer, Wolf, and Risley, 1968). The metaphor for this model is the machine. The second major theory, no less deterministic than the behavioristic, is the organismic-structural approach of Piaget. As discussed later in greater depth, development according to Piaget is a sequence of structural changes of an organism interacting within an environment (Loevinger, 1976). An extreme behavioral theory does not provide stages of development, but would stress principles by which a parent would train a child in a given setting. Most behavioral programs would draw upon the more descriptive theory of maturational age-stage description, which is largely based on notions of physical development. (Note that the term "infancy" means without language and a toddler is one who "toddles" before complete mastery of walking, and so on.)

Gagné's theory is hierarchical and sequential. The stages are achieved through training and are not specifically age normed. Piaget's cognitive theory is hierarchical, sequential, irreversible, and both age independent and age dependent. Sigmund Freud's theory is a genetic theory of affect. Unlike Piaget and Gagné, Freud believed that children can fixate on a level or regress from higher to lower levels. Anna Freud's (1965) lines of development are a refinement of Freud's later work and the work of Rapaport (1960) and his followers on the development of ego psychology. Ego, roughly translated into the "I" or "self," has had many conflicting labels in psychology (Loevinger, 1976), yet each theory assumes some aspect of the socioemotional development. The theories differ markedly in the processes by which maturity is achieved. Erikson's theory describes development as a series of resolutions or accomplishments. Loevinger's theory focuses on the "I"—ego attainments; it postulates hierarchies to be achieved, but it does not postulate all stages at which they are achieved.

However, although all models assume a posture toward a developmental theory and work toward the child's attainment of physical, cognitive, and socioemotional skills, the theories are too broad to be a basis for specific lesson plans. Therefore, project personnel have had to construct specific developmental sequences. We call those lists of skills "developmental guidelines."

Developmental Guidelines

Each developmental perspective is insufficient for program planning. Thus, developmental scales have had to be constructed. Children babble, talk, walk, and say their first word at about the same time. Developmental guidelines indicate specific attainments normal children make by age or stage. Those working with impaired children have to know whether a child is unable to perform a task due to his age or impairment. In almost every case, every early childhood handicapped program has had to come to terms with this issue. A quick perusal of the Technical Assistance Development System Tadscript #5 (TADS, n.d.) will indicate that the HCEEP programs have produced their own specific developmental guidelines or have sought permission to use those developed by others, such as Karnes (1975).

All programs, whether they feel developmental tasks are acquired through training, through genetic blueprints, or through environmental-biological interactions, have constructed some notion of milestones in development and have also divided development into such areas as motor, cognition, language, social skills, self-help skills, and socioemotional development. The models differ on how they perceive these skills to be acquired, but by and large they agree that the milestones should be met.

Reinforcement

While the amounts, timing, and method of reinforcement vary, all models provide guidance as to the manner in which reinforcement is to be administered. The overwhelming majority, if not all the models, employ positive reinforcement in response to the performance of desired behaviors. Positive reinforcement is any event following a response that increases the performance level of that response (Adams, 1976). Negative reinforcement works the same way, but as a consequence of its removal not its application. Negative reinforcement refers to a behavior that increases in frequency as a result of terminating a stimulus (aversive). Punishment, more rarely used, is used to stop a behavior. Ignoring a behavior to reduce its frequency is normally part of the process of extinction.

Reinforcement is a key construct in both behavioral and cognitive theories and is at the heart of learning theories. Much confusion has arisen over the term "reinforcement" because it is too often perceived as an exclusive element of the misnamed behavior modification programs. This author freely admits that he has not been free of his own misuse of the term. Currently, behavior modification as a technique is broadly conceived as the systematic programming for increase in desirable behaviors and the

Table 1. Developmental theories

Maturational	Learning	Cognitive	Dynamic/psychosocial			
Gesell/Spock	Gagné [a]	Piaget	Freud	Erikson	A. Freud [b]	Loevinger [a]
Infancy (0–2)	Signal; stimulus-response	Sensorimotor	Oral	Trust vs. mistrust	Biological unity; (dependence) part object; object constancy	Presocial; symbiotic
Toddlerhood (2–3)	Verbal association	Preoperational	Anal; phallic	Autonomy vs. shame →	Ambivalent	Self-protective
Preschool (3–5)	→	→	Latency →	Inactive vs. guilt →	Object centered	→
Elementary school (8–10)	Multiple discrimination →	Concrete operational →	→	→	Latency	Conformist →

Strategies and Models 93

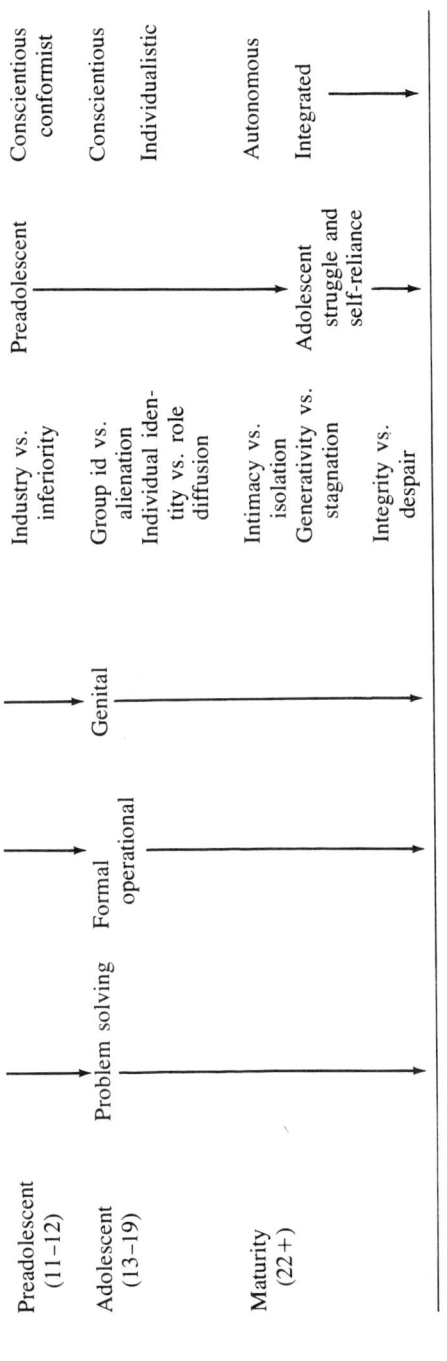

Age	Cognitive	Psychosexual	Psychosocial	Self-concept[b]	Ego development
Preadolescent (11–12)	Problem solving →		Industry vs. inferiority	Preadolescent →	Conscientious conformist
Adolescent (13–19)	Formal operational →	Genital →	Group id vs. alienation Individual identity vs. role diffusion		Conscientious Individualistic
Maturity (22+)	→	→	Intimacy vs. isolation Generativity vs. stagnation Integrity vs. despair	Adolescent struggle and self-reliance →	Autonomous Integrated →

[a]No age norms implied.
[b]Prototype of basic developmental line.

reduction or removal of behaviors deemed as undesirable. In behaviorally oriented programs both techniques are utilized. In psychodynamically oriented programs, constructs such as needs, drives, and unresolved impulses may be evoked to account for the undesired behavior, whereas in behavioral programs all emitted behavior is perceived as a product of teaching and learning, under some schedule of reinforcement, and there is resistance to evoking any other interpretation.

To perceptual-theorist Gibson (1975), reinforcement is internal and is achieved through the reduction of uncertainty through the child's own learning.

Structure

All teachers must plan and structure the classroom in some way, whether the teacher provides small step instruction, plans small group activity, or arranges the environment so that a child encounters objects from which he or she will learn. Structure, as we define it, has to do with how the teacher plans and organizes—not how the teacher commands or disciplines. Structure is the way things are related to each other to form a whole. Each part of the structure is defined by relationships. Whereas the individual parts (i.e., the curriculum) may vary, they nonetheless go together to make sense (Loevinger, 1976). The amount and type of structure vary among models but are present in all. As we shall see, programs that differ markedly in philosophy may still be high-structure programs. Weikart's (1976) research suggests that the element of structure is a critical element in contributing to program success.

Play

Most programs consider play as a dominant means of child-learning. To some, such as Vygotsky (Anastasiow et al., 1974), impaired children are perceived as sharing the common inability to learn how to play naturally. Thus, the impaired child must be taught to learn how to play. Even in the most structured preschool centers, play at some point in the day occurs; however, it may occur for very diverse reasons. In a behavioral program, play may be a break from a learning task, whereas in a cognitive program, play is the framework for the learning task. Toys are another common feature. It follows, almost without comment, that toys, the tools of play, exist in every center.

In-Service Training

Most models, with rare exceptions, include the need for supervision and continuous in-service training of the staff. It would appear that the preschool handicapped models have fully recognized and accepted what the public school has not been able to put into practice: the fact that there is no one set of techniques and strategies available for facilitating development of all children. These strategies must be discovered and developed. One method by which they can be discovered or invented is by planned experimentation: trying a technique with a child, and having an independent person observe the act and collect data. This is followed by analyzing and critiquing the results. To the author this procedure is at the heart of in-service training. Other models include special seminars and guest speakers. In addition, due to the experimental or developmental nature of most new programs, teachers, aides, and other personnel learn how to implement the program while employed—making in-service training mandatory for the program's success. Tyler and Smith (1942) estimated that it took three years for a teacher to master a new program, and Weikart's report (1976) suggests that this ongoing interaction of teacher-supervisor contributes to any model's success.

Low Ratio

Early childhood handicapped programs also share the common need for low teacher to child ratios. In the case of infant programs, it is most likely a one teacher to one child ratio. With toddlers, the ratio tends to be three to one. The maximum number appears to be about five to one for children with special needs.

Major Differences: Perception of the Learner

The area in which models differ markedly is in the way the learner is perceived. These differences have been conceptualized on an active-passive dimension (Anastasiow and Mansergh, 1975). At one extreme is the position that the learner is to be taught by a trainer-teacher who perceives the child as a receptor. Another extreme perceives the child as the discoverer and inventor of all of his or her learnings. Somewhere near the discoverer extreme is the position of the child as a transactor within an environment. And finally, a more moderate laissez-faire group views the child as a receptor who matures at a fixed rate.

Behaviorism has a long history in psychology and probably was as prominent with Watson and Mary Cover Jones in the 1920s as it has become today with Skinner (1953), Lindsley (1964), and Bandura (1971). (See Adams, 1976, for an excellent discussion.) Watsonian behaviorists believed it was possible to produce whatever kind of person was desired by controlling the conditions of training. Skinner (1948) in *Walden Two* appears to be similar to Watson in orientation. However, Skinner was able to specify and delineate the principles of training and acquisition. I perceive Skinner's first aim as the development of a technology for teaching and socialization. The technology proposed by Skinner was atheoretical and, in my opinion, later models of behaviorism are closer in philosophy to Skinner's earlier statements than they are to his later ones. Where behaviorists such as Tolman (1951) differed was in the way that they look at a cognitive domain of intentions, maps, and purposeful activity.

Social learning theory appears to have been derived from psychoanalytic theory as an active attempt to translate psychoanalytic principles into behavioral terms (Sears, Maccoby, and Levin, 1957). Social learning theory attempted to identify those parenting techniques that lead to later stages and processes such as dependency, identification, sex role adoption, and so on. Bandura's (1969) *Principles of Behavior Modification* has combined elements of social learning theory and behaviorism more closely associated earlier with the followers of Skinner. However, Bandura's behaviorism added to the theory the importance of modeling and imitation. At the core of behaviorism is the notion that learning is the result of a trainer (teacher) who shapes the behavior of the learner. Hence, all behavior is learned and is a direct result of teaching in a broadly based set of environmental influences. All nonobservable behaviors such as needs are not accepted in the theory; however, constructs such as friendliness, love, and aggression have observable behaviors and—though one must at times interpret their intent—are therefore considered learned behaviors. Nonobservable processes such as attention, motivation, and motor reproduction processes which are closely related to observable behaviors are perceived as mediators of observed behaviors.

Reinforcement of behavior is the key to the theory, as are schedules of reinforcement, imitation of observed behavior, modeling, small step instruction, extinction, and feedback. Excellent discussion of these principles can be found in Bandura (1969).

To Piaget and the other cognitive theorists, the child is the active agent in learning. Piaget and cognitive psychologists conceive of the child as motivated to grow and to learn. As Loevinger (1976) points out, most learning theories ignore growth motivation.

MODELS

The task of ameliorating a child's impairment so that the child can reach his or her full level of functioning is enormous. It is a long distance from the early competencies of birth to Erikson's (1950) "integrity," Freud's (1965) "adult sexuality," Loevinger's (1976) "integrated persons,"

Gagné's (1965) "problem solver," or Piaget's (Piaget and Inhelder, 1969) "abstract reasoner." What is implied in the "mature" adult is a person who has developed cognitive, behavioral, and social skills. Appleton, Clifton, and Goldberg (1975, p. 161) have provided a complete analysis of what is expected of a normal child:

> These abilities can be categorized as cognitive, behavioral, and social skills. Cognitive skills include: (1) attentional skills such as persistence, curiosity, and exploration; (2) perceptual skills, including the ability to notice discrepancies and learn from observation; and (3) conceptual skills such as the anticipation of consequences, taking the perspective of another person, planning and carrying out activities, developing strategies for problem-solving, and the acquisition of basic knowledge. Behavioral abilities consist of: (1) motor skills such as manipulation of objects and control of body position; (2) control skills, including the ability to carry out instructions and to inhibit impulsive behavior; and (3) self-care skills such as toileting, eating in a regular manner, and so on. Finally, social skills include: (1) the understanding and use of language; (2) the ability to use adults as resources by getting their attention and help at appropriate times; and (3) the development of such personal attributes as feelings of self-worth, independence, ability to express feelings, warmth, flexibility, and cooperation. These skills prepare the child for successful learning in school, independent behavior, and effective communication with people.

The impaired child has a condition (inability to see) or symptom (requires additional examples before learning) that points to a potential need for the application of learning strategies to compensate/ameliorate/replace the impairment. Thus, a mildly developmentally delayed child may need to have a task presented in smaller steps, with greater frequency, and/or for a longer period of time (Doman, 1974).

As noted earlier, there are four models in existence: *behavioral, normal developmental, cognitive developmental,* and *cognitive learning.* These categories are similar to classifications used earlier (Anastasiow and Mansergh, 1975).

Behavioral Model

The techniques emphasized in programs based on the behavioral model have been derived from the work of Skinner and are called "applied behavioral analyses" (Baer, Wolf, and Risley, 1968) or "functional analyses of behavior" (Spradlin, Karlan, and Wetherby, 1976). For a complete discussion of the principles see Spradlin, Karlan, and Wetherby's excellent analysis. As they suggest (see Table 2), analysis of behavioral events is based on the notions that these events can be observed and recorded; that classes of behavior are established and maintained by the

Table 2. Behavioral model

Learning stance	Teaching strategy	Developmental theory

Reinforcement
Instrumental learning
Classical conditioning
Verbal learning
Shaping and fading
Discrimination
Response generalization
Stimulus control and
  generalization
Stimulus and response
  classes
Feedback
Modeling
	Assess child's current status
	  in skill development
	Develop lessons in small
	  discrete steps based on task
	  analysis for each child
	Develop a diagnostic data
	  collection system
	Determine reinforcers
	Provide sequential lessons
	  at child's pace
	Determine pace of reinforcers
	Ignore undesirable behaviors
	Reinforce desired behaviors
	Prompt, model, and shape
	  desired behaviors
		Maturational stages
		Infancy
		Toddler
		Early childhood
		Preadolescent
		Adolescent
		Adult

consequences of the behavior; that different consequences and situations will produce different rates of behavior; that reinforcement should be continuous when a behavior is first established, but on a variable schedule later; and that behavior tends to be more persistent when reinforced on a variable schedule (pp. 242-243).

Several HCEEP programs are specifically designed to follow behavioral principles and concentrate on observed events. These projects avoid speculations about internal, nonobservable states of a child and attempt to specify the nature of the training based on diagnosis/evaluation of the child and data collected on a daily basis regarding the child's progress. Progress is measured on individual children and developmental norms are used as guides for assessing instruction.

One of the most highly visible and popular behavioral models is the Bereiter and Engelmann (1966) model, which was developed originally to train poverty-level children. Principles of behaviorism were systematically applied to assist children in the acquisition of basic skills of reading, language arts, and writing. Several HCEEP projects have developed programs utilizing these techniques. (See TADS (n.d.) for the names and locations of all the model types discussed in this section.)

Other behavioral preschool handicapped programs have been very successful with acting-out or oppositional and disturbed children. The term "behavior modification program" has been loosely applied to most of the behaviorally oriented programs. The principles of reinforcement applied systematically appear to be reasonable measures for controlling frantic, aggressive children.

Many of the behavioral programs that work with severely retarded children begin by focusing on teaching self-help skills. What becomes confusing is that behavioral techniques are utilized in a variety of pseudobehavioral programs.

I believe that most behavioral models were set up to deal with children who were not making normal developmental progress. These programs were primarily behavior modification programs in the sense described above; that is, they were designed to increase desirable behaviors and reduce the appearance of undesirable behaviors. A case in point is the RIP project, Regional Intervention Project (Wiegerink and Parrish, 1974) as it was originally conceived and implemented by Ora, Wiegerink, and Ray at George Peabody College. The program focused on autistic and oppositional children. The pressing first task with most of the children was to bring undesirable behaviors under control and to systematically reward desirable behaviors. To begin, the technique of extinction was used to decelerate behaviors such as temper tantrums, acting-out, and aggressive behaviors. As the child reduced his acting-out and/or his aggressive behaviors and became able to attend to verbal directions, to focus on the trainer's lessons, and to verbally interact with his trainer and peers, new skills were taught to the point that the child could be placed in a preschool or school setting with normal children. In the meantime, the staff sought to train teachers in the normal classroom to utilize the techniques of the behavioral learning model. Thus, the diffusion went out to the normal school on the premise that the techniques were applicable to all children, and if used with all children, then the child who exhibited undesirable behaviors could be dealt with within the normal class rather than be excluded from it. As teachers in regular classrooms become trained, there would be the possibility of fewer and fewer oppositional referrals to special classes. Only the severely autistic or aggressive child would be placed in a special training class before joining a regular class.

The behavioral preschool program for normal children that has attained the degree of development of programs for impaired children is the Bereiter and Engelmann program. (See Wiekart, 1976, for an excellent description of the program's application in elementary school setting.)

In summary, the behavioral model is applicable to children with impairments and appears to have been demonstrated to be particularly effective with some extreme behavior problem children. The Bereiter-

Engelmann (now the Becker-Engelmann) model appears to be effective in the early elementary school for basic skill development up to the third grade when compared to other programs (Weikart, 1976).

Normal Developmental Model

Gibson (1975) in another context has claimed that, although there is no one way children can master a skill, all teaching strategies must be based on a psychology of learning to be effective. As discussed earlier, there are marked differences among learning theories, and practitioners draw upon one, a combination of them, or none of them. By drawing upon "none of them" is meant that the practitioner states that he or she has an intuitive feel for how instruction is to be carried out and may or may not be able to support the intuition with evidence or to indicate references to specific learning theorists.

The normal developmental model (see Table 3) is a case in point. Its philosophical roots reside in Dewey, but its learning position has never been well explicated. The movement toward establishing the nursery schools during the 1930s had many goals. In the opinion of this author, the major impact of the progressive movement on education at large (Cremin, 1961) was to educate teachers and parents in how to raise their children in a more humane fashion. In this respect, the movement was successful. It was

Table 3. Normal developmental model

Learning stance	Teaching strategy	Developmental theory
Child is active	Utilize a unit approach that includes a range of activities around a central theme	Maturational—Gesell or Spock
Child is motivated to learn		Items on a Bayley Developmental Scale
Child learns through activity	Provide large group activity, small activity, variety, songs, dance, construction	Specific skill attainment by age expectancy
Child learns if parents have facilitated learning and helped establish: attachment, dependency, independence, mature self-concept	Provide verbal direction	Stages—infancy, early childhood, etc.
	Encourage conformity to school rules	Psychodynamic orientation toward emotional development, (i.e., healthy child-rearing relationship between mother and child equals healthy child)
	Encourage independence in self care (toileting, finding things, putting toys away, buttoning coats)	
	Reward	

supported by magazines and the press (Bigner, 1972; Lavatelli, 1970), and the mass of middle-class parents now hold very similar child-rearing attitudes which appear to facilitate children's growth (Martin, 1975). These attitudes are the use of praise, warmth, and reasoning, along with a firm setting of limits and a strong press for achievement. The press for achievement is made on the basis of the child's "readiness" to accomplish a new task. Age norms such as those of Gesell (1975) or Spock (1957) are used to determine when a child should be able to sit, walk, talk, climb, tie his shoes, and perform other similar tasks. The nursery schools reinforce these training attitudes, and mothers and teachers of kindergartners are often in high agreement on how they perceive a child according to the child's level of skill development (Mlodnosky, 1962). Experiences are provided in the classroom setting to reflect that level of development. For example, children who should be at an age when lacing or tying their own shoes is typical, are provided with toy shoes for practice. Toy manufacturers have followed the demand of the nursery and regular school and provide age norms for the toys they sell.

The kindergartens are readiness centers where children are prepared for first grade. The term "readiness" is an apt descriptor for the model, and "preschool" is an excellent descriptor of the major thrust of such classes, "pre-" meaning both before school and as preparation for regular school. Thus, emphasis on readiness for reading, for arithmetic, and for social control is the core of the program. However, the guiding spirit of the curriculum is social control, with great emphasis on taking turns, sitting quietly, listening to oral instructions, and controlling impulses. As stated earlier, these are the behaviors of the work ethic of this country; they are more highly prized by, and therefore more instrumental in achieving success in, the business and corporate communities than such behaviors as creativity and independence (Bowles and Gintis, 1976). The major teaching strategy of the normal developmental model is group instruction, which strives to bring children up or down to a mean or average as stated by some developmental guideline. Comparisons of individual children are made to the group. Given this basic framework of a press toward group performance and a mean level of achievement of motor, cognitive, and language skill development, it should not surprise the reader that the impaired child was almost universally excluded from such centers.

As we have implied earlier in this chapter, the normal developmental model is, with few exceptions, the major model of public education. There are some allowances for individual differences in classrooms, but most of the nursery-preschool and public schools in this country measure success according to grade-by-grade mean level achievement in all types of skill development and continue to do so in spite of a rash of reforms to individualize instruction. Examples of these reforms are team teaching, ungraded instruction, programmed instruction, open space, open education, and cross-grade groupings. It has been estimated that eighty to ninety percent of elementary school teachers still use a basic textbook in reading; and most of these teachers use a text that is of the grade level they are teaching, even though it is commonly known that the spread in reading ability among children in any one classroom is across many levels. (For example, at fourth grade it can range from second grade to high school (Russell, 1949).)

A major concern of teachers in "normal developmental" centers is the child's "self-concept," a much overused and unclear concept in psychology (Loevinger, 1976). Generally speaking, the preschool stresses conformity to the standards of the school, and children who readily conform and participate in the activities of the school are perceived as socioemotionally healthy. Fortunately, the preschool has the mass of support of the training of parents at home—the so-called hidden curriculum of the middle-class home that has been discussed at length elsewhere (Anastasiow and Haynes, 1976). Given home-school agreement of goals, the child achieves success in the preschool (Mlodnosky, 1962). Obviously, from what has been stated so far, the impaired child would not fare well in such a classroom. Individualization of instruction or treatment of deficits is practically nonexistent in such centers. I believe that the failure of the normal developmental model to provide for individual differences is what led parents of impaired children to set up their own schools and experiment with ways to facilitate impaired children's learning.

Thus, the strength of the normal developmental model is the utilization of normal guidelines in development; but its strength is also its major weakness, for practitioners of the model rarely ameliorate or otherwise try to deal with the child other than according to an average pace of development. The unusual child is usually referred out of the classroom for diagnosis and treatment, after which, in many cases, nothing is done.

Each of the experimental preschool handicapped programs that has adopted the normal developmental model has had to make massive revisions in its original design to develop curriculum, train teachers, and invent strategies in order to offset the deficit in the model. In my opinion, there are no actual normal developmental models for impaired children, and the model is inappropriate for them. The Hodges, McCandless, and Spicker (1967) program, which began as a normal developmental model, became successful when the curriculum was developed and strategies were invented to remediate weaknesses in the normal model. The program drew upon psychological theory to guide its practices.

Cognitive Developmental Model

To educators, the term "cognitive" usually refers to the human processes associated with thought. Whereas many writers have dealt with cognition, for educators the most prominent psychologist identified with the term is Piaget. Given the difficulty of Piaget's more than fifty books, it is probably his followers who have made his work accessible to educators. (The reader is referred to Furth (1970) and Wadsworth (1971) for excellent beginning analyses, and to Piaget and Inhelder (1969) for a comprehensive but complex treatment of his theory.)

The basis of a cognitive theory is that cognitive processes are unconscious and are derived from primitive schema available at birth from which, through environmental interaction, all other structures are built. The genetic or biological basis of thinking is a fundamental principle in Piagetian theory (Piaget, 1971). There is also a very deterministic-nativistic aspect of the theory in that, given environmental interaction with objects, stages of development will appear in an orderly fashion. To Piaget, the child is not a miniature adult but one whose thinking capacity and approach to the world are markedly different from those of the adult.

According to Piaget, children develop through four distinct stages: sensorimotor (zero to two years of age), preoperational (two to five years of age), concrete operations (five to twelve years of age), and abstract reasoning (twelve years to maturity). To Piaget, through the processes of "assimilation" the child changes the primitive schema by "taking in" objects in the environment. A child who is confronted with a heretofore unencountered object or experience is forced to change his or her schema to account for the new or unknown. The child does this through the process of "accommodation." "Equilibration" is the mechanism hypothesized to balance the assimilation-accommodation actions. "Decentration" is hypothesized to be the growing ability of the child to separate himself from the world and gain identity and perception as a distinct individual. Although this process begins early in life, with object permanence at eight months, it is not complete until full maturity at around twenty-two years of life (see Table 4).

The theory postulates that development is sequential, hierarchical in organization, universal, and irreversible. Piaget's developmental theory is part of the French structural position (Piaget, 1970).

The child in Piaget's theory is perceived as the active learner constructing his or her own intelligence. In this regard, his position resembles Dewey's description of the child "who learns through his own experimentation and thinking" (Cremin, 1961). The notion of the child's actions as a key to learning is fundamental to the cognitive approach toward under-

Table 4. Cognitive developmental model

Learning stance	Teaching strategy	Developmental theory
Assimilation Accommodation Decentration Decálage Child active as: discoverer/ inventor, knowledge seeker, competence seeker	Plan environment to allow for child's major encounters to: discover physical knowledge of shapes, texture, function; discover logicomathematical knowledge of classification numbers, socialization, and reversibility Develop attachment and object permanence Provide objects for name learning Provide experiences for social rule learnings Present skill development directly through lessons and large-small group games Base plans, environment, and lessons on observation of children's current status	Piaget: sensori-motor, pre-operational, concrete operations, abstract reasoning Developmental milestones à la Gesell or Spock Erikson's psychosocial development

standing development. Piaget's appeal to American educators is probably best understood by the similarity of his philosophy to Dewey's.

To Piaget, the child learns how the physical world operates (causality, time, space, and the laws of physics and chemistry, such as conservation) through six distinct stages in the sensorimotor period, which ends with the child having the capacity of insight. Following the end of the sensorimotor period, the child constructs reality through deferred imitation, symbolic play, drawing, internalized imitation (mental images), and verbal evocation of events (Piaget and Inhelder, 1969). (For a complete analysis of Piaget's conception of the first two years of life, the reader is referred to Morehead and Morehead (1974).) As the child matures, his or her knowledge of the physical world and logicomathematical knowledge continues while social knowledge accelerates. (The reader is referred to Kamii (1972) for a description of an application of Piagetian theory to curriculum development.)

The teaching strategies for each of these types of knowledge require a different stance. Physical knowledge is obtained through the child's action on objects, that is, shaking, smelling, tasting, feeling, and throwing. Logicomathematical knowledge is derived from the child's native curiosity of how things work and go together or make sense. Social knowledge comprises the man-made rules or names given things in the language the child speaks (chair, hat, bed). The teacher must provide the physical objects for a child to experience and experiment with and also the experiences whereby the child can experiment. Thus, objects of different textures, sizes, and shapes are found in "cognitive developmental" classrooms for the direct purpose of children's learning. Classification of objects must be discovered by the child. One technique to encourage the development of classification is to provide experiences that lead to classification. For example, metals which can be attracted by a magnet and metals which cannot, along with a magnet, might be provided to stimulate the child's discovery. The experiences the teacher provides have to be appropriate to the age of cognitive development of the child or near the age when the child will make a transition. To Piaget, development cannot be speeded up; it can only be facilitated. The teacher, however, can focus the child on the dimension to be mastered through questions such as, "Do you think she is taller or shorter than you?" The child can be guided to form hypotheses through questioning and by being allowed to confirm or reject those hypotheses through his or her own activity. To Piaget, major learnings occur by both the confirmation and the rejection of hypotheses.

One of the examples of a model based on much of Piagetian reasoning is the English informal school (Weber, 1971). The following statement from Weber (1971, p. 11) makes clear the relationship between the cognitive developmental model and the informal school of open education model:

> The active force of such learning is considered to be curiosity, interest, and the needs of a child's own search for definition and relevance. The school setting or environment must be rich enough to foster and maintain this curiosity; it must be free enough to allow and even to help each individual follow the path indicated by his curiosity. Entwined with the experience gained through a child's own use of the school environment is the learning of skills, because skills are needed in the process. How a child would learn in the school setting was also individual—he would learn in his own way, at his own pace, exploring his own interests, for his own purposes.

Cognitive Learning Model

A new model developed by the Brickers (1974) has been called by this author a "cognitive learning model" for lack of a better name. The name was chosen because the Brickers integrate the utilization of operant procedures for lesson strategies and remediation while drawing upon cognitive, psycholinguistic, and perceptual theories to diagnose the child's level of development and to plan intervention programs. The Brickers state: "The experimental analysis of behavior is a method for seeking and documenting functional relationships between and among antecedent events, behavioral moments and subsequent events" (p. 437). It is an open system for collecting data about child-environment interactions. The method they use is,

"... a method of looking at behavior and not, necessarily, a basis for explaining it..." (p. 438). Thus, the language production of a child would be analyzed to determine what level his or her production reflects and to determine how to facilitate the acquisition of more complex forms. The experimental analysis would be the means used to determine what intervention might best enhance the acquisition.

In using such an approach (see Table 5), the Brickers draw upon the theories of Piaget and Bruner for their conception of the child. They perceive the normal child as an active explorer of the environment who is able to make his or her own discoveries and syntheses. Hence, they believe it may be necessary with an impaired child to initiate and teach active exploration of the environment. To both the cognitive developmental and cognitive learning theories, exploration is a mediator of knowledge, as it is to Piaget; however, the cognitive learning theorists stress the importance of teaching exploration to impaired children who do not initiate it on their own. This notion, I think, is very close to Vygotsky's notion of the necessity to teach play to impaired youngsters. To Vygotsky it would appear to be the motivational tool for learning. To the cognitive learning theorist, exploration can be encouraged through a variety of instructional strategies and, thus, accelerate learning.

Table 5. Cognitive learning model

Learning stance	Teaching strategy	Developmental theory
Cognitive: assimilation, accommodation, decentration, decálage, information processing	Diagnoses (evaluate child's skills development)	Piaget, cognitive: sensorimotor, preoperational, concrete operations, abstract reasoning
Learning takes place through child-environmental interactions	Plan small step lessons	Gesell-Spock-Bayley types of developmental skill attainment; normal development
Adherence to generative grammar psycholinguistic development	Utilize positive reinforcement	
	Ignore undesirable behaviors	Developmental scales: Uzgiris-Hunt, Haring-Hayden
	Utilize behavior modification and cognitive strategies	Psycholinguistic development: Bloom, Brown
	Collect data daily	
	Evaluate daily	
	Plan lessons on child's current developmental status	Information processing/mediation: Bandura, Gibson

The cognitive learning theorists believe that the impaired child should be dealt with as soon as possible and that maturational guidelines per se are a poor source for planning instruction. The work of the Brickers has been largely with infants and toddlers. Thus, they perceive prelinguistic forms of behavior as a prelude to linguistic forms, thereby placing language in the larger framework of communications. In their infant stimulation work, the Uzgiris and Hunt (1975) scales, or others based on Piagetian notions of the sensorimotor period, are used to assess the domain of the child's strengths and weaknesses. Recently, Diane Bricker (personal communication) has recommended the use of the Uniform Performance Assessment System (Haring and Hayden, 1976). The assessment techniques utilized break a large skill area into smaller skills, such as twelve steps in visual tracking, eight steps in prehension, five steps in object permanence. To the Brickers, the test-teach system would be applicable for normally developing children up to the age of four and for retarded children as old as fifteen, but who are behaving in a defined developmental space (Bricker and Bricker, 1974, p. 445).

Guralnick (personal communication) also uses a cognitive learning model, but with somewhat older youngsters than those in the Bricker program. Emphasis is placed on translating concepts from developmental psycholinguistics (Bloom, 1970; Brown, 1973), information processing and perceptual strategies (e.g., Gibson, 1969), and mediational/learning processes (Bandura, 1969; Mahoney, 1974) into developmental programs for handicapped youngsters. Instructional and evaluative strategies are carried out within a behavioral framework (Guralnick, 1975).

In summary, the cognitive learning model is an outgrowth of the application of behavioral analysis as a technology for diagnosing/teaching/evaluation. Psycholinguistic theory is drawn upon for language development, cognitive theory for cognition, perceptual theory for perceptual training, and normal-developmental scales for self-help skills.

PRESCHOOL MODEL PROGRAMS AND THE INTEGRATION OF HANDICAPPED CHILDREN

From the outset, the normal developmental model is perceived to have many weaknesses for both normal and impaired children. The behavioral model can serve both groups of children, but it has not yet demonstrated that it can focus both on remediation and on complex skill development. Of the two remaining models, each has much to offer. The cognitive developmental model is an attractive means of developing creativity and problem-solving techniques, and its focus on individualization would do much to remediate an impaired child's deficits. Clearly it is not a suitable model for the severely impaired. The cognitive learning model can serve the severely impaired well and, as the Brickers attest, would be suitable for the normal preschool child as well. Further development of the model by Guralnick would make it a viable model for both impaired and normal children.

Clearly, some type of environmental modification (remediation) is necessary to meet the needs of children who are impaired, and must be considered when choosing a model for the integration of handicapped children into preschool settings for normal children. The normal developmental model is currently the most prevalent model but probably provides the least desirable situation in which to place children with special needs. In most cases it is so unyielding that it even rarely meets the needs of the normal child. In addition, children from different ethnic and racial groups may be considered developmentally delayed when placed in a normal developmental model-based setting (Mercer, 1973). In the normal developmental model, competence is meeting the expectations of the setting. From an ecological point of view, no one is handicapped if the setting can be modified so that the impairment is not an impairment (Carlson, 1976).

Our analysis suggests that the cognitive developmental and the cognitive learning models pay a great deal of attention to individual differences of children across a wide set of behaviors. These settings may be the most adaptable to the environmental changes required to successfully integrate the handicapped and the nonhandicapped child.

REFERENCES CITED

Adams, J. A. 1976. Learning and Memory: An Introduction. Homewood, Ill.: The Dorsey Press.

Anastasiow, N. J., and Mansergh, G. P. 1975. Teaching skills in early childhood programs. Exceptional Children, 41, 309-317.

Anastasiow, N. J., and Haynes, M. L. 1976. Language Patterns of Poverty Children. Springfield, Ill.: Charles C Thomas.

Anastasiow, N. J., Gallagher, J. J., Hewett, F. M., and Matthews, J. 1974. Educational research and development. In J. J. Gallagher (Ed.), Windows on Russia. Washington, D.C.: U.S. Department of Health, Education, and Welfare.

Appleton, T., Clifton, R., and Goldberg, S. 1975. The development of behavioral competence in infancy. In F. D. Horowitz (Ed.), Review of Child Development Research. Chicago: University of Chicago Press.

Baer, D. M., Wolf, M. M., and Risley, T. F. 1968. Some current dimensions of applied behavior analysis. Journal of Applied Behavior Analysis, 1, 91-97.

Bandura, A. 1969. Principles of Behavior Modification. New York: Holt, Rinehart and Winston.

Bandura, A. 1971. Analyses of modeling processes. In A. Bandura (Ed.), Psychological Modeling. Chicago: Aldine-Atherton.

Bereiter, C., and Engelmann, S. 1966. Teaching Disadvantaged Children in the Preschool. Englewood Cliffs, N.J.: Prentice-Hall.

Bigner, J. J. 1972. Parent education in popular literature: 1950-1970. Family Coordinator, July, 313-319.

Bloom, L. 1970. Language Development: Form and Function in Emerging Grammars. Cambridge, Mass.: MIT Press.

Bowles, S., and Gintis, H. 1976. Schooling in Capitalist America. New York: Basic Books.

Bricker, W. A., and Bricker, D. D. 1974. An early language training strategy. In R. L. Schiefelbusch and L. L. Lloyd (Eds.), Language Perspectives—Acquisition, Retardation, and Intervention. Baltimore: University Park Press.

Broudy, H. S. 1972. The Real World of the Public Schools. New York: Harcourt Brace Jovanovich.

Brown, R. 1973. A First Language. Cambridge, Mass.: Harvard University Press.

Bruner, J. S. 1973. Beyond the Information Given: Studies in the Psychology of Knowing. New York: W. W. Norton.

Carlson, N. A. 1976. The Contents of Life: A Socio-Ecological Model of Adaptive Behavior and Functioning. Washington, D.C.: U.S. Department of Health, Education, and Welfare, Bureau of Education for the Handicapped.

Cremin, L. 1961. The Transformation of the Schools. New York: Random House.

DeWeerd, J. 1974. Federal programs for the handicapped. Exceptional Children, 40, 441.

Doman, G. 1974. What To Do About Your Brain Injured Child. New York: Doubleday & Company.

Erikson, E. H. 1950. Childhood and Society. New York: W. W. Norton.

Eysenck, H. J. 1960. Behavior Therapy and the Neuroses. New York: Pergamon Press.

Feldman, D. H. 1976. The child as craftsman. Phi Delta Kappan, 58, 143-149.

Freud, A. 1965. Normality and Pathology in Childhood. New York: International Universities Press.

Furth, H. G. 1970. Piaget for Teachers. Englewood Cliffs, N.J.: Prentice-Hall.

Gagné, R. M. 1965. The Conditions of Learning. New York: Holt, Rinehart and Winston.

Gesell, A. 1954. The ontogenesis of infant behavior. In L. Carmichael (Ed.), Manual of Child Psychology (2nd ed.) New York: John Wiley & Sons.

Gibson, E. J. 1969. Principles of Perceptual Learning and Development. New York: Appleton-Century-Crofts.

Gibson, E. J. 1975. Theory-based research on reading and its implications for instruction. In J. B. Carroll and J. S. Chall (Eds.), Toward a Literate Society. New York: McGraw-Hill.

Greenberg, P. 1969. The Devil Has Slippery Shoes. New York: Macmillan.

Guralnick, M. J. 1975. Early classroom-based intervention and the role of organizational structure. Exceptional Children, 42, 25-31.

Haring, N., and Hayden, A. 1976. Uniform performance assessment system. (Mimeograph). Seattle: University of Washington.

Hodges, W. L., McCandless, B. R., and Spicker, H. H. 1967. The development and evaluation of a diagnostically based curriculum for preschool psychosocially deprived children. Washington, D.C.: U.S. Department of Health, Education, and Welfare.

Kamii, C. 1972. An application of Piaget's theory to the conceptualization of preschool curriculum. In R. K. Parker (Ed.), The Preschool in Action. Boston: Allyn & Bacon.

Karnes, M. B. 1969. Research and development program on preschool disadvantaged children. Final Report, Vol. 1. University of Illinois, Contract OE-6-10-235, U.S. Office of Education.

Karnes, M. B. 1975. Developmental Scale. Champaign, Ill.: Generators of Educational Materials, Enterprises.

Klein, J. W. 1976. Comparison of model preschool programs. In K. F. Riegel and J. A. Meacham (Eds.), The Developing Individual in a Changing World. The Hague: Mouton.

Lavatelli, C. S. 1970. Contrasting views of early childhood education. Childhood Education, 46, 239–246.

Lindsley, O. R. 1964. Direct measurement and prosthesis of retarded behavior. Journal of Education, 147, 62–81.

Loevinger, J. 1976. Ego Development. San Francisco: Jossey-Bass.

Lord, F. E. 1971. Complete individualization of instruction: An unrealized goal of the past century. In M. C. Reynolds and M. D. Davis (Eds.), Exceptional Children in Regular Classrooms. Minneapolis: Department of Audio-Visual Extension, University of Minnesota.

Lortie, D. C. 1975. School-teachers: A Sociological Study. Chicago: University of Chicago Press.

Mahoney, M. 1974. Cognition and Behavior Modification. Cambridge, Mass.: Ballinger.

Martin, B. 1975. Parent-child relations. In F. D. Horowitz (Ed.), Review of Child Development Research. Chicago: University of Chicago Press.

Mercer, J. R. 1973. Labeling the Mentally Retarded. Berkeley: University of California Press.

Mlodnosky, L. B. 1962. Some child-rearing antecedents of readiness for school. Unpublished doctoral dissertation, Stanford University.

Morehead, D. M., and Morehead, A. 1974. From signal to sign: A Piagetian view of thought and language during the first two years. In R. L. Schiefelbusch and L. L. Lloyd (Eds.), Language Perspectives—Acquisition, Retardation, and Intervention. Baltimore: University Park Press.

Piaget, J. 1970. Structuralism. New York: Basic Books.

Piaget, J. 1971. Biology and Knowledge. Chicago: University of Chicago Press.

Piaget, J., and Inhelder, B. 1969. The Psychology of the Child. New York: Basic Books.

Rapaport, D. 1960. The structure of psychoanalytic theory. Psychological Issues, 2(2, whole no. 6).

Russell, D. H. 1949. Children Learn to Read. New York: Ginn & Company.

Sears, R. R., Maccoby, E., and Levin, H. 1957. Patterns of Child Rearing. New York: Harper & Row.

Skinner, B. F. 1948. Walden Two. New York: Macmillan.

Skinner, B. F. 1953. Science and Human Behavior. New York: The Free Press.

Smith, B. O., Cohen, S. B., and Pearl, A. 1969. Teachers for the Real World. Washington, D.C.: American Association of Colleges for Teacher Education.

Spock, B. 1957. Baby and Child Care. New York: Pocket Books.
Spicker, H. J., Anastasiow, N. J., and Hodges, W. L. 1976. (Eds.), Children with Special Needs: Early Development and Education. Minneapolis: Leadership Training Institute.
Spradlin, J. E., Karlan, G. R., and Wetherby, B. 1976. Behavior analysis, behavior modification, and developmental disabilities. In L. L. Lloyd (Ed.), Communication Assessment and Intervention Strategies. Baltimore: University Park Press.
TADS. (n.d.). Technical Assistance Development System Tadscript 5. Chapel Hill: University of North Carolina.
Tolman, E. C. 1951. Behavior and Psychological Man. Berkeley: University of California Press.
Tyler, R., and Smith, E. 1942. Appraising and Recording Students' Progress. New York: Harper & Row.
Uzgiris, I. C., and Hunt, J. McV. 1975. Assessment in Infancy: Ordinal Scales of Psychological Development. Urbana, Ill.: University of Illinois Press.
Wadsworth, B. J. 1971. Piaget's Theory of Cognitive Development. New York: David McKay.
Weber, L. 1971. The English Infant School and Informal Education. Englewood Cliffs, N.J.: Prentice-Hall.
Wiegerink, R., and Parrish, V. 1974. A parent implemented preschool program. In: Training Parents to Teach. TADS monograph. Chapel Hill: University of North Carolina.

INTEGRATED PRESCHOOL PROGRAMS:
Description, Design, Evaluation, and Research

INTEGRATED PRESCHOOLS AS EDUCATIONAL AND THERAPEUTIC ENVIRONMENTS:
Concepts, Design, and Analysis

Michael J. Guralnick, Ph.D.

The design of educational and therapeutic environments that are sensitive to the varied, complex, and often subtle needs of young children provides a critical challenge to programs that integrate children at various developmental levels, including nonhandicapped children. A decade of experience with preschool intervention programs carried out mostly in nonintegrated settings, although often producing equivocal results, has nevertheless confirmed the value of a systematic approach to developmental programming (Bronfenbrenner, 1975; Hunt, 1975; Tjossem, 1976). Components of successful classroom-based programs include a strong reliance on organization and systems related to planning, design, feedback, and evaluation while conducted within a carefully specified theoretical framework (Guralnick, 1975; Karnes, 1973; Weikart, 1972). It is likely that these findings will also be applicable to integrated programs, although demands on organizational and staff resources will undoubtedly increase. In addition, the rather unique nature of integrated programs suggests that they have the potential

---

Portions of this work were supported by Grants OEG-0-74-0546, G00-76-03992, and G00-76-04055 from the United States Office of Education, Bureau of Education for the Handicapped.

for generating new developmental strategies. It is this latter aspect that is the focus of this chapter.

The existence of substantial numbers of integrated programs reflects the influence of a complex array of factors. In part, it is a response to reverse society's historical pattern of segregating its atypical groups, and the insensitive and unresponsive treatment that apparently inevitably results. For certain groups of handicapped individuals, the effects of this pattern have been documented all too vividly (Blatt, 1970; Kanner, 1964; Martin, 1974). From this awareness and our concern about the effectiveness of even well designed and well intentioned segregated programs (Dunn, 1968; Filler et al., 1975; Kaufman and Alberto, 1976), in conjunction with labeling issues for many groups of children (MacMillan, 1973; Mercer, 1973), new concepts and ideologies have emerged, finding expression in the terms "normalization" and "mainstreaming" (Birch, 1974; Wolfensberger, 1972). Although many points need to be resolved, especially when attempts are made to translate the principles into actual programs (MacMillan, Jones, and Meyers, 1976), these concepts have provided an impetus and direction for the creation of models, techniques, and administrative procedures that can effectively accommodate children within a wide range of developmental levels.

Efforts to integrate children at the preschool level have been most prominent, perhaps because of the comparative ease with which this can be accomplished (Caldwell, 1974; Wolfensberger, 1972) and the strong federal mandates in this regard. Interestingly, we are discovering that integration not only can serve to prevent some of the deleterious effects that can result from separation, but also, from a developmental and therapeutic perspective, the presence of nonhandicapped children may well have an independent positive effect on their handicapped peers (Guralnick, 1976a). More specifically, we are finding that more advanced peers can serve as valuable resources by providing instruction, applying adaptive consequences, or modeling appropriate social, play, and communicative behaviors. In addition, benefits of a more pervasive nature exist in that integrated groups tend to alter the entire climate of previously segregated classrooms in positive ways. Factors associated with this latter effect include the facts that (1) overall, fewer inappropriate behaviors tend to occur; (2) teachers' observations of nonhandicapped children provide a framework for understanding varying patterns of behaviors within a developmental context (Bricker and Bricker, 1972); and (3) the social, play, and linguistic environments tend to be of a richer quality. Accordingly, these circumstances provide opportunities and benefits for the handicapped child that are uniquely associated with integrated settings.

In this chapter, a number of concepts, issues, and findings with regard to classroom-based integrated programs for preschool children are explored. First, a description of an integrated preschool program consisting of children with widely varying skills is presented. This provides a framework for examining certain issues and principles related to the design of integrated programs. Next, techniques that have successfully utilized nonhandicapped peers as direct resources, the design implications of these techniques, and the relevance of various developmental processes to the organization of integrated programs are analyzed. Finally, the concept of integrated preschool programs as educational and therapeutic environments and the conditions that must be established to optimize the benefits and impact of these environments are discussed.

THE EXPERIMENTAL PRESCHOOL

Framework for Individualization and Togetherness

Nicholas Hobbs (1975) has pointed out that an enlightened application of the mainstreaming principle does not at all imply a melting pot concept where special needs tend to lose their identity, but rather that meaningful integrated programs require numerous arrangements, each geared to unique child and group needs with children remaining in as close contact with one another as possible. He states:

> In schools that are most responsive to individual differences in abilities, interests, and learning styles of children, the mainstream is actually many streams, sometimes as many streams as there are individual children, sometimes several streams as groups are formed for special purpose, sometimes one stream only as concerns of all converge. We see no advantage in dumping exceptional children into an undifferentiated mainstream; but we see great advantages to all children, exceptional children included, in an educational program modulated to the needs of individual children, singly, in small groups, or all together. Such a flexible arrangement may well result in functional separations of exceptional children from time to time, but the governing principle would apply to all children: school programs should be responsive to the learning requirements of individual children, and groupings should serve this end (p. 197).

Over the past few years, the Experimental Preschool of the National Children's Center has provided an integrated model demonstration program primarily supported by the Bureau of Education for the Handicapped and constituting part of what is referred to as the "First Chance" network. In doing so, we have explored a variety of arrangements in an attempt to optimize the developmental environment for a diverse population of preschool children in a manner that is consistent with Hobbs' position. To demonstrate this, four- to six-year-old children were specifically selected to ensure representation of a wide range of developmental levels. Although preschoolers with severe sensory or orthopaedic handicaps were not included, the program consisted of children exhibiting a considerable range of handicapping conditions, from those with little or no communicative or appropriate social behaviors to a group (twenty-five to thirty-five percent) with no developmental delays whatsoever.

The design of the integrated setting was intended to optimize resources such that: (1) the needs of individual children were met through specialized curricula, programs, and activities; (2) interactions among peers at various developmental levels would occur in a manner that maximized the potential value and satisfaction of those contacts; and (3) the instructional and social environment was sufficiently flexible to accommodate specialized peer-peer programs to benefit the handicapped child.

Structural Aspects of the Integrated Preschool

The architectural design of the preschool is compatible with the "many streams" concept and lends itself to numerous arrangements. Large double classrooms that can be divided if necessary are separated by a central area for indoor gross motor play. The size of the classrooms provides adequate space for play and lesson activities, and large observation rooms with one-way mirrors permit unobtrusive observations by parents, staff, and visitors. Children with relatively mild handicaps and the nonhandicapped children occupy one double classroom and are completely integrated for all activities. Children with severe handicaps and those with more moderate delays, characterized by emerging speech and poorly developed social behaviors, are located in the second double classroom and are involved with more advanced peers on a selective basis.

Decisions regarding the extent of each child's involvement in integrated activities are based on the child's responsiveness to social interactions and reinforcement, the level of development of his or her observational and imitative repertoires, and the severity and extent of any behavior problems. Although it has been suggested that these factors tend to limit the benefits derived from integrated experiences (Evers-Pascale and Sherman, 1975; Guralnick, 1976a; Strain, Shores, and Kerr, 1976), the proportion of time spent in integrated activities, even for children with extremely underdeveloped skills in this regard, is nevertheless quite substantial in our program. Moreover, as discussed below, more advanced children are frequently employed in assisting less advanced children to develop in these areas so as to enable them to benefit more fully from integrated activities.

Classroom events consist of a variety of structured and unstructured activities common to most preschool programs but with a strong emphasis on systematic observation, planning, and evaluation-feedback systems for each developmental area (Guralnick, 1975). Lessons, with a primary focus on cognitive and language development, are arranged for children grouped in terms of their progress in particular curriculum components. In addition, heterogeneous groups of children participate in lessons, often with the composition of the group and the selection of specific lesson activities designed to foster the development of the less advanced children in the group. Within the group format, planned interactions are geared to each individual child. Observations of these lessons would find the teacher moving from one child to another, adjusting her interactions to each, asking questions of the entire group from time to time, providing for extensive utilization of materials, requiring action sequences and child-child interactions whenever possible, and in general, orchestrating the elements of the lesson for all children as a social unit.

In addition to instructional or therapeutic teacher-child interactions conducted on a one-to-one basis as needed, numerous less structured activities, including various play, music, art, and other events, form additional key components of the program and constitute the majority of the day's activities. In these latter instances, especially play activities, children from all developmental levels, without restriction, are integrated, and the processes and techniques related to reaping the potential benefits from the interactions of children at various developmental levels are systematically applied. The extensive involvement of children at different developmental levels during play and other social and cultural activities reflects both the relative ease with which integration can occur in these more dynamic and free-flowing activities as well as the potential benefits of these interactions for the less advanced children. It should be noted, however, that the principles of peer modeling, peer reinforcement, peer support, and other social learning processes, discussed in detail at a later point, are applied in lesson situations as well as in the less structured activities.

The content and sequence of the curriculum components themselves are based on data derived from the structure and strategies associated with normal developmental patterns and have been subjected to various empirical tests. In general, our approach can best be described as a cognitive learning model (see preceding chapter). The organization of the curriculum accentuates the role of the social context, facilitates individualizing even in group lessons, and provides a systematic basis for structuring interactions in an integrated setting. Our series of language programs provides a good example. Based upon a variety of semantic, syntactic, and functional aspects of language development (see Bloom, 1975; Brown, 1973; MacDonald and Blott, 1974; Miller and Yoder, 1974), and utilizing a highly individualized instructional format within a behavioral framework (Guralnick, 1975, 1977), the program focuses on the development and generalization of linguistic concepts and the spontaneous use of language. Intrinsic to the program is an emphasis on communication in a social context, both in the lesson format as well as in play and other social and semistructured activities. In fact, many of the more advanced peers directly assist teachers in encouraging the application of newly acquired concepts and in arranging natural appearing circumstances for formalized probes with respect to the generalization of language concepts and usage.

Accordingly, the design of the preschool provides for varying degrees of integration carried out in proportion to the expected benefits that can be derived from such interactions; at the same time, it is governed by the principle of responsiveness to individual needs and the recognition of the critical importance for the sharing of physical and psychological space. This structure also establishes a means whereby small groups of children tend to be more frequently linked to one or two teachers ("home room"). This occurs to a greater degree for those with more severe delays and reflects an awareness of the fact that significant social agents (parents, teachers, etc.) require intense contact across diverse circumstances to enable them to recognize the developmental significance of and to build upon each child's emerging and often idiosyncratic characteristics. This is especially true with regard to the interpersonal aspects of communicative behavior (Mahoney and Seely, 1976).

Approaches to Facilitate Integration

In the design of our program, we were aware that integration efforts with primary age children have produced equivocal results. In general, sociometric and observational data (Gottlieb and Davis, 1973) have indicated that handicapped children are not readily accepted by their nonhandicapped peers regardless of whether the context is a nongraded elementary school (Goodman, Gottlieb, and Harrison, 1972), a regular classroom with supportive services (Iano et al., 1974), or a no-interior wall nongraded school (Gottlieb and Budoff, 1973). On the positive side, however, recent gains have been achieved in identifying the characteristics of children and conditions that will increase the likelihood of success (Budoff and Gottlieb, 1976).

Similarly, existing research with preschool children has documented that, especially for widely heterogeneous groups of children, spontaneous interactions are not likely to occur (Allen, Benning, and Drummond, 1972;

Feitelson, Weintraub, and Michaeli, 1972; Ray, 1974; but see Ispa, 1976). The available evidence suggests that the systematic arrangement of events and other specialized procedures to encourage and support integration may need to take place, especially if peer interactions are intended to serve as an educational or therapeutic resource (Guralnick, 1976a). Within the overall structure and design of the preschool described above, two general approaches have been adopted in order to maximize interactions among children at different developmental levels. The first approach includes attention to the following structural, organizational, and programmatic characteristics: (1) a careful selection of social play activities and related games and materials (see Quilitch and Risley, 1973), (2) a flexible design of the content and organization of the curriculum, (3) the matching of children's interests, (4) the provision for and arrangement of certain spatial layouts and equipment (see Twardosz, Cataldo, and Risley, 1974), and (5) systematic modeling and prompting activities by teachers. Conceptually, these activities are compatible with a broad-based ecological approach (Gump, 1975) in that the proper structuring of the social and physical environments is designed to set the occasion for the occurrence of frequent and productive interactions among handicapped and nonhandicapped children.

The second approach is to build the observational, imitative, group involvement, and social interaction skills of the less advanced children. Gains in these areas would increase the probability of productive interactions. To some degree this can be facilitated with the help of more advanced peers (Guralnick, 1976a; Hartup, 1970), but especially for children with very limited skills or severe behavior or emotional problems, techniques implemented by staff members for gradually developing these behaviors, such as those described by Koegel and Rincover (1974) for achieving group involvement, may need to be employed. In general, an entire range of social learning and direct reinforcement principles and techniques can be utilized to build specific skills and to establish peers and adults as meaningful social agents (Bandura, 1969; Kozloff, 1974).

NONHANDICAPPED PEERS AS POTENTIAL RESOURCES

Social Play Interactions

A variety of techniques have been successfully used to foster social interactions among preschool children. These have included systematic and direct reinforcement of play behavior through contingent praise and attention by adults (Allen et al., 1964; Buell et al., 1968; Hart et al., 1968), by peers (Nordquist and Bradley, 1973; Wahler, 1967), through the use of toys and games (Quilitch and Risley, 1973), by providing certain types of play equipment (Keogh, Miller, and LeBlanc, 1973), through symbolic modeling (O'Connor, 1969), and by direct training in sociodramatic play (Strain and Wiegerink, 1976).

The diversity of these methods is a reflection of the significance we attach to the growth of reciprocal social play interactions among young children and the development of the child's constructive use of toys and materials. It has been suggested that play activities permit exploration of actions and interactions in nonthreatening situations, and provide an atmosphere conducive to the practice of subskills and the testing of contingencies that will be employed later as part of a more complex and integrated behavior pattern (Bruner, 1972; Slobin, 1964; Weisler and McCall, 1976). It appears that the absence of social play interaction skills has a significant negative impact on later personality development (Bandura, 1969), and a number of observers have traced the development of social play and provided useful descriptive information of both normative and theoretical interest (Barnes, 1971; Eckerman, Whatley, and Kutz, 1975; Mueller and Lucas, 1975; Parten, 1932, 1933). Accordingly, despite some cloudy conceptual and empirical issues regarding exploration and play, Weisler and McCall (1976, p. 492) point out that "... it is widely acknowledged that such behavior is a key ingredient in... adaptability, learning, cognition, education, and social behaviors...".

Structuring Social Interactions The existence of integrated programs provides a potential and perhaps unique opportunity for using nonhandicapped peers as an additional resource for promoting social development. Prior work by O'Connor (1969), Nordquist and Bradley (1973), and Wahler (1967), and the observations by Hartup (1970) suggesting the feasibility of systematically utilizing peers as agents of change, have provided a framework and point of departure for our efforts directed toward children manifesting more severe delays and a wider range of handicapping conditions.

Our early exploratory work on the effects of integrating handicapped and nonhandicapped children in a free-play setting produced a number of interesting results (Devoney, Guralnick, and Rubin, 1974). As might be expected, we found that simply introducing nonhandicapped children into a play setting had virtually no effect on the quality of play of a heterogeneous group of handicapped children. However, when the teacher structured the setting so as to promote interactions (by arranging equipment and other prompts), a substantial increase in the proportion of associative and cooperative play was noted for virtually all of the handicapped children.

Perhaps the most striking aspect of this demonstration, however, was anecdotal evidence suggesting the occurrence of substantial changes in the nature of the play of the handicapped children. Specifically, the teachers observed that, especially in the absence of the nonhandicapped children, the play of the handicapped children was more sophisticated, organized, and contained more fantasy play elements than ever previously noted. Interestingly, there is some evidence (Freyberg, 1973) to suggest that changes such as these are associated with gains in the cognitive and social-emotional domains.

Additional work (Guralnick, 1976a) analyzed in more detail the procedures and effects of utilizing nonhandicapped peers to modify less advanced peers' social play behavior. A setting was arranged whereby two nonhandicapped peers focused on promoting the social play of a designated handicapped child. The experimental procedures were based, in part, on Wahler's (1967) experimental analysis of child-child interactions in free-field settings in which he established the important role of contingent peer attention as a means of controlling a diverse set of preschool children's social behaviors. In our work, through role playing and direct training, nonhandicapped children were instructed to model and encourage interactive and constructive play with a particular toy and to selectively reinforce only the appropriate social play behaviors of the handicapped child. Observations and recordings of the handicapped child's behavior were carried out on a time-sampling basis utilizing the social play categories described by Parten (1932) and validated by Wintre and Webster (1974).

Figure 1 illustrates the various components and sequence of this procedure. During baseline sessions, the handicapped child engaged primarily in solitary play and addressed very few positive comments to the nonhandicapped children (percentage data are based on the number of time-sampled intervals in which the behavior occurred). No effect was noted by simply having the handicapped child observe his peers playing associatively or cooperatively in the modeling condition (panel 2). Consequently, the peer modeling and selective reinforcement procedure was initiated and, as is evident in panel 3, a rapid and marked change occurred in the percentage of intervals in which the handicapped child engaged in associative and cooperative play. In addition, a substantial increase in the number of positive verbalizations occurred as well. Since there were three toys in the setting, we were able to assess the nature of control by the peers by having the nonhandicapped children select a second toy (toy B) and carry out the same procedures that were in effect when toy A was the focus of activity. Again, the handicapped child's social play shifted from solitary to that

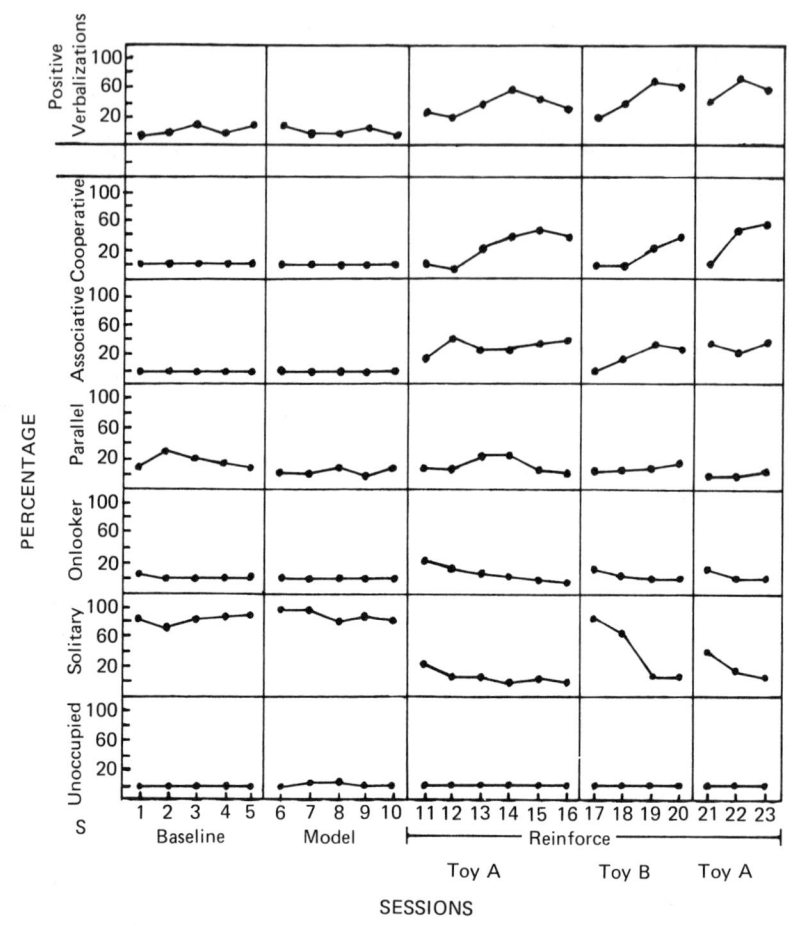

Figure 1. Changes in social play behavior and positive verbalizations for a handicapped child as a result of peer modeling and reinforcement. (Based on Guralnick, 1976a.)

categorized as associative and cooperative. A final return to toy A again replicated these findings, as did a similar procedure carried out with a different group of children.

This technique has worked well for children with both mild and moderate developmental delays. An observational analysis suggested that the social play interactions of the handicapped children were facilitated by a sequential process that was frequently repeated by the nonhandicapped children. Specifically, it included encouragement to interact, demonstrations of appropriate toy use and play roles, and then the provision of appropriate social and activity consequences.

Need for Further Analysis Unquestionably, further analysis of this process is warranted. It remains to be determined how durable these changes are and to what extent they generalize to other settings and children. The compatibility of the groups, the willingness of the nonhandicapped children to participate, as well as the developmental levels and interpersonal characteristics of the handicapped children are factors that are likely to affect that efficacy of this technique. In fact, our current research strongly suggests that generalization of these play patterns to other more diverse free-play settings tends to be reduced by the presence of competing activities, especially those involving other advanced peers. Perhaps the application of the aforementioned technique with larger groups of handicapped and nonhandicapped children will reduce the impact of these competing variables. In any event, it is important that we recognize the value of improved social development that occurs even in the small play groups, since the development of social skills and constructive play in these settings is likely to facilitate generalization to more complex environments.

In addition, it is important to establish the extent to which this process simply facilitates the occurrence of play and social play interaction skills already existing in the handicapped child's repertoire and to what extent new learning, both in terms of toy use and interpersonal skills, actually takes place. This latter analysis relates to observational learning studies in which efforts to tease out the processes of vicarious desensitization, vicarious reinforcement, and the acquisition of new behaviors (and ultimately direct reinforcement procedures) are vital issues (Bandura, 1971; Keller and Carlson, 1974; O'Connor, 1972).

Peers as Therapeutic Agents

The development of social play skills using peers as agents of change actually consists of many processes and could be categorized equally well as a "therapeutic" intervention in which peers prompt others, serve as models, and provide feedback for appropriate interpersonal behaviors. The therapeutic value of peers in this regard has not gone unrecognized. Early efforts by Mary Cover Jones (1924) explored a number of techniques designed to eliminate fears of young children. She observed that the method of social imitation, in which nonfearful children were used to induce actions in others incompatible with the fear response, was an extremely valuable technique. The work of O'Connor (1969, 1972) on vicarious processes that promote social interactions is relevant here as well. Further documentation for the potential therapeutic significance of peer relationships can be found in the remarkable account by Freud and Dann (1951) on the group upbringing of children orphaned during World War II (highlighted by Hartup in the second chapter of this volume) and the review by Hartup (1970) of a variety of studies establishing the significance of peer influence during early childhood. Taken together, these efforts and a number of direct and systematic attempts to induce therapeutic change by peers that have been developed recently appear to have important programmatic implications for integrated settings.

Reducing Severe Avoidance and Self-Directed Behaviors Through Peer Contact Although less directive and more symbolically oriented techniques can be effective in reducing even the extreme social withdrawal of many young children (O'Connor, 1969, 1972), for those with more generalized deficits and maladaptive behaviors, including highly developed self-directed behaviors, other more direct treatment procedures are generally necessary. One technique that has served as a prototype for our efforts in this area can be found in the work by Suomi and Harlow (1972) in which isolate-reared monkeys, who normally manifest profound and generally irreversible social deficits as a result of their isolation, were successfully rehabilitated through the use of "therapist" monkeys. The rehabilitation procedure consisted of the selection of nonisolate peer monkeys in order to deliberately and persistently force contact with the isolates whose behavior was dominated by a variety of self-directed activities. In order to achieve the therapeutic effect, Suomi and Harlow chose therapist monkeys that were younger than the isolates such that their emerging social repertoire matched, in a predictable fashion, the stages of the therapeutic program. The results showed that social rehabilitation was complete after twenty-six weeks of this form of intervention. An analysis of the processes involved led Suomi and Harlow to suggest that the constant clinging by the therapist monkeys was responsible for the breakdown of the self-directed behaviors. Following this, opportunities arose for the therapist monkeys to reinforce alternative prosocial behaviors and to assist in the development of a complex social repertoire.

In an application of this general technique in the preschool, we used systematic instructions to nonhandicapped "therapist" peers in order to increase the appropriate social interactions of a child who displayed many severe isolate behaviors. Specifically, during certain activities, we asked some of our nonhandicapped preschoolers to tag along with the designated child despite the fact that he exhibited a complex repertoire of bizarre, self-directed, and well devised pattern of avoidance behaviors. The analysis of the program revealed that by having the nonhandicapped children remain physically close, to constantly initiate interactions, and to respond to any positive overtures on the part of the designated child, we were able to produce a substantial change in a behavior pattern of that child that had previously resisted all other efforts. In addition, these changes set the occasion for the child's introduction into the natural reinforcing environment provided by the preschool community (Baer and Wolf, 1970).

Although this procedure can be used only on a limited basis, since it requires the extensive involvement of nonhandicapped peers and certainly varies with their patience, understanding, and willingness to participate, it suggests the availability of a treatment approach that, even in modified form, may have extraordinary potential. In practice, this technique is likely to be most useful in conjunction with other direct and vicarious procedures, many of which may also involve more advanced peers. However this is accomplished, a systematic structuring of many of the peer-peer interactions appears essential to ensure a successful outcome.

Language Usage

The results of the social play study summarized earlier (see Figure 1, top panel) revealed increases in the frequency of positive speech addressed by handicapped to nonhandicapped children which correlated with increases in advanced social play. This finding suggests that perhaps other aspects of the handicapped child's language can be similarly altered through interactions with more advanced peers. In general, integrated settings provide a much more diverse and complex linguistic environment for the handicapped child than is normally available in nonintegrated settings. It is this characteristic, unique to integrated settings, that suggests the possibility for formulating new strategies to promote the language development of handicapped children.

Peer Modeling of Advanced Speech The heterogeneous grouping of children in lesson and nonlesson activities affords numerous opportunities for handicapped children to listen to the speech of more advanced peers as well as to observe any consequences related to that speech. Given the availability of these language models, one question that can be asked is whether and under what conditions the modeling of more advanced speech can affect the language usage of handicapped children.

Although there are many controversial issues regarding the roles of modeling and reinforcement by adults as techniques for facilitating language development (Mahoney and Seely, 1976; McNeil, 1970), evidence does indicate that modeling of appropriate speech, in conjunction with feedback highlighting that the more advanced speech is the desirable form, can be an effective technique. In fact, even though investigations focusing exclusively on the role of peer models as a means of facilitating language are only at the early stages of development, some recent research has indicated that, by systematically reinforcing a more advanced peer for using a particular class of a well developed syntactic construction, the frequency of usage of that form by handicapped children who observed the interaction will increase (Guralnick, 1976a). It is important to note that the effectiveness of this procedure, perhaps best described as vicarious expansion, may be limited to circumstances in which comprehension of the linguistic concepts is already part of the handicapped child's repertoire (Whitehurst, Ironsmith, and Goldfein, 1974; Whitehurst and Novak, 1973). Of course, children's observational skills and current levels of expressive language development are critical variables moderating this effect, but teachers who properly and judiciously employ this procedure will have available a very efficient instructional strategy.

Kazdin (1973) has indicated that vicarious learning in situations such as this can occur as a direct result of the fact that the observer simply imitates the model who was reinforced or that reinforcement contains cue properties that indicate to the observer which behaviors will be reinforced. These explanations are, of course, not mutually exclusive, and it is likely that both processes, in conjunction with other variables known to influence modeling (Akamatsu and Thelen, 1974), operate in governing the effects of the observations of advanced language by handicapped children.

Whatever processes may be operative, it is important to underscore the potential significance of language models in integrated settings. As Whitehurst, Ironsmith, and Goldfein (1974) point out:

> Language development certainly involves processes other than modeling and selective imitation and these processes themselves have prerequisites and corequisites such as comprehension and reinforcement. Nevertheless, a full account of language development must have at its core a consideration of the frequency with which models use language that displays particular characteristics, the contexts in which that language is modeled, and the situations in which the observing child is encouraged to respond (p. 301).

Clearly, integrated preschool settings are likely to provide greater opportunities for handicapped children to benefit from language models.

Adaptive Communication

The work outlined in the preceding sections has clearly revealed that, through the proper arrangement of events and activities, environments can be organized to increase the frequency and quality of interactions among children at different developmental levels, thereby setting the occasion for a variety of additional learning experiences. For the most part, the interactions discussed thus far have been directed or arranged by adults through specific instructions, training, or systematic reinforcement. However, it would also be useful to obtain more detailed information regarding the nature of these contacts, especially language interactions, as they occur under conditions in which adults do not specify the form or precise nature of the interactions that the more advanced children are expected to provide.

It is quite common in integrated settings to find the more advanced children, especially nonhandicapped children, engaged in instructional interactions with less advanced children. In some instances the teacher has directly requested that some instructional help be given, while on other occasions these interactions develop spontaneously. In either instance, it is hoped that the quality of these interactions would be such that the handicapped child would derive certain benefits. Before discussing some experiments that bear directly on this issue, it may be useful to highlight some findings for normally developing children in order to provide a relevant framework.

Expectations from Language Interaction Research There is a considerable body of research on mother-child interactions with normally developing children that indicates that mothers carefully adjust the complexity of their interactions in accordance with their child's cognitive and linguistic abilities (Broen, 1972; Mahoney and Seely, 1976; Moerk, 1977; Snow, 1972). In addition, detailed analyses have suggested that these interactions are arranged in such a manner as to facilitate language acquisition of the developing child. For example, Mahoney (1975, pp. 142-143) notes that " . . . simplified and redundant language to young children may serve to facilitate language acquisition by providing children with a linguistic model which is within their range of semantic and syntactic complexity." Although data have been reported that mothers of handicapped children provide a linguistic environment that is less complex and generally not as adaptive or progressive as that of mothers of nonhandicapped children (Howlin et al., 1973; Marshall, Hegrenes, and Goldstein, 1973), Rondal (1976) has recently suggested that parents of Down's syndrome children do indeed make appropriate linguistic adjustments when delayed and nondelayed children are matched in terms of mean utterance length.

The mother-child interaction studies clearly recognize the significance of the nature of the linguistic input and its relationship to the development of language competencies. However, the nature of child-child interactions in this regard has not been explored to any substantial degree, although there are a few notable exceptions (e.g., Shatz and Gelman, 1973; see Bates, 1975, for a review). This is an unfortunate omission since it is likely that child-child interactions will take on even more significance given the current and projected extent of day care and preschool programs. Moreover, the nature of these interactions is especially significant for programs that integrate children at various developmental levels. Interestingly, the results of the study by Shatz and Gelman (1973), which compared the verbal interactions of four-year-olds when addressing adults, other four-year-olds, and two-year-olds, revealed that the four-year-olds do tend to adjust their speech as a function of the listener and that these adjustments parallel the adjustments mothers make when addressing children at different ages (Broen, 1972; Snow, 1972). For example, they noted that, "When talking to two-year-olds as opposed to peers or adults, four-year-olds produced shorter utterances, they were less inclined to use coordinate constructions, subordinate conjunctions, and certain forms of predicate complements; and they were more inclined to use words which attracted or maintained attention" (Shatz and Gelman, 1973, p. 30).

Verbal Interactions Among Handicapped and Nonhandicapped Children Accordingly, focusing on the language that occurs during instructional interactions, it is important to ask if nonhandicapped children do in fact adjust their communications as a function of the listener's developmental level. Some adjustments certainly appear necessary in order to achieve effective communication and, given that these modifications occur, it is important to ascertain whether these adjusted forms of linguistic input are likely to benefit the handicapped child.

In an effort to answer some of these basic questions, Guralnick and Paul-Brown (1977) recently analyzed the speech of nonhandicapped children in an instructional setting as they addressed children at different developmental levels. Specifically, for experimental purposes, children were classified as evidencing either mild, moderate, severe, or no handicaps whatsoever. Classification was based jointly on the American Association on Mental Deficiency's classification scheme (Grossman, 1973) and utterance length. For reference, children in the moderate group expressed a maximum of three words per utterance with children comprising the severe group expressing a maximum of one word per utterance. For the mild group, utterance length generally ranged from four to seven words, most often characterized by complete grammatical phrases, although a number of speech problems were evident.[1]

---

[1] The mean IQ's (and chronological ages (CA)) for the mild, moderate, and severe groups were 62.5 (5-6), 51.75 (5-2), and less than 30 (5-5), respectively. For the nonhandicapped children, we selected the most verbal children and recorded their speech (mean IQ = 105; CA = 4-3) to the handicapped groups as well as to a group of nonhandicapped children (mean IQ = 90.25; CA = 4-3).

The speech of a group of designated nonhandicapped children only was recorded in a setting in which the "speaker" was asked to provide instruction on certain drawing tasks to children in each of the four "listener" groups on an individual basis. This speech was then analyzed in terms of forty-one linguistic parameters. The results clearly revealed that the nonhandicapped children did make communication adjustments. In general, their speech was more complex and more diverse, with a greater overall output (words and utterances) when speaking to the more advanced children. Results for two key variables are illustrated in Figure 2 and represent the pattern of results common to the other language variables that showed significant changes. For the instructional setting, the figure notes the effect of the developmental level of the listener for mean length of utterance (MLU) and total complex sentences. These and related data are based on the group means for each of the four developmental levels.

Interestingly, the same pattern of results occurred when the nonhandicapped children's speech was recorded in a separate experiment during free play. Figure 3 illustrates this similarity for the MLU and total complex sentence measures. It is important to note that no instructions whatsoever were provided during free play, yet similar communicative adjustments

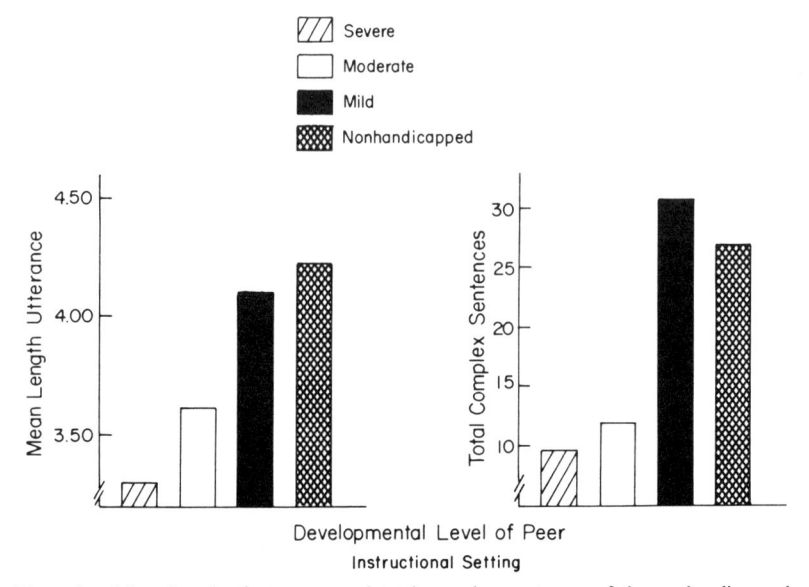

Figure 2. Mean length of utterance and total complex sentences of the nonhandicapped children as a function of the developmental level of peers in the instructional setting. (Based on data (means) from Guralnick and Paul-Brown, 1977.)

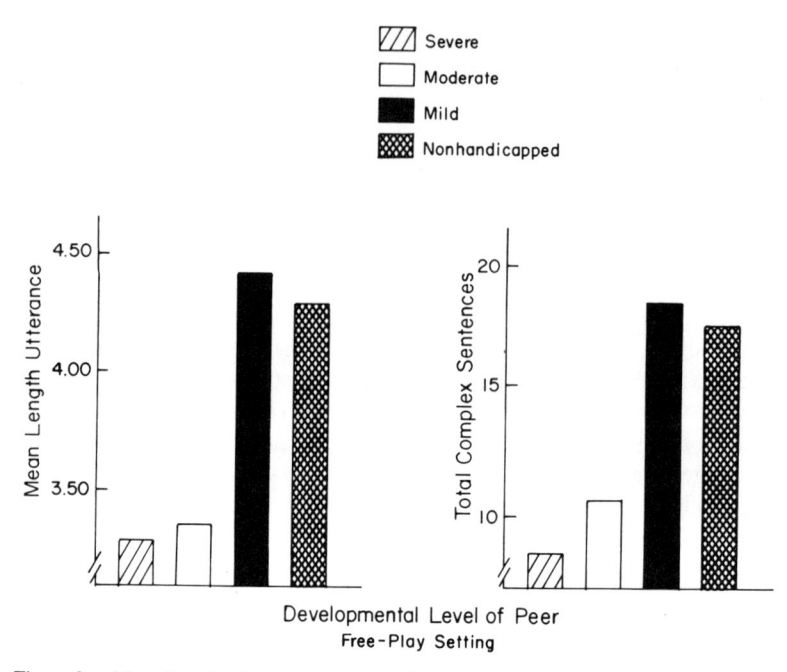

Figure 3. Mean length of utterance and total complex sentences of the nonhandicapped children as a function of the developmental level of peers in the free-play setting. (Based on data (means) from Guralnick and Paul-Brown, 1977.)

were obtained. Both figures also reveal the consistent finding that the nonhandicapped children tended to respond similarly to children with severe and moderate delays on the one hand, and to children with mild and no delays on the other. Although some differences occurred within these major classifications, most of the results indicate that differences occurred between these two groups.

Value of Communication Adjustments by Peers In many respects, the overall results of this study reveal a pattern similar to that obtained in the parent-child studies noted earlier. Differences in child-directed speech appear to reflect adjustments on the part of the nonhandicapped children in a manner consistent with the notion that they were responding to the cognitive and linguistic levels of the listener. Extrapolating from the parent-child interaction data, it may well be that these adjustments provide a positive impact on the language learning of less advanced preschool children. As discussed by Guralnick and Paul-Brown (1977), a closer inspection of our data provided additional support for this hypothesis.

First, it was noted that, despite average MLU differences across groups, utterance lengths were widely distributed even within the different developmental levels. This ensured that even the less advanced peers were exposed to more complex speech but to a degree commensurate with their developmental level. Similarly, other measures reflected the fact that the complexity and diversity of speech, as well as the use of numerous grammatical categories, remained in proportion to the child's developmental level.

Functional Interactions Taken together, it appears that the linguistic environment of children at varying developmental levels as provided by nonhandicapped peers consists of progressive input that is sufficiently complex to stimulate language development but remains within the broad boundaries of the listener's developmental level. It remains to be determined, however, how "finely tuned" these adjustments are to the developmental levels of the children, especially to children with relatively mild handicaps. In addition, a much more detailed analysis of the dialogue among children at different developmental levels is essential to help clarify some of our findings in which the relationships between the outcomes for a number of our linguistic parameters and their impact on speech development were unclear or inconsistent (and perhaps even counterproductive), although, as noted, the overall pattern did suggest a positive effect. Moreover, an assessment of communication patterns going beyond semantic and syntactic categories would be valuable. Specifically, this would take the form of a sequential analysis of the dialogue to functionally assess the more immediate and dynamic adjustments of the children (see Moerk, 1976). As Mahoney and Seely (1976) suggest, this should include an analysis of response variables, such as imitation, interpretation, expansion, correction, responses to questions, and reinforcement, as well as stimulus variables comprised of behavior and information requests, and information statements. Although this task is certainly complex and demanding, such an analysis should provide additional valuable information on the potential usefulness of child-child interactions for the language-learning child.

THE INTEGRATED PRESCHOOL AS AN EDUCATIONAL AND THERAPEUTIC ENVIRONMENT

The contention offered here is that a significant independent, positive contribution to the development of handicapped preschool children can be achieved through appropriate involvement in integrated programs. Conversely, we may state that the absence of nonhandicapped children may well limit the developmental opportunities for those who are handicapped.

It must be admitted, however, that the boundary conditions related to this proposition remain to be established, and a wide variety of factors, including the availability and distribution of resources, the type of intervention model employed (Anastasiow and Mansergh, 1975), and the developmental levels and related social-personal characteristics of the children are likely to interact with and limit the outcomes and the nature of child-child interactions in many integrated programs. Nevertheless, as summarized below, the preponderance of a variety of supportive developmental concepts across a number of dimensions, in addition to the experimental evidence regarding the potential effectiveness of nonhandicapped peers as resources described in the preceding sections, strongly argues for the tenability of this notion.

Alternative Instructional Strategies

One of the most significant aspects of the involvement of nonhandicapped children is that it makes available to program planners and teachers an entire array of instructional strategies that are unique to integrated settings. As we have seen, these strategies consist, in part, of directly utilizing nonhandicapped peers as educational and therapeutic resources (Guralnick, 1976a, b). The form this intervention has taken is to provide direct training and instruction to nonhandicapped peers to model, prompt, or provide social consequences on a systematic basis. This process has been effective with regard to the development of social play behavior, the reduction of social withdrawal, and the reduction of self-directed behaviors. Similarly, efforts in the language area have revealed that modeling of advanced speech can serve to increase usage of specific speech forms by less advanced children.

At a less formalized level, it appears that teachers can feel confident that when nonhandicapped peers are asked to help teach less advanced children, their language interactions are adjusted to the level of the listener and that these adjustments appear to have developmental significance for the language-learning child. Moreover, similar communication adjustments occur when children at different developmental levels naturally come into contact during social play (Guralnick and Paul-Brown, 1977). Frequently, these play contacts turn out to be instructional in nature such as when children at varying developmental levels engage in joint ventures in the block corner or adopt different roles in fantasy-type play. Of course, we do not know at this time whether the nonverbal behavior of the nonhandicapped children in these situations is adaptive as well, but additional work in this area, perhaps analogous to the maternal-child teaching style interaction studies, should be useful (see Filler, 1976; also see Mahoney and Seely, 1976, on "communicative matching").

Integrated programs also give teachers the option of enlisting the aid of more advanced children in numerous other respects as well. For example, these children may assist in arranging probes to systematically test the extent to which various cognitive and language skills of the handicapped child generalize to different contexts. Similarly, teachers in integrated settings can more effectively utilize the procedures involving group contingencies (Hayes, 1976; Walker and Hops, 1973).

Generalization of Social Interactions One might effectively argue that in certain circumstances, especially in the social play domain, the direct use of peers as agents of change is the strategy of choice. It is assumed that by establishing behaviors more naturally in the social context, with opportunities available for the handicapped child to experience and cope with contingencies and relationships that normally occur in this environment, conditions essential for the maintenance of adaptive and advanced behavior will exist. The importance of this state of affairs is evident since, after all, the true measure of a program's success is reflected in the extent to which the intervention produces long-lasting and generalized effects.

Unquestionably, in the area of promoting social interactions, contingent adult attention and related adult-directed techniques can and have been effective. For example, contingent teacher attention can bring children into situations in which they are more likely to encounter positive social interactions (Buell et al., 1968) as well as provide consequences that reduce collateral behavior that has tended to interfere with prosocial interactions (Twardosz and Sajwaj, 1972). Moreover, children with severely limited behavioral repertoires or serious behavior disorders will probably require the direct assistance of adults. Nevertheless, despite the recognition that there are circumstances where adults play critical roles, evidence is accumulating which suggests that their effectiveness as agents of change in the context of play is limited by a number of factors. For example, there are many situations in which the child's behavior following an adult-controlled intervention program remains dependent upon the presence of the adult (Redd, 1970). In fact, O'Connor (1972) points out that contingent teacher attention designed to encourage interactions of socially withdrawn children can have the opposite effect by actually distracting the child from ongoing peer interactions. Moreover, Shores, Hester, and Strain (1976) noted that the presence of adults during play tended to reduce the extent of child-child interactions. They also observed that circumstances in which teachers prompted and structured play activities and then removed themselves from the situation produced the highest proportion of child-child interactions. Accordingly, since programmed generalization to more natural consequences must occur in instances such as these in any event, it is probably most expedient to utilize peers directly at the outset. The ideal strategy, it would seem for many circumstances, would include the joint efforts of adults and peers (see Baer and Wolf, 1970).

Developmental Opportunities in Integrated Settings

Beyond the direct planned use of more advanced peers functioning in a variety of roles to assist less advanced children, there are a host of factors which suggest that, by their very nature, integrated settings can indeed serve as educational and therapeutic environments. The following description of the potential developmental opportunities that exist in integrated settings should be tempered by the comment that we should not permit ourselves to envision integrated settings as paragons of highly nurturant, wholly integrated, and totally supportive social groups. As mentioned at various points in this chapter, even under ideal circumstances, this is not a realistic expectation. Nevertheless, focusing on these potential benefits, it can be noted that the diversity of actions, the variations in behaviors, and the overall richness of the environment tend to be more characteristic of integrated programs than those consisting of homogeneous groups of handicapped children. Consequently, this state of affairs provides a wealth of opportunities for less advanced peers to interact with and potentially benefit from everyday events.

For example, in the area of play, Bricker and Bricker (1971) have indicated that nondelayed children may well provide better models in this regard than teachers, and Devoney, Guralnick, and Rubin (1974) have demonstrated how observed variations of advanced play can be readily incorporated into the repertoires of handicapped children. In fact, it may well be that delayed imitation effects such as these, many of which tend to develop during parallel play, may prove to be the most significant aspect of the benefits children with relatively extensive behavioral deficits receive as a result of their experiences in integrated settings.

Along similar lines, a recent study by Rubenstein and Howes (1976) with toddlers suggested that the presence of peers enhances various aspects of play, including its frequency, maturity, and the creative use of objects. Since integrated settings tend to be more active and interactive, there appears to be a greater likelihood that handicapped children will be productively involved. Moreover, Eckerman, Whatley, and Kutz (1975) have suggested that novelty factors may play a role in establishing social play with peers, and that these peer-peer interactions may become dominant over adult-child interactions by two years of age. The saliency of peers as contrasted to adults does certainly seem to be a relevant factor. The novelty of children's displays, their often unusual uses of materials, and the nature of their relationships seem likely candidates for eliciting and maintaining the attention of peers.

Another factor relevant here is the sheer frequency of child-child interactions that occurs within a classroom on a daily basis, many of which are of potential benefit to less advanced children. Even under ideal circumstances, teachers are limited in the extent to which they can interact individually with each child. Fortunately, integrated settings provide numerous opportunities for the less advanced child to interact with and to experience adaptive consequences from their peers. These consequences, of course, may need to be monitored by teachers in some cases to ensure their appropriateness; but in most instances it appears that the children's behavior will reflect the types of consequences that are sanctioned, modeled, and supported by teachers.

Research has also suggested that prosocial behaviors in preschool children tend to be reciprocated (Charlesworth and Hartup, 1967; Hartup, 1970). As a result, nonhandicapped children can benefit their handicapped peers not only by selectively reinforcing appropriate behaviors during the acquisition of those prosocial behaviors, but by maintaining those behaviors through the reciprocal pattern of interactions that occurs naturally within the social context. Baer and Wolf (1970) have referred to the "trapping" phenomenon whereby children's appropriate social behaviors are supported and maintained by the natural consequences existing in the preschool environment. The end product here is a more generalized set of appropriate social behaviors.

As discussed earlier, learning is further expedited through vicarious processes (Bandura, 1969). For example, through observation, peers can transmit information as to which behaviors are likely to be reinforced (Kazdin, 1973; Keller and Carlson, 1974) as well as new skills and information (Bandura, 1969; O'Connor, 1969). Given the extensive opportunities available for observational learning in integrated preschool settings, it is important to point out that available evidence suggests that the more competent the model the more likely it is that that model's behavior will be imitated (Akamatsu and Thelen, 1974; Strichart, 1974). As has been noted, the benefits that can occur through observation of more competent models during play and verbal interactions, as well as the attempts to replicate those behaviors, include the development of important skills and abilities. Finally, it is suggested that the extensive diversity and variations found in integrated settings tend to produce environments that are more challenging to all concerned. This has the effect of increasing the likelihood that events discrepant from the handicapped child's typical interactions will be experienced. Many theoretical positions suggest that experiencing and resolving such discrepancies are vital for cognitive development (e.g., Hunt, 1961).

Effects on Nonhandicapped Children

A salient characteristic of the design of integrated programs is its emphasis on meeting individual needs of children, including those who are nonhandicapped. To the extent that this is accomplished, we can expect that nonhandicapped children will be stimulated and supported in their own development. Our own data as well as those of others (Bricker and Bricker, 1971; Ispa, 1976) suggest that, as measured by standardized tests and later school success, nonhandicapped children benefit from integrated programs to at least the same degree (and usually better) as would be expected if they had attended nonintegrated preschools. In a recent review of the role of peers as change agents for classmates' social behavior, Strain, Cooke, and Apolloni (1976) noted the absence of any reports of negative effects as a result of peers' participation as active agents in intervention programs. Similarly, preliminary data from a current study at the Experimental Preschool on the quality of play revealed no differences whatsoever in the constructiveness or appropriateness of the play of nonhandicapped children when playing in a homogeneously grouped setting as compared to a setting composed of children with widely varying developmental levels. However, there did appear to be some reduction in the frequency of associative play in the heterogeneous setting, which seems to be diminishing over time as interaction patterns become more firmly established.

These positive findings are consistent with results reported by cross-age tutoring programs in which benefits to those providing the tutoring, as well as the tutored, appear to be substantial (Gartner, Kohler, and Reissman, 1971). Similarly, Zajonc (1976) has advanced the notion that the tutoring of younger siblings by older children can perhaps explain some of the differences in intelligence found for certain family configurations. He notes, "One who has to explain something will see from the other's reactions whether the explanation was well understood, and be prompted to improve the explanation, with the consequence that his or her own understanding of the matter is improved" (Zajonc, 1976, p. 231). This may have relevance to instructional interactions among children at different developmental levels.

Although the findings to date are reassuring, extensive explorations of the social and attitudinal effects of integrated experiences on nonhandicapped children have not yet been attempted. Before we move too rapidly in our programming efforts, these vital issues should be thoroughly addressed.

CONCLUSIONS

Taken together, the evidence relating to integrated preschool programs suggests that this environment does indeed contain unique characteristics that may be utilized to promote the development of handicapped children. In addition, this chapter further underscores the critical need for designing and organizing these programs so as to accommodate as many streams as are necessary to respond to each child's needs. Although the feasibility for designing programs within this framework appears to be well established, we must be keenly aware that, to be effective, integrated programs must attend to the many concepts, methods, and techniques that relate directly to the integration process. Specifically, they must include an environmental design that seeks to arrange encounters between children at varying developmental levels that are likely to be productive, that considers the reward value of peers and the compatibility of the children involved, that carefully reinforces and highlights positive behaviors, that increases the likelihood of less advanced peers observing and effectively interacting with more advanced peers, and that carefully monitors the observational and cognitive skills of the handicapped children to ensure that interactions are challenging but not overwhelming. Clearly, the implementation of these strategies is no easy task.

Finally, it is suggested that the issues that remain to be resolved should be conceptualized as attempts to find optimal environments that meet each child's needs. Fortunately, available evidence indicates that not only are integrated settings feasible and consistent with that goal but, by their very nature, provide a unique and effective educational and therapeutic environment.

ACKNOWLEDGMENTS

A willingness to explore new ideas and models has characterized the staff members with whom I have had the privilege of working over the past few years. The results of this project are clearly a reflection of their creativity, energy, sensitivity, and technical skills. A special debt of gratitude is also owed the children, especially those who diplomatically and graciously participated in our attempts to understand the values and limits of peer-peer interactions in integrated settings. Finally, Vivian Ottenberg is thanked once again for transforming my illegible scratchings into a reasonably coherent form.

REFERENCES CITED

Akamatsu, T., and Thelen, M. 1974. A review of the literature on observer characteristics and imitation. Developmental Psychology, 10, 38–47.

Allen, K. E., Benning, P. M., and Drummond, W. T. 1972. Integration of normal and handicapped children in a behavior modification preschool: A case study. In G. Semb (Ed.), Behavior Analysis and Education. Lawrence, Kan.: University of Kansas Support and Development Center.

Allen, K. E., Hart, B. M., Buell, J. S., Harris, F. R., and Wolf, M. M. 1964. Effects of social reinforcement on isolate behavior of a nursery school child. Child Development, 35, 511-518.

Anastasiow, N. J., and Mansergh, G. P. 1975. Teaching skills in early childhood programs. Exceptional Children, 41, 309-317.

Baer, D. M., and Wolf, M. M. 1970. The entry into natural communities of reinforcement. In R. Ulrich, T. Stachnik, and J. Mabry (Eds.), Control of Human Behavior (Vol. 2). Glenview, Ill.: Scott, Foresman.

Bandura, A. 1969. Principles of Behavior Modification. New York: Holt, Rinehart and Winston.

Bandura, A. 1971. Analyses of modeling processes. In A. Bandura (Ed.), Psychological Modeling. Chicago: Aldine-Atherton.

Barnes, K. E. 1971. Preschool play norms: A replication. Developmental Psychology, 5, 99-103.

Bates, E. 1975. Peer relations and the acquisition of language. In M. Lewis and L. A. Rosenblum (Eds.), Friendship and Peer Relations. New York: John Wiley & Sons.

Birch, J. 1974. Mainstreaming: Educable Mentally Retarded Children in Regular Classes. Reston, Va.: Council for Exceptional Children.

Blatt, B. 1970. Exodus from Pandemonium. Boston: Allyn & Bacon.

Bloom, L. 1975. Language development. In F. D. Horowitz (Ed.), Review of Child Development Research (Vol. 4). Chicago: University of Chicago Press.

Bricker, D., and Bricker, W. 1971. Toddler research and intervention project report: Year I. IMRID Behavioral Science Monograph 20, Institute on Mental Retardation and Intellectual Development. Nashville, Tenn.: George Peabody College.

Bricker, D., and Bricker, W. 1972. Toddler research and intervention project report: Year II. IMRID Behavioral Science Monograph 21, Institute on Mental Retardation and Intellectual Development. Nashville, Tenn.: George Peabody College.

Broen, P. A. 1972. The verbal environment of the language-learning child. American Speech and Hearing Association Monograph, 17.

Bronfenbrenner, U. 1975. Is early intervention effective? In B. Z. Friedlander, G. M. Sterritt, and G. E. Kirk (Eds.), Exceptional Infant (Vol. 3). New York: Brunner/Mazel.

Brown, R. 1973. A First Language: The Early Stages. Cambridge, Mass.: Harvard University Press.

Bruner, J. 1972. Nature and uses of immaturity. American Psychologist, 27, 687-708.

Budoff, M., and Gottlieb, J. 1976. Special-class EMR children mainstreamed: A study of an aptitude (learning potential) × treatment interaction. American Journal of Mental Deficiency, 81, 1-11.

Buell, J., Stoddard, P., Harris, F. R., and Baer, D. M. 1968. Collateral social development accompanying reinforcement of outdoor play in a preschool child. Journal of Applied Behavior Analysis, 1, 167-174.

Caldwell, B. M. 1974. The importance of beginning early. In J. B. Jordan and R. F. Dailey (Eds.), Not All Little Wagons are Red. Reston, Va.: Council for Exceptional Children.

Charlesworth, R., and Hartup, W. W. 1967. Positive social reinforcement in the nursery school peer group. Child Development, 38, 993-1002.

Devoney, C., Guralnick, M. J., and Rubin, H. 1974. Integrating handicapped and non-handicapped preschool children: Effects on social play. Childhood Education, 50, 360-364.

Dunn, L. M. 1968. Special education for the mildly retarded—Is much of it justifiable? Exceptional Children, 35, 5-22.

Eckerman, C. O., Whatley, J. L., and Kutz, S. L. 1975. Growth of social play with peers during the second year of life. Developmental Psychology, 11, 42-49.

Evers-Pasquale, W., and Sherman, M. 1975. The reward value of peers: A variable influencing the efficacy of filmed modeling in modifying social isolation in preschoolers. Journal of Abnormal Child Psychology, 3, 175-189.

Feitelson, D., Weintraub, S., and Michaeli, O. 1972. Social interactions in heterogeneous preschools. Child Development, 43, 1249-1259.

Filler, J. W. 1976. Modifying maternal teaching style: Effects of task arrangement on the match-to-sample performance of retarded preschool-age children. American Journal of Mental Deficiency, 80, 602-612.

Filler, J. W., Jr., Robinson, C. C., Smith, R. A., Vincent-Smith, L. J., Bricker, D., and Bricker, W. 1975. Mental retardation. In N. Hobbs (Ed.), Issues in the Classification of Children (Vol. 1). San Francisco: Jossey-Bass.

Freud, A., and Dann, S. 1951. An experiment in group upbringing. Psychoanalytic Study of the Child, 6, 127-168.

Freyberg, J. T. 1973. Increasing the imaginative play of urban disadvantaged kindergarten children through systematic training. In J. L. Singer (Ed.), The Child's World of Make-Believe. New York: Academic Press.

Gartner, A., Kohler, M., and Reissman, F. 1971. Children Teach Children. New York: Harper & Row.

Goodman, H., Gottlieb, J., and Harrison, R. H. 1972. Social acceptance of EMRs integrated into a nongraded elementary school. American Journal of Mental Deficiency, 76, 412-417.

Gottlieb, J., and Budoff, M. 1973. Social acceptability of retarded children in nongraded schools differing in architecture. American Journal of Mental Deficiency, 78, 15-19.

Gottlieb, J., and Davis, J. E. 1973. Social acceptance of EMR children during overt behavioral interactions. American Journal of Mental Deficiency, 78, 141-143.

Grossman, H. J. 1973. Manual on Terminology and Classification in Mental Retardation. Washington, D.C.: American Association on Mental Deficiency.

Gump, P. V. 1975. Ecological psychology and children. In E. M. Hetherington (Ed.), Review of Child Development Research (Vol. 5). Chicago: University of Chicago Press.

Guralnick, M. J. 1975. Early classroom-based intervention and the role of organizational structure. Exceptional Children, 42, 25-31.

Guralnick, M. J. 1976a. The value of integrating handicapped and nonhandicapped preschool children. American Journal of Orthopsychiatry, 46, 236-245.

Guralnick, M. J. 1976b. Early childhood intervention: The use of nonhandicapped peers as educational and therapeutic resources. Paper presented at the International Congress of the International Association for the Scientific Study of Mental Deficiency, Washington, D.C.

Guralnick, M. J. 1977. A planning process for developmental programming for handicapped preschool children: Language development as a model. Paper presented at the annual meeting of the Council for Exceptional Children, Atlanta.

Guralnick, M. J., and Paul-Brown, D. 1977. The nature of verbal interactions among handicapped and nonhandicapped preschool children. Child Development, 48, 254-260.

Hart, B. M., Reynolds, N. J., Baer, D. M., Brawley, E. R., and Harris, F. R. 1968. Effects of contingent and non-contingent social reinforcement on the cooperative play of a preschool child. Journal of Applied Behavior Analysis, 1, 73-76.

Hartup, W. W. 1970. Peer interaction and social organization. In P. H. Mussen (Ed.), Carmichael's Manual of Child Psychology (Vol. II). New York: John Wiley & Sons.

Hayes, L. A. 1976. The use of group contingencies for behavioral control: A review. Psychological Bulletin, 83, 628-648.

Hobbs, N. 1975. The Futures of Children. San Francisco: Jossey-Bass.

Howlin, P., Cantwell, D., Marchant, R., Berger, M., and Rutter, M. 1973. Analyzing mothers' speech to young autistic children: A methodological study. Journal of Abnormal Child Psychology, 1, 317-339.

Hunt, J. McV. 1961. Intelligence and Experience. New York: Ronald Press.

Hunt, J. McV. 1975. Reflections on a decade of early education. Journal of Abnormal Child Psychology, 3, 275-330.

Iano, R. P., Ayers, D., Heller, H. B., McGettigan, J. F., and Walker, V. S. 1974. Sociometric status of retarded children in an integrative program. Exceptional Children, 40, 267-271.

Ispa, J. 1976. A cognitively oriented approach to preschool mainstreaming. Paper presented at the annual meeting of the National Association for the Education of Young Children, Anaheim.

Jones, M. C. 1924. The elimination of children's fears. Journal of Experimental Psychology, 7, 383-390.

Kanner, L. 1964. A History of the Care and Study of the Mentally Retarded. Springfield, Ill.: Charles C Thomas.

Karnes, M. B. 1973. Evaluation and implications of research with young handicapped and low-income children. In J. C. Stanley (Ed.), Compensatory Education for Children Ages Two to Eight: Recent Studies of Educational Intervention. Baltimore: Johns Hopkins Press.

Kaufman, M. E., and Alberto, P. A. 1976. Research on efficacy of special education for the mentally retarded. In N. R. Ellis (Ed.), International Review of Research in Mental Retardation (Vol. 8). New York: Academic Press.

Kazdin, A. E. 1973. The effect of vicarious reinforcement on attentive behavior in the classroom. Journal of Applied Behavior Analysis, 6, 71-78.

Keller, M. F., and Carlson, P. M. 1974. The use of symbolic modeling to promote social skills in preschool children with low levels of social responsiveness. Child Development, 45, 912-919.

Keogh, W. J., Miller, R. M., and LeBlanc, J. M. 1973. The effects of antecedent stimuli upon a preschool child's peer interaction. Paper presented at the biennial meeting of the Society for Research in Child Development, Philadelphia.

Koegel, R. L., and Rincover, A. 1974. Treatment of psychotic children in a classroom environment: I. Learning in a large group. Journal of Applied Behavior Analysis, 7, 45-59.

Kozloff, M. 1974. Educating Children with Learning and Behavior Problems. New York: John Wiley & Sons.

MacDonald, J. D., and Blott, J. P. 1974. Environmental language intervention: The rationale for a diagnostic and training strategy through rules, context, and generalization. Journal of Speech and Hearing Disorders, 39, 244-256.

MacMillan, D. L. 1973. Issues and trends in special education. Mental Retardation, 11, 3-8.

MacMillan, D. L., Jones, R. L., and Meyers, C. E. 1976. Mainstreaming the mildly retarded: Some questions, cautions, and guidelines. Mental Retardation, 14, 3-10.

Mahoney, G. 1975. An ethological approach to delayed language acquisition. American Journal of Mental Deficiency, 80, 139-148.

Mahoney, G. J., and Seely, P. B. 1976. The role of the social agent in language acquisition: Implications for language intervention. In N. R. Ellis (Ed.), International Review of Research in Mental Retardation (Vol. 8). New York: Academic Press.

Marshall, N. R., Hegrenes, J. R., and Goldstein, S. 1973. Verbal interactions: Mothers and their retarded children vs. mothers and their non-retarded children. American Journal of Mental Deficiency, 77, 415-419.

Martin, E. W. 1974. Some thoughts on mainstreaming. Exceptional Children, 41, 150-153.

McNeil, D. 1970. The development of language. In P. H. Mussen (Ed.), Carmichael's Manual of Child Psychology (Vol. 1). New York: John Wiley & Sons.

Mercer, J. 1973. Labeling the Mentally Retarded. Berkeley: University of California Press.

Miller, J. F., and Yoder, D. E. 1974. An ontogenetic language teaching strategy for retarded children. In R. L. Schiefelbusch and L. L. Lloyd (Eds.), Language Perspectives—Acquisition, Retardation, and Intervention. Baltimore: University Park Press.

Moerk, E. L. 1976. Processes of language teaching and training in the interactions of mother-child dyads. Child Development, 47, 1064-1078.

Moerk, E. L. 1977. Pragmatic and Semantic Aspects of Early Language Development. Baltimore: University Park Press.

Mueller, E., and Lucas, T. 1975. A developmental analysis of peer interaction among toddlers. In M. Lewis and L. A. Rosenblum (Eds.), Friendship and Peer Relations. New York: John Wiley & Sons.

Nordquist, V. M., and Bradley, B. 1973. Speech acquisition in a nonverbal isolate child. Journal of Experimental Child Psychology, 15, 149-160.

O'Connor, R. D. 1969. Modification of social withdrawal through symbolic modeling. Journal of Applied Behavior Analysis, 2, 15-22.

O'Connor, R. D. 1972. Relative efficacy of modeling, shaping, and the combined procedures for modification of social withdrawal. Journal of Abnormal Psychology, 79, 327-334.

Parten, M. B. 1932. Social participation among preschool children. Journal of Abnormal Social Psychology, 27, 243-269.

Parten, M. B. 1933. Social play among preschool children. Journal of Abnormal and Social Psychology, 28, 137–147.
Quilitch, H. R., and Risley, T. R. 1973. The effects of play materials on social play. Journal of Applied Behavior Analysis, 6, 573–578.
Ray, J. S. 1974. Ethological studies of behavior in delayed and non-delayed toddlers. Paper presented at the annual meeting of the American Association on Mental Deficiency, Toronto.
Redd, W. H., 1970. Generalization of adult's stimulus control of children's behavior. Journal of Experimental Child Psychology, 9, 286–296.
Rondal, J. A. 1976. Maternal speech to normal and Down's syndrome children matched for mean length of utterance (Research Report 98). Minneapolis: University of Minnesota, Research, Development, and Demonstration Center in Education of Handicapped Children.
Rubenstein, J., and Howes, C. 1976. The effects of peers on toddler interaction with mother and toys. Child Development, 47, 597–605.
Shatz, M., and Gelman, R. 1973. The development of communication skills: Modifications in the speech of young children as a function of listener. Monographs of the Society for Research in Child Development, 38, No. 5.
Shores, R. E., Hester, P., and Strain, P. S. 1976. The effects of amount and type of teacher-child interaction on child-child interaction during free-play. Psychology in the Schools, 13, 171–175.
Slobin, D. I. 1964. The fruits of the first season: A discussion of the role of play in childhood. Journal of Humanistic Psychology, 4, 59–79.
Snow, C. E. 1972. Mothers' speech to children learning language. Child Development, 43, 549–565.
Strain, P. S., Cooke, T. P., and Apolloni, T. 1976. The role of peers in modifying classmates' social behavior: A review. Journal of Special Education, 10, 351–356.
Strain, P. S., Shores, R. E., and Kerr, M. M. 1976. An experimental analysis of "spillover" effects on the social interaction of behaviorally handicapped preschool children. Journal of Applied Behavior Analysis, 9, 31–40.
Strain, P. S., and Wiegerink, R. 1976. The effects of sociodramatic activities on social interaction among behaviorally disordered preschool children. Journal of Special Education, 10, 71–75.
Strichart, S. 1974. Effects of competence and nurturance on imitation of nonretarded peers by retarded adolescents. American Journal of Mental Deficiency, 78, 665–673.
Suomi, S., and Harlow, H. 1972. Social rehabilitation of isolate-reared monkeys. Developmental Psychology, 6, 487–496.
Tjossem, T. D. (Ed.). 1976. Intervention Strategies for High Risk Infants and Young Children. Baltimore: University Park Press.
Twardosz, S., Cataldo, M. F., and Risley, T. R. 1974. An open environment design for infant and toddler day care. Journal of Applied Behavior Analysis, 7, 529–546.
Twardosz, S., and Sajwaj. T. 1972. Multiple effects of a procedure to increase sitting in a hyperactive, retarded boy. Journal of Applied Behavior Analysis, 5, 73–78.
Wahler, R. G. 1967. Child-child interactions in free-field settings: Some experimental analyses. Journal of Experimental Child Psychology, 5, 278–293.

Walker, H. M., and Hops, H. 1973. The use of group and individual reinforcement contingencies in the modification of social withdrawal. In L. A. Hamerlynck, L. C. Handy, and E. J. Mash (Eds.), Behavior Change: Methodology, Concepts and Practice. Champaign, Ill.: Research Press.

Weikart, D. P. 1972. Relationship of curriculum, teaching, and learning in preschool education. In J. C. Stanley (Ed.), Preschool Programs for the Disadvantaged: Five Experimental Approaches to Early Childhood Education. Baltimore: Johns Hopkins Press.

Weisler, A., and McCall, R. B. 1976. Exploration and play: Résumé and redirection. American Psychologist, 31, 492-508.

Whitehurst, G. T., Ironsmith, M., and Goldfein, M. 1974. Selective imitation of the passive construction through modeling. Journal of Experimental Child Psychology, 17, 288-302.

Whitehurst, G., and Novak, G. 1973. Modeling, imitation training, and the acquisition of sentence phrases. Journal of Experimental Child Psychology, 16, 332-345.

Wintre, M. G., and Webster, C. D. 1974. A brief report on using a traditional social behavior scale with disturbed children. Journal of Applied Behavior Analysis, 7, 345-348.

Wolfensberger, W. 1972. The Principle of Normalization in Human Services. Toronto: National Institute on Mental Retardation.

Zajonc, R. B. 1976. Family configuration and intelligence. Science, 192, 227-236.

INTEGRATED PROGRAMMING AT THE INFANT, TODDLER, AND PRESCHOOL LEVELS

Tony Apolloni, Ph.D., and
Thomas P. Cooke, Ph.D.

The 1960s represented a period in which an imposing amount of theory and empirical evidence was presented in support of the proposition that human ontogeny is profoundly influenced by the timing, degree, and contingent nature of environmental stimulation. Scholars and scientists from a variety of orientations generated evidence that educational intervention produces its maximal impact while children are young (less than five years old). It has been generally agreed that this early childhood period is the occasion when developmental processes and behavioral characteristics are undergoing rapid change and are most malleable (Bijou and Baer, 1965; Bloom, 1964; Hebb, 1966; Hunt, 1961).

Recognizing the importance of early stimulation to development, a number of investigators began experimental attempts to accelerate the development of children who seemed potentially handicapped based on apparent experiential deprivation (Bronfenbrenner, 1974; Karnes and Teska, 1975). Other researchers studied the effects of early intervention programs with mentally retarded children (Hayden and Haring, 1976; Heber and Garber, 1970; Kirk, 1958). These attempts largely substantiated beliefs in the malleability of developmental sophistication or intelligence. Additionally, as research and program development with exceptional children

---

The work reported in this chapter was supported in part by State of California Grants 49-00000-3029-7-05 and 49-00000-3029-7-03, Title VI-B, of the United States Elementary and Secondary Education Act.

began to suggest more optimism regarding the therapeutic effects on developmental anomalies, service delivery agents began to consider less exclusionary educational alternatives for handicapped children. Programs began to emerge that enrolled integrated groups of handicapped and nonhandicapped children (Bricker and Bricker, 1972, 1973). In addition to new and more hopeful attitudes toward disability, other factors that began to prompt the development of such integrated services were: (1) litigation and legislation on the social inequity of segregated services for handicapped children (Cohen and DeYoung, 1973; Warfield, 1974), (2) the disappointing results of efficacy studies of segregated services for school-age handicapped children (see Meyer, Vergason, and Whelan, 1975), (3) a growing philosophical commitment to the principle of normalization (Wolfensberger, 1972), and (4) increased financial support for such services (Wynne, Ulfelder, and Dakof, 1975). Additionally, including nonhandicapped and handicapped children in the same programs was viewed by some as offering definite programmatic advantages (Bricker and Bricker, 1972, 1973). It was presumed that developmentally more advanced children could be induced to serve as models and as reinforcing agents for handicapped classmates and that exposure to normally developing children would favorably influence teacher expectations of handicapped youngsters (Guralnick, 1976; Snyder, Apolloni, and Cooke, 1977).

We have been involved for the past two years with integrated programs for infant, toddler, and preschool-age children. This chapter reviews some of the information we have obtained during the course of this involvement. We begin by describing our classroom programs. Next we review literature on the outcomes associated with integrated programming and summarize the results of analyses that we have conducted on procedures to increase handicapped toddlers' and preschoolers' imitation of nonhandicapped classmates. Finally, we conclude the chapter with suggestions for needed research in the area of integrated programming for infants, toddlers, and preschoolers, and with a discussion of some of the practical implications of our work for educators.

INTEGRATED PROGRAMS IN SONOMA

The Sonoma County Office of Education, in collaboration with Santa Rosa Junior College and California State College, Sonoma, directs three empirically based intervention projects providing integrated educational experience to handicapped and normally developing youngsters from six months to six years of age. The functioning level of the handicapped children ranges from severely/multiply impaired (IQ < 25) to mildly delayed (IQs, 65–85).

The Sonoma projects systematically investigate intervention strategies that produce educationally desirable outcomes at the infant, toddler, and preschool levels. Guralnick (1973) has termed such programmatic organization the "research-service model." This model applies to those programs which offer services of the highest quality possible based on the results of direct observation data on child performance. These data are collected to determine the most effective educational strategies for the population served.

Organizational Characteristics

In many respects the classrooms resemble other empirically based special education preschool projects. That is, the programs organize instruction around the traditional major areas of (1) language, (2) motor, (3) perceptual-cognitive, (4) self-help, and (5) social-emotional development. Each child, handicapped or normal, is administered a comprehensive battery of criterion-referenced assessments (Popham, 1971) to determine his or her level of behavioral sophistication in the above areas of performance. Emphasis in assessment is placed upon a sensitivity to developmental sequences of skills emergence while employing operant stimulus control tactics to ensure each child's optimal performance. Following the identification of developmentally appropriate goals, each child receives daily intensive instruction in the five aforementioned curricular areas. The format of this instruction, typically characterized as behavioral, may be individual (adult and one child), small group with adult teacher, or peer "tutoring" with adult supervision. Peer tutoring dyads and triads are systematically arranged so that one child (often normally developing) is established as a behavioral model to one or two children who are less developmentally advanced. These handicapped children are initially trained with a procedure that reliably produces generalized imitative repertoires. A delayed child with an imitative repertoire paired with a model child who performs comparatively high rates of developmentally appropriate behavior has produced some of the most exciting educational results of our integrated programming. This process and its results are discussed in more detail later in this chapter.

The ratios of adults to children in these projects is particularly fortuitous. Inasmuch as the projects are associated with institutions that train both special education teachers and aides, a large cadre of manpower is available. The projects are utilized as laboratories for Santa Rosa Junior College and California State College, Sonoma, thus heightening the quality and quantity of professional resources. Typically, the projects are staffed with one-to-one or one-and-one-half-to-one ratios of children to adults. Although many of the adults have not completed professional or paraprofessional training, they are provided with daily instruction and are closely monitored. This desirable ratio of "teachers" to children makes possible the maintenance of a detailed and systematic record of each child's developmental progress. The accouterments of each "teacher" typically include behavior coding forms, a wrist counter, and a stop watch. The children are observed closely and their behavior is coded daily in each of their targeted areas. When the children have completed their day, the staff tabulates and graphs each child's performance for that period. Following this, staffings are held to review the progress of each child in relationship to the specific educational procedures implemented. There is a continuous effort to identify instructional tactics that will reliably produce developmental progress in handicapped infants, toddlers, and preschoolers. Whenever several (approximately four) days of a particular variety of intervention have occurred with no related improvement observed in child behavior, the procedure is modified and data collection continues. Thus, effective tactics are empirically validated on a continuing basis. This "research-service" model has been presented elsewhere as an approach that is compatible with quality control and accountability (Guralnick, 1973).

The ratios of normally developing children to handicapped children at any point in time vary somewhat as a function of activity and schedule fluctuations. However, in terms of program enrollment, there are typically two to four nonhandicapped children integrated with a group of six to eight handicapped youngsters. The specific way in which the normal children are paired or grouped with their handicapped peers depends upon the nature of the activity underway. The ratio of normal to handicapped children in an activity group, then, would vary from one-to-one to one-to-six. It is also noteworthy that handicapped children of varying skill levels are often used as behavioral models for their peers in the same way the normal children are used.

Parent Component

Another significant component of the integrated infant, toddler, and preschool programs in Sonoma is their heavy emphasis on parental involvement. The leadership and staffs of the programs are committed to the notion that parents should be trained and involved in their children's educational process (Cooke and Apolloni, 1975). The experience in Sonoma and elsewhere has clearly indicated that parental involvement is associated with desirable outcomes of schooling (Johnson and Katz, 1973). The parents of the children in the Sonoma programs are initially provided with basic functional training in behavior principles and teaching procedures as well as in developmental sequencing. They are then slowly but systematically shown how to implement what they have learned with their own children. In many cases, they work as a teacher in the program with their child as well as with other children. Perhaps most important, the parents continue the educational interventions that have begun at school in their own homes and gauge their efforts via continuous direct observation data on their children's progress. It is strongly felt that this "transition programming" from school to home plays a large part in the success of the projects. While parents often demonstrate a predictable hesitancy to perform such functions, their first successes in controlling their child's behavior in a therapeutic fashion nearly always secure their firm commitment. Parents meet with the project directors at least weekly to review their children's progress as it is reflected in the data they have collected.

Summary of the Sonoma Projects

In summary, the Sonoma integrated infant, toddler, and preschool projects operate within a developmental view of child behavior paired with an applied behavior analytic instructional paradigm. Many of the procedures analyzed have focused on methods of engineering peer integration between children of varying developmental sophistication (generally a normal child serving as a peer model to a handicapped child). The goals of the projects revolve around generating technologically replicable and educationally effective instructional strategies, thereby providing top quality service delivery to the children and families enrolled. The projects are also characterized by high ratios of "teachers" to children. The most significant of these teachers, we believe, are the parents of the children served. Through parent training and participation as educational agents, both at school and at home, the probability of successful intervention is markedly increased.

PROGRAMMING FOR SOCIAL INTEGRATION

Reviews of the child development literature on the nature and extent of early child-peer interaction (Apolloni and Cooke, 1975; Hartup, 1970) and recent direct observational studies (Apolloni and Tremblay, in press; Eckerman, Whatley, and Kutz, 1975) indicate that normally developing children under two years of age imitate and socially interact with familiar peers. Observers of integrated toddler and preschool settings, however, have consistently noted minimal levels of free-field peer imitation and interaction between handicapped and nonhandicapped classmates, especially if differences in development or behavior are substantial (Allen, Benning, and Drummond, 1972; Devoney, Guralnick, and Rubin, 1974;

Guralnick, 1976; Porter et al., in press; Ray, 1974). Apparently, some form of therapeutic intervention is often needed for handicapped and nonhandicapped preschoolers to socially benefit from attending school together. Investigations are needed regarding ways to: (1) establish nonhandicapped children as agents of social reinforcement for appropriate behavior by handicapped classmates, and (2) bring handicapped children's imitative behavior under the stimulus control of nonhandicapped peers' appropriate behavior. Our studies have focused on the latter of these research needs.

There has been little direct experimental assessment of training procedures to increase handicapped children's imitation of nonhandicapped classmates. Our review of this literature has resulted in the identification of numerous experimental arrangements wherein nonhandicapped children were observed to learn through imitating peers (Apolloni and Tremblay, in press; Bandura and Kupers, 1964; Christy, 1975; Clark, 1965; Hartup and Coates, 1967; Miller and Dollard, 1941). Moreover, school-age nonhandicapped (Csapo, 1972; Ross, 1970; Ross and Ross, 1972; Strichart, 1973) and handicapped children (Berkowitz, 1968; Cooke and Apolloni, 1976; Whalen and Henker, 1969, 1971) have served as models for teaching behaviors to handicapped children. Fewer studies, however, have been reported on educational programming to establish nonhandicapped preschoolers as behavioral models for handicapped classmates. O'Connor (1969, 1972) employed a filmed demonstration by peer models to increase the social interaction of withdrawn preschoolers, and Devoney, Guralnick, and Rubin (1974) initiated "structured activities" to increase free-play behavior, including imitation, between handicapped and nonhandicapped preschoolers. More recently, Guralnick (1976) presented evidence supporting the efficacy of two training strategies for inducing handicapped four- and five-year-olds to imitate the toy use and language behaviors of nonhandicapped age-mates.

Peer Imitation Training

We have recently completed a series of studies on the effects and side effects associated with a direct conditioning procedure for training developmentally delayed toddlers and preschoolers to imitate nonhandicapped classmates. We have termed the procedure "peer imitation training," hereafter referred to as PIT. The procedure consists of verbally and physically, if necessary, prompting a child to imitate the behavior of a classmate and then fading the prompt, with adult praise provided for imitative behavior. We have monitored the effects of PIT on the behavior of two- and three-year-old delayed children using time-sample, direct observation data collection systems. Our observations of delayed children under twenty-four months of age have indicated that they generally do not yet possess the perceptual and motor capabilities needed for peer imitation.

Thus far we have systematically evaluated the outcomes of various forms of PIT with ten separate delayed children. The major procedural variations investigated have included training focused on delayed children (unidirectional) under structured and free-play conditions and training focused on both delayed and nondelayed children (bidirectional) under structured and free-play conditions. We have also assessed the maintenance of the effects of training following PIT under nontraining conditions, both in structured settings and in naturalistic, free-play situations. Our completed studies have demonstrated the feasibility and validity of PIT at the toddler and preschool-age levels and have provided some tentative information regarding the stimulus and response generalization side effects that are associated with implementing the procedure. Before reviewing our studies, it seems pertinent to first define two important operational constructs: stimulus generalization and response generalization.

Stimulus and Response Generalization Stimulus generalization, as we use the term, refers to the appearance of a particular response event or category of behavior under stimulus conditions that are somehow different from those present when the behavior was originally trained. Stimulus generalization always involves response maintenance after the removal of programmed reinforcers (i.e., under extinction conditions). Stimulus generalization effects include transfer of conditioned responding across time, settings, and individuals (e.g., Cooke and Apolloni, 1976). Programming to achieve stimulus generalization is obviously important since responses that are evident under a narrow range of stimulus conditions are of limited practical value (Cooke, Cooke, and Apolloni, 1976).

Response generalization is another important construct. This term applies when untrained responses shift with alterations in conditioned responses of the same class. Thus, response generalization, as we use the term, implies a generative repertoire. When a specific response is trained, responses in the same general class also increase. Such effects are the result of functional interrelationships in topographically dissimilar behaviors (e.g., McCarty et al., in press) and are educationally most desirable. Educational programming is particularly efficacious when widespread increases in appropriate behaviors accompany training to modify a narrow range of performance.

Peer Imitation by Delayed Toddlers and Preschoolers Each of our studies on peer imitation training has included assessments of stimulus and response generalization. Our first studies (Apolloni, Cooke, and Cooke,

1977; Cooke, Cooke, and Apolloni, in press) investigated the feasibility of training delayed toddlers to imitate motor, material use, and verbal responses emitted by nondelayed age-mates. Stimulus generalization outcomes were evaluated by measuring the subjects' responsiveness to trained, peer-modeled stimuli when the training procedure was not in effect. Response generalization effects were monitored by having nondelayed peer models present untrained peer-modeled stimuli under nontraining conditions. Peer imitation of and vocalizations to peers were recorded in the case of one study during a free-play generalization setting without the adult teacher present.

The three delayed subjects and the two nondelayed peers for these first studies were all under three years of age. The delayed children's IQs ranged from 67 to 70. One child evidenced Down's syndrome, the second manifested auditory and visual impairments in addition to delayed development, and the third was generally delayed in all areas of behavioral development. Two of the subjects were females and one was male. Both nondelayed peers were females.

The results of these first two studies indicated that we could successfully train delayed toddlers to imitate nondelayed age-mates under highly structured conditions. Each subject successively increased his or her imitation of the trained responses concurrent with the application of PIT. Moreover, the generalization session data generally indicated response maintenance under nontraining conditions and increased levels for the untrained responses. The subjects' levels of verbal peer imitation did not increase, however, in a free-play setting without the adult present. The subjects verbalized more toward the peer models and their other classmates following training, but these effects could have been attributable to historical or maturational variables. Our anecdotal observations for both investigations suggested that the nondelayed children did not increase their imitation of the delayed children's behavior.

Our third study (Peck et al., 1976) was directed toward developing peer-imitative behavior that would be maintained under nontraining, free-play conditions in the absence of an adult experimenter. Since previous research had substantiated that stimulus generalization effects are likely to be obtained when there is a high degree of correspondence between training and generalization situations (Strain, Cooke, and Apolloni, 1976, pp. 131–141), we applied PIT directly in free-play settings. Two experiments were carried out. The three subjects for the first experiment were three-year-old developmentally delayed preschoolers (Down's syndrome), two males and one female. Their IQs ranged between 55 and 64. The three peer models were four-year-old nondelayed children, two males and one female.

A dyadic data collection system was employed. This system permitted recording the levels at which the delayed and nondelayed children imitated and socially interacted with one another. The data were recorded in a free-play setting, under training and nontraining conditions, with all of the delayed subjects and peer models present. An adult experimenter prompted and praised the subjects for imitating the ongoing free-play behavior of the nondelayed children (unidirectional training). Peer imitation was defined as, "A response similar in topography to one emitted 5 seconds or less previously by another child, and which was observed by the subject" (Peck et al., 1976, p. 7). The adult experimenter left the play area during the generalization sessions.

The results of this experiment demonstrated that PIT could be effectively applied to teach developmentally delayed preschoolers to imitate the free-play behavior of nondelayed classmates. Additionally, the small but consistent increases evident in the delayed subjects' imitative responding under nontraining conditions indicated success in training peer-imitative behavior that was maintained in the absence of the training agent. Reciprocal increases in the social interaction between the delayed subjects and the nondelayed children were also evident under training and nontraining conditions once PIT was in effect with all three subjects. In addition, the data clearly showed that the nondelayed children did not increase the rates at which they imitated the delayed children.

The second experiment of this study was a replication and extension with two toddler-age subjects. Dyadic data were again coded. Bidirectional training was applied; that is, both delayed and nondelayed participants were trained to imitate one another in a variety of material use and motor activities, and the experimenter left the play area following the training sessions. The results of the second experiment replicated those of the first, with one very important exception. The nondelayed children imitated the delayed children. The bidirectional training procedure had apparently resulted in reciprocal imitation between the delayed and nondelayed participants. It is important to note, however, that the behavior imitated by the nondelayed children was not considered inappropriate.

Finally, in our fourth study (Cooke, Apolloni, and Cooke, 1976), we again assessed the effects of a bidirectional PIT procedure. We had anecdotally observed, consistent with recent ethological reports (Porter et al., in press; Ray, 1974), that more developmentally advanced children preferred nondelayed to delayed playmates. We decided to assess this issue through observing the interaction and imitation between delayed and more advanced children in three environmental arrangements: (1) a PIT setting with a delayed and nondelayed child present, (2) a nontraining setting with the same two children, and (3) a second nontraining setting with the same two children plus a second nondelayed child. We also replicated the experiment with a second nondelayed child. One delayed subject, a two-year-old female, earned a social quotient of 47 on the Vineland Social Maturity Scale and was medically diagnosed as cerebral palsied. The second subject was also two years old; he manifested Down's syndrome and scored 65 on an individualized IQ test.

In general, the results of this study indicated that PIT, applied in a bidirectional fashion, was effective for producing increases in the reciprocal peer imitation and social interaction between delayed and nondelayed children in the training setting. Moreover, the nondelayed children who participated in PIT demonstrated higher rates of imitation and interaction with the delayed subjects in the generalization setting not offering a second nondelayed peer as a social option. Consistent with ethological reports, our option setting observations indicated a deceleration in the nondelayed children's imitation and interaction with the delayed child and a corresponding increase in the nondelayed children's social behavior toward one another. These data support the notion that nondelayed children, when provided the choice of a nondelayed or a delayed playmate of similar age, prefer to interact with children who are functioning at a developmental level that is similar to their own.

Summary of PIT Training

In summary, the four studies we have conducted thus far clearly support the feasibility of training young delayed children to imitate the behavior of nondelayed classmates. Furthermore, once trained, generalized peer imitation has been consistently observed across stimulus conditions and to responses never directly trained. Generalized increases in social interaction also seem to accompany this procedure. It appears that bidirectional training produces increased reciprocal peer imitation by delayed and nondelayed children while unidirectional training results in increased peer imitation by only delayed participants. It also appears that, given an option, nondelayed children prefer nondelayed to delayed playmates, PIT notwithstanding. Our interpretations regarding the effects of bidirectional versus unidirectional training and the extent and influence of nondelayed children's social preference for nondelayed playmates are as yet based on insufficient data to permit firm conclusions. Additional PIT studies are needed, some of which are outlined in the concluding sections of this chapter.

IMPLICATIONS AND RECOMMENDATIONS

In this final section of the chapter we review the implications of existing knowledge on effective educational programming in integrated infant, toddler, and preschool settings. The implications are presented as recommendations of two sorts: those applicable to researchers, and those relevant to educational program personnel. In this section we move somewhat beyond "hard data" to extrapolate experimental and programmatic suggestions. The reader should be alerted to the shift from data-based results to more general discussions.

Recommendations to Researchers

Before any totally substantiated claims can be made regarding the relative values and varieties of social interaction in integrated preschool settings, much more normative data are needed on the interaction patterns of children in such settings. The early data that are available suggest largely neutral outcomes for the handicapped participants (Devoney, Guralnick, and Rubin, 1974; Porter et al., in press; Ray, 1974). We cannot make judgments regarding the widespread advisability or necessity of behavior change strategies in integrated settings until we know more about the social behavior that is natural in such ecologies.

Another fundamental area in need of research is that of the effects of systematic variations in the developmental levels of the children who are placed in integrated settings. Researchers have noted therapeutic changes in the social behavior of isolate-reared rhesus monkeys as a consequence of integrating them into play sessions with younger species mates (Gomber and Mitchell, 1974; Suomi and Harlow, 1972). It seems plausible that developmentally delayed children would respond quite differently to exposure to peers of varying developmental sophistication. Researchers should begin to determine what constitutes the optimal developmental skill blend for integrated intervention programs. It may prove best to match handicapped and nonhandicapped children on the basis of similar developmental levels. A related topic worthy of investigation concerns the ratios of handicapped to normal children and the concomitant social arrangements that maximally facilitate the likelihood of positive outcomes. Certainly we should expect differential effects of various ratios and grouping arrangements. However, to date, little empirical data have been reported that shed direct light on these questions.

Educational Effects of Integration Perhaps the most fundamental question concerns the relative outcomes of mixing handicapped and nonhandicapped children for educational purposes. More specifically, what are the language, motor, cognitive, and social outcomes to preschool children, both handicapped and nonhandicapped, with and without integrated programs? Clearly, this was one of the salient initial questions regarding integration. It is perplexing to note that this question has not yet been the subject of direct empirical scrutiny. In all likelihood this area of research will emerge as one that is influenced by the legal, ethical, and value judgments of the individuals involved in the analysis. In fact, to many current educational decision makers, the moral, ethical, and perhaps legal aspects of segregated versus integrated schooling probably loom as more significant issues than the educational data available on the topic.

We have analyzed several forms of PIT in integrated settings to determine their effects on handicapped and normally developing participants. There currently exist, however, no experimental reports on the relative effectiveness of integrated preschool programming with and without PIT. In all likelihood PIT will demonstrate varying degrees of effectiveness when used with children with different behavioral characteristics. The performance areas in which PIT will be most effective will probably also depend in large measure on the nature of the participants. A next logical direction for investigation with PIT might be to determine how this procedure could be systematically modified to be maximally effective with various objectives and across a continuum of developmental sophistication.

It would also seem valuable to shed some empirical light on the behavioral concomitants of PIT. We have reported data which suggest that increases in social interaction between handicapped and normal children accompany PIT. It thus seems plausible that PIT or similar training procedures might increase both the quality and the quantity of social interaction between handicapped and nonhandicapped children in integrated settings. More research is needed on procedures to produce desirable social interaction effects in integrated settings.

PIT has been shown to produce generalized imitative repertoires in handicapped children. While it seems self-evident that developing such repertoires would be developmentally advantageous to handicapped children in integrated schools, no data have yet been reported on long-term effects. We would like to encourage and collaborate with any colleagues interested in this area of research.

Imitation by Nondelayed Children   A question quite often voiced by observers of PIT sessions relates to the effects on the normal participants. Observers have often asked whether the normal participants begin to imitate the behavior of handicapped peers. The early results of our research indicate that such imitation does not occur unless it is reinforced as a part of the training procedure. It was only during the two experiments in which normal children were directly reinforced for imitating the behavior of handicapped classmates that nonhandicapped children were observed to imitate handicapped children. The behaviors imitated by the normal children were appropriate material use in nature. Moreover, there is no reason to believe that any behavior of a handicapped child which is imitated by a normal child will necessarily be detrimental. Reciprocal imitation probably facilitates social integration in many cases. It is important for researchers to determine what types of training will produce imitation of particular predictable forms of behavior among normal children involved in PIT.

Research Design The topics for research suggested herein are obviously wide ranging and will be demanding of those who pursue them. The research designs that seem most appropriate would be combinations of single subject, behavior analytic designs for intrasubject evaluations of specific procedures, and group designs that rely on inferential statistical analysis of results for intergroup comparisons. The latter variety of research should be aimed at answering questions relevant to the overall programmatic outcomes associated with integrated versus segregated educational arrangements and for assessing the external validity of specific teaching procedures. This suggestion for interaction between single subject and group modes of research is made to discourage the reader from perceiving the area as one that is specific to behavior analytic designs. Although the current authors have relied on single subject designs to the present point, it should be recognized that other research designs and methodologies have important contributions to make to this area of research (O'Leary and Kent, 1973).

Recommendations to Educators

A primary goal of integrating infant, toddler, and preschool educational environments is to facilitate the overall positive behavioral, attitudinal, and emotional development of all children enrolled. Although optimal procedures will be clarified through future research, sufficient data are available to provide recommendations for educators. Specifically, teachers in such settings can arrange certain physical and social aspects of their classrooms to maximize positive outcomes. Programming to achieve social integration of handicapped children represents a logical first step toward generating a wide range of desirable educational outcomes. It is commonly believed that the social learning of children is facilitated by positive social contacts with peers (Hartup, 1970). Additionally, when handicapped children are accepted by and interact with their nonhandicapped classmates, more structured forms of teaching between children can be readily organized. Such interactions should also be beneficial to nonhandicapped children as well, by providing them with opportunities to develop sensitive and well informed feelings of acceptance for human diversity. In short, it seems wise to structure events in classrooms to maximally integrate handicapped children to promote accepting attitudes, positive social-emotional interactions, and structured educational activities. With this in mind, it seems important to offer some concrete suggestions for programming high levels of positive social interaction between handicapped and nonhandicapped children in integrated settings.

Teacher Reinforcement First of all, teachers should be sensitive to the social interaction that is occurring naturally between children. They should be careful to facilitate children's ongoing positive social interaction without interrupting it. Teacher praise, contingent upon children's interactive behavior, has proved to be an effective behavior modification tactic to increase the social integration of preschool children (Hart et al., 1968; Strain and Timm, 1974). But teacher-delivered social reinforcement programs can also interfere with children's ongoing social play, and teachers should consider using other techniques including dramatic play activities (Strain and Wiegerink, 1976). For example, Shores, Hester, and Strain (1976) found that dramatic play or role-playing activities were more successful in producing social interaction between preschool children than were arrangements that relied heavily on continued adult involvement. Teachers should be no more obtrusive and obvious than necessary in structuring positive social-emotional experiences between handicapped and nonhandicapped children. This policy will be much more likely to produce maintenance of responding when the children are outside the teacher's direct influence. This kind of generalized outcome, of course, represents a goal of nearly every educational endeavor.

Materials and Their Use Teachers should also recognize that the kinds of materials provided for children's use will influence the nature and duration of their social interaction. Research has shown that the type and amount of available play materials are important determinants of children's social play levels (Johnson, 1935; Quilitch and Risley, 1973; Updegraff and Herbst, 1933). Peterson (1976, personal communication) has recently completed observations that replicate these findings in an integrated preschool setting.

It is also important to make sure that all children in a play setting have the necessary skills to utilize the available materials. Observers have reported that some children must first learn to use play materials before successful programming can be implemented to increase their level of peer interaction (Allen, Turner, and Everett, 1970; Buell et al., 1968). Teachers should also be sure that sufficient materials are present to permit interactive participation by all children present. It is particularly important that sufficient sets of duplicate materials be available to permit imitative behavior by handicapped children who might observe and imitate a model child enjoying a material.

Grouping of Children Remembering that handicapped children can learn a great many new skills by observing and imitating the behavior of nonhandicapped peers, teachers should engage the children in small groups of two, three, or four for structured learning activities. When such arrangements are planned, teachers should be cautious to organize children according to developmentally appropriate groupings. Optimally, normal children would serve as "teachers" of handicapped peers only slightly less developmentally advanced than themselves. In this way normal models will receive the benefits of appropriate practice while sharing their skills with handicapped peers. Along a similar vein, teachers should be careful to arrange learning groups with children who are interpersonally compatible. If children do not seem capable of positive social relations, it would be foolhardy to attempt to have them serve as teachers or models. A handicapped child is more likely to learn from a peer with whom he or she has shared good social rapport. Socially isolated or aggressive children, handicapped or nonhandicapped, will often need special help in learning how to socially interact with peers. We have previously reviewed appropriate educational procedures for assessing and modifying deficient social interaction patterns (Strain, Cooke, and Apolloni, 1976). It is important to remediate such problems speedily, since their existence serves as a block to many productive forms of learning.

Research-Service Strategies in Integrated Settings

Our final, but certainly not least important suggestion, is to advocate the systematic collection of information that will provide feedback on the effectiveness of teaching procedures. Only when information is available on the relative success of various strategies can the most effective ones be identified. If the integration of handicapped and nonhandicapped children in educational programs is to develop into an effective, broadly based, and socially significant practice, then the most viable and effective strategies for its implementation must be identified. Part of this analysis and identification will come from applied educational research. Another, equally important form of "research" must be pursued by every educational professional charged with responsibility in integrated settings. Research-service activities should be aimed at answering questions like, "What kinds of integration work with my children in the available environment? What methods of grouping produce desired effects for both handicapped and nonhandicapped children? How can I generate productive forms of social interaction among my children? Which children can best fill particular roles in my integrated setting?" These are difficult questions, for this is a demanding task. The need to systematize and utilize feedback data renders the task somewhat more demanding, but certainly more promising. Perhaps in this way, with competent teachers applying and evaluating their best efforts at successful integration strategies, young handicapped and nonhandicapped children will begin to reciprocally benefit from their developmental diversity and mutual growth.

ACKNOWLEDGMENTS

The authors are grateful for the collaboration of Dr. Robert Reiland, Sonoma County Office of Education, who provided administrative guidance for the projects described herein. Gratitude is also expressed for the research contributions of Sharon Cooke and Charles Peck, the individuals who directly supervised the present research on a day-to-day basis.

REFERENCES CITED

Allen, K. E., Benning, P. M., and Drummond, T. W. 1972. Integration of normal and handicapped children in a behavior modification preschool: A case study. In G. Semb (Ed.), Behavior Analysis and Education. Lawrence: Kan.: University of Kansas Press.

Allen, K. E., Turner, K. D., and Everett, P. M. 1970. A behavior modification classroom for head start children with problem behaviors. Exceptional Children, 37, 119-127.

Apolloni, T., Cooke, S. A., and Cooke, T. P. 1977. Establishing a normal peer as a behavioral model for delayed toddlers. Perceptual and Motor Skills, 44, 231-241.

Apolloni, T., and Cooke, T. P. 1975. Peer behavior conceptualized as a variable influencing infant and toddler development. American Journal of Orthopsychiatry, 45, 4-17.

Apolloni, T., and Tremblay, A. (In press). Peer modeling between toddlers. Child Study Journal.

Bandura, A., and Kupers, C. J. 1964. Transmission of patterns of self-reinforcement through modeling. Journal of Abnormal and Social Psychology, 69, 1-9.

Berkowitz, S. 1968. Acquisition and maintenance of generalized imitative repertoires of profound retardates with retarded peers functioning as models and reinforcing agents. Unpublished doctoral dissertation, University of Maryland.

Bijou, S., and Baer, D. M. 1965. Child Development II: Universal Stages of Infancy. New York: Appleton-Century-Crofts.

Bloom, B. S. 1964. Stability and Change in Human Characteristics. New York: John Wiley & Sons.

Bricker, D. D., and Bricker, W. A. 1972. Toddler research and intervention project report: Year II. IMRID Behavioral Science Monograph 21, Institute in Mental Retardation and Intellectual Development. Nashville, Tenn.: George Peabody College.

Bricker, D. D., and Bricker, W. A. 1973. Infant, toddler, and preschool research and intervention project report: Year III. IMRID Behavioral Science Monograph 23, Institute on Mental Retardation and Intellectual Development. Nashville, Tenn.: George Peabody College.

Bronfenbrenner, U. 1974. Is early intervention effective? Publication (OHD) 74-25. Washington, D.C.: U.S. Department of Health, Education, and Welfare, Office of Child Development.

Buell, J., Stoddard, P., Harris, F. R., and Baer, D. M. 1968. Collateral social development accompanying reinforcement of outdoor play in a preschool child. Journal of Applied Behavior Analysis, 1, 167-173.

Christy, P. R. 1975. Does use of tangible rewards with individual children affect peer observers? Journal of Applied Behavior Analysis, 8, 187-196.

Clark, B. S. 1965. The acquisition and extinction of peer imitation in children. Psychonomic Science, 2, 147-148.

Cohen, J. S., and DeYoung, H. 1973. The role of litigation in the improvement of programming for the handicapped. In L. Mann and D. A. Sabatino (Eds.), The First Review of Special Education (Vol. 2). New York: Grune & Stratton.

Cooke, S. A., Cooke, T. P., and Apolloni, T. 1976. Generalization of language training with the mentally retarded. Journal of Special Education, 10, 299-304.

Cooke, S. A., Cooke, T. P., and Apolloni, T. (In press). Developing nonretarded toddlers as verbal models for retarded classmates. Child Study Journal.

Cooke, T. P., and Apolloni, T. 1975. Parental involvement in the schools: Ten postulates of justification. Education, 96, 168-169.

Cooke, T. P., and Apolloni, T. 1976. Developing positive social-emotional behaviors: A study of training and generalization effects. Journal of Applied Behavior Analysis, 9, 65-78.

Cooke, T. P., Apolloni, T., and Cooke, S. A. 1976. The effects of a second nondelayed playmate on the free-play imitation and interaction of delayed and nondelayed children. Unpublished manuscript.

Csapo, M. 1972. Peer models reverse the 'one bad apple spoils the barrel' theory. Teaching Exceptional Children, 4, 20-24.

Devoney, C., Guralnick, M. J., and Rubin, H. 1974. Integrating handicapped and non-handicapped preschool children: Effects on social play. Childhood Education, 50, 360-364.

Eckerman, C. O., Whatley, J. L., and Kutz, S. L. 1975. Growth of social play with peers during the second year of life. Developmental Psychology, 11, 42-49.

Gomber, J., and Mitchell, G. 1974. Preliminary report on adult male isolation-reared Rhesus monkeys caged with infants. Developmental Psychology, 10, 298.

Guralnick, M. J. 1973. A research-service model for support of handicapped children. Exceptional Children, 39, 277-282.

Guralnick, M. J. 1976. The value of integrating handicapped and nonhandicapped preschool children. American Journal of Orthopsychiatry, 42, 236-245.

Hart, B. M., Reynolds, N. J., Baer, D. M., Brawley, E. R., and Harris, F. R. 1968. Effect of contingent and noncontingent social reinforcement on the cooperative play of a preschool child. Journal of Applied Behavior Analysis, 1, 73-76.

Hartup, W. W. 1970. Peer interaction and social organization. In P. H. Mussen (Ed.), Manual of Child Psychology (3rd ed.). New York: John Wiley & Sons.
Hartup, W. W., and Coates, B. 1967. Imitation of a peer as a function of reinforcement from the peer group and rewardingness of the model. Child Development, 38, 1003–1016.
Hayden, A. H., and Haring, N. G. 1976. Early intervention for high risk infants and young children: Programs for Down's syndrome children. In T. D. Tjossem (Ed.), Intervention Strategies for High Risk Infants and Young Children. Baltimore: University Park Press.
Hebb, D. O. 1966. A Textbook of Psychology (2nd ed.). Philadelphia: W. B. Saunders.
Heber, R., and Garber, H. 1970. An experiment in the prevention of cultural-familial mental retardation. Paper presented at the Second Congress of the International Association for the Scientific Study of Mental Deficiency, September, Warsaw, Poland.
Hunt, J. McV. 1961. Intelligence and Experience. New York: Ronald Press.
Johnson, C. A., and Katz, R. C. 1973. Using parents as change agents for their children: A review. Journal of Child Psychiatry and Psychology, 14, 181–200.
Johnson, M. W. 1935. The effect on behavior of variation in amount of play equipment. Child Development, 6, 56–68.
Karnes, M. B., and Teska, J. A. 1975. Children's response to intervention programs. In J. J. Gallagher (Ed.), The Application of Child Development Research to Exceptional Children. Reston, Va.: The Council for Exceptional Children.
Kirk, S. A. 1958. Early Education of the Mentally Retarded. Urbana: University of Illinois Press.
McCarty, T., Griffin, S., Apolloni, T., and Shores, R. E. (In press). Increased peer-teaching with group-oriented contingencies for arithmetic performance in behavior disordered adolescents. Journal of Applied Behavior Analysis.
Meyer, E. L., Vergason, G. A., and Whelan, R. J. 1975. Alternatives for Teaching Exceptional Children. Denver: Love Publishing.
Miller, N. E., and Dollard, J. 1941. Social Learning and Imitation. New Haven: Yale University Press.
O'Connor, R. 1969. Modification of social withdrawal through symbolic modeling. Journal of Applied Behavior Analysis, 1, 15–22.
O'Connor, R. D. 1972. Relative efficacy of modeling, shaping, and the combined procedures for modification of social withdrawal. Journal of Abnormal Psychology, 79, 327–334.
O'Leary, D. O., and Kent, R. 1973. Behavior modification for social action: Research tactics and problems. In L. A. Hammerlynck, L. C. Handy, and E. J. Mash (Eds.), Behavior Change: Methodology, Concepts, and Practice. Champaign, Ill.: Research Press.
Peck, C. A., Apolloni, T., Cooke, T. P., and Cooke, S. R. 1976. Teaching developmentally delayed toddlers and preschoolers to imitate the free-play behavior of nonretarded classmates: Trained and generalized effects. Unpublished manuscript.
Popham, W. E. 1971. Criterion-Referenced Measurement. Englewood Cliffs, N.J.: Educational Technology Publications.
Porter, R. H., Ramsey, B., Tremblay, A., Iaccobo, M., and Crawley, S. (In press). Social interactions in heterogeneous groups of retarded and normally

developing children: An observational study. In G. P. Sackett and H. C. Haywood (Eds.), Observing Behavior, Vol. 1: Theory and Applications in Mental Retardation. Baltimore: University Park Press.

Quilitch, H. R., and Risley, T. R. 1973. The effects of play materials on social play. Journal of Applied Behavior Analysis, 6, 573-578.

Ray, J. S. 1974. Behavior of developmentally delayed and nondelayed toddler-age children: An ethological study. Unpublished manuscript, Nashville, Tenn.: George Peabody College.

Ross, D. M. 1970. Effect on learning of psychological attachment to a film model. American Journal of Mental Deficiency, 77, 137-142.

Ross, D. M., and Ross, S. A. 1972. The efficacy of listening training for educable mentally retarded children. American Journal of Mental Deficiency, 77, 137-142.

Shores, R. E., Hester, P., and Strain, P. S. 1976. Effects of teacher presence and structured play on child-child interaction among handicapped preschool children. Psychology in the Schools, 13, 171-175.

Snyder, L., Apolloni, T., and Cooke, T. P. 1977. Integrated settings at the early childhood level: The role of nonretarded peers. Exceptional Children, 43, 262-266.

Strain, P. S., Cooke, T. P., and Apolloni, T. 1976. Teaching Exceptional Children: Assessing and Modifying Social Behavior. New York: Academic Press.

Strain, P. S., and Timm, M. S. 1974. An experimental analysis of social interaction between a behaviorally disordered preschool child and her classroom peers. Journal of Applied Behavior Analysis, 7, 583-590.

Strain, P. S., and Wiegerink, R. 1976. The effects of sociodramatic activities on social interaction among behaviorally disordered preschool children. Journal of Special Education, 10, 71-75.

Strichart, S. A. 1973. Effects of competence and nurturance on imitation of non-retarded peers by retarded adolescents. American Journal of Mental Deficiency, 78, 665-673.

Suomi, S. J., and Harlow, H. F. 1972. Social rehabilitation of isolate-reared monkeys. Developmental Psychology, 6, 487-496.

Updegraff, R., and Herbst, E. K. 1933. An experimental study of the social behavior stimulated in young children by certain play materials. Journal of Genetic Psychology, 42, 372-391.

Warfield, G. J. (Ed.). 1974. Mainstream Currents: Reprints from Exceptional Children 1968-1974. Reston, Va.: Council for Exceptional Children.

Whalen, C. K., and Henker, B. A. 1969. Creating therapeutic pyramids using mentally retarded patients. American Journal of Mental Deficiency, 74, 331-337.

Whalen, C. K., and Henker, B. A. 1971. Pyramid therapy in a hospital for the retarded: Methods, program evaluation and long term effects. American Journal of Mental Deficiency, 75, 414-434.

Wolfensberger, W. 1972. The Principle of Normalization in Human Services. Toronto, Canada: National Institute on Mental Retardation.

Wynne, S., Ulfelder, L. S., and Dakof, G. 1975. Mainstreaming and Early Childhood Education for Handicapped Children: Review and Implications of Research. Final Report, Contract OEC-74-9056. Washington, D.C.: Bureau of Education for the Handicapped.

INTEGRATING HANDICAPPED PRESCHOOL CHILDREN WITHIN A COGNITIVELY ORIENTED PROGRAM

Jean Ispa, Ph.D., and
Robert D. Matz, Ph.D.

The current High Scope Cognitively Oriented Preschool Curriculum is the result of fifteen years of work in education by David P. Weikart and his associates. Over this time, the evolution of this curriculum has been guided by cognitive developmental theory. The influence of this theory can be described by referring to some basic concepts about how children learn:

As they mature, children develop new thinking abilities in a somewhat predictable sequence. The stages described by Piaget and his colleagues are helpful in gaining insight into these new abilities.
Given at least a minimum amount of emotional security, children are intrinsically motivated to exercise their emerging abilities. Intrinsic motivation is maximized when children have an opportunity to make choices, experience success, and pace themselves.
Intellectual development occurs through active transactions with adults, peers, real materials, and events.
Language development proceeds naturally in an environment where children are encouraged to communicate their needs and ideas in day-to-day social interactions.

The research reported herein was carried out as part of High/Scope's First Chance model demonstration project supported by Grant OEG-0-74-2720 from the United States Office of Education, Bureau of Education for the Handicapped.

A variety of media including gesture, drawing, construction, and dramatic play are involved in symbolic functioning.

A setting designed to foster active learning and intrinsic motivation will also enhance children's self-esteem and promote positive social interaction among children and adults.

These principles of development are applicable to almost all children, including the majority of handicapped children.

CURRICULUM STRUCTURE

The curriculum structure is an open framework because it provides general principles and strategies from which teachers can generate their own specific programs tailored to the resources and cultural heritage of their community. This approach contrasts with programmed curricula, in which the instructional procedures and materials are so specific as to be virtually "teacher proof." The open framework curriculum, on the other hand, requires a thinking, creative teacher who can relate the actions and language of young children to underlying developmental principles. Furthermore, what sets it apart from child-centered curricula is the expectation that both the teacher and the child will provide input into the direction of daily classroom activities (Weikart, 1974).

The coherence of the goals for children and the strategies for teachers helps make possible the mutual initiation of activities by teacher and children. This coherence can be outlined by describing four basic components of the curriculum. First, teachers are encouraged to keep in mind a set of "key experiences" through which emerging cognitive skills may be broadened and strengthened rather than "accelerated" or "taught." These experiences suggest ways to involve children in active learning, in using language, in representing, in classification, seriation, number concepts, temporal relations, and spatial relations. The three other basic curriculum components—room arrangement, the daily routine, and daily planning and evaluation by teachers—are described below.

Room Arrangement

A good room arrangement can help provide children with the message that they can make decisions about what they are going to do and how they are going to do it. It also imparts a sense of order. The cognitively oriented preschool classroom is divided into several distinct areas. These typically include a block area, an art area, a housekeeping area, a quiet area, a workbench area, and a sand and water area.

In each area, there are "real" things for the children to use, such as real tools, real kitchen items, etc. Storage cabinets and displays are at the child's eye level. Equipment that encourages active manipulation is available. Items that are similar are stored together, and shelves and drawers are labeled with pictures of the contents. This helps children locate things and put them away themselves; it also stimulates use of their developing abilities to classify objects and to understand the relationship between objects and symbols of objects.

Daily Routine

The central purpose of the consistent daily routine is to give both adults and children a focus allowing them to use their creative energies on the task at hand without worrying about what comes next. Children are made to feel more secure and more in control of their actions when they can predict the order of events. In addition, the routine helps children develop an understanding of time in terms of a sequence of events they participate in each day. A capsule description of each element in the daily routine follows:

Planning time—Each child decides what he or she is going to do during work time and indicates the plan to an adult, who helps the child think through and elaborate his or her ideas. The adult also records the plan so he or she can help during work and recall times and also help the child get to the proposed work area.

Work time—With the support and assistance of adults and peers, children actively pursue the ideas, activities, and projects they planned for at planning time. Teachers move about the room, conversing with children, asking them questions about what they are doing, and helping them follow through on the plans they made. Children who complete their initial plans, make and work on another set of plans.

Clean-up time—Children sort, order, and put away materials they have used during work time. They store unfinished projects.

Recall, snack, and small group time—The same small group of five to eight children meets together each day with an adult to snack, recall work time activities, and work with materials in an activity usually planned by the adult to provide one of the key experiences. A small group time activity might involve each child making a batch of Playdoh and observing changes that occur, for example, or each child building with boxes and blocks and talking about spatial relations.

Activity time—Outside if possible, indoors if it rains, children and adults are involved in large motor play and conversation about what they are doing.

Circle time—All children and adults meet together as a total group to sing and make up action songs, play musical instruments, move to music, play games, and sometimes briefly review an upcoming social event (Hohmann et al., in press).

Of course, there are specific strategies related to each element of the routine. For example, individual children come to preschool at different levels of ability to plan and make decisions. Accordingly, teachers using the Cognitively Oriented Curriculum learn to support the planning process at the child's present level. The rationale for the daily routine includes other concepts of typical concern to teachers such as classroom management. When children are accustomed to the routine, they are able to wait for the teacher's attention, allowing the teacher to work one-to-one with separate children as necessary. In our opinion, the blend of freedom and structure in the daily routine helps foster social competence in young children (see Baumrind, 1973).

Daily Evaluation and Planning

In an open framework classroom where teachers and children generate the specific agenda, teachers need to engage in daily evaluation and planning. Evaluation concentrates upon the actions of children and the activities provided during the course of the day—the appropriateness of an activity for individual children and the success of an activity in providing one or more key experiences. Planning concentrates upon ways of supporting and enriching children's actions in the coming day.

Planning and evaluation are a team process of problem solving and mutual support. All the adults involved in the classroom play an active role. Planning and evaluation are more productive when team members keep organized, written records. Teachers therefore keep daily notes on individual children. General assessments of the progress of each child are completed bimonthly, and a detailed form, the High/Scope Child Observation Record, is completed three times per year for each child.

INTEGRATING HANDICAPPED AND NONHANDICAPPED CHILDREN WITHIN THE COGNITIVELY ORIENTED CURRICULUM

High/Scope preschool staff are currently involved in ongoing efforts to adapt the preschool curriculum for classrooms in which handicapped and nonhandicapped children are integrated. While the focus of integration is relatively new for High/Scope, interest in handicapped or potentially handicapped children is not. The curriculum, in fact, first evolved out of a five-year project to develop preschool programs for low income children diagnosed as "functionally mentally retarded." Follow-up studies comparing children who attended the preschool during those five years and their controls have indicated that the project was successful both in terms of standardized intelligence tests scores and in terms of various measures of school success (Weikart, 1974).

Characteristics of Handicapped Children

With funding from the Bureau of Education for the Handicapped, the effort has now been expanded to include children with moderate perceptual or sensory impairment, motor disability, emotional disturbance, and/or delayed mental development. Two half-day High/Scope First Chance preschool classrooms in Ypsilanti, Michigan, serve as demonstration sites. Each classroom is staffed with two teachers and includes five handicapped and ten nonhandicapped children. During the school year 1975-1976, the list of handicaps shown by the children included severe cardiac defects, hemiplegia, muscular dystrophy, failure of lungs to clear, spinal scoleosis and kyphosis, language delay, delayed mental development, emotional disturbance, epilepsy, learning disabilities, partial hearing loss, and Down's syndrome. Several children received supplementary speech and/or physical therapy at local hospitals and universities.

Cognitively Oriented Curriculum and Children with Special Needs

What makes the curriculum appropriate for children with special problems? It is our belief that most of the curriculum components are universalistic and can work for the benefit of both handicapped and nonhandicapped children. A number of points can be made in this regard. The attention teachers give to the individual developmental levels and interests of children creates a setting in which each child can be actively involved in broadening and strengthening those particular abilities that are emerging. Because each child works at activities that are developmentally appropriate, he or she has the opportunity to grow and experience success without infringing on the needs of other children for a faster (or slower) pace or for an activity that is more personally interesting.

Second, while teachers' plans are built upon their observations of children's differing abilities, their focus remains on the universalities of development and on the children's strengths more than on their weaknesses. This means that teachers' expectations are kept high and that they are encouraged to see the potential in each child. The tendency to lump handicapped children together, to see them as a separate, uniformly disabled group, is thus reduced. Moreover, handicapped children's expressions of normal development are supported and stimulated, rather than, as too often happens, seen as being of secondary importance to their deficits. It is believed that this results not only in their continued progress in those areas in which they are already strong, but also in progress in those areas most affected by their handicaps.

This catching up, or evening out, of abilities may result from the self-confidence and independence that children develop when their strong points are recognized. It then becomes possible for them to become active in those areas in which they are weaker, to develop them as if in the service of interests and strengths. To illustrate, one child who attended the preschool this past year was severely language delayed but very socially aware and quite interested in exploring classroom objects. Support for his skills and interests seems to have been a factor contributing to the great improvements seen in his speech comprehension, vocabulary, and syntax. Encouraged to develop positive relationships with peers and teachers, which he did relatively easy and well, he was, in effect, also being encouraged to communicate with them verbally. It is noteworthy that, even toward the end of the academic year, a speech therapist whom he saw on a regular basis was unable to elicit as much language from him as he typically used in the preschool classroom. It may be presumed that her methods, which involved very didactic situations with almost no direct child involvement with materials or natural interactions with peers or adults, simply did not motivate him to speak.

This brings us a third, related, characteristic of the Cognitively Oriented Curriculum that makes it appropriate for handicapped children. Therapeutic exercises are introduced by the teachers in such a way that they become extensions of activities the children already understand and enjoy. Artificial exercises are avoided. The above example illustrates this point. A second example was provided by teachers who incorporated exercise into role play and circle time activities. For a child with muscular dystrophy who enjoyed role playing in the house area, pretending to be a mother carrying groceries was a good way to exercise her weak arm and shoulder muscles. At circle time, having the class pretend to be elephants gave her the opportunity at once to be part of a group and to get the arm, shoulder, and neck exercise she needed.

For classrooms in which handicapped and nonhandicapped preschoolers are integrated, the Cognitively Oriented Curriculum also offers opportunities for the two groups to interact on more than a superficial basis. Because children are not expected to focus primarily on their teachers, they are free to interact with peers during much of the day. Second, during snack and small group times, groups of seven or eight children meet with the teacher to eat, recall what they have done that day, and work with materials either together or in parallel. The groups are integrated. This means that there are times each day when the routine provides a structure that facilitates communication between diverse kinds of children. Positive experiences during group times may engender positive feelings about group-mates that are reflected in peer interactions during the rest of the day. No systematic attempts to "train" handicapped and nonhandicapped children to relate positively to one another are made; it is hypothesized that in the environment that is provided, positive interactions will occur naturally.

NATURALISTIC OBSERVATIONS OF SOCIAL AND EMOTIONAL BEHAVIOR IN INTEGRATED CLASSROOMS

During the winter of 1975-1976, systematic naturalistic observations were carried out in the two High/Scope First Chance Preschool classrooms. The aims of the research were twofold: first, to determine whether or not the frequency and style of interaction between classmates were significantly affected by the presence of a handicap on the part of one or more of them, and second, to determine whether or not and how teachers related differently to handicapped and nonhandicapped children.

The research was motivated both by the need to evaluate the social atmosphere in our own preschool and by the call that has been made for naturalistic studies of programs that integrate handicapped and nonhandicapped children (Baldwin and Baldwin, 1974; Wynne, Ulfelder, and Dakof, 1975). In particular, we aimed to respond to some of the concerns that have been raised by these programs, among them fears that handicapped children will necessarily receive either a disproportionately greater or smaller amount of their teachers' attention, will be ostracized by their nonhandicapped peers, will be disruptive and serve as models of inappropriate behavior for nonhandicapped children, and/or will be frustrated by classroom demands they cannot possibly meet.

Our own perspective on these issues had led us to expect that, while in individual cases integration may not be advisable, in many more cases the exposure of handicapped children to models of normal peer functioning could lead to gains in terms of social, cognitive, and motor skills. We were also optimistic that handicapped and nonhandicapped preschoolers would of their own accord, as well as with some teacher encouragement, involve each other in their play and that their interactions would generally be positive in tone.

The research literature, however, gave no conclusive support for our optimism regarding social interactions in integrated preschool classrooms. In the one preschool program that has reported clearly positive effects attributable to integration, nonhandicapped children were trained to be models and to reward certain behaviors of their handicapped peers. Early attempts to integrate handicapped and nonhandicapped children without special training have produced only limited effects for widely heterogeneous groups of children (see Guralnick, 1976).

As pointed out by Guralnick (1976), whose own work was based on direct observations of the level of social play, few studies on the social integration among handicapped and nonhandicapped children have been based on observations of actual interactive behaviors. Results of sociometric and projective testing have suggested that children become aware of other children's physical handicaps at about the age of four, and that during the next few years their attitudes toward the handicapped waver between acceptance (Kennedy and Bruininks, 1974) and rejection (Billings, 1963; Jones and Sisk, 1967). However, because young children's responses to such attitude tests are known to lack stability (Lawrence and Winischel, 1973) and often to be unrelated to their actual behavior (Goodman, 1952), these findings must be interpreted with caution. It should also be noted that young children's reactions to peers whose handicaps are emotional or mental rather than physical have not been explored.

Moreover, researchers who have relied on sociometric and projective techniques with older children have suggested that the type and severity of the handicapped children's disabilities, the attitudes of parents and teachers (Kennedy and Bruinicks, 1974; Lazar, Gensley, and Orpet, 1971), and the length of time children have been integrated (Monroe and Howe, 1971) are important variables influencing the attitudes of nonhandicapped children toward handicapped peers. These qualifications supported our own hopes that, given an accepting, stimulating environment with much attention to and respect for individual needs, children would be open to children different from themselves.

In addition, despite apparently widespread concern that, in integrated classrooms, either handicapped or nonhandicapped children (or both) will be cheated in terms of the amount of individualized teacher-attention they experience (e.g., Joslin, 1976), the literature search turned up no previous studies on this issue. Nor have there been any data on the differential behaviors directed toward teachers by handicapped and nonhandicapped children.

It thus became clear that, both for program evaluation and for the sake of supplementing the existing body of basic research on these issues, a study examining classroom interactions in some detail was needed. In addition, because of the limitations of projective and sociometric testing, it was important that the study be based on systematic but naturalistic observations of the classrooms.

Classroom Interactions: Method

Participating Children The subjects of the study included four female teachers and twenty-eight children attending the two High/Scope First Chance Preschool classrooms during the 1975-1976 winter months. The children included eight handicapped boys, two handicapped girls, eight nonhandicapped boys, and ten nonhandicapped girls. When observations began, the mean chronological ages of the nonhandicapped and handicapped children were 4.00 (range = 2.83-5.17) and 5.13 (range = 3.04-7.06) years, respectively.

Observational Procedures Using a standard thirty-second time-sampling procedure, the two authors acted as nonparticipant observers. Observations were made only during work time and only when at least two handicapped children were present. Observers were careful to stay within earshot of the children but to interact with them as minimally as possible. Most children ignored the observers entirely. Each child was observed four times, each time for twelve minutes. No two observations on a given child occurred less than three days apart.

Code sheets contained checklists of behavior categories chosen to measure children's general affective state and to capture the tenor of social behaviors directed to, and received from, peers and teachers. For each category except "facial expression," the name(s) of the child(ren) toward whom the behavior had been directed (or from whom it had been received) was noted. When the interaction with a target child involved a teacher, the letter "T" was recorded for that interval next to the appropriate behavior category. When the interaction involved other children, each child's name was written down. If more than three children were involved, "group" was written. The categories were not revealed to teachers until the research had been completed; nor were they aware that their actions as well as those of the children were being observed.

Behavior Categories The behavior categories and the directions for the observers were as follows:

Facial expression—Rate according to the following seven-point scale: (1) crying with tears; (2) whimpering, whining, no tears; (3) frowning, sighing, eyes downcast; (4) neutral, sober attentive; (5) brightening, fleeting smile; (6) smiling broadly; (7) laughing.
Type of social play—Indicate whether the child is engaged in unoccupied behavior, in solitary, parallel, associative, or cooperative play. Use Parten's (1932) definitions with the exception that her category, "onlooker," is to be omitted; the categories "unoccupied" and "observes" are to be marked in its stead. Mark down all types of play that occur during the thirty seconds.

Converses—Child is engaged in a conversation with another child or teacher. Both participants speak at least twice.

Leads—Child is imitated, followed, and/or his or her orders are obeyed. Includes all instances in which the child becomes a leader of sorts, whether or not he or she so intended. Does not include instances when the child is being helped without having asked to be helped. If, however, he or she asks to be helped, and the request is heeded, then "leads" is to be checked as well as "asks help" and "receives help."

Orders—Child consciously tries to initiate and/or structure another persons's activity. Includes statements such as "You be the baby." The category is not mutually exclusive with "leads." The difference is in the fact that "orders" takes into account the intention of the target child, and "leads" implies the reactions of those around the child.

Follows—Behaviors to be included under this category are the direct opposite of those under "leads." Here the child is complying with the command of another or imitating actions whether or not he or she has been asked to do so. Does not include helping that was not requested.

Asks help—Child asks for direct physical assistance, such as "Make me a house," "Help me carry this." Does not include requests for explanations or information. May include statements like, "I can't do this" if the intent is clearly to get assistance.

Gives help—Child helps another person by doing something for him or her such as helping clean up, showing how to make something, giving necessary information, etc.

Receives help—Child is given help, as defined under "gives help."

Refuses to comply—Child refuses to comply with another person's order or request for help, information, etc. Includes refusing to share with another child, to play the role another person has asked him or her to play, etc. The category also includes instances when a child is misbehaving according to the established norms of the classroom, even if the child has not at that moment been given a direct sanction. For example, if the child is throwing toys around, the category would be marked with a "T" (for "teacher") even if the teacher takes no notice of the event.

Is refused by others—Behaviors included here come not from the child being observed but from others who have not complied with an explicit request or command the child has made. The wishes of the target child must be verbal and explicit (although in the case of a speech-impaired child clear gestures indicating desire are sufficient), but the other's noncompliance may be either verbal or simply seeming not to pay attention.

Hurts—Child attempts to physically or verbally hurt another. Does not include accidents or noncompliance that is not overtly aggressive.

Abused—Child is the object of verbal or physical aggression. Does not include accidents or noncompliance that is not overtly aggressive.

Defends rights—Target child asserts his or her rights to property, to position, etc., when in fact the child does have a just claim. Child protects her- or himself from being hit, stops a name-caller, refuses to allow someone to take away materials or position. If the defense is aggressive in nature, as defined under "hurts," check both categories (as well as "refuses to comply").

Doesn't defend rights—Child surrenders to attacker, does not protect rights. Includes instances of child being hit and "taking it," of allowing another person to grab something away, etc.

Gives affection—Child shows physical and/or verbal affection.

Receives affection—Child is the recipient of affectionate behavior.

Shows pride—Child comments on own accomplishment or ability, shows work to teacher (when teacher has not asked to see it), etc. Includes statements such as, "Look what I made!" May also include comparative statements such as, "My tower is bigger than his!"

Takes—Child takes object from another person whether or not it is offered. This category may be checked in conjunction with "receives help" or "hurts."

Gives/Shows—Child gives or shows an object to another person. May be checked in conjunction with "orders," "shows/pride," or "gives help."

Requests materials—Child asks for materials. Includes statements such as, "I need the red one," "Give me the tractor."

Is observed—Someone watches target child for at least four consecutive seconds.

Observes—Child watches someone for at least four consecutive seconds.

Reliability Percentage agreement between the two observers was assessed on the basis of simultaneous, independent scoring of the behavior of eleven children. Reliability was calculated separately for each behavior category by dividing the number of agreements by the combined number of agreements and disagreements. Across categories, the mean agreement between observers was 95.1 percent.

Data Analysis For each child, ratings of facial expression were averaged and separate sums were computed for each of the levels of social play. In cases in which two levels of social play had been marked for one thirty-second interval, each received one-half point, regardless of the actual proportion of the interval it occupied. For each of the remaining categories, first the number of intervals in which either the name of a child or a "T" had been marked was computed. In cases in which children were involved with more than one child during an interval, each child was counted separately, even when the interactions were described by the same behavior category. Student's t tests were then performed to determine whether or not there were significant differences between handicapped and nonhandicapped children in terms of either the number of interactions involving peers or the number of interactions involving teachers.

Additional scoring involved determining for each child both the observed and expected number of times social behaviors were directed to (or received from) handicapped and nonhandicapped classmates. The two scores for observed behaviors were simply sums of the number of intervals in which the child had been involved with handicapped and nonhandicapped children. Expected scores were derived on the basis of the proportion of handicapped to nonhandicapped children present in the classroom on the days when observations were made. Thus, for example, the expected number of times a given nonhandicapped child would have "followed" handicapped children was determined by dividing the number of handicapped children present by the total number of children present and multiplying this fraction by the total number of times the child had "followed" children. This computation resulted in a figure that indicated how often the child would have "followed" handicapped as opposed to nonhandicapped children, had his or her choices of partners been random with respect to handicappedness. Finally, Student's t tests for paired samples were performed to compare the observed and expected frequencies with which (1) handicapped children interacted with handicapped children, and (2) nonhandicapped children interacted with handicapped children. The small sample sizes did not permit testing for sex differences.

Analysis of Social and Emotional Behavior

Teacher-Child Interactions In terms of interactions involving a teacher, the only difference to reach significance ($p < .05$) revealed nonhandicapped children to show pride by calling a teacher's attention to their work more frequently than did handicapped children ($t(26) = 2.45, p < .05$). Near-significant results suggested that handicapped children refused to follow teacher requests and classroom rules more often than did their nonhandicapped peers. A second trend suggested that handicapped children also asked teachers for materials more often than did nonhandicapped children.

Children's Emotional Tone, Social Play, and Peer Interactions Among handicapped children, the mean rating for facial expression was 3.93, or slightly less than "neutral." The mean rating for nonhandicapped children, 4.53, was between "neutral" and "bright." This difference approached but did not reach statistical significance.

As shown in Table 1, there were no differences between handicapped and nonhandicapped children in terms of the level of social play. Comparisons of the total mean frequencies with which handicapped and nonhandicapped children engaged in behaviors described by the remaining behavior categories, however, yielded several significant differences ($p < .05$). Compared to nonhandicapped children, handicapped children less frequently: (1) conversed with peers ($t(26) = 2.13, p < .05$); (2) verbally expressed pride to peers ($t(26) = 2.27, p < .05$); and (3) gave and showed materials to peers ($t(26) = 2.15, p < .05$). Although not reaching statistical significance the results also suggested that handicapped children were somewhat more likely to ask peers for help than were nonhandicapped children. Finally, there was a tendency for children to be somewhat less willing to comply with the wishes of handicapped children than with those of nonhandicapped children.

These results do not, however, tell us anything about the degree to which handicapped and nonhandicapped children interacted with each other; they do not, for example, tell us to whom handicapped children went for help. Consequently, we compared the observed and expected number of times children interacted with handicapped or nonhandicapped children. The results of these analyses gave little indication that handicapped and nonhandicapped children were not socially well integrated, since the expected and observed frequencies of interaction for the various observational categories were highly similar.

Among the handicapped children, the only difference between ob-

Table 1. Mean frequencies and standard deviations for the levels of social play

Levels of social play	Handicapped children [a] Mean	S.D.	Nonhandicapped children [b] Mean	S.D.
Unoccupied	4.45	3.93	2.78	3.30
Solitary or parallel	24.45	7.44	27.64	6.73
Associative	8.75	9.03	7.31	7.38
Cooperative	0	0	0.92	3.04

[a] N = 10.
[b] N = 18.

served and expected frequencies to even approach significance was in terms of asking for help. Handicapped children were never observed to turn to other handicapped children for help. Among nonhandicapped children, there was a tendency to refuse to comply with the wishes of handicapped children more frequently than would have been expected on the basis of chance alone. Yet nonhandicapped children also observed handicapped children more frequently than would have been expected ($t(16) = 2.48, p < .05$). No other differences even approached significance.

Upon first examination of these results, we suspected there might have been a greater number of significant differences had the sample size been larger. While we could not, at this point, increase the number of subjects, we could create summary scores for those nonoverlapping categories that were conceptually related. For example, we summed "play" and "conversing," "asks help" and "receives help," "gives help" and "gives affection," "gives materials" and "takes materials," "refuses to follow" and "others refuse," and "hurts" and "abused." Despite this, the only difference between observed and expected summary scores to even approach significance suggested that nonhandicapped children gave affection to and received affection from handicapped children more often than might have been expected.

Classroom Interactions: Discussion and Implications

For the two High/Scope First Chance Preschool classrooms, the results create a general picture of social integration among handicapped and nonhandicapped children. There is no indication that the two groups segregated themselves from each other. With one exception, the differences between observed and expected scores that did emerge instead suggest positive interaction.

Handicapped children seem to have perceived nonhandicapped children as persons to whom they could go for help. Very possibly, their apparent preference for nonhandicapped over handicapped classmates in terms of asking for help reflected accurate perceptions of the former group's greater strength and skill. At the same time, taking into account the other behaviors observed, there was no indication that handicapped children shunned other handicapped children.

The finding that nonhandicapped children joined handicapped children more frequently than expected in the giving and receiving of affection suggests active involvement between the two groups and perhaps some degree of solicitousness on the part of nonhandicapped children toward handicapped children. That handicapped children asked nonhandicapped children for help more often than was expected supports this interpretation;

it may be supposed that handicapped children approached nonhandicapped children for help because past experiences had given them reason to expect that their requests would be heeded.

It is interesting that teachers' informal observations supported this conclusion. They themselves were touched by the gentleness with which children interacted with their more severely handicapped classmates. This was true even for the "rougher" of the nonhandicapped children. Several nonhandicapped and one moderately handicapped child spent time trying to "teach" a Down's syndrome child to talk, to pass out napkins at snack time, etc. Children also learned to encourage a child with a spastic arm to use it, pretending to fall over when he touched them with his affected arm, not when he touched them with his good arm. In other instances, stronger children spontaneously helped the frailer handicapped children to carry heavy objects. In several cases, remarks made by children suggested that they saw some of the handicapped children as younger, and therefore as in need of more care. This, interestingly enough, did not always depend on who was older and taller, the handicapped child or the nonhandicapped child.

Interpretation of the finding that nonhandicapped children observed handicapped children more often than was expected is somewhat more difficult. It may be that nonhandicapped children were interested in watching handicapped children because they saw some of their behaviors to be unusual; one handicapped child who was observed by children a great deal, for example, was emotionally disturbed and also very active. At times it was almost inevitable that he caught the children's attention.

In this study there was no direct test of the proposition that, in integrated classrooms, nonhandicapped children will imitate the inappropriate behaviors of the handicapped. There was, however, evidence that nonhandicapped children refused to follow more of the suggestions of handicapped children than would have been expected had they been operating randomly with respect to handicappedness. Whether or not this was attributable to handicapped children trying to get nonhandicapped children to join them in inappropriate activities cannot be discerned from our data. If this was the case, then it can be said that nonhandicapped preschoolers do resist suggestions that they take to be inappropriate. Of course, the difference between observed and expected scores for the category "refuses to follow" may have resulted from other factors, such as handicapped children being less adept at offering suggestions or less involved in activities that nonhandicapped children would find interesting.

Results in terms of teacher-child interaction are perhaps most remarkable in giving no clear indication that teachers treated handicapped children very differently from nonhandicapped children. While some teachers in integrated classrooms may tend to devote most of their attention to the handicapped children (or, the converse, to ignore them), it seems that skillful teachers following a coherent open framework curriculum can avoid such partiality.

Certain predictable differences emerged between the way teachers interacted with handicapped and nonhandicapped children. For example, nonhandicapped children, as compared to their handicapped classmates, more often "showed off" their work to teachers. Our figures for the category, "shows pride," give no way of knowing whether nonhandicapped children were in fact more proud of their work or whether they engaged in more activities that resulted in products that might be displayed. Another possibility is that, because the category "shows pride" was defined in such a way as to stress verbal expressions of pride, the observers missed nonverbal manifestations of pride. This possibility is particularly important since seven of the ten handicapped children showed language impairment.

The near-significant finding that handicapped children tended to be less compliant with classroom rules and teacher requests than the nonhandicapped children supports the common understanding that, as a group, handicapped children do seem to pose somewhat more behavior problems than do nonhandicapped children.

The trend suggesting that handicapped children asked teachers to bring them materials more often than did nonhandicapped children is perhaps not surprising. It stands to reason that children with physical and/or mental handicaps cannot be as independent as most children; their asking more frequently for the teacher's help in finding, reaching, and carrying materials is simply a manifestation of their greater dependence on adults. Teachers who work with handicapped children will have to remember that these children may need more support than other children to locate and obtain materials.

On the whole, the results of the study are most encouraging. Teachers using the Cognitively Oriented Curriculum at the High/Scope First Chance Preschool seem to have been successful in running their classrooms in such a way as to truly integrate handicapped and nonhandicapped children. A word of caution must be raised, however, before the results are generalized either to other preschools following the Cognitively Oriented Curriculum or to preschools in general. First, it is possible that more significant differences may have been found had the sample sizes been larger. Second, the results must be seen as characterizing a particular set of teachers and children and a particular curriculum. With a different curriculum, different teachers, and children with different handicaps, results may have been quite different. Only further studies of the same nature will be able to answer the question of the specificity of the present results to the present samples.

SUMMATIVE EVALUATION OF CHILDREN'S ABILITIES IN THE INTEGRATED PRESCHOOL

(The McCarthy Scales of Children's Abilities)

For the purpose of summative program evaluation, we pre- and posttested children with the McCarthy Scales of Children's Abilities (MSCA). We are well aware of the shortcomings of norm-referenced tests (see Ginsburg, 1972; Sattler, 1974) and the limitations of traditional procedures for child assessment (Bond, Epstein, and Matz, 1976). However, because of the difficulty in finding a comparison group with the same combination of characteristics as the children in our First Chance project, the use of a norm-referenced test is the only currently available means of determining whether the children progress more than could be expected on the basis of maturation alone.

The MSCA (McCarthy, 1970) is a standardized test with five reliable scales measuring verbal, perceptual-performance, quantitative, memory, and motor skills. The general cognitive scale is a weighted summary of the verbal, perceptual, and quantitative scales. The MSCA has been validated in terms of its ability to predict school achievement. We selected it because it covers a wide range of items and because it is designed for use with children as young as two and one-half years.

Overall Results

Previous evaluations of the open framework curriculum (see Weikart et al., 1970) led us to expect the children to achieve marked increases in MSCA scaled indexes between September and May. The results confirm this expectation. Frequency distributions of pre- and posttest scores of handicapped and nonhandicapped children for the general cognitive scale are portrayed in Figures 1 and 2. The distributions for the other MSCA scales resemble the distributions in these figures.

The scale index is analagous to an IQ score in that both reflect the relationship of a child's mean raw score to the mean and standard deviation of a national sample. Thus, an increase in a child's scale index is assumed to represent advancement in comparison to his or her age-mates. As shown in Table 2, paired Student's t tests revealed dramatic changes for all the scales of the MSCA for the combined group of children.

Another way of looking at the practical significance of this result is in terms of "mental age" scores. Each child's scale index may be converted

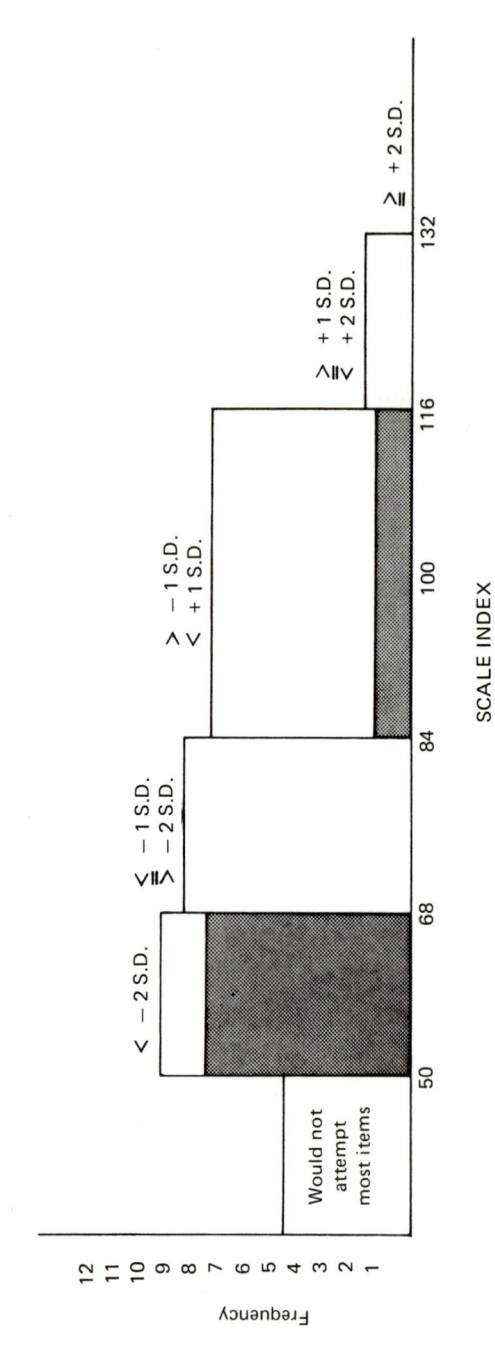

Figure 1. Distribution of pretest MSCA general cognitive scores. (Shaded area indicates placement of handicapped children.)

Cognitively Oriented Program 185

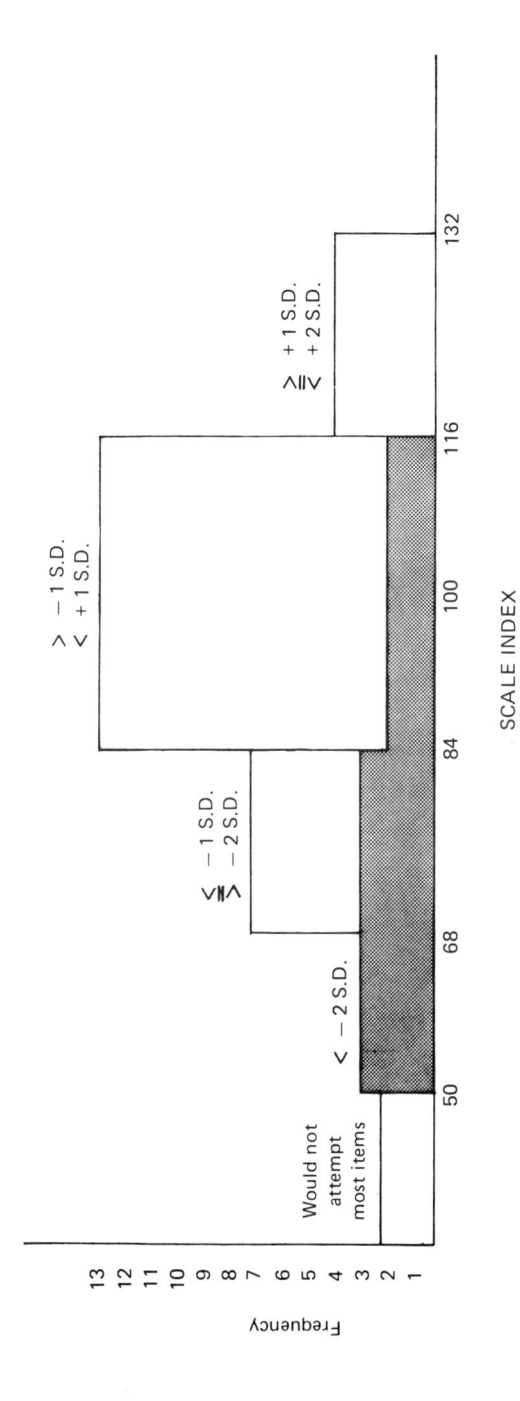

Figure 2. Distribution of posttest MSCA general cognitive scores. (Shaded area indicates placement of handicapped children.)

Table 2. Paired Student's t tests comparing pretest and posttest indexes for the MSCA [a]

Scale	Pretest Mean	S.D.	Posttest Mean	S.D.	$p<$
Verbal	38.16	11.56	45.36	11.87	0.001
Perceptual-performance	37.04	12.27	47.16	13.43	0.001
Quantitative	41.04	13.05	46.40	12.61	0.01
General cognitive	77.20	22.36	92.60	22.33	0.001
Memory	41.64	11.70	46.48	12.06	0.002
Motor	37.20	11.36	43.24	12.94	0.002

[a] $N = 25$.

to a mental age score, which roughly estimates the age level at which the child functioned in the test situation. According to the test scores, attendance in the First Chance Preschool project has been associated with an average gain of 2.07 months in mental age for each month of preschool, or 7.2 months total growth more than could be expected on the basis of maturation alone.

We decided against using pretest results in formative-diagnostic planning for individual children because of the potential dangers of stereotyping and of increasing teacher-directed activity at the expense of child-directed activity. In part, this decision was based upon our confidence in the efficacy of the High/Scope daily planning and evaluation process. The posttest results support this confidence: In all but one instance, those children whose pretest scores were more than two standard deviations below the mean on three or fewer of the McCarthy Scales showed more even profiles in the spring. Their posttest scores on each of the scales were all above two standard deviations below the mean. That is, the children for whom we might have used the McCarthy Scales diagnostically at the beginning of the year did not demonstrate the need for such use at the end of the year.

Gains of Handicapped Children

The preferred statistical method for testing whether nonhandicapped students achieved significantly greater gains in MSCA scores than their handicapped peers is to employ an analysis of covariance with the spring score as the dependent variable and the fall score as the predictor variable, or covariate (O'Connor, 1972). Table 3 provides a summary of these analyses.

The only comparison near statistical significance is for the motor scale. (Because of the nature of some children's physical disabilities, it may be unreasonable to expect progress analogous to that of nonhandicapped children.) With the exception of motor skills, these results indicate that both handicapped and nonhandicapped children achieved similar average gains in MSCA indexes. Another way to examine the performance of the handicapped group is to compare scores for the handicapped group only. For this group the pre- and posttest indexes respectively were: verbal, 27.88, 34.75; perceptual-performance, 27.50, 35.63; quantitative, 30.00, 36.25; general cognitive, 56.00, 72.38; memory, 30.38, 35.88; and motor, 25.63, 28.63. Of course, the size of the sample requires caution in generalizing from these results. (Additionally, the handicapped children made advances similar to the nonhandicapped on the Child Observation Record and the Preschool Productive Language Assessment Tasks, two instruments we are developing. In our Program Performance Report (Banet, 1976) we discuss other aspects of our evaluation work, including the issue of possible artifacts affecting the summative outcomes.)

Table 3. Analysis of covariance summary: Comparison between handicapped and nonhandicapped children on posttest means adjusted for pretest scores

MSCA scale	Nonhandicapped [a] or handicapped [b]	Mean (posttest)	Adjusted mean	$p<$
Verbal	Nonhandicapped	50.35	46.41	
	Handicapped	34.75	43.13	
Perceptual-performance	Nonhandicapped	52.59	48.65	
	Handicapped	35.62	43.99	
Quantitative	Nonhandicapped	51.18	48.07	
	Handicapped	36.25	42.85	
General cognitive	Nonhandicapped	102.12	93.25	
	Handicapped	72.38	91.23	
Memory	Nonhandicapped	51.47	47.40	
	Handicapped	35.88	44.54	
Motor	Nonhandicapped	50.12	47.72	
	Handicapped	28.62	33.72	0.01 [c]

[a] $N = 17$.
[b] $N = 8$.
[c] For this comparison only, the assumption of equal slopes did not hold.

SUMMARY AND CONCLUSIONS

The results of our research have buoyed our confidence that the Cognitively Oriented Curriculum is well suited for preschool classrooms integrating nonhandicapped children and handicapped children represented by the handicapping conditions described earlier. Systematic, naturalistic observations of social and emotional behaviors in the two High/Scope First Chance Preschool classrooms indicated that handicapped and nonhandicapped children were socially well integrated and that teachers' interactions with handicapped children were similar to their interactions with nonhandicapped children. In addition, over the course of the school year, handicapped children achieved equivalent gains to nonhandicapped children on each of the McCarthy Scales of Children's Abilities except the motor scale.

The favorable results probably can be attributed to several factors. Elements of the curriculum that support active exploration and developmentally appropriate use of materials, the natural use of language through child-child and teacher-child conversations about ongoing and past events and feelings, the emphasis on first planning, then carrying out, and finally reviewing activities, all seem to be important in this regard. It may be supposed that these curriculum components help children develop self-sufficiency and the ability to organize their time while supporting intrinsic interest in learning and in social communication. These abilities and interests may, in turn, enable children to interact in a positive way with others different from themselves.

Aspects of the program that are less specific to this particular curriculum have no doubt been important as well. Most simply, preschoolers are young, too young perhaps, to have the preconceived negative attitudes toward handicappedness that seem to interfere with the development of positive relationships between older children and adults and the handicapped. Second, being exposed to nonhandicapped peers probably enabled the handicapped children to develop, or continue to develop, "normal" behavior. Nonhandicapped children seem to have stimulated handicapped children to become involved in activities they might not otherwise have attempted, encouraged them both by serving as models and by offering them the challenge of and reinforcement for interactive play. In turn, the more skilled the handicapped children became, the greater were the chances for interaction between the two groups. The tenderness that the needs of some of the weaker handicapped children brought out in even the most boisterous children suggests that nonhandicapped children were also able to make necessary adjustments and to gain from the experience.

During the course of the year, particularly during the latter half, visitors, teachers, and the authors noted that, because all of the children, handicapped and nonhandicapped, had their own strengths as well as their weaknesses, their interactions were little different from those characterizing an all nonhandicapped group. This pattern was facilitated by the attitudes and strategies of teachers, which were aimed at keeping each child's strengths in the foreground.

ACKNOWLEDGMENTS

The authors are indebted to all of the staff of the High/Scope Demonstration Preschool Project (Bernard Banet, director; Linda J. Rogers, assistant director) for their cooperation. Teachers Marilyn Adams, Sara Jane Adler, Sharon Bixby, and Isabel Flores not only accepted our frequent presence in their classrooms, but also were a ready and critical audience for our initial drafts. Bob Hanvey and Arthur Granville assisted with the processing and analysis of the data. The typing was done by Sarah Prueter and Becki McLaughlin.

REFERENCES CITED

Baldwin, C. P., and Baldwin, A. L. 1974. Personal and social development of handicapped children. In C. Sherrick, R. Haber, W. Wickelgren, P. Suppes, E. Lenneberg, B. S. Long, V. Douglas, C. and A. Baldwin, J. Swets,and L. Elliot (Eds.), Psychology and the Handicapped Child. Washington, D.C.: U.S. Government Printing Office.

Banet, B. 1976. Program Performance Report. High/Scope Demonstration Preschool Project. Ypsilanti, Mich.: High/Scope Educational Research Foundation.

Baumrind, D. 1973. Will a day care center be a child development center? Young Children, 28, 154–160.

Billings, H. K. 1963. An exploratory study of the attitude of noncrippled children toward crippled children in three selected elementary schools. Journal of Experimental Education, 31, 381–387.

Bond, J. T., Epstein, A., and Matz, R. D. 1976. Methods for assessing the language production of the young child (Mimeo). Ypsilanti, Mich.: High/Scope Educational Research Foundation.

Goodman, M. E. 1952. Race Awareness in Young Children. Reading, Mass.: Addison-Wesley.

Ginsburg, H. 1972. The Myth of the Deprived Child. Englewood Cliffs, N.J.: Prentice-Hall.

Guralnick, M. 1976. The value of integrating handicapped and nonhandicapped preschool children. American Journal of Orthopsychiatry, 46, 236–245.

Hohmann, M., Coppersmith, G., Banet, B., and D. Weikart. (In press). The Cognitively Oriented Preschool Curriculum. Ypsilanti, Mich.: High/Scope Educational Research Foundation.

Jones, R. L., and Sisk, D. A. 1967. Early perceptions of orthopedic disability. Exceptional Children, 34, 42–43.

Joslin, N. H. 1976. Teachers' experiences in Massachusetts. Today's Education, March-April, 24-25.

Kennedy, P., and Bruininks, R. H. 1974. Social status of hearing-impaired children in regular classrooms. Exceptional Children, 40, 336-342.

Lawrence, E. A., and Winischel, J. F. 1973. Self-concept and the retarded: Research and issues. Exceptional Children, 39, 310-319.

Lazar, A. L., Gensley, J. T., and Orpet, R. E. 1971. Changing attitudes of young mentally gifted children toward handicapped persons. Exceptional Children, 37, 600-602.

McCarthy, D. 1970. Manual for the McCarthy Scales of Children's Abilities. New York: The Psychological Corporation.

Monroe, J. D., and Howe, C. E. 1971. The effects of integration and social class on the acceptance of retarded adolescents. Education and Training of the Mentally Retarded, 6, 21-24.

O'Connor, E. F. 1972. Extending classical test theory to the measurement of change. Review of Educational Research, 42, 73-97.

Parten, M. B. 1932. Social participation among preschool children. Journal of Abnormal and Social Psychology, 27, 243-269.

Sattler, J. M. 1974. Assessment of Children's Intelligence. Philadelphia: W. B. Saunders.

Weikart, D. P. 1974. Curriculum for early childhood special education. Focus on Exceptional Children, 6, 1-8.

Weikart, D. P., Deloria, D. J., Lawser, S. A., and Weigerink, R. 1970. Longitudinal Results of the Ypsilanti Perry Preschool Project. Ypsilanti, Mich.: High/Scope Educational Research Foundation.

Wynne, S., Ulfelder, L., and Dakof, G. 1975. Mainstreaming and Early Childhood Education for Handicapped Children: Review and Implications for Research. Washington, D.C.: Wynne Associates. (Report prepared for the Division of Innovation and Development, Bureau of Education for the Handicapped, U.S. Department of Health, Education, and Welfare.)

INTEGRATING THE MODERATELY AND SEVERELY HANDICAPPED PRESCHOOL CHILD INTO A NORMAL DAY CARE SETTING

H. D. Bud Fredericks, Ed.D., Victor Baldwin, Ed.D., David Grove, Ph.D., William Moore, Ed.D., Cheryl Riggs, and Barbara Lyons

We are currently faced with a bandwagon movement to mainstream the mildly handicapped child into normal classroom settings. This mainstreaming effort presumes that the child will spend the bulk of his or her time in the normal setting and will receive special education support from specialists or resource personnel. The additional resources assist children to overcome specific deficits to enable them to function more effectively in the normal setting, as well as to help the teacher in that setting by providing training in special teaching techniques for the handicapped children. As yet, there has been little effort to mainstream moderately or severely handicapped children. Yet, it may be appropriate to consider integration of such children into regular programs.

It is necessary to distinguish between our use of the terms "integration" and "mainstreaming." Mainstreaming, as noted, assumes that the handicapped child will be primarily maintained in the normal setting and receive whatever special education support is necessary. Integration, on the other hand, implies that the child's primary educational environment is special and that the bulk of the child's time will be spent in that special education environment except for certain activities or certain times of the day during which the child will be with normal children.

Integration actually occurs at a number of different levels. First, there is the integration of self-contained special education classrooms into public school buildings. This is technically a misuse of the term in that the classrooms in this case are mainstreamed into the normal public schools although the children within the classrooms are still segregated. Integration of children from those self-contained classrooms into various activities conducted with the normal children, however, is a bona fide form of integration. Children may be integrated for certain activities such as recess, lunch, music, or physical education. A more difficult type of integration to achieve is the placement of handicapped children in specific academic settings for the teaching of academic or developmental skills. It is in this latter sense that this chapter talks of integration.

A fundamental question to ask is why we even consider integration of the moderately or severely handicapped. The answer is that the concept of normalization requires it (Wolfensberger, 1972). There are two underlying aspects of this concept. One is that the environment for the handicapped individual be as normal as possible so that he or she can have the rights and privileges to which every individual is entitled. The second suggests that exposure to a normal environment will promote the development of the handicapped person.

Smith and Arkans (1974) argue that services for the severely handicapped can be best delivered in a special class. Yet Devalk (1966) makes the case that for preschool children it is not only possible but economical to mainstream them. Few have systematically examined the effects of integration on preschool moderately and severely handicapped children. Certainly the problem of training teachers to teach mildly handicapped children in regular classrooms is so involved that to expand the concept of mainstreaming to the severely handicapped may seem unreasonable at this time.

The problems associated with integrating and mainstreaming moderately and severely handicapped children (especially the latter) reflect the complex needs of these children. Although a definition of their characteristics is elusive because of the wide range of individual differences, for purposes of this chapter we define severely handicapped children as those with a major deficit in more than one of the basic developmental areas of language, self-help skills, motor skills, or socialization and who require extensive structure for learning to occur (see Justen, 1976). Since we are focusing on developmental programs, we have chosen to describe the deficits in developmental terms. A similar description can be provided for moderately handicapped children. However, in view of the complexities and the uneven developmental rates common to preschool children, the reader is referred to standard classification manuals (e.g., Grossman, 1973) as a first approximation only. A more detailed behavioral description of the children in our project is presented in the next section.

EVALUATING THE INTEGRATION OF MODERATELY AND SEVERELY HANDICAPPED PRESCHOOL CHILDREN

In an effort to determine more precisely the difficulties or benefits of integrating moderately and severely handicapped children into a setting with normal children, a study was recently conducted by the Teaching Research Infant and Child Center. In designing this study, we assumed that the moderately or severely handicapped child would not be likely to benefit from an integration program without specialized procedures. This was based on the recognition that the handicapped child's level of skill development and behaviors are so different from those of the normal child's that it would be asking far too much of a regular classroom teacher of normal children to accommodate to the significant deficits presented by these children without these additional supports. However, it was hypothesized that, given a level of prerequisite behaviors and specialized treatment, there may be some benefits which could accrue to the handicapped child by systematic exposure to normal peers.

It was believed that these beneifts would be manifested in two major areas. The first of these is socialization, namely, the ability to relate with and to play with peers. Devoney, Guralnick, and Rubin (1974) and Guralnick (1976) have demonstrated some positive effects on the social play of the handicapped population by mixing handicapped with nonhandicapped children, although most of the children were not classified as severely or moderately handicapped. The second area where integration might have a favorable effect is language. Therefore, the purposes of this study were to examine the effects of integration on (1) the socialization skills of moderately and severely handicapped children as manifested in their play behavior, and (2) the language behavior of the handicapped children.

Promoting Social Play and Language Behaviors: Method

Description of Children The data reported herein were gathered from six children who participated in an integration program over a six-month period. Socialization and language skills of the six participating children were monitored to determine if integration affected these two areas. The children chosen to participate in the study were enrolled in a preschool program for handicapped children. The site chosen for integration was a day care center for normally functioning children. Selection of the handicapped children was based on the following criteria: (1) each child could emit and imitate some language behavior in the preschool handicapped program; and (2) the handicapped children were within one year of chronological age of the day care center children with whom they were integrated.

Two of the six children were classified as autistic. One (child A) engaged in frequent echolalic language, responded to questions with inappropriate or nonsense language, and engaged in much self-stimulatory behavior. The other autistic child (child C) also used echolalic language and frequently failed to respond to requests or questions; she exhibited no social responses to other children. Three mentally retarded children were also included in the group to be integrated. Child B was diagnosed as brain damaged. He exhibited severe language delay although he could speak in two- to three-word phrases; his delay was also apparent in his fine and gross motor abilities and in prereading and writing skills. Child E had phenylketonuria and exhibited inappropriate social behaviors and significant delays in prereading and writing skills. Child F, a Down's syndrome child, exhibited language delay, poor motor coordination, and delays in prereading and writing skills. The sixth child to be integrated (child D) had cerebral palsy with severe lower limb motor dysfunction, severe language delay, and delays in prereading and writing skills. The age range of the handicapped children was from four to seven years; the age range of the nonhandicapped children in the day care center was three to six. The mean age of the handicapped children at the start of the academic year was five years, one month. The mean age of the nonhandicapped population was four years, nine months.

Outcome Measures and Observation Methods Language skill was monitored by looking at three aspects of the verbal and nonverbal behavior of the handicapped children. The first was a measure of the number of verbal initiations and responses that were emitted. The second was the length of sentences or phrases emitted, and the third was the percentage of time that a child interacted with his peers, both handicapped and nonhandicapped, either verbally or nonverbally. It is recognized that these language interactions are also a form of socialization and relate to the socialization measures used.

The second major area of measurement was the social behaviors of the children in relation to activities with other children. The Parten scale (Parten, 1932) was utilized as the instrument to conduct that measurement. This developmental scale provides definitions of children's social play behaviors and classifies them into unoccupied, solitary, onlooker, parallel, associative, and cooperative play. For purposes of this study, the definitions of associative and cooperative play as specified in the Parten scale were combined into one category.

The language data were gathered in continuous samples of ten minutes each. Samples on the Parten scale were taken over a ten-minute period on an intermittent observation schedule. The observer observed for ten seconds, recorded the major social behavior which occurred during that ten-second interval, did not observe for twenty seconds, reobserved again for ten seconds, and so on for the ten-minute period. Consequently, twenty observations were recorded for each child during the course of a ten-minute period.

In order to have a standard against which the behaviors of the handicapped population could be measured, observations were also taken on five nonhandicapped children in the day care center to establish a baseline of normal performance in the areas of language and socialization as measured by the instruments utilized.

Settings It was necessary that all data be obtained in settings where children could freely interact socially and verbally. Two environmental settings were chosen that had this characteristic. The first of these was the motor room where children could engage in free play on various apparatus or with toys. The other was during art sessions where children were able to communicate, interact, and engage in cooperative projects with minimum environmental constraints.

It is important to note that the primary placement of the handicapped children was in a special class, but they joined the regular classroom for art, gross motor play, lunch, and various other special activities. The ratio of handicapped to nonhandicapped children was 7.5:1, and this ratio was maintained even when smaller groups were formed. The typical teacher-child ratio in the integrated setting was 15:1. A daily average of five trained volunteers were also included to assist in the facilitation process (see Fredericks et al., 1975 for a description of the training process and procedures).

Procedure and Design Pretreatment baseline data were taken over a five-day period for both the nonhandicapped and the handicapped children in each of the environmental settings for each of the language and socialization measures. Once pretreatment baseline data had been gathered, the plan was to have the staff assist or facilitate the handicapped children to increase their socialization and language skills through modeling and by reinforcing normal peers and the handicapped children for interacting with one another. This was accomplished in the context of materials-use so that, for example, the handicapped children were required to ask a nonhandicapped child for items or toys or to respond when receiving those items or toys from the nonhandicapped child. This facilitation procedure was to be conducted three days per week in only one environmental setting, the motor room. The other setting, the art area, was to continue without such adult facilitation in order to provide a basis for assessing generalization across environmental settings. Specifically, recordings were taken during treatment conditions in each of the settings twice each week to determine if the language and social behaviors were increasing (generalizing) in the environment in which the adult was facilitating (motor room) and whether they were also generalizing to the environment in which no facilitation was occurring (art area). It is important to note that data for the treatment setting (motor room) were collected on "probe" days, that is, when no treatment was in effect. All data were based on changes that developed over a six-month treatment period.

Reliabiltiy was obtained by comparing ratings by two independent observers during baseline, treatment (sample only), and the last two observations of the treatment period. All correlations were high, never falling below .85.

Guidelines for Facilitating Social Behavior Using the Parten scale as a developmental guide, general procedures were developed for the staff in order to facilitate movement through the categories of social behavior. The facilitation program was designed to change children's social behavior to the next, more advanced, Parten category. Examples of the facilitation procedures follow:

1. To facilitate movement from unoccupied behavior into solitary independent play, or even onlooker activity, the child is placed near other children and is encouraged to participate with a toy or an object. The child is reinforced for manipulating that toy or object while remaining within that environment or observing other children.
2. To facilitate movement to parallel activity from either the onlooker or solitary play levels, the adult reinforces the child for proximity to other children and for playing with toys similar to the others. The adult encourages the normal children to share toys with the handicapped children, and reinforces the children when they do share. During this type of activity the child should be placed among the normal children, not on the fringes of the group. For instance, if there are five children sitting at a rectangular table, the child should not be placed at the end of the table but in a position where normal peers are on all sides.
3. To facilitate associative play, the adult arranges a setting where all normal peers are engaging in play with the handicapped peer, and reinforces the normal peers for conversation and sharing of objects

with the handicapped child. The handicapped child is also reinforced for playing with normal peers. During associative play, if the handicapped child steps out of the setting, the adult should direct the handicapped child to engage in that activity once again and reinforce when the child enters or reenters the group.

Guidelines for Facilitating Language Behavior The procedures to facilitate the increase in appropriate language interactions were as follows:
1. The adult reinforces all verbal and nonverbal communication emitted by the handicapped child while in the treatment setting.
2. The adult directs child-child interactions. For example, if the handicapped child is standing back as an onlooker, the adult directs the nonhandicapped peers to verbalize to the handicapped child and reinforces the peers for these interactions.
3. The adult reinforces nonhandicapped children when they initiate and/or respond to handicapped children in the treatment setting.
4. To increase the percentage of time that a handicapped child interacts with a nonhandicapped child, the adult should encourage and/or direct the handicapped child into appropriate play situations. For example, if a child is playing with a given toy, the adult could direct a peer to play with the child with that toy or vice versa.
5. If a peer does not respond to the handicapped child, the adult should model a response for the peer. If the peer adopts the response, the adult should then reinforce the peer for responding to the handicapped child.
6. The handicapped child should be encouraged to increase usage of word phrases at all times when interacting with peers. If a child does not use spontaneous intelligible language with word phrase lengths appropriate for the child's current level of language development, then the adult should model this usage and encourage the handicapped child to imitate the adult's language. The child is then reinforced for appropriate language.

Effects of Directly Facilitating Social and Language Behaviors

The results of this study were analyzed separately for social and language interactions. As pointed out earlier, the purpose of the study was not simply to demonstrate that the facilitation techniques would influence behavior while the treatment was in effect, but that such techniques would generalize to the environment in which they were utilized as well as to another untreated environment.

Pretreatment Baseline: Social Play Table 1 shows the social play pretreatment baseline data for both normal and handicapped children as measured by the Parten scale in the motor and art rooms. Data were reported in terms of the mean percentage of time spent in each activity. A more detailed examination of our data for each setting revealed that the five nonhandicapped children spent approximately seven percent of their time in the combined categories of unoccupied behavior, solitary independent play, and onlooker behavior. The vast majority of the nonhandicapped children's time was spent either in parallel or associative play.

The pretreatment baseline data for the handicapped children are also shown in Table 1. An examination of the individual data indicated that only one child (F) spent more than ten percent of the time in associative play. No handicapped child exceeded forty-five percent total time in parallel and associative play, and three of the handicapped children spent less than four percent of their time playing at those levels. At the other end of the scale, we noted that, with the exception of two children who spent more than forty percent of their time in parallel or associative play, four of the children were spending better than forty percent of their time as onlookers, being unoccupied, or in solitary play. Thus, the pretreatment baseline patterns for the normal children and the handicapped children are almost reversed, with the normal children spending the majority of their time in parallel and associative play and the handicapped children spending the majority of their time being unoccupied, in solitary play, as onlookers, or in adult-directed activities.

Treatment Effects: Social Play Table 1 shows the final treatment data in terms of the means of the last two observations for each of the handicapped children in the motor and art rooms. No data were obtained for the nonhandicapped children following treatment. For the motor room, the data shown here and elsewhere are data obtained during which no treatment (probe days) was in effect. The results indicated that during the last two observations in the motor room following treatment, each handicapped child was spending nearly fifty percent or more of his or her time either in parallel or associative play and that there was a concurrent reduction in the amount of time spent in unoccupied, solitary play, and onlooker behavior. Three children (C, D, and E) were engaged in a total amount of associative and parallel play comparable to our earlier measures on the normal children, exceeding eighty percent of the time that they were observed. Child F, whose performance at the beginning of the study was the highest, now engaged in parallel and associative play 73.5 percent of the time and showed a decided increase from parallel to associative play.

Since these results were achieved in the motor room, it is important to determine if the effects generalized to the art activity room where no

Table 1. Pretreatment baseline and treatment data for art area and motor room for social play [a]

Level of social play	Pretreatment[b]				Treatment[c]	
	Art (NH)	Motor (NH)	Art (H)	Motor (H)	Motor room (H)	Art area (H)
Unoccupied	0.3 (0.5)	0.6 (0.6)	21.6 (15.7)	25.0 (17.7)	3.3 (3.0)	4.7 (5.0)
Solitary	4.0 (0.8)	5.3 (2.4)	28.0 (19.4)	20.7 (12.1)	7.3 (4.8)	6.0 (8.5)
Onlooker	3.1 (2.4)	0.7 (0.4)	20.3 (21.6)	20.7 (8.3)	13.2 (9.5)	18.4 (7.2)
Parallel	63.3 (21.6)	59.8 (30.6)	14.0 (11.3)	16.8 (16.0)	35.8 (15.9)	44.9 (20.6)
Associative	16.2 (7.4)	32.7 (17.8)	3.0 (6.8)	3.2 (6.62)	34.8 (15.3)	17.1 (16.8)

Note: Totals will not add to one hundred percent because another category, children directing their attention to adults, accounts for the missing percentages.
[a] NH, nonhandicapped children; H, handicapped children.
[b] Data represent mean percentages of all children in the group; in parentheses are the standard deviations.
[c] Data are reported only for the handicapped children and represent the means and standard deviations of the last two observations only.

treatment was provided. The last columns of Table 1 show those results. At the conclusion of the time period, which corresponded to the treatment in the motor room, a substantial increase in the quality of play resulted in the art room as well. In fact, the social play for three of the handicapped children (C, D, and E) approximated that of the nonhandicapped children. Children A and B showed increases in parallel and associative activities as well. Thus, for all children we see a generalization effect with regard to increases in parallel and associative play to a different environment with a corresponding reduction in the amount of time in unoccupied, solitary, adult-directed, and onlooker behavior.

Treatment Effects: Language The other part of the study examined whether or not the effects of integrating moderately and severely handicapped children into a normal environment under structured situations would result in an increase in the language activity of the child. It should be emphasized that many of these handicapped children had demonstrated little language fluency, although all had demonstrated that they could make sounds or words, could be reasonably understood, and could communicate their wants. Thus, they are different from many other children classified as moderately or severely handicapped who do not have these communication abilities. Certainly in the case of the two autistic children who were integrated, there was initially a great deal of inappropriate verbalizations, repetition of words, and echolalic behavior.

The data for verbal initiations, responses, and interactions are presented in two ways: (1) an examination of the percentage of time interacting to include both verbal and nonverbal interaction with another child, and (2) an analysis of the actual verbal initiations and verbal responses. Again, the data were recorded in two environmental areas, the motor room and the art activity center, although treatment was only conducted in the motor room.

Figures 1 and 2 show the percentage of time interacting in the motor and art rooms either verbally or nonverbally with another child during pretreatment baseline conditions and during the last twenty-five percent of the posttreatment observations. This is shown for each handicapped child, with group means only presented for the nonhandicapped children. For the handicapped children, during pretreatment baseline conditions in the motor room, child F spent the largest percentage of time (twenty-seven percent) interacting. For three children it was ten percent or less. In the art room, only one child exceeded ten percent. During the final twenty-five percent of the posttreatment observations, however, all children were interacting in the motor room more than thirty-three percent of the time and two of the children were interacting more than sixty percent of the time. Looking at the generalization data in the art activity room, only one child was still

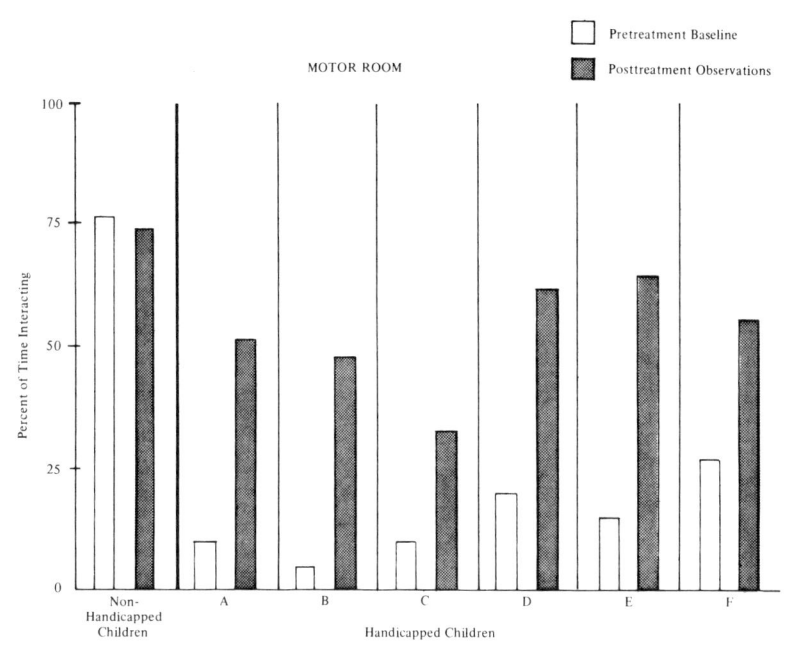

Figure 1. The percentage of time interacting either verbally or nonverbally for children in the motor room during pretreatment baseline and posttreatment observations. Handicapped children's data are presented individually. Group means only are presented for the nonhandicapped children.

interacting less than ten percent of the time. It should be emphasized that these figures reflect both verbal and nonverbal interactions.

Tables 2 and 3 present the number of appropriate verbal initiations and the number of appropriate verbal responses made by the handicapped children in pretreatment baseline conditions and during the last two posttreatment observations in the motor and art environments. Our examination of the individual data for verbal initiations summarized in Table 2 indicated that all children except one increased the number of their initiations in the motor room. In three cases (children C, D, and E), those increases were quite large. Child F had a reduction in the number of initiations, a fact that we cannot explain. In the art activity area, child A showed no increase, child B showed a sizable increase, child C showed a loss, child D showed a sizable increase, child E a very slight increase, and child F showed a loss. Thus, we see that verbal initiations were increased in five out of six cases in the area where treatment was conducted, but in the area where treatment was not conducted only three children showed gains and one of these was very slight.

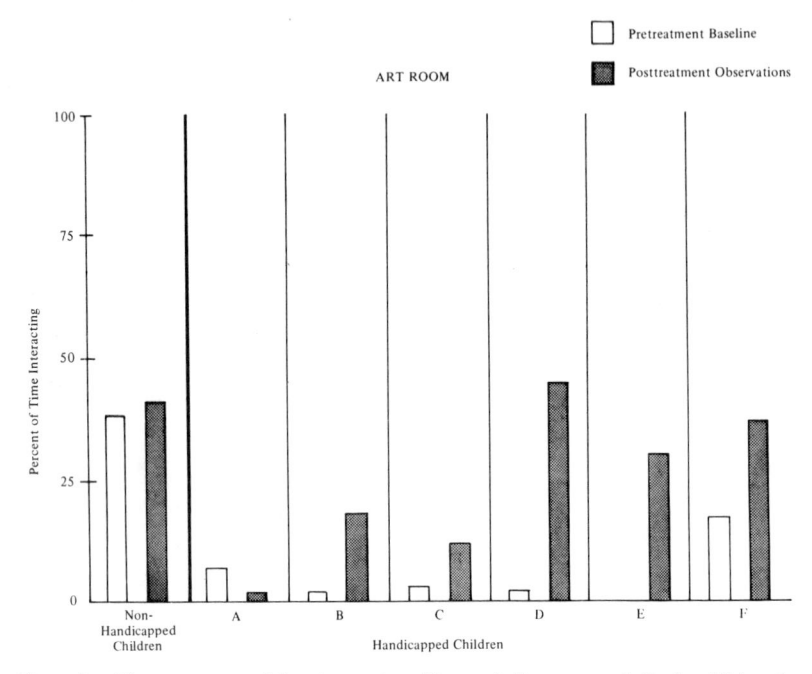

Figure 2. The percentage of time interacting either verbally or nonverbally for children in the art room during pretreatment baseline and posttreatment observations. Handicapped children's data are presented individually. Group means only are presented for the nonhandicapped children.

Relative to verbal responses (Table 3), when other children initiated verbalizations, the pretreatment baseline data showed that the rate of responding by the handicapped children in both environments was initially quite low. However, during the last two treatment sessions in the motor room, four of the six children showed increases in verbal responses al-

Table 2. Pretreatment baseline and treatment data for verbal initiations

Condition	Nonhandicapped: motor room	Handicapped: motor room	Handicapped: art area
Pretreatment baseline	19.8 (8.4)	3.3 (2.1)	0.7 (.9)
Treatment, final	21.7 (8.7)[b]	13.1 (11.2)[b]	3.0 (3.6)[b]

Group and setting [a]

[a]Data represent means and standard deviations of frequency of verbal initiations.
[b]Data are based on the means and standard deviations from the last two observation periods.

Table 3. Pretreatment baseline and treatment data for verbal responses

	Group and setting [a]		
Condition	Nonhandicapped: motor room	Handicapped: motor room	Handicapped: art area
Pretreatment baseline	17.1 (11.6)	0.8 (0.6)	0.8 (1.0)
Treatment, final	16.5 (8.9)[b]	1.9 (1.8)[b]	0.8 (0.9)[b]

[a]Data represent means and standard deviations of frequency of verbal responses.
[b]Data are based on the means and standard deviations from the last two observation periods.

though these increases were relatively small. In the art activity room only two children showed increases and in both cases these increases were small as well. Therefore, we see that the number of verbal responses did not increase to any great extent as a result of the treatment either in the motor room or in the art activity room.

The length of phrases, as measured by the number of words in these phrases, was the final measure of language behavior. It was believed that the length of phrases would reflect, in part, whether or not the children were modeling their behavior after their normal peers who generally used longer phrases than the handicapped children. The results, obtained only for the motor room, were mixed. Child A, during pretreatment baseline conditions, was using longer phrases than he was at the conclusion of the treatment. Child B showed an increase in the use of three-word phrases and a decrease in the use of one-word statements. Child C showed very little difference between baseline conditions and the final observations. Child D showed an increase in the length of phrases by adding three-, four-, and five-word phrases where these did not exist under baseline conditions. Similarly, Child E also showed an increase in longer phrases where they did not exist under baseline conditions. Data in this area were not available for child F.

IMPLICATIONS FOR INTEGRATING MODERATELY AND SEVERELY HANDICAPPED PRESCHOOL CHILDREN

The data indicate that, in an integrated setting when structured activities are provided, handicapped children will increase their social and language interactions. The results also definitely indicate that moderately and severely handicapped children can be taught to play with nonhandicapped children either in a parallel or associative manner. In the area of verbal and nonverbal interactions, the results indicate that the handicapped children benefited from the program. However, although verbal initiations in the structured environment did show a general increase, the rate of verbal responses increased only slightly or not at all. Moreover, the generalization of verbal initiations and responses, except in isolated instances, either did not occur in the nontreatment environmental setting or were extremely small changes. In four out of five cases the children did show an increase in the number of words that they utilized, but these data must be weighed against the fact that in only one of these cases was there a substantial increase in the number of verbal initiations and responses.

Thus, overall, the data indicated mixed results. Nevertheless, they do suggest the potential benefits that can result from having handicapped children placed in free-time type activities with nonhandicapped children, given that a structured program is provided which teaches the handicapped children how to play and interact with normal children. The social play behaviors generalized not only to the environment in which the teaching was conducted but also to another dissimilar environment. Certainly one of the possibilities may be that language improvement may not occur in as rapid a time as the ability to socially interact in other ways. Therefore, a longer period of integration might have produced different results. This is currently under investigation. Moreover, we recognize that more controlled investigations are needed to establish direct and clear relationships between our procedures and the changes that have occurred as a result of the integration process. Nevertheless, the suggestive evidence appears to be very strong.

However, a major question raised by the procedures used is whether or not it is feasible to expect day care or Head Start centers to carry out the kind of facilitation procedures that were done in this study. To answer this question we must recognize the improvements that occurred in the handicapped children's social and language interactions, as well as recognize what the children's behavior would be like in the free-play situation without the facilitation process. With regard to the latter point, the pretreatment baseline conditions demonstrated that handicapped children will engage in behaviors that mark them as isolates. Observations indicated large amounts of unoccupied and self-stimulatory behaviors. The children avoided contact with the other children, and the other children did not interact with them. There is no reason to believe that this pattern of behavior would change without intervention. Admittedly, if the pretreatment baseline conditions were continued for more days, change might have occurred and the children might have begun to interact with each other. However, previous observations over a period of a week of moderately handicapped children in kindergarten settings, where one teacher was supervising twenty-five children, indicated no change in the handicapped children's isolate status. Verbalizations by the teacher to include the children in some activities would create an immediate response to the handicapped child by other children but would have little generalization effect.

Observations in this study also indicated that the handicapped children could not keep pace with routine day care center activities without special help. For instance, they frequently could not understand group instructions and would fail to move to the appropriate place at the right time. Admittedly, teachers can be trained to present their instructions so that a moderately or severely handicapped child can understand them and make other special arrangements in the same manner that teachers have learned to accommodate hearing-impaired children or children with other handicapping conditions in the classroom. But it is critical to emphasize that, for moderately and severely handicapped children to benefit from placement in day care, Head Start, of any other preschool environment, the type and extent of training that must be provided to the staff is complex and of long duration. Specifically, it has been suggested here that carefully structured procedures are probably necessary to facilitate the child's improvement of social play and language interactions and to generate interactive behaviors with nonhandicapped children. This procedure requires considerable staff time, either paid or volunteer, and it requires training of that staff in those procedures. In addition, assurance must be obtained that the staff has the time, willingness, and other resources (such as the volunteers used here) to provide the handicapped children with the special assistance that will be needed even in general classroom activities. Therefore, a hasty effort to generalize the procedures described in this study to day care and Head Start centers without adequate staff preparation may not yield a beneficial effect, and may even impede the progress of the handicapped children by placing them in a situation where they may engage in even fewer verbal and social exchanges with peers than might have existed in an environment designed solely for handicapped children.

Thus we suggest that integration and especially mainstreaming of moderately and severely handicapped children at the preschool level are a difficult process. It requires a substantial expenditure of effort to train the staff in places serving nonhandicapped children, and even with a trained staff it requires an extensive expenditure of their time and resources once the handicapped child is in that environment. Therefore, the preschool environment in which such children are integrated must be chosen carefully. That the children will benefit if the environment has been adequately prepared is not questioned by the data in this study. Whether or not it is feasible to adequately train staff and conduct the programming necessary, however, is a serious concern.

REFERENCES CITED

Devalk, I. 1966. The preschool child goes to school, a special kindergarten program in the Netherlands. International Child Welfare Review, 19, 183-190.

Devoney, R., Guralnick, M., and Rubin, H. 1974. Integrating handicapped and non-handicapped preschool children: Effects on social play. Childhood Education, 50, 360-364.

Fredericks, H. D., Jordan, V., Gage, M. A., Levak, L., Alrick, G., and Wadlow, M. 1975. A Data Based Classroom for the Moderately and Severely Handicapped. Monmouth, Ore.: Instructional Development Corporation.

Grossman, H. J. 1973. Manual on Terminology and Classification in Mental Retardation. Washington, D.C.: American Association on Mental Deficiency.

Guralnick, M. J. 1976. The value of integrating handicapped and nonhandicapped preschool children. American Journal of Orthopsychiatry, 46, 236-245.

Justen, J. E. 1976. Who are the severely handicapped? A problem in definition. AAESPH Review, 1, 1-12.

Parten, M. 1932. Social participation among preschool children. Journal of Abnormal Social Psychology, 27, 243-269.

Smith, J. O., and Arkans, J. R. 1974. Now more than ever: A case for the special class. Exceptional Children, 40, 497-502.

Wolfensberger, W. 1972. The Principle of Normalization in Human Services. Toronto, Canada: National Institute on Mental Retardation.

INTEGRATING THE PREPRIMARY HEARING-IMPAIRED CHILD:
An Examination of the Process, Product, and Rationale

Winifred H. Northcott, Ph.D.

> "Anything less than a commitment to total integration into a hearing society is a goal that cannot be acceptable to parents of deaf children."
> —Leo E. Connor

Today, on the threshold of the twenty-first century, it is increasingly evident that discerning critical thinking is an essential tool for coping in a future complex society. Individuals will be forced to live with ambiguity and demonstrate reasoning and problem-solving competencies that can be applied to jobs not yet identified and to the satisfying use of leisure time.

As a result of current federal, state, and local policies and laws, rising human expectations of individual fulfillment have led general and special educators and allied specialists to identify the opportunities that a socially responsible public school system must provide for every child without exception. The new three R's—development of reasoning, responsibility, and resourcefulness in children—can be relevant goals for educators seek-

---

The development of the model described in this chapter was supported in part by Grant OEG-0-72-5367 from the United States Office of Education, Bureau of Education for the Handicapped, under the Handicapped Children's Early Education Program.

ing to provide a responsive learning environment that will ensure a match between individual potential and performance during the formal school years. In the case of a child with special needs, it offers added assurance that "It's O.K. to be different."

Dr. Edwin Martin (1973), Deputy Commissioner, Bureau of Education for the Handicapped, U.S. Office of Education, charges educators with the responsibility for viewing children as exhibiting a variety of learning and behavior styles that fall along a continuum of uniqueness. This contrasts with the more common perception of two discrete groups (exceptional versus not exceptional), with corresponding assumptions about sharp distinctions in the basic nature and learning styles between each. He urges "an end to dichotomous constructs" that lead to segregated educational environments, and the reconceptualization of teacher education that would permit teachers to broaden their range of competencies to deal with a wider range of educational behaviors in the classroom.

Public Law 94-142, the Education for All Handicapped Children Act of 1975, reinforces today's focus on individualized education through its mandate that every state agency, in order to remain eligible for federal funds for the education of handicapped children, is required to adopt a formal state plan that assures a "free appropriate education," including special education and related services, for all handicapped children (ages three through eighteen, by September 1978; ages three through twenty-one, by September 1980).

MAINSTREAMING THE HANDICAPPED CHILD

The concept that children, regardless of their handicapping condition, should mingle with their peers to the greatest extent possible is based on the assumption that all children should be exposed to as many varied learning experiences and situations as possible in order to generate as much intellectual and social stimulation as the child can handle.

P.L. 94-142 addresses this philosophy in specific terms; it describes procedural safeguards for parents and clarifies what is meant by a "free and appropriate" education for all handicapped children based on an individualized educational program plan. With regard to integration, the law notes:

> Section 612. Subdivision 5. (Eligibility for funds) "The State has established... (b) procedures to assure that, to the maximum extent appropriate, handicapped children, including children in public or private institutions or other care facilities, are educated with children who are not handicapped, and that special classes, separate schooling, or other removal of handicapped children from the regular educational environment occurs only when the

nature or severity of the handicap is such that education in regular classes with the use of supplementary aids and services cannot be achieved satisfactorily."

The focus today is on a flexible educational system offering a variety of educational options ranging from partial or full-time regular class placement to full-time special education day classes or residential school-based program. The system must remain fluid in order to accommodate handicapped children from preprimary ages through secondary years who are ready for integration with nonhandicapped age-mates. For certain children, the least restrictive environment may be the special class taught by a special educator with appropriate certification.

Dr. Edwin Martin has reminded educators of the deaf that the message of P.L. 94-142 is not the same educational setting for every child with special needs but equality of educational opportunity. "Equality does not mean *sameness,* it means *appropriateness.*"

EARLY EDUCATIONAL INTERVENTION: THE CORNERSTONE OF INDIVIDUALIZED SERVICES

A symphony of voices recorded in major documents of this decade reflects the recurring theme of a systems approach to early educational intervention for the handicapped (Abt Associates, 1973; Martin, 1974; Minnesota Department of Education, 1974). There is a consensus that the design of an individualized educational program and related services for the young child should be based on certain premises and have the following characteristics:

1. Children are identified on the basis of their developmental and behavioral needs rather than on categorical criteria related to their handicap
2. There is assurance of active parent/family involvement in the program of learning
3. The public education agency (school district of the child's residence) is the case finder, case manager, and coordinator of educational services in partnership with parents and the health care system
4. A school district may subcontract with public, private, or voluntary agencies in implementation of services based on a "zero reject" concept of equal access for all children with special needs
5. The placement of selected handicapped children in community-based programs for nonhandicapped children for their group educational experience is an integral component of a comprehensive program
6. When family-oriented education begins at the earliest stages of a child's development: (a) the coping skills of the child and family are

advanced; (b) the handicap is reduced to the level of underlying defect, and (c) greater long-term cost effectiveness is realized

The Education of All Handicapped Children Act of 1975, through its Preschool Incentive Grant authorization (Section 619), has provided an incentive for the direct administration of a full-service goal of educational services for handicapped children between the ages of three and five inclusive, by the state education agency. Major education associations are beginning to form coalitions to urge that public schools be given the primary role in early childhood education programs supported in whole or in part by federal funds.

THE PREPRIMARY HEARING-IMPAIRED CHILD

In the introductory sections, I have attempted to provide a broadly based philosophical and sociopolitical context within which one can consider the nature of young children, including the handicapped, and the process of the integration of the hearing-impaired child. It is intended to serve as a structural framework to highlight the complexity and uniqueness of behavioral phenomena among the preprimary hearing-impaired population and the need to provide responsive school and community environments to meet that challenge.

Historical Perspective

General community recognition of the value of early confirmation of hearing loss, the fitting of wearable hearing aids, the initiation of therapeutic support to families, and the immediate enrollment of parents and child in a home-centered, family-oriented infant program dates back to the 1950s in England (Ewing and Ewing, 1954) and the early 1960s in the United States (Davis, 1965).

Participants in the 1967 National Conference on Education of the Deaf in Colorado Springs, in response to the rubella epidemic of 1964–1965, recommended that the age group, birth to three years, be considered a special entity within the preschool category "because of the compelling need for valid and reliable detection techniques, the significance of this period for language stimulation and acquisition, the necessity for parent guidance and counselling, and the possibility of prevention and therapeutic medical intervention." Earlier, in 1964, an international conference on the young deaf child in Toronto offered overwhelming evidence on the statistical validity of definitive tests of hearing in neonates and infants. It further supported the value of early prescription of wearable hearing aids and immediate infant stimulation for the active and informal development of listening skills through the dynamic use of residual hearing in connection with the child's daily activities.

Federal grants spawned a variety of demonstration home projects across the country in the mid-1960s, which resulted in the Nashville Conference in 1968. This combination of workshop and forum for personnel activity teaching and supporting parents in operational programs for deaf infants revealed certain commonalities despite wide variation in infant populations, physical settings, and community support. Common elements were: (1) an individually designed aural and oral program, (2) utilization of child care and daily household activities for demonstration and home training, (3) group experience with hearing children (all but three programs), and (4) supportive medical, audiological, and psychological services (McConnell, 1968; Northcott, 1971a).

The annual report of the National Advisory Committee on Education of the Deaf (1973) included among its basic rights for deaf persons, "... early educational programs for deaf infants and their families, which should be available as soon as a hearing loss is identified" (p. 1). In turn, the National Advisory Committee on the Handicapped (1977) recommended that all state plans for special education include a section on the delivery of educational services to preschool handicapped children and that "... whenever possible, handicapped children be integrated into regular early childhood education programs" (p. 2).

Barriers to Individualized Programming

The field of education of the deaf is a parochial and insular one in many ways, and the road to individualized programming including group educational experience in regular nursery schools at times resembles a walk through a briar patch more than a "tiptoe through the tulips." This intransigence persists despite ample evidence of the deleterious effect of medical labels and segregation on the exceptional child's self-concept, attitudes, and behavior (Jordan and Daily, 1973; Warfield, 1974) and the need to program for children on the basis of developmental characteristics identified through psychoeducational assessment in essential life skill areas (Neisworth, 1975; Minnesota Department of Education, 1974).

Observers have labeled the continuing controversy related to the method of instruction of hearing-impaired children as the Hundred Years' War. When I am asked, "Which method of instruction are you for?" I respond, "For which child?" More recently, headlines such as, "Mainstreaming—Friend or Foe?" point to the emergence of a second "either-or" question, "Are you for mainstreaming or not?", to which the same response, "For which child?", seems equally appropriate.

In June 1976, a landmark resolution entitled, "Individualized educational programming for the hearing impaired (deaf and hard of hearing)," was unanimously affirmed by the Executive Committee of the Council on Education of the Deaf (CED) after having been approved by the individual boards of directors of the three major organizations that comprise the constituent members of CED: (1) the Alexander Graham Bell Association for the Deaf, (2) the Convention of American Instructors of the Deaf, and (3) the Conference of Executives of American Schools for the Deaf. Recognizing this to be a landmark policy statement, the Council on Education of the Deaf forwarded the resolution to directors of all schools and classes and teacher training centers for the deaf in the United States. It reaffirmed the intent of P.L. 94-142 as applied to the hearing impaired and stated in part that "no single method of instruction and/or communication (oral or total communication) or educational setting can best serve the needs of all hearing impaired (deaf and hard of hearing) children."

Insularity in this field of special education seems to exist partly because invitational seminars and conferences, as well as conventions for continuing professional growth where national priorities and policies are established, are too often restricted to topics, speakers, and registrants whose title, supporting agency, or institution and preservice coursework bear the title, "for the deaf." The focus is on remedial, not developmental, prescription. Furthermore, many nursery school programs that accept handicapped children, including the child with communication difficulties, in actuality include A.B.D. This means not the doctoral candidate who is unable to harness at one time the discipline, energy, and creative thinking to write a dissertation, but "all but the deaf."

Myths and Stereotypes

The incidence of deafness in the United States, according to the Bureau of Education for the Handicapped, is .075 percent in the school age population, or three in four thousand children. It is further suggested that fifty percent of this figure be used in the instance of the preschool population, due to the difficulty of identification and diagnosis. The medical definition of deafness relates to the physiological degree of hearing loss in the speech range as indicated on an audiogram following audiological assessment that measures the sensitivity of hearing to pure tones offered at different frequencies (91+ decibels, ISO).

There is no standard set of acoustic cues to which a child must respond in formal examination, and nothing of an intrinsic nature in the medical label "deaf" that precludes the possibility of language acquisition by means of amplified hearing through the wearing of individual binaural hearing aids. McConnell (1973) points out that such antiquated diagnostic terminology is a deterrent to the implementation of contemporary infant/preschool management programs that seek to establish the degree to which amplified hearing can become the primary modality for language development as a result of "learning to listen." This is in sharp contrast to the visual-oral approach of earlier years where a standard statement to parents was, "Wait until your child looks at you, and then begin to speak."

In general, a number of unwarranted assumptions and myths about the hearing-impaired child include: (1) a certain degree of hearing loss (above ninety decibels) is evident; (2) a three- to five-year language delay exists; (3) a certain educational setting—usually self-contained—is necessary; (4) the primary channel for language acquisition is visual; (5) intelligible speech is rarely attainable; (6) "the deaf prefer their own kind"; and (7) integration means you "deny your deafness."

Categories and Labels

Hobbs (1975)—in his book, *The Futures of Children,* relating to categories, labels, and their consequences—points out that mismanagement of a person with a moderate impairment, for example, may result in evidence of a more significant communicative handicap than for a person with a severe hearing loss. He notes, "Thus, the terms educational, social, or occupational deafness may be used to refer to any individual who has not received proper management, regardless of the type and degree of hearing loss" (p. 171). Assuming evidence of an intact central nervous system, I would agree.

The audiological term "deaf" is unsuitable when applied to preschool children who may become partially hearing through suitable training in the development of listening skills (Calvert and Ross, 1973; Calvert and Silverman, 1975; Davis, 1965; McConnell, 1968). The degree of hearing loss is no barrier to integration in a regular nursery school for social and linguistic stimulation during the preprimary years, nor does it prevent assimilation during the elementary school years (Kennedy and Bruininks, 1974; Kennedy et al., 1976; Liff, 1973; Northcott, 1973a; Rister, 1975). Luterman (1976), in a research study, reevaluated the language skills of forty-nine graduates of a parent-oriented nursery program, twenty-seven of whom had received visual/oral treatment and twenty-two of whom had received auditory/oral treatment. Clear evidence of the educational advantage in the auditory/oral approach compared to the more traditional visual/oral approach is seen in the fact that thirty-six percent of the auditory/oral trained children were in totally integrated educational settings as compared to less than ten percent of those trained in the visual/oral approach. Despite a two-year age advantage for the visual/oral trained children, language tests (The Illinois Test of Psycholinguistic Abilities and the Northwest Syntax Screening Test) indicated no statistically significant differences between the two groups.

Conversely, ample evidence indicates that the absence of early sensory stimulation causes neurological deterioration through disuse (Davis, 1965). The dynamics of the "self-fulfilling prophecy" argue for the use of the term "hearing impaired" during the preprimary years. It is a generic term indicating a continuum of hearing loss ranging from mild to profound as indicated on an audiogram. It includes the subclassifications "deaf" and "hard of hearing" (Northcott, 1973a). It is an emotionally neutral label and carries no automatic stereotyping. This is in contrast to the term "deaf," which leads to the premature categorizing of a child in four general areas: diagnosis, parent-child interaction, decision as to educational placement and method of instruction, and expectations for achievement (Calvert and Ross, 1973; Davis, 1965).

For example, Elliott (1967) examined 177 children at Central Institute for the Deaf and found that only 6 percent showed no response when audiometers with an extended range to 130 decibels were used, in contrast to 78.5 percent who had been labeled as profoundly deaf on a conventional audiometer. "If he is treated as non-hearing, he will indeed not hear" (McConnell, 1971, p. 175). Since amplified hearing permits an extended range of volume to 140 decibels, varying degrees of residual hearing are available to nearly every hearing-impaired child for utilization through early auditory experiences integrated into daily play and natural parent/child interactions.

The Hearing-Impaired Child's First Language: A Parental Decision

The rights of a parent are paramount in any decision about the method of communication/instruction to be used with their infant/preschool hearing-impaired child. As mentioned, two methods of instruction/communication are available for consideration, the auditory/oral method and the simultaneous method.

Auditory/Oral Method Synonyms for the auditory/oral method are: aural/oral, unisensory, auditory/global, acoupedic, natural. The assumption is that, "The primary, although not always exclusive, channel for speech development is auditory and... the input is connected speech" (Calvert and Silverman, 1975, p. 148). The focus is on learning to listen through binaurally aided hearing, when recommended, in a carefully sequenced program of activities designed to foster the child's development of short- and long-term auditory memory for the English language. Oralism is the philosophy undergirding these methods of "... educating hearing-impaired children through development of speech communication skills, which include the use of residual hearing, speechreading and speech but exclude signs and fingerspelling" (Northcott, 1973a, p. 280).

Simultaneous Method The simultaneous method adds a form of American Sign Language and fingerspelling to the use of residual hearing, speech, and speechreading. Undergirding this method is total communication, "a philosophy requiring the incorporation of appropriate aural, manual, and oral modes of communication in order to assure effective communication with and among hearing impaired persons" (American Annals of the Deaf, 1976, p. 358). A total of four years was spent in a nationwide study culminating in the adoption of this definition in May 1976 at the 48th Meeting of the Conference of Executives of American Schools for the Deaf in Rochester, New York. It should be noted that Nix (1975), in a comprehensive review of the studies offered in support of total communication, found that all of the ex post facto studies used only students from public residential schools where subjects were described as "oral" but did not use auditory/oral communication as their exclusive mode of communication. In addition, it was noted that the findings of the studies were inappropriately generalized beyond the children examined despite some investigators' warning against this practice, and that the results "... are truncated through the total absence of data on successfully mainstreamed auditory/oral deaf students" (p. 493).

Given the opportunity to observe functionally deaf and hard of hearing children and youth in special classes and integrated settings, and to review their audiograms, nearly all parents elect an auditory/oral method of communication and instruction for their infant/preschool child initially. The simultaneous method can then be introduced as a second language based on English syntax, by joint decision of parents and staff as the changing needs and responses of individual children dictate (Luterman, 1976; Northcott, 1977a).

Channel Selection for Primary Reception of Information

An accumulation of research data led Gaeth (1967) to conclude that a deaf child learns originally either through the visual or auditory channel but not through both simultaneously, selecting one channel initially for primary linguistic information. The research of Goetzinger (1974) and Goetzinger and Proud (1975) and their analysis of the research of Stuckless (1971) and Gates (1970) indicate that a hearing-impaired individual cannot process two visual stimuli (speechreading and sign language) at the same time. When multiple modes of visual communication are used simultaneously, synchronization has been demonstrated to be poor as compared to an auditory-visual input consisting of vocalized speech and speechreading (Goetzinger and Proud, 1975). Carson and Goetzinger (1975), in an experiment involving unisensory and bisensory stimulation with deaf children eight to ten years of age, found that results under the speechreading, sign, and auditory condition were not statistically different from the speechreading and auditory condition, and concluded that "... our results would cast doubt upon the superiority of the so-called 'total communication approach' in teaching the deaf" (p. 14).

A recent and extensive study by the Office of Demographic Studies (Gallaudet College, in press) involving six thousand hearing-impaired (deaf and hard of hearing) students supports these findings. Their results revealed a substantial positive correlation between speech communication proficiency and academic achievement. In addition, the study found that as the amount of speech increased, the amount of signs used decreased, so that the sum of the two remained the same. The conclusion by the investigators was that, in the actual classroom situation, teachers and students do not use large amounts of both methods simultaneously. These results then tend to negate the "additive" model of communication usage.

Recognizing that both speechreading and sign language are imprecise methods of receiving linguistic information, Simmons-Martin (1976) cites the research of Erber (1972) and Blesser (1972) in challenging educators to assist the audiometrically deaf child with proper amplification to make use of the prosodic patterns of speech (rhythm, duration, stress, accent, and pitch) that are potentially available. These time and intensity features, perceptible through training, can aid speechreading and help the deaf child to achieve better rhythm and voice quality. In an integrated nursery, normal hearing peers supply the motivation to listen and to talk.

Hearing Parents of a Young Deaf Child

"What will be the mother tongue, the child's first language?" asks van Uden (1970) rhetorically. Each family must make this judgment independently on the basis of its own value code and lifestyle. When parents with normal hearing decide to learn sign language in formal classes, communication with a child does not automatically follow. The young child's primitive gestures and approximations of correct signs cause ambiguity of meaning. Parents are required to learn, as must those employing the oral method, the techniques of modeling and expanding the child's early attempts at self-expression.

In the process of gaining fluency in the language of signs, with its paucity of vocabulary, a parent may unconsciously use deliberate, sloweddown speech, thus eliminating the distinctive tonal patterns and rhythm of spoken language that assist in code learning. Children soon learn whether their signed message or attempt at speech is rewarded by the desired action from adults, with improvement noted in the modality which is reinforced.

Northcott (1973b) investigated the competencies needed by teachers of hearing-impaired infants, ages zero through three, and their parents in a questionnaire completed by teachers in one hundred seventy infant programs in the United States in a variety of educational settings. The abilities to use sign language, fingerspelling, and Cued Speech were consistently ranked as the three competencies of lowest value and as skills not required in teaching the infant.

Deaf Parents of Preschool Children

Oral and manual interpreting must be available to accommodate to the broad range of communication skills among deaf parents (Northcott, 1977b). This can ensure their motivation to learn and participate in group discussions and individual parent teaching sessions where their insight and shared observations are invaluable. At Lexington School for the Deaf in New York, oral deaf parents are learning to listen along with their toddlers, as part of an individualized program for family and child (Held, 1975).

INTEGRATION OF HEARING-IMPAIRED CHILDREN IN REGULAR NURSERY SCHOOLS

Developmental Implications for Hearing-Impaired Children

As an icebreaker, when meeting parents for the first time I often ask, "How's your child doing?", and too often the response is, "Fine, he's integrated," or on the other hand, "Not so well, he's in a special class." Integration, the physical placement of a child with normal hearing peers, is an option in educational programming. It must not become a magnificent obsession or a parent's status symbol. The potential of a particular child for being assimilated (Watson, 1973), which Webster's Dictionary defines as "rendering alike by environmental influences," depends on consideration of the child's chronological age (CA); the disparity between the CA and the child's listening age (beginning with full-time hearing aid usage); the developmental age in critical skill areas such as cognitive, psychomotor, and social/adaptive behavior; and the linguistic age as related to performance levels of receptive and expressive language (Northcott, 1975a).

An illustration of the interaction among these critical variables, and the usefulness of information relating to them that can be used as guidelines for prediction of high or low potential for assimilation in integrated settings, would be the case of a three-year-old child who established full-time hearing aid usage at one and one-half years. The child's CA is three years and his listening age is one and one-half years. The developmental lag in the area of listening skill development (audition) is one and one-half years. Judgment as to the linguistic age of the child must be reserved until all available information about the child's current level of functioning has been considered. Additional sources of developmental lag should be explored in several major areas. When designing a comprehensive direct service program, they include: (1) the child's physical condition: assessment of the presence or absence of notable secondary physiological handicaps that require medical intervention, reassignment to another program, or give assurance that the child is physically intact for optimum learning; (2) the child's learning environment: analysis of the characteristics of the child's home and school environment that may contribute to developmental delay or distortion or hasten the child's acquisition of useful language and motor skills. This would include a search for the optimum condition in learning to hear, in which adults in the child's daily environment encourage the dynamic use of residual hearing as an integral component of daily functioning in contrast to an auditory training program restricted to formal "sit-down" periods during the school day and at home; (3) the child's current skill repertoire: assessment by means of norm-referenced and criterion-referenced procedures as well as parent and teacher observations and exchange of information related to the significant knowledge and skills the child has already acquired in communication, psychomotor, cognitive, and social/adaptive behavioral areas (see Minnesota Department of Education, 1974).

In the instance of children whose primary handicap is severe or profound hearing impairment, most children are realistic candidates for placement in a regular nursery school around the age of three as one dimension of a parent-oriented comprehensive program. However, the following conditions should be present: early fitting of binaural hearing aids (Ross, 1976), the existence of a fragment of residual hearing, and enrollment in a family-oriented infant program with a focus on natural listening, natural language, and natural learning. The neighborhood nursery with its structured teacher and unstructured toddlers can offer a responsive environment in which attention can be focused on the basic questions, "What does he hear?" and "What can he do?" (Northcott, 1970, 1971b; Pollack and Ernst, 1973; Stern, 1969; Weinstein, 1968).

Schumacher (1975) points out that the essence of education is to transmit values through ideas that are shaped by experience and observation. Prejudice based on blind judgment has little chance to grow when hearing and hearing-impaired children begin nursery school together and continue classes together, which Birch (1975) considers a fully operational definition of mainstreaming. This is a hospitable environment, where we see "children playing, unlearned and unlabored . . . without the tarnish of 'must' or 'maybe' . . . (absorbing) values of courage and curiosity, of commitment without reserve, of self-acceptance, of eager expectation, of optimism, of gaiety" (Hartley, 1976). It has the potential for making each child more accepting of another on the basis of shared group activity, with a naturalness and lack of fear or self-consciousness that permits the hearing-impaired child, in this instance, to realize the ability to control his or her own life (Blumberg, 1973; Klein, 1975).

Play and Motivation   Piaget charmingly referred to play as "the work of childhood." Bruner (1972) explains it permits observational learning to take place and develops the visually directed manipulatory skills that have survival value for flexibility in coping with an increasingly complex technological world upon reaching adulthood. The traditional nursery school, with its appreciation of individuality among children, permits what Isaacs (1974) calls "living integrative learning" in contrast to "passive receptivity."

For the hearing-impaired child, it is an environment that encourages good speech attitudes and motivates the child to use expressive language, however primitive at first, to get more attention and an earned share of the rewards at hand. "Mo mil (more milk)" the child demands, holding out an empty cup. "My 'urn (my turn)" the child shouts, when it is time to feed the fish.

Communication   The special educator is concerned with communication readiness, with particular attention to increased comprehension in the context of child-centered activities offering situational meaning to the language being supplied by the nursery teacher. Here in the integrated setting, one finds no focus on articulation, no "baked sentences" ("I see a fish." "The box is on the table."), a kind of constructionalism often practiced by traditional teachers of the deaf that van Uden (1970) refers to as "the grave of the oral way." Gone are the controlled vocabulary, formally taught, and the unrealistic and prolonged language drills to which deaf children were subjected a generation ago. Instead, the hearing-impaired child is encouraged to make the transition from what may be a sheltered environment of home and family with excessive maternal-child interdependence, to one without artificiality or rote learning.

The process of language learning is developmental. Once full-time hearing aid usage has been accomplished, every sentence (given appropriate levels of sentence complexity and its relation to the child's experience at the moment) is equally easy for the nursery-age child to process through his or her own auditory and vocal mechanism through encouraged imitation. For example, the child babbles, "No!" and pushes a plate of food away. "I don't want any," says the adult, modeling the appropriate language as the child would say it, if he or she could. "Wah-eh-e" parrots the child, with coaxing, and the plate is taken away. A nursery teacher will need assistance in developing the techniques of modeling and expanding a child's first natural attempts at verbal self-expression; these skills are learned behaviors even for parents of normal hearing children (Giattino and Hogan, 1975; Ling and Ling, 1974).

In the instance of any young child, the semantic system has to be learned through experience. At the same time, there is a semantic matching of the child's interests with the language offered by a staff member of hearing peers. In the case of a hearing-impaired child, babbling or telegraphic speech elicits a response, and he or she begins to get a sense of the value of speech and the reward it brings—more companionship, more fun, and more related experiences. Conveying and receiving meaning through shared activity and the action-oriented language connected with it is a natural concomitant to placement in a regular nursery school. The hearing-impaired child gains enough speaking and listening experience to begin to induce the rules of language naturally and learns that there is functional value to verbal self-expression in manipulating the environment and the people in it. Guralnick (1976) stresses the need for systematically designing interactions that involve specific modeling and peer reinforcement experiences in order to encourage increased frequency and complexity of verbalizations among handicapped children. This potential for higher level language and social functioning cannot be left to chance.

Many of the prosodic patterns of speech (pitch, intonation, rhythm, and duration) are available to the audiometrically deaf child much of the time in integrated settings, and from them a child gets his or her first linguistic information while achieving better rhythm and voice quality in the child's own speech (Ling, 1976; Ross, 1972; Simmons-Martin, 1976). In addition to the group educational experience in a regular nursery school, it is important to have individual or small group sessions offered by a teacher of deaf children for additional auditory and linguistic experience related to the concepts presented by the nursery teacher in songs, readiness training, creative experimentation with manipulative materials, and association and classification activities.

Resources for the Integrated Nursery School

Educational Audiologist Recognizing the primacy of the auditory channel for basic language development, the relative effect of noise on speech comprehension must be considered. Since distance from the teacher, intensity, and background noise are factors that cause distortion of the speech signal with amplification, integrated placement requires the intimate and continuing involvement of an audiologist (Hanners, 1973; Ross, 1972).

The person's responsibilities would include the measurement of hearing and a description of the variables of acoustic environments and their implications for auditory perception. This staff member (or consultant) would also be a "facilitator" in the home. In addition, through observation of the child in the special education program and nursery school, the educational audiologist would advise on matters such as the child's ability to integrate environmental and linguistic sound into total behavior patterns and the design of an individualized plan for the systematic development of listening skills by the adults in the child's daily environment.

Analysis of classroom listening conditions on speech intelligibility argues strongly for the installation of a wireless amplification system as a routine part of related support services at the time a hearing-impaired child is enrolled (Gaeth, 1967; Ross, 1972; Ross, Giolas, and Carver, 1973).

Nursery School Teacher Experience and research have shown that teacher attitudes associated with the integration of handicapped children are strongly influenced by labels and observation of children in special classes, the presence or absence of supportive special education personnel, and, in some instances, the provision of a management aide in the classroom (Shotel, Iano, and McGettigan, 1972; Valletutti, 1969). The range of parental response to the presence of a handicapped child in the family is broad; a nursery teacher may require guidance to be alert to the problem and gain knowledge of the resources available in dealing with it (Almy, 1975). Each of these variables has direct implications for the child's feeling of competence and motivation to learn in the integrated nursery program. For example, Gorelick (1974), in sampling preschools in Los Angeles, found that sixty-two percent of nursery teachers would accept a child with partial deafness, but the label "deaf" reduced the acceptance level to thirteen percent.

In attempting to match a single hearing-impaired child with an individual nursery teacher, critical variables to be considered in objective observation would include the teacher's conceptual tempo (reflective/impulsive), teaching style, voice quality, ability to individualize responses to children of varying abilities, openness to new ideas about deafness, and willingness to include parents in observations of the child's interactions with a group and as a partner in the design of activities to promote a better match between potential and performance (Northcott, 1975a; Porter, 1975).

Teacher of Hearing-Impaired Children Original placement of a hearing-impaired child should be preceded by a formal assessment of the nursery school environment (physical, acoustic, scheduling, learning) and a joint agreement with the child's parents as well as special education and nursery school staff on a grouping that is based on the child's interests and abilities rather than on his or her linguistic level of functioning. The schedule of individual teaching sessions in the special education setting should also be arranged as an essential supplement to the group placement.

Monitoring of a hearing-impaired child's progress in the nursery school requires realignment of the special educator's professional time to permit periodic site visitation for shared observation about the child's social and cognitive levels of performance, and joint participation in the design of a formal in-service training program and its implementation for the nursery staff.

As the level of mutual trust and usefulness rises, a variety of alternative patterns of integration can be discussed. In Sweden, for instance, one out of four chairs in every nursery school is reserved for a hearing-impaired child, and team teaching by an early childhood educator and teacher of the deaf is a common pattern. Reverse integration is a considered alternative, particularly in the instance of a residential school for the deaf where neighborhood children with normal hearing are brought into special classes for nursery/kindergarten children with severe and profound hearing losses (Connor, 1976; Rankhorn, 1974).

INTEGRATION OF HEARING-IMPAIRED CHILDREN IN A NEIGHBORHOOD NURSERY: A MODEL, A PROCESS, A PHILOSOPHY TRANSLATED INTO PRACTICE

The UNISTAPS Project is one of six models in the First Chance network (Title VI-C) that has been validated for national dissemination by the U.S. Office of Education. The oldest component of the eight-year project is the Regional Program for the Hearing Impaired, for children from birth through four to five years (Minneapolis Public Schools, 1975). The grantee is the Minnesota Department of Education.

The acronym UNISTAPS highlights the diverse project roles of three agencies—the University of Minnesota, the State Department of Education, and the Minneapolis Public Schools (laboratory program)—in developing a systems approach to early educational intervention for preschool age handicapped children. The UNISTAPS Project enables the Minnesota Department of Education to develop and disseminate a model of preschool services for handicapped childeren, from birth through four or five years. This model includes: (1) a multicategorical laboratory program (the Family-Oriented Special Education Preschool, ages birth to four or five years); (2) a written state plan for preschool services for handicapped children (Minnesota Department of Education, 1974); (3) an evaluation handbook (Minneapolis Public Schools, 1975), which defines program objectives, treatment strategies, and instrumentation that are applied in five major areas: clinical assessment, child development profiles, parent/family education, interagency communication/coordination, and family management; (4) criteria for placement and continuation in a regular nursery school; and (5) a curriculum for hearing-impaired children from birth to age three based on neurological, cognitive, and language developmental milestones for children with normal hearing (Northcott, 1977a). Responsibility for coordinating policies on preschool handicapped children and conducting training workshops for professionals is vested in the State Department of Education under my direction as project director, with the assistance of a broad representative advisory committee.

The rest of this chapter addresses the process of integrating hearing-impaired children into regular nursery schools in the Minneapolis program (see Figure 1). Upon enrollment, each hearing-impaired child is referred to the prescriptive nursery for initial child/family orientation and assigned a case manager and prescriptive nursery coordinator for the purpose of determining processes and procedures for program management and parent/staff determination of initial target objectives. The prescriptive nursery (see Figure 2) is a concept, not a physical setting, of staff observation in whatever settings the child is presently functioning, including the home.

The multidisciplinary staff members, not the child, are labeled: family adviser/teacher of the deaf, social worker/family education adviser, education adviser, educational audiologist, speech clinician, physical therapist,

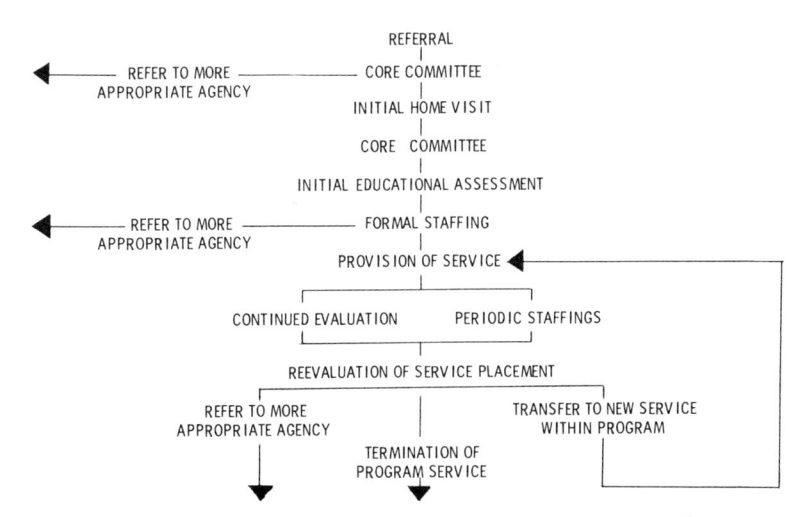

Figure 1. A description of the delivery of preschool program services.

PROCESS/PROCEDURE

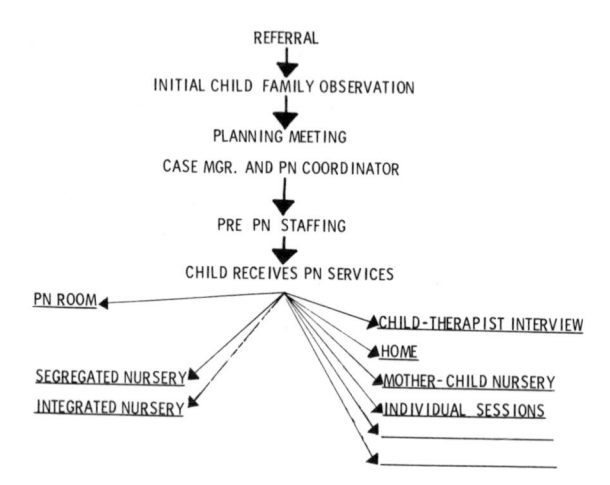

```
                    REFERRAL
                       ↓
          INITIAL CHILD FAMILY OBSERVATION
                       ↓
                 PLANNING MEETING
            CASE MGR. AND PN COORDINATOR
                       ↓
                  PRE PN STAFFING
                       ↓
             CHILD RECEIVES PN SERVICES
     PN ROOM ←                    → CHILD-THERAPIST INTERVIEW
                                  → HOME
     SEGREGATED NURSERY ←         → MOTHER-CHILD NURSERY
     INTEGRATED NURSERY ←         → INDIVIDUAL SESSIONS
```

Figure 2. Sequence of activities in the diagnostic prescriptive nursery (PN).

occupational therapist, coordinator, and program evaluator. The multidisciplinary team follows the child until school entry. Individual parent/child teaching sessions are scheduled once a week even as the child grows older and is placed in a neighborhood nursery school.

Parent Component

Family Guidance and Counseling An intensive parent/family education program is offered in a demonstration center and family residences with a dual focus on teaching parenting skills. First, assistance in developing "response-ability" in dealing with chronic sorrow that parents often feel following the diagnosis of an educationally handicapping condition is provided (Auerbach, 1968; Ross, 1964; Solnit and Stark, 1961). This leads in turn to the incorporation of family values and priorities into the school program. Oral and manual interpreting/translating are provided selectively by staff members for parents who are deaf. Overall, one goal of the program is a transfer of competencies and confidence from multidisciplinary staff members to parents; this enables the adults in the immediate family to enhance the hearing-impaired child's responses to learning opportunities during the preschool years.

Another goal is to reduce the debilitating effects of the child's handicap to the level of genuine defect so that increased numbers of children reaching school age will be candidates for partial or full-time integration in available educational programs for the nonhandicapped, or will be capable of being effectively served in comprehensive public school special education programs.

Individual Parent/Child Teaching Sessions Every hearing-impaired child and family is scheduled to meet with the family adviser/teacher of the deaf once a week. The systematic training of each child's residual hearing is the fundamental emphasis. In addition, training is focused on: (1) guidance on the "when" and "how" of verbal reinforcement in home-like activities for child and parent in the demonstration center or family home; (2) application of the principle of alternation (speak to child, wait for verbal response, answer); and (3) modeling and expansion of the child's attempts at speech, using functional language and interesting inflection. The parent gradually assumes a teaching responsibility while the family adviser/teacher relinquishes the lead role. A portion of the visit is devoted to informational exchange relating to the child's behaviors, family interactions, and concerns about the child's achievements and developmental delays.

Mounting evidence of the educational advantage of the auditory/oral approach (see earlier discussion) compared to the visual/oral method supports the decision by the majority of parents in the Minneapolis Public School program (Davis, 1965; Kennedy et al., 1976; McCauley, Bruininks, and Kennedy, 1976) to adopt this method. Under teacher guidance, parents learn to use appropriate auditory and verbal cues related to the listening age of the child and to make use of their daily living experiences for the content of the natural language directed to the child. However, a simultaneous method of communication (speech, fingerspelling, and signs) is available for certain hearing-impaired children as an adjunct to informal speechreading and the use of residual hearing. This method may be implemented under circumstances in which: (1) the child's parents are hearing impaired or wish this mode of communication to be used with their child; (2) the child is diagnosed late (three and one-half years or older), profoundly deaf (ninety-five decibel loss or greater, unaided, throughout the speech range), and shows evidence of being unable to integrate what is heard; (3) there is evidence of inability to make reasonable progress in an aural/oral program initiated in infancy; or (4) the child gives evidence of significant developmental delays in other areas.

The simultaneous method may be applied in two ways. For children who are psychologically and physiologically intact and are making normal gains in other developmental skills, a form of sign language that follows the syntax of the parent's language model would be used. For children who are developmentally delayed, basic signs only would be used. The addition of word endings an indications of tenses in signs or fingerspelling would present a sensory overload for such children.

The topic of selection of a method of communication/instruction follows the visit by parents to schools and classes representing the full range of settings and modes of communication, with lively discussion among staff and parents following each trip. Under any of the methods of communication/instruction, the parents and the multidisciplinary team work together to develop appropriate behavioral objectives and to determine which techniques should be used in implementing the educational program. Together, they evaluate the child's progress toward achieving these goals, making adjustments in the educational programs where needed.

Nursery School Placement with Nonhandicapped Peers

Enrollment in a neighborhood nursery program may be recommended by the family adviser/teacher for children around the age of three years. Selection of an appropriate nursery program is based on the child's specific needs and accessibility to the nursery. The family adviser/teacher visits the nursery program before the child's enrollment to determine if the physical facilities, educational program, and nursery staff can meet these needs. (The Special Education Preschool Program pays for any tuition charged by the neighborhood/special nursery program. State special education aids are applicable here, with Minnesota laws permitting a school district to contract with a private, public, or voluntary agency.)

Placement eligibility for hearing-impaired youngsters in neighborhood nursery schools (Northcott, 1977) consists of the following: (1) the hearing-impaired child is a full-time hearing aid user; (2) the child has advanced in the use of audition for language acquisition; and (3) the child has developed speech and language skills to a level where peer interaction is possible. Criteria have also been established relating to licensing, curriculum, and teacher/pupil ratio.

Criteria to determine the appropriateness of a nursery school stipulate that the nursery school should provide: (1) an opportunity for social interaction with normally hearing age-mates, (2) exposure to peer group behavior models, (3) exposure to peer group language, (4) an opportunity to follow routine and structure, and (5) an opportunity to relate to adults other than parents. Site visitation by the parent and parent adviser/teacher is part of the ongoing monitoring process on a scheduled basis, usually six weeks apart.

Formal In-Service Training Program for Nursery School Teachers

Each fall, the Preschool Special Education staff provides an intensive in-service training workshop for nursery school teachers who will be working with Preschool Program children. Each year the content of the program, as jointly designed by an advisory committee of parents and early childhood educators and staff, varies according to responses on a formal needs-assessment questionnaire. Group discussions relating to adapting experiential activities, developing the environment, encouraging language and communication, maximizing hearing aid usage, facilitating coping skills, and managing behavior are supplemented by features such as a panel of parents of integrated children "telling it like it is" and a panel of experienced nursery teachers who have successfully integrated hearing-impaired children in early years, discussing, "We've been through it—may we help you?"

In addition, consultant support is provided throughout the year. This support includes site visitation, assistance with lesson planning and activities that meet individual child needs, demonstrations of methods that will facilitate working with the child, provision of toys and materials on a loan basis, and assistance in working with the child's family.

Parent/Child Nursery: An Alternative

Program options exist beyond the integrated nursery. A self-contained parent/child nursery is operated three mornings a week, primarily for children who have been identified late, have a profound hearing loss, or whose rate in developing listening skills and oral language patterns is delayed. Here, a specific sequence of auditory experiences involving parent and child is provided for application in daily family-child interactions at home. Sentence cards, experience charts, and story sequencing are used to stimulate auditory attention, discrimination, and recall. Parents are helped to become more proficient at modeling and expanding their child's attempts at verbal self-expression, and ongoing interactions are stressed. This is a transitional program between the individual parent counseling and guidance of the Preschool Program and the full-day, school-based, self-contained, nonintegrated nursery program provided for four-year-olds.

Prekindergarten Nursery (Four-Year-Olds)

Most children who enter the integrated nursery go on to the prekindergarten nursery for four-year-olds, in addition to continuing in an integrated nursery school. Placement in the prekindergarten nursery for specialized instruction (two half-days per week) is determined by the child's auditory functioning level, not by audiogram. Hearing-impaired/language-delayed children for whom regular kindergarten placement would seem appropriate are eligible when they meet the following criteria: (1) the child has integrated listening skills; (2) strong parent or surrogate parent support is evident; (3) the child has demonstrated an ability to learn new language and concepts through listening; (4) the child has appropriate listening skills for age level (based on the Minnesota Child Development Inventory and nursery school observations); and (5) the child has communicative and cognitive skills approaching age level. (Tests here include the Houston Language Test, the McCarthy Scales of Children's Abilities, the Boehm Tests of Basic Concepts, and the Peabody Picture Vocabulary Test.)

As noted, the prekindergarten nursery meets two half-days a week. The home school's kindergarten curriculum and readiness for reading programs are utilized to plan the extensive language and structured cognitive activities. In addition, the children continue to attend their neighborhood nursery school at other times and have an individual language and auditory stimulation session at least one hour a week with their parent(s) and family adviser/teacher.

Children who are integrated into a regular kindergarten program the following year are accompanied by a special education teacher of the hearing impaired. This teacher works in the classroom with the regular classroom teacher to provide a full educational program for the youngsters.

Summary of the Model

The UNISTAPS Project has enabled the Minnesota Department of Education to offer a direct service model while proceeding with child advocacy activities, interagency advisory committees, and a series of special study institutes, graduate courses, and state parent conferences over a period of time beginning in 1969. The noncategorical family-oriented program in the Minneapolis Public Schools (laboratory) ensures individually prescriptive programs for children and families. In the instance of the hearing-impaired child, it dispels the notion of one educational setting for all children once they reach the age of mandated school services. The full cascade or continuum of educational settings ranging from full-time regular class placement to special classes in a day of residential school is in operation, and "graduates" of the Family-Oriented Special Education Preschool are found in each level of service.

Active family involvement includes individual parent teaching sessions, family workshops, parent meetings (weekly), couples' evening, and "men only" meetings. The laboratory program is based on the premise that a child's parents are his or her first and best informal teachers. Thus, parents are the first learners in the redirection process involving family and child. Staff members help parents to view their child in terms of normal developmental expectations (cognitive, motor, social-emotional, and linguistic) for each chronological age. The long-range goal is to enable the child to succeed in the least restrictive educational alternative when he or she reaches mandatory school age.

RESEARCH DATA: CHALLENGING SOME UNWARRANTED ASSUMPTIONS

Dr. Edward Zigler, former director of the Office of Child Development, expressed to members of a congressional committee his belief that without careful research and evaluation efforts, the concepts of normalization, mainstreaming, and deinstitutionalization are little more than slogans. Currently, there are few data on how children in integrated settings have fared after they leave the preschool.

Accountability is an essential goal of the UNISTAPS Project. Several pieces of empirical evidence generated by the UNISTAPS Project staff and faculty from the University of Minnesota support the application of the principle of accountability to a direct service program for hearing-impaired children, birth to four or five years of age.

Identification and Cost Effectiveness

For the UNISTAPS program, certain significant changes over time were noted. During the five-year period, 1968–1969 to 1973–1974, the mean age of diagnosis for profoundly deaf children (fifty-six percent) dropped from twenty-four months to ten months of age, while the age of enrollment dropped from thirty-five months to nineteen months of age. The cost per family and child enrolled in 1974–1975 was $2,339. This includes community site visitation, nursery schools, staff salaries, pro rata share of building space and maintenance, travel, evaluation, and report writing. The per pupil direct instructional costs were $1,739. The cost efficiency principle is emphasized when one considers that the average per capita cost in 1974–1975 at the Minnesota School for the Deaf was $8,029.

Follow-Up Data

Educational Placements Data from the fall of 1974 on the placements of hearing-impaired "graduates" of the program (the last year that statistics were kept by disability) highlight the necessity of maintaining a continuum of educational services. Of the fifty-two graduates, forty-four percent were in a full-time integrated program, six percent in a partially integrated program, and forty-one percent in self-contained programs (nine percent moved or no information was available).

Since a comparable control group of children who had not received the benefit of auditory/oral instruction in the Minneapolis Public School Program was not available, these findings can only be indirectly assumed to relate to its effectiveness. However, our findings clearly indicate that the presence of a severe or profound hearing loss is not an automatic deterrent from assimilation into a regular classrrom during the elementary school years.

Substantiation of this conclusion is available in the studies conducted and/or cited by Davis (1965), Liff (1973), Pollack (1974), McConnell (1968), and Luterman (1976). Rister (1975) offered further supportive data in a longitudinal follow-through study of eighty-eight audiometrically deaf children, ages six to sixteen, who had graduated from the preschool program at the Speech and Hearing Institute in Texas. Here, the children were provided early amplification and the oral language skills "... necessary for education in the mainstream of society. ... Loops, auditory training units and total communication frequently associated with more traditional preschool programs were not a part of the program at this Institute" (Rister, 1975, p. 280).

Social Status of Hearing-Impaired Children in Regular Classrooms In the Minneapolis study, Kennedy and Bruininks (1974) examined the peer status and self-perceived peer status of fifteen first and second grade hearing-impaired preschool "graduates" enrolled in thirteen separate regular classrooms as compared with a random sample among two hundred seventy-seven normal hearing age-mates, on three sociometric tests. All of the subjects had experienced nursery school with normal hearing children and were binaural hearing aid users. The method of communication/instruction in school and at home was auditory/oral.

There were seven boys and eight girls in the study, thirteen in grade one and two in grade two. Hearing loss was congenital, except for one child who became deaf at thirteen months from meningitis. The etiologies of deafness included rubella (nine), unknown (two), jaundice (one), drugs (one), and premature birth (one). The average decibel loss (pure tone average) ranged from fifty-five to one hundred ten unaided. Eleven of the fifteen subjects had a severe or profound hearing loss ranging from seventy-five to one hundred ten decibels (ISO).

The results indicated no significant difference between the level of peer status for the two groups. In addition, the hearing-impaired children were as perceptive of their own social status as the normal hearing children. During the next two years of the longitudinal study (1972–1974) on social status (McCauley, Bruininks, and Kennedy, 1976), the subjects were eleven children of the original fifteen with severe and profound hearing losses (seventy-five to one hundred ten decibels, pure tone average) each with a congenital hearing loss except for one child (onset thirteen months). The

Moreno peer nominations scale (Gronlund, 1959) indicated that the hearing-impaired children declined in social status over a three-year period whereas the social acceptance data revealed no significant difference in social status. In mutual choice data, designed to assess the group status of children who are nominated by their peers through questions that specify a criterion such as working, playing, or sitting together, examination revealed that hearing-impaired children were chosen significantly more often in first grade but no significant differences were found in subsequent years. They continued to be as perceptive as normal hearing children concerning their in-class social status.

Cross-Sectional Data: Pupil Observational Schedule The overall quality of behavioral interactions of these hearing-impaired children is not significantly different from that of their normal hearing classmates as far as positive/negative and verbal/nonverbal behavior directed to teachers, peers, and total classroom group is concerned. However, hearing-impaired children interacted positively and verbally to a significantly greater degree with teachers and with a significantly fewer number of peers (McCauley, Bruininks, and Kennedy, 1976).

Academic Achievement Data: Children in Grades Three and Four The language and achievement data as measured by the Woodcock Word Recognition, Peabody Individual Achievement Test, Metropolitan Achievement Test (MAT: Word Knowledge), and data from the KeyMath Achievement Test indicated no significant differences between the two groups except for the MAT word knowledge measure, where normal hearing children scored significantly higher (Kennedy et al., 1976).

Future research is designed to determine whether certain characteristics associated with these graduates of the Minneapolis program are critical variables related to relative success in an integrated setting in later years. Such variables to be investigated include individual binaural hearing aids, the severity of hearing loss, type of nursery school placement, the nature of individualized instruction (auditory/linguistic), continuing parent guidance, counseling and training, and the role of in-service training of staff.

TOMORROW'S SPECIALISTS: IMPLICATIONS FOR TEACHER TRAINING INSTITUTIONS

The traditional authority on education of deaf persons has been the university and its tenured faculty, with focus on preparation for one role—teacher of the deaf, certified to teach grades kindergarten through twelve; one model—the school for the deaf; one education setting—the self-contained classroom; and one certifying body—the state department of education.

Currently, however, any consideration of an educational program for preprimary hearing-impaired children must involve parents in the teaching/learning process and recognize the differential staffing patterns required to match each individual child's developmental skill repertoire with available educational alternatives including group educational experience with nonhandicapped peers. This is a preferred option for competitive learning for most children enrolled.

Thus, the Council on Education of the Deaf has identified preprimary certification as one area of specialization. The focus is on the competencies (skills, knowledge, and attitudes) needed for a teacher of young hearing-impaired children to assume the role of speech, hearing, and language specialist as a member of the multidisciplinary team including specialists in child development, family life, and social welfare. Differentiated staffing patterns in direct service programs for the hearing impaired dictate a focus on the process of making decisions on curriculum content, methods of instruction, and the nature of participatory learning experiences. The recurring theme in the guidelines developed by the Professional Standards and Guidelines Committee, Council for Exceptional Children, is that all available professional talent within a university must be utilized to offer needed kinds of specialized training. This concept of transdisciplinary, transdepartmental coordination of planning efforts for preservice and continuing professional growth training permits role differentiation to occur. It also requires use of preprimary teachers of deaf children in direct service educational programs as adjunct instructors for orientation of nursery school teachers and other early childhood educators to the "tricks of the trade" that are required to stimulate the development of communication skills in language-delayed children, including the hearing impaired. In addition, these professionals will pay attention to attitudinal and conceptual barriers in order to facilitate the assimilation of hearing-impaired youngsters into classes with nonhandicapped peers.

Dimensions of participatory learning for the preservice teacher of deaf children would include practica with these dimensions: observation and site visitation, parent interviewing (supervised), home visitation, precision teaching, experience in a microteaching center, individual and group parent guidance, behavior management of hearing-impaired children, in-basket simulated procedures, integration procedures, and participation in research as appropriate (Northcott, 1975b).

Certain managerial skills are required of the preprimary communications specialist, who may be certified as a teacher of deaf children or a speech clinician, under the rubric of demonstrated ability to individualize educational instruction. These include behavior modification techniques, task analysis, written behavioral objectives, and planning skills applicable to group implementation. The flexibility of a university in establishing a working partnership between teacher trainers and consumers will determine its relevance in assuring the least restrictive educational environment for the majority of hearing-impaired children of preprimary age.

A LOOK TO THE FUTURE

During the student demonstrations at Berkeley some years ago, a lettered placard caught the imagination and attention of citizens everywhere. "I am a human being . . . please do not spindle, fold, or mutilate." This thought underscores the right of every infant and preschool hearing-impaired child to receive an individualized educational program based on his or her developmental and behavioral needs and utilizing the mode of communication chosen by the family as one of their formally recognized rights in a participatory management role.

Today in the United States, deaf children are learning to hear[1] at an increasingly early age in family-oriented public school regional programs that include placement in a regular nursery school with normal hearing peers as a preferred option for group educational experience. An overwhelming majority of enrolled families initially elect an auditory/oral method of communicating with their young children. As a result of functional language presented with good inflection and received through amplified hearing, a growing number of children with severe and profound hearing losses are realistic candidates for placement in regular classes during the elementary school years. This is one option that must be available in addition to special classes required by others for competitive learning. Regardless of placement in the continuum of services, current research findings and empirical evidence have shattered the myth that very young children labeled "deaf" by physiological degree of hearing loss must be taught in a highly visual way and that they can rarely develop intelligible speech. The assumptions made about the capabilities of children thus classified are diagnostically and psychologically unsound as a basis for individualized program planning and may sharply limit the preschool child's opportunities to make functional use of aided residual hearing.

The role of the preprimary teacher of deaf children is more challenging than ever before, demanding an outreach to new audiences—nursery school staff, the child's family, and multidisciplinary team members—thus

---

[1]Hearing Alert! Public Information Program: Early Detection of Hearing Impairment. Alexander Graham Bell Association for the Deaf, Washington, D.C.

providing an antidote to the cartoon statement, "I'm sorry I can't be more specific. I'm a generalist." This individual must exercise leadership by presenting the case for mainstreaming, the budget required for implementation, and acting as a child advocate in the community. In addition, this person must identify the critical behaviors of teachers, children, parents, and nonhandicapped peers, behaviors that can enhance the potential for assimilation of each hearing-impaired child, in this instance, on the basis of matched characteristics (Wynne, Ulfelder, and Dakof, 1975).

The early placement of hearing-impaired children in regular nursery schools is one component of a comprehensive program supplemented by parent guidance and individual teaching by a special educator. The integrated school experience focuses on carefully managed play as a natural means of social adjustment, creative cooperation, motivation to speak, and development of confidence under the direction of a disciplined teacher. It equips many hearing-impaired children for continued assimilation in regular classes and friendships therein; for others, it is a short-term useful experience. It holds great promise for the development of independent thinking and of inner-directed human beings, each capable of speaking for him- or herself in later years and being understood by those who can hear. Integrated preschool experience can give an assurance to hearing and hearing impaired alike that, in the words of A. A. Milne, "the world belongs to me."

ACKNOWLEDGMENTS

The forms related to this chapter (see Northcott, 1977a) and most of the description of the program options were developed by the following staff in the Family-Oriented Special Education Preschool, zero to five years, either as a group or as individuals: Nancy Short, program evaluator; Lou Erickson, program coordinator; Doris Anderson, family adviser/teacher; Harriet Kaplan, family adviser/teacher; Pat Kennedy, family adviser/teacher; Vicky Ruppenthal, family adviser/teacher; Ann Sieving, family adviser/teacher; Anne Gearity, social worker; Shirley Fowler, family education adviser; Marla Frank, speech clinician; Donna Heiman, physical therapist; Ruby Starr, occupational therapist.

This very dedicated and competent staff is committed not only to providing direct and indirect services to children and families, but also to eliciting feedback regarding the quality and effectiveness of services provided. The staff is creative and flexible, and provides the impetus and direction for programming options which implement the objective of an individualized educational program plan for each child with special needs and his or her family.

REFERENCES CITED

Abt Associates. 1973. Exemplary programs for the handicapped. Early childhood education: Case studies. Vol. III. Washington, D.C.: National Institute of Edu-

cation for the Handicapped, U.S. Department of Health, Education, and Welfare.
Almy, M. 1975. The Early Childhood Educator at Work. New York: McGraw-Hill.
American Annals of the Deaf. 1976. Total communication definition adopted. Volume 121, 358.
Auerbach, A. B. 1968. Parents Learn through Group Discussion: Principles and Practices of Parent Group Education. New York: John Wiley & Sons.
Birch, J. W. 1975. Hearing Impaired Children in the Mainstream. Reston, Va.: The Council for Exceptional Children.
Blesser, B. 1972. Speech perception under conditions of spectral transformation, I. Phonetic characteristics. Journal of Speech and Hearing Research, 15, 5-41.
Blumberg, L. 1973. The case for integrated schooling. Exceptional Parent, 3, 15-17.
Bruner, J. S. 1972. Nature and uses of immaturity. American Psychologist, 27, 687-708.
Calvert, D. R., and Ross, M. 1973. The semantics of deafness. In W. H. Northcott (Ed.), The Hearing Impaired Child in a Regular Classroom: Preschool, Elementary and Secondary Years. Washington, D.C.: Alexander Graham Bell Association for the Deaf.
Calvert, D. R., and Silverman, S. R. 1975. Speech and Deafness. Washington, D.C.: Alexander Graham Bell Association for the Deaf.
Carson, P. A., and Goetzinger, C. P. 1975. A study of learning in deaf children. Journal of Auditory Research, 15, 73-80.
Connor, L. E. 1976. Mainstreaming a Special School. Teaching Exceptional Children, 8, 76-81.
Davis, H. (Ed.). 1965. The young deaf child: Identification and management. Proceedings of the Conference held in Toronto, Canada. Acta Otolaryngologica, Supplementum 206.
Elliott, L. 1967. Descriptive analysis of audiometric and psychometric scores of deaf students. Journal of Speech and Hearing Research, 10, 209-224.
Erber, N. P. 1972. Auditory, visual and auditory-visual recognition of consonants by children with normal and impaired hearing. Journal of Speech and Hearing Research, 15, 413-422.
Ewing, A. W. G., and Ewing, I. R. 1954. Speech and the Deaf Child. Manchester, England: University Press.
Gaeth, J. H. 1967. Learning with visual and audiovisual perceptions. In F. McConnell and P. H. Ward (Eds.), Deafness in Childhood. Nashville, Tenn.: Vanderbilt University Press.
Gallaudet College. (In press). Communication methods and educational achievement: Patterns and relationships. Washington, D.C.: Office of Demographic Studies.
Gates, R. R. 1970. The differential effectiveness of various modes of presenting verbal information to deaf students through modified television formats. Unpublished doctoral dissertation, University of Pittsburgh.
Giattino, J., and Hogan, J. 1975. Analysis of a father's speech to his language learning child. Journal of Speech and Hearing Disorders, 40, 524-537.
Goetzinger, C. P. 1974. Psychological considerations of hard of hearing children. In R. L. Cozad (Ed.), The Speech Clinician and the Hearing Impaired Child. Springfield, Ill.: Charles C Thomas.

Goetzinger, C. P., and Proud, G. O. 1975. The impact of hearing impairment upon the psychological development of children. Journal of Auditory Research, 15, 1–60.

Gorelick, M. C. 1974. What's in a label? Unpublished paper. California State University, Northridge.

Gronlund, N. E. 1959. Sociometry in the Classroom. New York: Harper and Brothers.

Guralnick, M. J. 1976. The value of integrating handicapped and nonhandicapped preschool children. American Journal of Orthopsychiatry, 46, 236–245.

Hanners, B. A. 1973. The role of audiological management in the development of language by severely hearing impaired children. Paper presented at the annual meeting of the Academy of Rehabilitative Audiology, Detroit.

Hartley, R. E. 1976. Play and values. International Journal of Early Childhood, 8, 21–27.

Held, M. 1975. Oral deaf parents communicate with their deaf infants. Volta Review, 77, 309–312.

Hobbs, N. 1975. The Futures of Children. San Francisco: Jossey-Bass.

Isaacs, N. 1974. Children's ways of knowing. In M. Hardeman (Ed.), Nathan Isaacs on Education, Psychology, and Piaget. New York: Teachers College Press.

Jordan, J. B., and Dailey, R. F. (Eds.). 1973. Not All Little Wagons are Red: The Exceptional Child's Early Years. Arlington, Va.: The Council for Exceptional Children.

Kennedy, P., and Bruininks, R. H. 1974. Social status of hearing impaired children in regular classrooms. Exceptional Children, 40, 336–342.

Kennedy, P., Northcott, W., McCauley, R., and Williams, S. M. 1976. Longitudinal sociometric and cross-sectional data on mainstreaming hearing impaired children: Implications for preschool programming. Volta Review, 78, 71–82.

Klein, J. 1975. Mainstreaming the preschooler. Young Children, 30, 317–327.

Liff, S. 1973. Early intervention and language development in hearing impaired children. Unpublished master's thesis, Vanderbilt University.

Ling, D. 1976. Speech and the Hearing Impaired Child: Theory and Practice. Washington D.C.: Alexander Graham Bell Association for the Deaf.

Ling, D., and Ling, A. H. 1974. Communication development in the first three years of life. Journal of Speech and Hearing Research, 17, 146–159.

Luterman, D. M. 1976. A comparison of language skills of hearing impaired children trained in a visual/oral method and an auditory/oral method. American Annals of the Deaf, 121, 389–393.

Martin, E. W. 1973. An end to dichotomous constructs: A reconceptualization of teacher education. Paper presented at the Dedication of Thorndike Hall, Columbia University, New York.

Martin, E. W. 1974. Public policy and early childhood education. Paper presented at the Education Commission of the States' Symposium: "Implementing child development programs," Boston.

McCauley, R. W., Bruininks, R. H., and Kennedy, P. 1976. Behavioral interactions of hearing impaired children in regular classrooms. Journal of Special Education, 10, 277–284.

McConnell, F. (Ed.). 1968. Proceedings. Current practices in educational management of the deaf infant (0–3 years). Nashville, Tenn.: Vanderbilt School of Medicine.

McConnell, F. 1971. The psychology of communication. In L. E. Connor (Ed.), Speech for the Deaf Child: Knowledge and Use. Washington, D.C.: Alexander Graham Bell Association for the Deaf.

McConnell, F. 1973. Children with hearing disabilities. In L. M. Dunn (Ed.), Exceptional Children in the Schools (2nd ed.). New York: Holt, Rinehart and Winston.

Minneapolis Public Schools. 1975. Evaluation report of the family-oriented special education preschool (0–4/5 years), Minneapolis, Minn.

Minnesota Department of Education. 1974. State Guidelines: Preschool Educational Programs for the Handicapped in Minnesota. St Paul: Minnesota Department of Education.

National Advisory Committee on Education of the Deaf. 1973. Annual report. Basic education rights of the hearing impaired. Publication 73-24001. Washington, D.C.: U.S. Department of Health, Education, and Welfare.

National Advisory Committee on the Handicapped. 1977. Annual report. Full educational opportunity under the law. Washington, D.C.: U.S. Department of Health, Education, and Welfare.

Neisworth, J. T. 1975. Functional similarities of learning disability and mild retardation. Exceptional Children, 42, 17–24.

Nix, G. W. 1975. Total communication: A review of the studies offered in its support. Volta Review, 77, 470–493.

Northcott, W. H. 1970. Candidate for integration: A hearing impaired child in a regular nursery school. Young Children, 25, 367–380.

Northcott, W. H. 1971a. Infant education and home training. In L. E. Connor (Ed.), Speech for the Deaf Child: Knowledge and Use. Washington, D.C.: Alexander Graham Bell Association for the Deaf.

Northcott, W. H. 1971b. The integration of young deaf children into ordinary educational programs. Exceptional Children, 38, 29–32.

Northcott, W. H. 1973a. The Hearing Impaired Child in a Regular Classroom: Preschool, Elementary and Secondary Years. Washington, D.C.: Alexander Graham Bell Association for the Deaf.

Northcott, W. H. 1973b. Competencies needed by teachers of hearing-impaired infants, birth to three years, and their parents. Volta Review, 75, 532–544.

Northcott, W. H. 1975a. Normalization of the preschool child with hearing impairment. In M. E. Glasscock (Ed.), Sensorineural hearing loss in children: Early detection and intervention. Otolaryngologic Clinics of North America, Number 8.

Northcott, W. H. 1975b. Preparation for specialized roles in early childhood education for the handicapped: Who prepares whom to do what? In Proceedings of the Conference on Research Needs Related to Early Childhood Education for the Handicapped. Princeton, N.J.: Bureau of Education for the Handicapped, U.S. Office of Education.

Northcott, W. H. (Ed.). 1977a. Curriculum Guide: Hearing Impaired Children—Birth to Three Years—and Their Parents (Rev. ed.). Washington D.C.: Alexander Graham Bell Association for the Deaf.

Northcott, W. H. 1977b. The oral interpreter: A necessary support specialist for the hearing impaired. Volta Review, 79, 136–144.

Pollack, D. 1974. Denver's acoupedic program. Peabody Journal of Education, 51, 180–185.

Pollack, D., and Ernst, M. 1973. Learning to listen in an integrated preschool. Volta Review, 75, 359–367.

Porter, G. 1975. The missing vital dimension in successful integration. Volta Review, 77, 416–422.

Rankhorn, B. 1974. Some effects of reverse integration on the language environment of hearing impaired children. New York: Lexington School for the Deaf.

Rister, A. 1975. Deaf children in mainstream education. Volta Review, 77, 279–291.

Ross, A. 1964. The Exceptional Child in the Family. New York: Grune & Stratton.

Ross, M. 1972. Classroom acoustics and speech intelligibility. In J. Katz (Ed.), Handbook of Clinical Audiology. Baltimore: Williams & Wilkins.

Ross, M. 1976. Verbal communication: The state of the art. Volta Review, 78, 324–328.

Ross, M., Giolas, T., and Carver, P. W. 1973. Effects of classroom listening conditions on speech intelligibility. Language, Speech, and Hearing Services in Schools, 4, 72–76.

Schumacher, E. F. 1975. Small is Beautiful: Economics as if People Mattered. New York: Harper & Row.

Shotel, J. R., Iano, R. P., and McGettigan, J. F. 1972. Teacher attitudes associated with integration of handicapped children. Exceptional Children, 38, 677–683.

Simmons-Martin, A. A. 1976. The auditory-global method. Paper presented at a meeting of the Louisiana State Advisory Committee for Education of the Deaf, New Orleans.

Solnit, A. J., and Stark, M. J. 1961. Mourning and the birth of a defective child. In R. S. Eissler (Ed.), Psychoanalytic Study of the Child (Vol. 16). New York: International Universities Press.

Stern, V. W. 1969. Fingerpaint on the hearing aid. Volta Review, 71, 149–154.

Stuckless, E. R. 1971. Assessing and supporting linguistic development in deaf adolescents. Paper presented at Hearing and Speech Conference, February, Kansas University Medical Center.

Valletutti, P. 1969. Integration vs. segregation: A useless dialectic. Journal of Special Education, 3, 405–409.

van Uden, A. A. 1970. A World of Language for Deaf Children. Part I. Basic Principles. The Netherlands: Rotterdam University Press.

Warfield, G. J. (Ed.). 1974. Mainstream Currents. Reston, Va.: The Council for Exceptional Children.

Watson, T. J. 1973. Integration of hearing impaired children in nursery schools in England. In W. H. Northcott (Ed.), The Hearing Impaired Child in a Regular Classroom: Preschool, Elementary and Secondary Years. Washington, D.C.: Alexander Graham Bell Association for the Deaf.

Weinstein, G. W. 1968. Nursery school with a difference—Deaf and normal children in New York. Parents, 43, 66–69.

Wynne, S., Ulfelder, L. S., and Dakof, G. 1975. Mainstreaming and Early Childhood Education for Handicapped Children: A Guide for Parents and Teachers. Washington, D.C.: Wynne Associates.

OPEN EDUCATION AND THE INTEGRATION OF CHILDREN WITH SPECIAL NEEDS

Samuel J. Meisels, Ed.D.

The program described in this chapter is one that integrates or mainstreams mildly to moderately handicapped preschool and kindergarten-age children into open structure classrooms. Although such an arrangement may appear to place this program in double jeopardy—given the history of innovations in American education—the objective of this chapter is to show that mainstreaming and open education are not only compatible, but reasonable educational partners as well.

The program that is described is known as the Eliot-Pearson Children's School. Eliot-Pearson is the laboratory school of the Department of Child Study, Tufts University. The school serves as a training site for graduate and undergraduate students and has an adult-to-child ratio of one to four or one to five.

Approximately one hundred children of ages two-and-a-half to six years attend Eliot-Pearson. Twenty percent of these children are handicapped. A wide range of handicapping conditions is represented in this population, although the range of severity is limited to mild and moderate impairment. Examples of the kinds of diagnostic categories represented in the school include cerebral palsy, developmental delay, speech impairment, orthopaedic impairment, hearing impairment, emotional disturbance, epilepsy, learning disability, Down's syndrome, and brain damage.

This chapter discusses the basic assumptions and elements of the open classroom. Next, it describes the applicability of this framework to integra-

---

Preparation of this chapter was supported in part by Grant G00-75-00230 from the United States Office of Education, Bureau of Education for the Handicapped.

tion. Finally, it explores the relationship between the interventions characteristic of open classrooms and the needs of integrated handicapped children.

OPEN EDUCATION

Model of Teacher-Child Interaction

Open education is a problematic phenomenon to discuss. Unlike several recent educational innovations, it cannot call upon single authorship, clear principles, or controlled experiments. In all the time that it has been practiced, no model, single philosophy, or set of universally endorsed assumptions have emerged. Although many books and articles have been written about the practice of open classrooms, few research or analytical studies have been published (see Barth, 1972; Bussis and Chittenden, 1970; Bussis, Chittenden, and Amarel, 1976; Central Advisory Council for Education, 1967; Eisner, 1974; Friedlander, 1975; Hawkins, 1974; Peters, 1969; Resnick, 1972; Weber, 1971; Wright, 1975).

As if to emphasize its pluralism, even its name has not been formally agreed upon. Some common variants are "integrated day," "informal education," "Leicestershire approach," "open classroom," "open space," and "open structure." In this chapter, these names are used interchangeably.

Several of its proponents insist that open education is actually a "nonmodel" (Bussis and Chittenden, 1970; Kallet, 1970) and as such resists uniform definition. Nevertheless, in recent years, the professional and nonprofessional American public has begun to associate open education with one type of educational practice, namely, that of the child-centered classroom. In this classroom, the teacher acts as a relatively passive "facilitator" while the child, as a spontaneous learner, is free to follow his or her interests and inclinations. One advocate of this viewpoint claims that the open classroom teacher "... is concerned with learning as opposed to teaching.... The teacher is largely a stagesetter, a stimulator, who encourages and guides but who does not direct" (Rogers, 1970, p. 289).

This conventional view of open education assimilates it to the model of the "permissive" or "laissez-faire" classroom. In the laissez-faire stereotype, all significant choices about learning are made by the child. The teacher plays a passive role. The converse of this position is represented by "authoritarianism." The authoritarian position holds that all significant choices belong to the teacher or the curriculum; the child's responsibility is to implement or follow these choices.

Open Education at Eliot-Pearson The Eliot-Pearson conception of open education embraces neither the laissez-faire nor the authoritarian position. Our conception of open education is based on a teacher-child relationship characterized by interaction and joint decision-making. To fully comprehend this approach, the one-dimensional permissive-authoritarian continuum must be abandoned. In its place, a view of teaching and learning is substituted that is simultaneously child centered and adult centered. This approach assumes that:

> ... the organization of experience and growth of knowledge can best take place when the child himself is located very much at the center of the learning process and acquires responsibility for learning.... [T]his does not imply that the teacher assumes a role that is merely understanding and supportive. While teachers certainly should strive to understand and support children, they are also perceived as active thinking adults whose job it is to extend and integrate children's learning in all spheres. (Chittenden and Bussis, 1971, p. 1)

Thus, "child centeredness" and "adult centeredness" are treated as independent dimensions, rather than as dependent points on a single continuum. Figure 1 shows a classification scheme that portrays this relationship in terms of the relative contributions of the teacher and the child to decisions governing the content and process of learning. Utilizing this framework, an open classroom can be defined as a classroom in which both

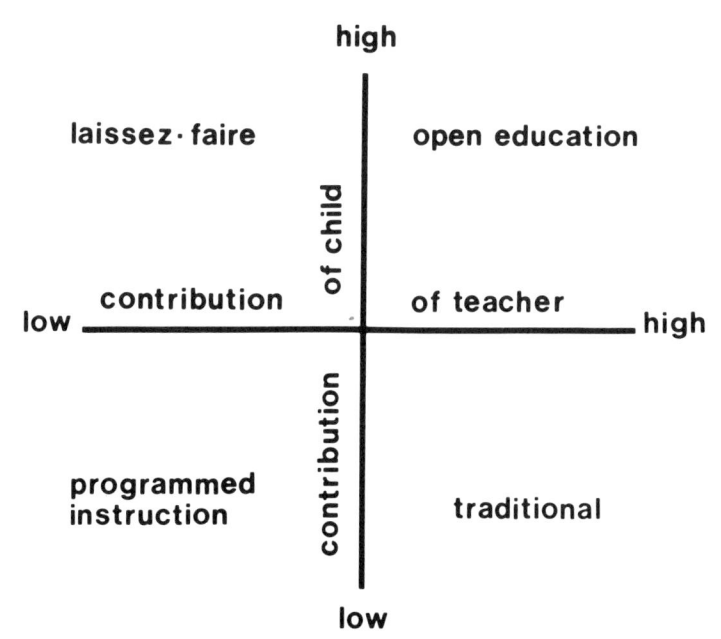

Figure 1. Double classification scheme based on extent to which the individual teacher and the individual child are active contributors to decisions regarding the content and process of learning. (Figure adapted from Bussis and Chittenden, 1970.)

teacher and child are active participants in the teaching-learning process. Most educational models are predicated on a "zero-sum" theory concerning activity and control in learning settings. Either the teacher takes the initiative and controls the direction of the classroom, or else the child does. To the extent that one relinquishes control, it becomes available to the other. At Eliot-Pearson, learning is seen as an interactive and additive process in which both children and teachers participate in framing and implementing objectives.

The teaching process in such a setting is hypothesis oriented or quasiexperimental. It usually begins with the accumulation of formal or informal diagnostic information about the child. The child is given extensive opportunities to express and follow interests and to become involved in the activities of the classroom. Based on this behavior and on the diagnostic information, the teacher begins to identify goals and corresponding subgoals that could have relevance for the child. These goals, which reflect the child's interests, abilities, and learning history, are then related to the context of the classroom space, time, materials, and grouping of children. In this manner, individualized outcome objectives are developed. Throughout the entire process, the teacher is engaged in evaluating and assessing the effects of interventions, the relationship of formal and informal diagnostic information to performance, the efficacy of certain materials and teaching strategies, and the participation of the child in the process as a whole.

Each decision undertaken in the course of the teaching process should reflect or contribute to the teacher's knowledge of the child's form of experiencing the physical, intellectual, and social world. In other words, in the open classroom, what the teacher has in mind is only part of the information that eventually structures the classroom experience. The other part is the child's response to the teacher, or the child's behavior to which the teacher responds. This type of interactive responsiveness is the foundation on which the open classroom program is built.

Individualization and Program Objectives

At the heart of open education and at the center of integration is individualization. Individualization refers to the practice of developing specific goals for individual children and specific strategies for implementing these goals. Although the same goals are frequently held for several children, this does not mean that all of these children are expected to learn the same thing at the same time, nor does it mean that all children are expected to learn in the same way.

In the open classroom, a teacher cannot claim to be individualizing instruction if he or she does not have multiple, intentional strategies for teaching. This is the difference between individualized instruction and individual experience. The teacher who uses goals for the purposes of individualization takes the data of personal or individual experience (the child's needs, abilities, moods, learning style, and history) and uses them to help the child find a personally rewarding and productive way of learning.

Individualization plays a fundamental role in the integrated program at Eliot-Pearson. Taken as a whole, the structure of the classroom experience for children with special needs does not differ significantly from the structure of experience for nonhandicapped children. Although supplementary services are provided only for special needs children, the fact that the program is individualized means that, to some extent, every child has a specific curriculum.

The goals and subgoals of the classroom program for handicapped and nonhandicapped children thus overlap. Most open educators do not specifically state behavioral objectives (see Central Advisory Council for Education, 1967); rather, they include their goals in statements of values, purposes, or general procedures. Chief among these purposes and values is that children work in art, music, math, reading, and writing; that they extend their activities beyond the initial encounter to more involved products; that they integrate their learning throughout all the activities of the classroom; that they utilize space, time, materials, and groupings functionally; and that they be happy, excited, involved, autonomous, cooperative, and creative.

At Eliot-Pearson, these value statements have been translated into three major domains or families of goals: personal/social development, cognitive development, and motor development. Each domain subsumes a noninclusive but extensive list of logically more specific subgoals, outcome objectives, and classroom activities. In any given classroom, handicapped or nonhandicapped children may share identical goals, subgoals, or outcome objectives while engaging in significantly different classroom activities designed to achieve those objectives. The planning process for all children is thus quite similar, although the execution of the plans shows diversity, variety, and extensive provision for individual difference.

Heuristic Environment

The ideal open classroom environment is a heuristic environment, an environment saturated with the possibilities of making choices and acquiring information (Meisels, 1973). In working with handicapped and nonhandicapped children in the same classroom, there is a fundamental need for reliable information concerning children's behavior. The term "heuristic environment" refers to an environment that is potentially differentiated, that is, one that can be put to a variety of uses. No undifferentiated environment can be optimal for a variety of learning styles, abilities, rates of comprehension, or moods. Differentiation and organization are critical for an open classroom; they are prerequisite for a mainstreamed classroom. The open educator plans and prepares the classroom so that it is personally functional or responsive in terms of generating and making use of information. The classroom must also be responsive or functional for each child, both in the way the child affects the environment and in the way that the environment affects the child.

Four major elements of the open classroom environment exist: space, time, materials, and the grouping of children. These are discussed below from the point of view of their information potential for both the child and the teacher. No sharp distinctions are made with respect to differential uses by handicapped or nonhandicapped children. In a program and environment designed to meet individual differences, modifications due to differences in physical, sensory, intellectual, or emotional development are made as a matter of intention, not exception.

Space The classroom space must be sufficiently flexible and ambiguous to allow children to adjust it to the function they wish it to perform. Accordingly, desks and chairs are not assigned permanent places or permanent occupants. If there is need for a few chairs in one part of the room, or several tables in another, then the appropriate changes are made. If a group of children wants to make a science museum, or to find a special place to display some of their work, the classroom should be designed so that these changes constitute reasonable adjustments. The important point is that the children must feel that it is possible for them to find the adequate setting for the type of activity in which they wish to engage. The classroom is designed so that each child—handicapped or nonhandicapped—can create this setting if it does not already exist. In this respect, the children structure the space in which their experiences take place.

In general, the classrooms at Eliot-Pearson are visually exciting. They contain climbing structures, locations that permit children to perceive things from different perspectives, dividers that function as barriers or walls, and small areas that serve as retreats and meeting places. All display areas (shelves, tables, wall areas, bulletin boards), consistent with the general scale of the classroom, are at child level. For children with physical disabilities, ramps, railings, and reinforced handholds have been installed. In general, the space is designed to be personally functional for each child.

In instances in which the space more explicitly prescribes functions for children, it still retains some ambiguity and flexibility. This is particularly true of the "interest areas": distinct areas in the classroom that are devoted to a unitary topic such as math, manipulatives, science, art, dress-up, blocks, reading, wood-working, sand and water play. Each of these areas is a separate environment contained within the classroom space. They are environments fixed by the kinds of materials available, the number of possibilities of rearranging them, and the contiguity of the environment to other interest areas within the room. Nevertheless, these spaces alone do not dictate specific outcomes or programs. Taken by themselves, they provide nothing more than materials and a physical location. Their primary functions are established by their users.

Time The temporal organization of the classroom is arranged so that time is as personally functional as possible for each child. Within broad limits, there is an absence of arbitrary scheduling in the open classroom. Not everyone works in the same way and at the same rate. Although class periods can roughly be divided into different forms of work time, group time, outdoor and indoor play, the ambiguity of these divisions serves to legitimize all rates and speeds. Children with long attention spans, or particularly vital interests, can work continuously and without interruption; those who prefer to work at several different activities in a single day can also do so. Thus, each child's feeling of subjective time—the sense of time generated by personal experiences—is maximized.

The ideal temporal organization in the open classroom is called the "integrated day" (see Taylor, 1971; Weber, 1971). This term refers to the simultaneity of activities available to children in an open classroom. At base, this concept is a temporal one: It deals with the division of the child's continuum of experience. In an integrated program, a number of different activities—such as sewing, cooking, reading, building, painting, climbing, experimenting, and play acting—go on at the same time. Usually these activities are designed to overlap spatially and temporally so that the different aspects of the classroom are seen by the child as continuous, as integrated into a whole. Traditional classrooms use time-tabling to separate activities; open classrooms use the form of the integrated day to combine activities and to make it possible for children to extend the skills they have acquired from one area to another.

The ideal of the integrated day is frequently modified for some preschool age children or for children who are intellectually and/or neurologically impaired. Without some external structuring, the behavior of these children may become random and unfocused. For these children, critical classroom objectives might include the development of the ability to attend, to delay gratification, to control perseverative behavior, or to acquire inner controls.

Materials The dual focus in the case of learning materials concerns: (1) the functions that the child organizes the materials to perform, and (2) the functions that the materials impose on the child. Often, children come to school with an explicit objective in mind—doing a puzzle, pounding on some wood, building with blocks, playing with dolls, and so on. In these cases, children frequently choose materials to work with that they believe will transmit to them the desired skills, knowledge, or experience. This is one way in which children organize materials for their own purposes.

Another example of how children use materials is evident in the way that materials function as a source of self-esteem. A child who masters a material, completes a project, or learns a skill usually gains a sense of accomplishment and control, and to this extent—when the child returns to or seeks out one of these experiences—is again organizing the materials for a particular purpose. Teachers in open classrooms frequently use materials as means to affective ends (Meisels, 1976). Children are encouraged to acquire mastery of a skill or material not only for its own sake, but for the feeling of "effectance" it transmits as well (see White, 1959).

The manner in which learning materials organize a child's experience depends on the teacher's discovery and recognition of a material's learning functions. This understanding of learning functions is essential for both the selection and the implementation of the materials. The concept of "learning function" is introduced to refer to the potential instructional use or value of a curricular material. This concept can be applied in any setting; it is particularly appropriate in a classroom that integrates children with a wide range of abilities. Through using the concept of learning functions, the task of individualizing different children's experiences with identical materials or objectives becomes clearer. For example, a partial listing of the cognitive learning functions of a set of attribute or logical blocks would include the following:

Matching	Class inclusion	Negation
Sorting	Building with	Conjunction
Classifying	unstructured materials	Disjunction
Ordering	Sets	Cardination
Learning colors	Mapping	Ordination
Deduction	Subtraction	Addition

This is not an exhaustive list. New functions could be added through the discoveries of its users or through extensions that involve other materials. The greater the learning functions contained in a material, the greater the density of that material. In the case of logical blocks, the learning functions are primarily cognitive. Other materials, for example, sand, pictures, animals, water play, or dress-up, are saturated with affective functions as well. The point is that these learning functions are potential uses to which the materials can be put. To the extent that the teacher seeks to diagnose, individualize, organize, and evaluate instruction—that is, to intervene in an interactive manner—to that extent, the teacher will have to plan, organize, and discover the learning functions of classroom materials.

A number of conclusions concerning the type of materials with which an open classroom should be equipped follows from the concept of learning functions. For one thing, the materials should be characterized by a variety of cognitive and affective learning functions. Another desirable feature of materials for children between the ages of three and five is that they be largely manipulable. Piaget (1964) has argued convincingly that young children "construct" their own reality. They learn by actively manipulating and assimilating experiences from the environment into already existing patterns of perception and conceptualization, while at the same time accommodating themselves to new data and new configurations from the environment. Hence, verbal abstractions about this environment, presented in the absence of the child's personal "construction" of reality, are often dysfunctional (see Kamii and Derman, 1971). In this regard, the open classroom shares a number of significant features in common with the cognitive-developmental classroom (Kohlberg, 1972; Meisels, 1976).

All of these features—the child's organization of materials, the affective dimension, learning functions, density, preoperational thought, as well as repetition and sequence—constitute heuristic content. Taken as a whole, this content forms the teacher's selection criteria for classroom materials.

Grouping of Children Typically, children in preschool classrooms are grouped vertically or heterogeneously by age, with a two- or three-year age span not uncommon. The open classroom does not depend on this form of grouping children, but it is desirable for a number of reasons and is practically a necessary condition for mainstreaming or integration. Vertically grouped classrooms are frequently called "family groupings" (Ridgway and Lawton, 1969) because each class, like a family, contains children of different ages. In mainstreamed classrooms, the handicapped children are often chronologically older than their other classmates. As in a family, mixed-age classrooms usually generate a great deal of cross-age tutoring, an advantageous feature for the developmentally delayed child. Cross-age tutoring also relates to the way children move from one level of intellectual organization to another. That is, a child who is at a certain point of intellectual development is most likely to move to a more complex level of development when exposed to the point of view of someone functioning just beyond his or her own stage of development (see Kohlberg, 1969). Nevertheless, since intellectual development is not strictly chronological, this type of change does not depend as much on age grouping as it does on social collaboration. If the classroom does not contain numerous opportunities for natural group experience, the developmental motivation will be sharply curtailed (Piaget, 1964).

In the integrated classroom, opportunities for developmental advance are maximized. Interpersonally, handicapped and nonhandicapped children are exposed to new information that challenges available intellectual schemas and may promote new patterns of accommodation. This process of adaptation is greatly facilitated when grouping within a classroom is not prescribed strictly by considerations of age or ability. An alternative to age and ability grouping is functional grouping. In a functionally grouped classroom, a child with special needs is less likely to be stereotyped, singled out, or continually assigned to the same role.

Functional grouping usually appears in two forms (see Palmer, 1971). First, there are interest or working groups in which children, with or without teacher intervention, organize and create their own groups based on their common interests. Children of varying abilities work together, each taking from the experience what they are able. By and large, these groupings by interest represent the majority of the types of groupings found in open classrooms and are highly appropriate for an integrated program.

The second form of functional grouping is the teaching group. These are groups chosen by the teacher in which children of relatively similar abilities in some specific area are brought together for special help and attention. It should be noted that teaching groups are temporary groups arranged to meet particular needs. They should be distinguished from systematic ability grouping, or tracking. Teaching groups derive much of their effectiveness from their potential for individualization. Thus, children with poor language skills but highly competent fine motor abilities do not need to be segregated into slower groups for all of their classroom experience simply because of their language disability. Alternatively, teaching groups can be formed around differing learning modalities, as opposed to abilities. Thus, to use the example of teaching reading, some children will be exposed to a linguistic reading approach, others to a phonetic approach, others to a language experience approach, and so forth. Discriminations along these lines highlight a child's preferred learning style rather than his or her learning deficiencies. The teaching group is used extensively at Eliot-Pearson to supplement the classroom experience of children with special needs.

As with the other elements of the physical environment, the animus is to use grouping for specific purposes and goals rather than to eliminate functions through rigid scheduling or planning. The open classroom environment must be an environment that is multiply responsive to, and alterable by, both the teacher and the children.

MAINSTREAMING AND OPEN EDUCATION

The Whole Child

The program at Eliot-Pearson is not the first open education program to be developed for children with special needs. Knoblock (1973) has described an open education program for emotionally disturbed children, and Winett (1973) has suggested that the technology of behavior modification can be merged with the humanistic concerns of open education. A small number of open structure programs have been funded by the Bureau of Education for the Handicapped in their Handicapped Children's Early Education Program.

Traditionally, education for children with handicaps has been deficit oriented (see Johnson, 1962). That is, the education program for the child with special needs has been narrowly confined to containing or remediating that child's area of greatest handicap or impairment. A child with a suspected disability is tested or evaluated to determine what he or she can or cannot do. Once the child's areas of disability have been identified, a program of remediation is designed and implemented. In such an approach, the child's areas of greatest strength or ability are frequently neglected.

In contrast to this approach, the program at Eliot-Pearson is not deficit oriented. In working with children with special needs, it is obviously critical to understand and be prepared to modify the classroom program to accommodate to the child's difficulties and disabilities. However, it is equally important to learn about and develop a program for the child's particular strengths. To the extent that it is possible, we try to utilize the child's strengths in the service of the child's weaknesses.

That education concerns the whole child is an axiom of open education. Our attempt at considering each child as an integrated whole person, combining strengths and weaknesses, follows from this assumption. Teachers at Eliot-Pearson continually seek to expand and extend the range of children's interests and abilities through maximizing each child's interactivity with the resources of the physical and social environment. In the sections that follow, the focus is on how these resources are employed for children with special needs.

Program Elements

In addition to the individualized classroom experience, children with special needs participate in several additional forms of instructional experience. Every special needs child is assigned a tutor who works with the child two to four hours per week. Additionally, several of these children participate in specialized small teaching groups. The small groups are led by a special needs resource teacher; the tutorials are supervised by the special needs resource teacher but are staffed by undergraduate or graduate students. In future years, home-based training will form the nucleus of the tutorial program.

The tutorial sessions serve a number of purposes. First, they provide each child with a one-to-one experience with an adult that is designed to be warm, accepting, and free from competition with other children. Second, they provide for additional individualization of instruction. In some respects the tutorial sessions are "deficit oriented" because they focus on the child's handicapping condition and seek to implement a program of remediation. Nevertheless, as in the classroom program, the child's limitations are addressed through his or her strengths. A third purpose of the tutorials is to extend the activities of the regular classroom program by teaching the child how to use some of the core materials of the classroom. A fourth purpose is to serve as an alternative learning setting free from the distractions and stimulation of the classroom.

The small teaching groups bring together children with similar abilities in particular areas. These groups might concentrate on language stimulation, fine motor skills, gross motor abilities, or movement and music. They are not exclusively composed of children with special needs, although their primary objective is to help children in a small group setting acquire competence in an area of weakness.

A final program element concerns service to parents of children with special needs. In addition to conferences, observations, room meetings, and opportunities to help in the classroom, parents of children with special needs are encouraged to participate in a number of single-topic didactic groups as well as in a special needs parent support group.

Each of these elements—the classroom program, tutorial sessions, small groups, and service to parents—forms one aspect of the Eliot-Pearson program. Although the individualized form of teaching practiced in the classroom is inherently responsive to the needs of the handicapped children, the coordinated supplementary instructional and parent support elements provide a critical reinforcement and extension for the classroom program. The classroom teacher is the critical member of this network of services and relationships. It is the teacher who synthesizes all of the information and who coordinates each child's program, thus enabling consistent and intelligent planning to take place.

The Program in Action

The rationale, assumptions, elements, and goals of the open classroom program have been presented thus far. An attempt has been made to relate the discussion to an integrated population of handicapped and nonhandicapped children. At this point, it is appropriate to analyze in greater depth the actual classroom program. Given the individualized nature of the Eliot-Pearson approach, the daily schedule in each classroom serves only as a general framework for the organization of each child's performance. The individualized programs developed for each child provide the major cohesiveness in the classroom. Nevertheless, a typical morning kindergarten program might reflect the following schedule:

9:00–9:20	Outdoors
9:20–9:30	Class meeting
9:30–10:40	Independent and small group work time at classroom interest areas
10:40–10:45	Cleanup and transition
10:45–11:00	Quiet time (reading, stories, puzzles, etc.)
11:00–11:20	Outdoors
11:20–11:45	Group time: songs, music, and story

Within this framework individual programs are implemented. Two case illustrations follow that demonstrate how the program planning procedures described earlier are put into practice.

Both of these cases involve children with special needs (children's names have been changed). The cases include a specific classroom example developed by each child's teacher. The assessment of behavior included in each example represents observational data accumulated by the teacher in the course of classroom interactions. Each classroom example is accompanied by a summary of the child's tutorial experience (see Tables 1 and 2). Finally, a discussion relating the work with the child to the open classroom framework follows each case.

> *Case 1: Nathan* Nathan is a four-and-one-half-year-old epileptic child whose behavior is often characterized as hyperactive and who shows signs of mild developmental delay across many developmental areas. This was Nathan's second year of group experience, his first at Eliot-Pearson. Although he was occasionally clumsy, his gross motor abilities were quite well developed and he was also able to make lasting one-to-one attachments with peers and adults. He is the youngest of three children. One of his siblings is moderately learning disabled. His parents have a high school education; his father is in a semiskilled profession.
>
> *Classroom Example 1*
> Goal:
>   Personal/social
> Subgoal:
>   To develop the ability to express one's feelings
> Assessment of behavior:
>   When trying to express his needs and feelings, Nathan shows angry facial expressions, aggressive thrusts of the body, clenched hands, head held down, movements becoming out of control, swearing, hitting, and spitting.

Table 1. Eliot-Pearson children's school partial summary of tutorial work, 1975–1976

Child's name Nathan　　　　　　　　　　　　　　　Handicapping condition Mild developmental delay; epilepsy

Objectives	Outcomes	Future objectives	Comments
To improve articulation and stimulate language usage through modeling and repetition, articulating sounds while looking in a mirror, blowing and peanut butter exercises, magazines, walks outside	Nathan articulates all letters except sibilants in at least one position in a word; he has begun to blend consonants; syntax is becoming more mature and descriptive language has increased	To complete a task cooperatively with another child through small group experience	Nathan functions best in a one-to-one relationship, in a familiar environment, and with minimal stimulation. Ability to attend to tasks improves when he is in an isolated setting. He was unable to "share" his tutor with other children, and worked best alone. It will be important next year for Nathan to begin to be able to use small group experience productively
To improve control of scissors and writing implements through experience with Magic Markers, chalk, cutting projects, stencils, sandpaper shapes, pegboard, puzzles	Nathan's pencil control has not improved; he has become competent with hammer and nails, and can cut on a line if paper is held by teacher	To label primary colors through experience with colored water and sand, colored cubes	
To label primary colors through Lotto games, color cubes, paint projects	Nathan does not consistently label colors correctly	To understand one-to-one correspondence	
To increase positive interactions with peers through small group experiences	Nathan's interest in sand and water has provided more opportunities for positive peer interaction	To improve control of writing and cutting implements through stencils, cutting projects, kinesthetic materials	
		To sustain attention for ten minutes while listening to a story on a record	

Table 2. Eliot-Pearson Children's School partial summary of tutorial work, 1975-1976

Child's name Carl   Handicapping condition Moderate developmental delay

Objectives	Outcomes	Future objectives	Comments
To improve visual attention through stencils, tracing, puzzles, shape sorting box	Carl attends more visually to tasks and can cut on a line, successfully complete a six-shape sorting box, and non-interlocking puzzles	To improve control of cutting and writing implements through stencils, tracing, sand writing, cutting	Carl's inattentiveness and lack of investment in activities were major obstacles to learning. Clear expectations and self-correcting materials were effective in increasing attention. His level of investment fluctuated constantly, and no single technique seemed to be consistently effective
To increase vocabulary of body parts through body tracing, songs, puzzles, faces	Carl recognizes and labels many body parts including neck, shoulders, eyes, nose, hair, head, arm, leg, hand, foot	To improve articulation through songs, modeling and repetition, consonant cards	
		To learn noun-verb-object constructions	
To increase understanding of directional prepositions through verbalization of the position of various objects, hide-and-seek games followed by verbalization of where the object was found, songs with finger plays	Carl follows directions involving "under," "over," "in front of," "behind," but needs prompting to verbalize prepositional directions	To increase descriptive vocabulary to include loud, soft, slow, fast through songs, direction games, modeling	
		To increase one-to-one correspondence, recognition and counting numbers to five, through matching games, board games, kinesthetic cards	
To familiarize Carl with time concepts through use of a calendar	Carl understands and verbalizes "yesterday" and "today"	To write Carl's name through tracing, kinesthetic cards, copying	
To increase descriptive vocabulary through stories, pictures, direction games, songs	Carl's descriptive vocabulary has increased and includes "near" and "far"	To increase concept of time	
		To generalize skills acquired in tutoring to classroom through coordination of materials and teachers	

Open Education and Integration   253

Outcome objective:
  To be able to use words instead of hitting and spitting
Approximate time period:
  Six weeks
Activities:
  1. State expectations in the classroom clearly, e.g., "No spitting here."
  2. Anticipate hitting and redirect his anger into another channel for expression, e.g., banging a nail or pounding Playdoh.
  3. Consistency throughout. Allow nothing to go by without an instant assessment. Watch all the time for emergence of anger.
  4. "Time out." Remove after incident and tell Nathan why he is being "timed out." "You forgot we don't hit." Do not condemn; rather, act in a neutral manner. Place a chair in a secluded part of the room (always the same spot). Hold if necessary. Set timer for two minutes. Do not talk or communicate with him. After bell goes off, redirect Nathan to an activity in which he feels safe. Always explain to other children why you are doing this: "I am helping Nathan learn not to hit."
  5. Give Nathan some words to use: "Don't hit me," "I want that." Give only simple statements to use so that he can grasp their significance and effectiveness.
  6. Very positive rewards for appropriate behaviors, e.g., hugs.
  7. Tell other children when he succeeds. "Look, Nathan shared his toy."
  8. Help or forewarn other children when danger signals show. "Nathan gets mad when someone takes his crayon; let's see if we can help him." "Nathan looks angry; let's find out what is making him angry." They can learn to help, too.
  9. Interpret for Nathan how he is feeling before he hits, e.g., "You must be mad because he took all the crackers. Tell him you want some."
Record keeping procedures:
  1. In team meeting report on time out incidents, what caused them, how they could have been avoided.
  2. Anecdotal records on child and critical incidents recorded to share with everyone.
  3. Share tutor's experiences to see if they can help.
  4. Have a neutral observer record or follow Nathan's movements during an afternoon to see if a pattern of behavior emerges.
Evaluation:
  1. "Time out" was completely effective. It was used six or seven times a day for the first week, and then the use declined until it was used rarely. After vacations it was used to deal with regressive behavior, which it dealt with quickly.
  2. Nathan has started to "time himself out"; e.g., one day he would not give me a puzzle piece and he became very aggressive. He yelled that he was going to the bathroom and off he went. He returned a few minutes later, threw himself in my arms, and gave me the puzzle piece. He had removed himself from a situation and returned to cope with it well.
  3. Children now expect a hug rather than a hit when Nathan approaches. They have started to make friends with him.
  4. Scapegoating has decreased.

Next steps:
Continue same program for a second six-week period.

Program and Open Classroom Framework The tutorial and parent work in this example extend the objectives of the classroom program. In the tutorial program, Nathan's ability to interact positively with a single peer and an adult is reinforced by including another child in one of the twice-weekly sessions. The tutor also assists Nathan in the development of his articulation skills so that he can make himself better understood to his peers.

His parents are given assistance, through conferences and didactic and support groups, in acquiring consistent management techniques. They are also given help in making contact with a neurologist to assess the advisability of Nathan's entering into a program of medication to modify his hyperactivity.

One primary classroom objective that emerges from this case study is the teacher's desire to help Nathan acquire inner controls. A fundamental assumption of open education is that, in developing competence and a feeling of mastery in the classroom, children will learn to subordinate the influences of the physical and social environment to their own sphere of control. In so doing, they increase their inner direction and autonomy. The teacher's description of Nathan "timing himself out" is an example of incipient acquisition of inner control and autonomy.

Another feature of this example that reflects the open classroom framework is the use of materials to redirect the inappropriate expression of feelings, e.g., carpentry and Playdoh. Where this strategy is not effective, and the extreme instance of segregation from the classroom is used, the teaching staff is continuously evaluating the effects of this technique. If it creates more problems than it solves, it would quickly be abandoned. Finally, the approach to individualization shown in this example should be noted. Not only does the teaching staff develop a personalized way of treating Nathan, they also try to help his classmates understand his behavior so that they can treat him in a personally responsive way as well.

Case 2: Carl Carl is a five-and-one-half-year-old boy who is diagnosed as moderately developmentally delayed. Born abroad, Carl has lived in the United States for most of his life. He has one younger brother. He is a very attractive and pleasant child. At Eliot-Pearson, in his first year of group experience, he receives four hours of individual tutoring per week and is in a small language stimulation group two hours per week. Carl's parents are both college educated. His father is a graduate student. English is spoken at home although it is not the native language of either parent.

Classroom Example 2
Goal:
Cognitive

Subgoal:
To increase exploration and mastery of a broad repertoire of curriculum experiences

Assessment of behavior:
Carl employs stereotyped, repetitive activity in the sandbox; minimal motivation or energy is focused in play; "listless" digging, filling, and dumping

Outcome objective:
Carl will involve himself in task-oriented, purposeful activities at the sandbox (defined by some initial planning, a variety of tool uses, and a clear ending)

Approximate time period:
Two to three weeks

Activities:
1. Whenever Carl is at the sandbox, ask him, "What are you making, Carl?"
2. Make a suggestion of a road or farm and structure the task so that he can accomplish it and knows when he is done, e.g., "Make a road from this house to this garage" (place props for house and garage in box); "Dig a hole until you get to the bottom of the sandbox."
3. Help him select appropriate tools for his tasks. Identify clear characteristics (help him acquire vocabulary by repetition of words): shovel for digging; bulldozer (flat shape) for flattening road.
4. Use teacher's presence and attention as reinforcement, e.g., "I'll be back when your hole is done," or "I'll be back when the timer rings (five minutes) and see how you're doing."
5. Help him structure next task. Re-identify big picture so he does not lose sight of the "project."
6. Occasionally exploit his primary learning style of observation and encourage his parallel play in the sandbox while other children are there. Identify for him verbally what they are doing.

Record keeping procedures:
Observe him twice a week while he is engaged at the sandbox, e.g.:

Time	Teacher contact—purpose	Child's behavior—include tasks accomplished by himself

Evaluation:
When teacher is available to support Carl, he is able to invest in purposeful activity at the sandbox, attending to a task from thirty to forty-five minutes with repeated reinforcing and structuring contact with an adult.

Next steps:
Continue for two more weeks in hopes of:
1. Gradual reduction of need for teacher's help at identifying project, smaller steps, and tools to be used.
2. Eventually playing with other children in sandbox.

Program and Open Classroom Framework With its emphasis on developing expressive and receptive language competence, longer attention span, and one-to-one correspondence, Carl's tutorial experience is primarily remedial in character. However, in the tutor's use of core classroom materials such as puzzles, a sorting box, classroom games, and songs, sand, blocks, and scissors, the teacher's objective of teaching Carl how to use the classroom productively is reinforced and extended.

The work with Carl's parents focuses primarily on expanding their awareness of his development. Efforts were made at overcoming their initial denial of his problems, securing needed evaluations, beginning supplementary treatment, and involving their local school district in Carl's educational program.

For Carl, this classroom objective centers on developing some of the skills basic to cognitive activity. These include developing goal-oriented behavior, using tools as means toward ends, acquiring a wider expressive vocabulary, following directions, obtaining and using feedback from actions in the structuring of subsequent reactions, isolating activities into distinct, temporal units with a beginning and an end, and developing internal motivation.

The choice of sand play is significant. Activities such as sand, water, blocks, and art media fulfill a central role in open classrooms. These activities can be called "expressive vehicles" (see Eisner, 1969). Expressive vehicles are highly suitable for developing nondeficit-oriented instructional programs. In general, they give children the opportunity to personalize the classroom's instructional means and to produce products that have subjective importance. For Carl, the vehicle of sand play provides an opportunity for the expression of earlier learned skills and knowledge. It also legitimizes a diversity of response, thus reducing frustration and failure. For Carl's teacher, this type of activity lends itself to ex post facto evaluation of significance rather than to exclusive specification of outcomes in advance. Consequently, it provides a good example of how instructional objectives can be formulated interactively, even when working with a moderately handicapped child.

When Carl's teacher began working with him at the sand table, she began to formulate a number of tentative or hypothetical outcome objectives. Her expectation was that, in the course of a number of interactions with Carl, these objectives would be expanded and revised, and some would be rejected.

The instructional experience described here is the product of this hypothetical, interactive approach. This case is an example that takes into account both Carl's strengths and his weaknesses and represents but one phase of the instructional process. The significance of this case, and that of the other case, rests with the open education principles and practices that it illustrates and with the context of integration from which it is derived.

CONCLUSION: THE DILEMMA OF MAINSTREAMING

This chapter has presented an educational framework, a set of assumptions, and partial documentation to support the position of integrating handicapped children into open structure classrooms. More systematic empirical data are being collected and analyzed. The effects on the subsequent development of preschool-age children who have been mainstreamed still remain to be studied. The potential pitfalls of mainstreaming are only now beginning to be discussed (Cruikshank, 1974; Scriven, 1976).

Although fundamental questions concerning the meaning of "integration" remain unanswered—for example, whether there is a critical criterion of integration, and what effects this approach has on nonhandicapped children—the experience at Eliot-Pearson suggests that the educational impact of a mainstreamed classroom program depends on some form of individualization.

By definition, mainstreamed classrooms include children with a wide range of skills and abilities. For such a diverse group of children to receive an educationally sound experience, the classroom program must be made appropriate for both handicapped and nonhandicapped children. Yet the needs of handicapped and nonhandicapped children are sometimes so widely divergent that what satisfies one may not satisfy the other. This is the dilemma of mainstreaming: While the needs of children in the mainstreamed classroom may be logically arrayed over a common continuum of development, these needs may be so radically different from one another—they may be at such opposite extremes of the continuum—that they cannot profitably be addressed in the same educational setting.

The open classroom framework does not eliminate the cause of this recurrent dilemma; however, for mildly and moderately handicapped children, it does provide a structure for its resolution. That is, instead of creating two or more curricula to accommodate to differences in the population of children, instruction in the open classroom can be individualized so that it is educationally appropriate for every child. The inherent ambiguity of the classroom materials, the flexibility of the spatial and temporal organization, the diversity in grouping of children, and the adaptability of the intervention process make possible a classroom program that supports differences and magnifies similarities. Such an approach goes beyond merely including children who are different from one another in the same classroom grouping; it increases the potential for significant social integration.

The open classroom program is fundamentally adaptive. As in the biological model of growth, adaptation refers to the changes imposed on an organism by its environment and the modifications required of the environment due to the structure, tendencies, and behavior of the organism. In this discussion, the open education framework represents the "environment"; the children are the "organism." In the typical intervention program, changes are mainly organism-outward. That is, the child accommodates to the demands of the instructional design. A program is followed or a sequence of activities is completed. However, the open structure, mainstreamed classroom relies on a different form of responsiveness in addressing the needs of the children who participate in it. Modifications are made in the "environment" (the instructional design) as well as in the "organism" (the child). It is an extremely demanding program for a teacher to implement, but it is one that is rational, that can be documented empirically, and that is attuned to the abilities and disabilities of both handicapped and nonhandicapped children.

ACKNOWLEDGMENT

Grateful acknowledgment is made to Virginia Chalmers and Florence Longhorn for their assistance in developing classroom illustrations.

REFERENCES CITED

Barth, R. 1972. Open Education and the American School. New York: Agathon Press.
Bussis, A. M., and Chittenden, E. A. 1970. Analysis of an Approach to Open Education. Princeton: Educational Testing Service.
Bussis, A. M., Chittenden, E. A., and Amarel, M. 1976. Beyond Surface Curriculum. Boulder, Colo.: Westview Press.
Central Advisory Council for Education (England). 1967. Children and Their Primary Schools (Vols. I and II). (The Plowden Report). London: Her Majesty's Stationary Office.
Chittenden, E. A., and Bussis, A. M. 1971. Open education: Research and assessment strategies. Paper presented at the annual meeting of the National Association for the Education of Young Children.
Cruikshank, W. 1974. The false hope of integration. Australian Journal on the Education of Backward Children, 21, 67–83.
Eisner, E. W. 1969. Instructional and expressive educational objectives: Their formulation and use in curriculum. In J. W. Popham, E. W. Eisner, H. J. Sullivan, and L. L. Tyler (Eds.), Instructional Objectives. Chicago: Rand McNally.
Eisner, E. W. 1974. English Primary Schools. Washington, D.C.: National Association for the Education of Young Children.
Friedlander, B. Z. 1975. Some remarks on "Open Education." American Educational Research Journal, 12, 465–468.
Hawkins, D. 1974. The Informed Vision. New York: Agathon Press.

Johnson, G. O. 1962. Special education for the mentally handicapped—A paradox. Exceptional Children, 29, 62–69.

Kallet, T. 1970. Some recent changes in the primary school. In S. Mason (Ed.), In Our Experience: The Changing Schools of Leicestershire. London: Longmans.

Kamii, C., and Derman, L. 1971. The Engelmann Approach to teaching logical thinking: Findings from the administration of some Piagetian tasks. In D. R. Green, M. P. Ford, and G. B. Flamer (Eds.), Measurement and Piaget. New York: McGraw-Hill.

Knoblock, P. 1973. Open Education for emotionally disturbed children. Exceptional Children, 39, 358–365.

Kohlberg, L. 1969. Stage and sequence: The cognitive-developmental approach to socialization. In D. A. Goslin (Ed.), Handbook of Socialization Theory and Research. Chicago: Rand McNally.

Kohlberg, L. 1972. The concepts of developmental psychology as the central guide to education. In M. C. Reynolds (Ed.), Proceedings of the Conference on Psychology and the Process of Schooling in the Next Decade. Minneapolis: Leadership Training Institute.

Meisels, S. J. 1973. An analysis of teacher intervention in open education. Unpublished doctoral dissertation, Harvard Graduate School of Education. (Dissertation Abstracts International, 1974, 34, 11; University Microfilms No. 74-11, 328, 230.)

Meisels, S. J. 1976. A personal-social theory for the cognitive-developmental classroom. Viewpoints (Bulletin of the School of Education, Indiana University), 52, 15–21.

Palmer, R. 1971. Space, Time, and Grouping. New York: Citation Press.

Peters, R. S. (Ed.). 1969. Perspectives on Plowden. London: Routledge & Kegan Paul.

Piaget, J. 1964. Learning and development. In R. E. Ripple, and V. N. Rockcastle, (Eds.), Piaget Rediscovered. Ithaca: Cornell University Press.

Resnick, L. B. 1972. Teacher Behavior in an Informal British Infant School. School Review, 81, 63–83.

Ridgway, L., and Lawton, I. 1968. Family Groupings in the Primary School. New York: Agathon Press.

Rogers, V. R. 1970. An American reaction. In V. R. Rogers (Ed.), Teaching in the British Primary School. New York: Macmillan.

Scriven, M. 1976. Some issues in the logic and ethics of mainstreaming. Minnesota Education, 2, 61–67.

Taylor, J. 1971. Organising and Integrating the Infant Day. London: George Allen and Unwin.

Weber, L. 1971. The English Infant School and Informal Education. Englewood Cliffs: Prentice-Hall.

White, R. W. 1959. Motivation reconsidered: The concept of competence. Psychological Review, 66, 297–333.

Winett, R. A. 1973. Behavior modification and open education. Journal of School Psychology, 11, 207–214.

Wright, R. J. 1975. The affective and cognitive consequences of an open education elementary school. American Educational Research Journal, 12, 449–465.

THE MARRIAGE OF SPECIAL AND GENERIC EARLY EDUCATION SERVICES

Charles Galloway, Ph.D., and Phyllis Chandler

It is clear that major shifts in social policy can and do occur in the absence of substantial empirical evidence to support those shifts. The development of "special education"—at least that dimension of special education characterized by separation and containment of children who are "too different"—was not based on argument, but rather on the assertion that education for these children could be better provided if the children were brought to a special place to receive it. Without dwelling on an examination of motives for that assertion, we must conclude that the containment policy was ideologically based and not a consequence of prior experimental study.

Similarly, we see the current shift in public policy toward the integration of persons with developmental disabilities into the larger body of social functions as reflecting new ideology rather than new evidence that contradicts the previous policy. For example, a frequently heard assertion marshalled against an integration policy is that the child with handicaps will not be "accepted" by his or her nonhandicapped peers. In fact, the available evidence regarding "acceptability" of young children with developmental disabilities supports conclusively neither the containment nor the integration models.

Bell (1977) reviewed the research literature related to educational integration of young children with handicaps and found, with a few excep-

---

Portions of this work were supported by Grant OEG-0-74-0464 from the United States Office of Education, Bureau of Education for the Handicapped.

tions, that the research was weak in a number of important areas. Bell identified the following gaps in the literature she reviewed. First, the popular methodology relies heavily on indirect measures of the "acceptability" of children with handicaps among their peers; the great majority of the investigators used children's responses to symbolic stimuli (such as pictures and interview questions) and did not perform direct observations of behavioral interactions between handicapped and nonhandicapped children. Second, the literature reveals an appalling scarcity of data regarding the integration of preschool populations; Bell found only three studies that involved children younger than elementary school age. This gap exists in spite of evidence (Richardson, 1970) that differential preference for nonhandicapped children (indirectly assessed) increases between the ages of five and eight years.

Bell's study of the literature also revealed that academic delay and physical disability are often confounded among the subject populations. Virtually all of the studies she reviewed involved children with the label "educationally mentally retarded" (EMR). Blatt's study (1958) of a group of children with the EMR label revealed more children with permanent or uncorrected physical impairments assigned to special classes than to regular classes. Until physical and learning handicap factors are separated, we will not know which dimensions of the child with disabilities are being discriminated, if at all, by the children responding to attitude probes. Understanding the part these factors play will be critical to the management of healthy attitude development within integrated educational settings. (For a more complete review of the literature on integrated early education, see Snyder, Apolloni, and Cooke, 1977.)

In summary, it appears that a major revision of social policy, expressed most clearly in recent federal legislation on the education of all children with handicaps (Public Law 94-142), is proceeding in spite of a substantial body of evidence in its support. It is not the first time that ideological assertions carried the burden of motivating social policy change.

HUMAN SERVICE SYSTEMS: ASSUMPTIONS AND VALUES

Before launching into a detailed description of how a mental retardation agency merged its early education services with the community's generic programs for young children, we would first like to identify a number of fundamental assumptions and values that, for us, dictate the design of human service systems in general. If, as we believe, logic follows from a set of values, the reader can decide early on whether or not he or she agrees with our values, and, if so, whether the subsequent decisions follow logically from our assumptions.

Early Education for Young Children with Handicaps Should Be as Normalized as Possible

Focusing the principle of normalization (Wolfensberger, 1972) on handicapped young children, we assert that *developmental growth of each handicapped child must be maintained in the most normal setting possible using the most normal teaching methods possible.* This general statement implies at least four important features of early education systems for handicapped young children:

1. A "normalized" service delivery system should be reasonably *dispersed* throughout the community to avoid congestion of children with special needs and to maximize accessibility to families.
2. The services and human talent provided to the handicapped child should be *specialized* according to his or her special needs; the needs the child shares with all children can be met by persons and settings not so specialized.
3. There should be *continuity* in the services planned for the handicapped child and the child's family; services should be triggered to start as soon as the child is identified as needing extraordinary assistance and continue through the time the child enters a public school program or comparable educational service.
4. And, very importantly, the extraordinary services the child requires should be woven (*"integrated"*) into early educational services offered to the community at large (i.e., the "generic" services).

Although our professional experience happens to be in the area of mental retardation, we firmly believe that the mandates described above apply to all children identified as "developmentally disabled"; the form the mandates take will certainly vary with the child's age, community, and unique needs.

The principle of normalization, in application, is not an automatic, clean machine for making programmatic decisions at all levels. To the contrary, it forces us to deal openly, and sometimes painfully, with the conflict between what is idealistic and what is realistic. For example, it is occasionally necessary to congregate individuals perceived as "deviant" in order to provide specialized services to each one of them; it is necessary because we cannot think of a more normal way to do it with the resources we have at the time. Sometimes forces beyond our control (such as funding sources) require us to attach stigmatizing labels to people before we can serve them. But labels can be confined to our agency files and ignored during day-to-day involvement with our students. And some services that are "normal" for the general population may not be a desirable state of affairs for anyone! Possibly the best examples of this conflict are the so-called "normal" services for the elderly citizens in this country. Resolving these conflicts often is a matter of compromise. But at least the compromises can be identified as such and not rationalized as ideal solutions. To paraphrase Wolfensberger, the principle of normalization keeps us from mistaking the better for the best.

Goals of Early Education for Handicapped Children Are Twofold: "Stigma Reduction/Removal" and "Competence Enhancement"

Stigma Reduction/Removal Psychologists, educators, physicians, and therapists are not the only people capable of spotting developmental deviations in young children. To the extent that the deviations are more extreme, more persons can identify the child as "different." All too often, these differences serve as *stigmata,* or characteristics of the person that reduce his or her perceived value as a human being. A stigma can be glaring (e.g., head size that is too large or too small), or it can be subtle (e.g., an unusual gait or an absence of smiling).

In order to deal with the issues of stigma and deviancy, we have to think of the child as living in an imperfect social context and not in a benign vacuum in which his or her only input comes from well-meaning, protective teachers and parents. How people perceive the child will affect how they respond to the child, how they respond will help determine how he or she behaves, and so on. As more and more severely and profoundly handicapped children remain in the local community and receive services there instead of being removed to remote, self-contained institutions, it becomes increasingly important to examine which characteristics of a person produce stigma and social avoidance.

Many techniques to reduce or remove stigma are already available to us. Some are simply cosmetic. The enlarged head of the child born with hydrocephalus can be visually diminished through proper hairstyling. Cleft palates can be repaired. Dental surgery and dentures can give a child an attractive smile and increase the frequency of positive social interactions.

Prosthesis is the artificial support or replacement of a body function. A prosthesis aimed at the reduction of stigma can be both physical and behavioral (Lindsley, 1964). Devices for people with neuromuscular deficits, such as orthopaedic bracing and wheel chairs, are familiar. Increasingly, we learn of ingenious inventions for people with severe communication problems—communication boards and symbol systems, electronic devices that allow the skin to serve as an alternative to the tympanic membrane in the ear. All of these devices, and hundreds more, sustain behavior that is more normal or more efficient than would occur in their absence, and thereby reduce the level of perceived stigma.

Behavioral technology based primarily on principles of reinforcement has demonstrated extensive utility in the reduction of behaviors that function as stigmata (e.g., Gardner, 1971). A child who abuses his or her own body or the bodies of others, engages in "autistic" behaviors (such as twirling in circles, or staring at his or her fingers for inordinate periods of time), or has frequent vocal outbursts will have a difficult time finding a niche in the natural social fabric. These behavioral stigmata, quite naturally, produce avoidance on the part of most people the child contacts. Quite a lot of productive study has gone into developing procedures that reduce or eliminate these behaviors and, incidently, the stigmata they produce. The real challenge, of course, is to design early learning environments that reduce the odds of such behavior being acquired in the first place.

Competence Enhancement Competence enhancement is the purpose of most early education programs and designers of "curricula." Currently, there are useful debate and research revolving around the question of what comprises "competencies" for young children. When a child's development deviates from that of most of his or her peers, when the child's growth is not so predictable and apparently effortless, we have to resort to exceptional means to support development within normal limits if not within normal time-frames.

If the child's learning delay is not an artifact of deficits in receiving normal behavioral stimulation and consequences resulting from an abnormal environment, then a more detailed examination of his or her developmental planning must take place. This planning can be organized through "task analysis." Gold (1976) describes task analysis as "... all of the activity which results in there being sufficient power for the learner to acquire the task" (p. 79). Gold and his associates demonstrated task analysis with sufficient power to teach the acquisition of complex assembly skills by severely and profoundly retarded persons who were also blind (1976). As Gold points out, the onus for learning is not on the learner but on the "power" of the task analysis. The mandate of normalization is that we ensure that the procedures comprising the task analysis are as normal as possible and do not themselves unduly stigmatize the learner.

So far, we have discussed the reduction or removal of stigma and the enhancement of competence primarily as a function of "personal factors," or means of behavior development focused on the individual learner relatively independent of the environmental context in which they are applied. Prosthetic devices and training through task analysis can be implemented in almost any environment, normalized or not. To a very large extent, this orientation parallels that of the vast majority of "special education" over the last decades. We have concentrated on what specially trained adults can do for children who are identified as developmentally delayed.

Environmental Factors Environmental factors also have an impact on both stigma reduction/removal and competence enhancement. Environmental factors, as the term is used here, are the setting conditions, physical and social, that support growth relatively independent of any particular child.

We are not aware of any supporting research, but our observations of parents, visitors, and teachers have convinced us that a handicapped child will be perceived as less different when immersed in a group of children who are not seen as different than when the child is among a group of children all of whom are handicapped. If this phenomenon is true, stigma reduction can often be accomplished simply by way of placing a child in a different setting. And the less deviant we perceive a child, the more likely we will treat the child with more normal expectations, the more we expect of the child, and so on.

The perception of competency merely provides the expectations that a delayed child can learn; but perceptions alone cannot teach. To do that we might take advantage of the natural learning opportunities available in the regular preschool (Guralnick, 1976). These opportunities include other children who are more competent in their social and linguistic achievement. It would be a mistake, however, to assume that the nondelayed children serve only as passive models of normal behavior. During the busy interplay of social exchange, they can provide both stimulation and feedback to the delayed child. The form and quality of stimulation and feedback are virtually impossible to approach in synthetic environments. To the extent that these natural events fall short of maintaining growth for the handicapped child across a broad range of developmental areas, supplementary resources need to be introduced into the setting to pick up the slack.

Early Education Settings Are Elastic

In the field of ecological psychology, the word "setting" refers to times, spaces, persons, and physical objects associated with fairly standard patterns of individual and group behavior. More precisely, "A setting is a homeostatic system with controls that maintain the setting intact and operating at a stable functional level under widely varying conditions" (Barker and Gump, 1964, p. 19). The setting "presses" some patterns of behavior on the part of its members and proscribes others.

Nurseries, preschools, and day care centers are typical early education settings. In the past, many educational planners acted as if they knew the tolerances these settings have for variances in children's competency. Under the apparent presumption that certain deviancies in a child's development will radically disrupt the equilibrium of the setting and send it out of control, we often hear statements such as, "The child is handicapped and is not *ready* for a regular preschool experience," or "What does this child have to learn *in order* to be accepted in a more normal preschool?"

By challenging our own preconceptions, we have found that the threshold of equilibrium can be stretched. The preschool center that never before enrolled a child called "retarded" can, with minor adjustments, incorporate a mildly involved child. When that adjustment becomes no longer remarkable, the new tolerances are ready to be extended through the progressive introduction of children whose delays are more and more significant. The adjustment required to bring certain children into the setting may include the times, spaces, persons, and physical objects that were previously foreign to the setting but in time can become natural.

Looking back over the last several years' experience, we would insist that the correct question to ask is, "What must *this* regular early education setting provide to get ready for *this* particular child who happens to be developmentally delayed?" Early education settings are much more dynamic and elastic than we have ever given them credit for. Consequently, the question of "readiness" calls for an ecological analysis rather than an intelligence test.

FROM IDEOLOGY TO ACTION: ENCOR

The Eastern Nebraska Community Office of Retardation (ENCOR) was formed as a five-county human service agency in July 1970. The geographic area served by ENCOR includes metropolitan Omaha (approximate population, 380,000), smaller cities, and farm communities for a total population of about 500,000.

ENCOR was established to provide a network of comprehensive community-based services that would prevent the need for any person in the service area having to be removed to Nebraska's sole state institution for mentally retarded people. Its second purpose is to return to community services all persons residing in the institution who originally lived in the ENCOR area. Component regional services include educational, vocational, and residential programs for children and adults with all levels of mental retardation (Lesink, 1976; Skarnulis, 1976).

By late 1972, ENCOR was operating six developmental daycare centers for retarded children. These centers served approximately one hundred eighty children between the ages of two and sixteen years. The centers were well dispersed within the region, but they served only retarded children and were thus completely segregated.

Forces of Change

At about the same time the ENCOR staff was confronting the conflict between espousing "normalization" on one hand and continuing to provide segregated services for children on the other, several other trends were beginning to be felt. The first was the experimental "Toddler Project" at Peabody College's Kennedy Center in Nashville, Tennessee. This project, started by Bill and Diane Bricker and their graduate students in 1970, brought together a group of toddlers, half of whom were identified as "developmentally delayed" and the other half assessed as developing normally (Bricker and Bricker, 1972). The project was basically research oriented, but the implications for educational systems, in terms of young student diversity, were compeling. Familiarity with the success of this integrated program created healthy questions about the ENCOR method of operation.

About this time, we also discovered a successful integrated child development center operation at the other end of the state, in Scotts Bluff. A visit to that program, operated under the auspices of the County Office of Mental Retardation, gave us local confirmation that Nebraska communities might accommodate even more extensive integration of delayed and nondelayed children. The final confirmation occurred when the parents of two children being served in ENCOR centers, on their own initiative, enrolled their children for two or three days a week in regular day care programs. Fortunately, ENCOR's educational data system (precision teaching) was prepared to reflect the acceleration in language behavior that occurred with both children during this mixed enrollment arrangement.

All of these events merged to make unavoidable the decision to integrate, system-wide, ENCOR's young children's program. The questions thereafter shifted from *whether* to *how*.

Integrating the Young Children's Program

The strategy question had been resolved: We would transfer the retarded youngsters ENCOR was serving and the related agency resources to regular early education programs around the five-county area. Some of the initial tactical questions we faced and the solutions we selected are discussed below.

How Do We Approach the Directors of Public and Private Generic Programs with Our Strategy? It is really a bit presumptuous to decide to marry other people's programs without at least some kind of proposal. That proposal was presented at a meeting of the local Association for the Education of Young Children. The majority of members of this group are the operators and teachers of regular early education centers, both public and private. After hearing a presentation on normalization and the additional resources they could expect, many of the members were warmly receptive to the idea that they could merge their services with those being provided by ENCOR. That professional exchange opened the door to the strategy of systemwide integration of young children with developmental delays.

Initially we decided to work with only one regular center. We anticipated that there would be a number of procedures and role definitions to be worked out, a process that would be a bit easier if we were not spread too thin. The first center was selected because the operator expressed a positive interest in collaboration, the center was centrally located, the facility was adequate, and the teaching staff of the center appeared to be cooperative even though they expressed some apprehensions about their preparation to work with retarded children. Meetings with the teachers to discuss the plan and their apprehensions sufficed to reduce their concerns enough for all of us to proceed.

How Can the Integrated Preschool Project Be Funded? The ENCOR children's education services had been funded all along primarily through federal social service monies, via the Nebraska Welfare Department. The amendments needed for ENCOR to subcontract some of these costs to private and public operations were negotiated with little trouble. In addition, we wrote a proposal to become one of the projects in the Bureau of Education for the Handicapped's (BEH) "First Chance" network of early education demonstration projects. The proposal was approved, assuring us of three years of support for activities that would not have been reimbursable under our base social services contracts. The combination of BEH and social service funding gave us the security we needed to plan a durable project.

How Should the First Group of Retarded Children be Selected? For the first attempt to merge ENCOR services with a regular early education center, we decided to stack the cards, to the best of our ability, in favor of successful integration. The first children to be selected were already enrolled in ENCOR developmental center programs; thus, we knew them and their parents very well. We decided to transfer children at first whose parents were supportive of the integration strategy, whose level of retardation was mild to moderate, who displayed minimal "behavior problems," who had no significant physical involvement, and who were otherwise delightful to be with. We felt that such children would quickly remove any lingering, amorphous fear of "retarded" children. We anticipated that within a short while we could begin transferring children whose handicaps were more extreme and whose behavior might be somewhat less than "delightful" at times.

Should There Be a Limit Placed on the Number of "Retarded" Children Integrated into Regular Programs? Our decision here was that the ratio of retarded to nonretarded children in any one program was more important than the absolute numbers. First, we did not want a center that was seen as a generic program to become perceived as a "retarded program" because of an inordinate ratio of delayed children being taught there. Such a change in program identity would be counter to the purposes of normalized services. Second, we were confronted with the expression of an interesting apprehension: namely, if one purpose of integration is to provide models of behavior for the retarded children, why would the reverse not take place as well? That is, would the "normal" children not be just as likely to start acting "retarded?" We were sure that this apprehension was groundless, or, if such a pattern emerged, that it could be controlled with a little common sense. But we had no hard evidence (or even personal experience) to allay the concern. At that time, we did not have access to a very pertinent study by Peterson, Peterson, and Scriven (1977). Their research indicates that both handicapped and nonhandicapped children are more likely to imitate a nonhandicapped child than one who displays "serious" developmental delays. We arbitrarily decided to limit the enrollment of retarded students to twenty percent of the total center population. This limit would reduce any tendency to saturate a regular center with handicapped children, and the odds of deviancy modeling would be reduced.

How Should the Retarded Children Be Grouped Within the Regular Center? We decided that the retarded students would not be "grouped" at all. A grouping arrangement would defeat, or limit, the goal of social integration. Instead, the children were dispersed among existing center groups according to age similarity. Exceptions to this rule could be made when special considerations arose, such as when there existed a wide disparity between age and developmental attainment.

How Can We Coordinate the Activities of All the People Who Are Participants in the Child's Education? The involvement of parents, early education program staff, ENCOR staff, and other resource persons had to be coordinated in some way. We accomplished this coordination by implementing the concept of a "teaching team," which consists of all those involved in the child's growth (parents, teachers, therapists, counselors, etc.). Each child's team meets at least quarterly to share their observations of the child's progress and to plan together the goals for the child for the next few months. Videotapes showing the child in activities designed to help meet previously set objectives are frequently shown. The behavior charts that teachers use to record the child's growth are shared with other members of the team. A written summary of the meeting is provided to each participant by the resource teacher.

What Should Be the Form of Parent Participation? A discussion of "parent involvement" is at least an obligatory cliché for all early education programs. In reality, it is often difficult to raise that involvement above the level of cliché. The "PTA" model of monthly group meetings has not worked well for us in the past, probably because it is seldom the case that the content of one meeting will be rewarding to each member of a group of otherwise unique parents with unique clusters of interest and informational needs.

Currently, the avenues of parent participation in the ENCOR preschool program focus on co-equal membership in the child's educational planning team. Parent attendance at these meetings (scheduled about every two months) has run about eighty-five percent. Therefore, the team meetings must serve some useful function for a large number of parents. The meetings are customized according to the parents' schedule and mobility. For example, meetings are often held in the home in the evening for the convenience of the parents. This kind of flexibility is seldom convenient for already overworked staff, but the effort has paid off in terms of coordinating the child's learning experiences across several settings, including the home.

Parents of handicapped children, like their children, tend to become isolated from the main body of the community. As their children become more and more integrated, the scope and definition of "parent participation" changes. Does it make sense to push for child integration and then encourage the continuation of separate meetings and "clubs" for their parents? We think not. Instead, we encourage the parents of handicapped children to participate in all the activities planned for parents by the regular education program. The rights and needs of handicapped children are a vital part of the "education" of parents of children who are not identified as handicapped. Television and radio spots are useful, but they cannot replace the communication that can exist between one parent and another. That communication will be retarded when agencies unconsciously reinforce arbitrary separateness among subgroups of parents.

What Should Be the Characteristics and Roles of Resource Staff Assigned to the Integrated Programs? The general term, "resource teacher," as used here, refers to an ENCOR employee who is assigned full-time to a regular early education program serving young retarded children placed through ENCOR. This resource person's major responsibility is to serve as a facilitator of integration by providing support to program staff in whose group the child is placed. This assignment may be accomplished by assisting the teacher directly in the classroom or by providing consultation in planning, as well as by encouraging and reinforcing the classroom teacher's efforts as the integration process takes place. In addition, it is the job of the resource teacher to supplement the educational program of the regular center when that program is not sufficient to support adequate growth in the development of the retarded child. Thus, the resource teacher plays a key role in the successful integration of the retarded children. A formal set of "competencies" was developed for the role of resource teachers, training was provided to staff in these areas, and written "probes" were developed to tap basic working knowledge of the various competency areas. The following is a brief description of the competencies identified for ENCOR resource teachers.

Normalization Through classes, reading, and personal contact, teaching staff are provided a thorough foundation in the principle of normalization. The way in which resource staff contribute to team planning, interact with parents and other teachers, and construct teaching routines is shaped by how well staff members understand the subtleties implied by the principle of normalization. Because of the nature of the program, the integration component of normalization is given special emphasis during training.

Agency History Resource teachers frequently meet and talk with tour groups, site visitors from funding agencies, politicians, parents of nonhandicapped children, and other interested persons. The teachers working in integrated programs must know the purpose of the agency that placed the children and how that agency came about. They must know the service scope of the agency and that it arose from the dreams and plans of parents of retarded persons. Not only must they "know" the history, they must be able to communicate it consistently and honestly.

Professionalism Professionalism refers to the manner in which the teacher interacts with colleagues, parents, and supervisors. Considerations such as confidentiality of information come under this heading.

Observation of Child Behavior Behavior observation includes identification of relevant aspects of the interaction between the child's behavior and his or her current environment, the ability to describe those aspects using common English with a low degree of personal interpretation, and the ability to communicate the description in writing. This competency provides the material for subsequent instructional analysis and planning.

Normal Child Development It seems obvious to say that the understanding of delayed, or deviant, development is difficult without a good foundation in what constitutes "normal" development. After all, the former is defined relative to the latter. Learning principles, such as stimulus discrimination, generalization, and reinforcement can be combined with cognitive developmental constructs, such as object permanence, means-ends relations, and schemes, to provide teachers with excellent tools with which to create educational plans for young children (Bijou and Baer, 1965; Robinson, 1976).

Educational Objectives Competencies in the areas of behavioral description and normal child development culminate in the skill of stating learning goals in behavioral, measurable terms. A good statement of educational objectives in such terms obviously facilitates communication with both professionals and parents and improves the documentation of child growth over time.

Behavior Analysis Many concepts related to child development place heavy emphasis on historical variables related to a child's pattern of behavior. Behavior analysis, based on principles of operant learning, balances this tendency by stressing the importance of assessing, and frequently rearranging, the environmental events that come before, during, and after the child's current behavior. A teacher who looks for "explanations" of the child's behavior in the current environment will more likely find manageable solutions than one who persists in exploring the child's remote past, the child's genes, or the child's nervous system. The two approaches, if the distinction is valid at all, are certainly not incompatible. Both are needed for a full understanding of the child's development.

Behavioral Measurement The glue that holds together all the competencies described so far is careful measurement of the delayed child's development. Behavioral measurement can be direct or indirect, continuous or intermittent (Lindsley, 1964). To monitor, forecast, and plan the child's growth, the resource teacher needs competency in various measurement tools. ENCOR teachers are expected to become proficient in direct measurement of behavior by using a system called "precision teaching" (e.g., Jordan and Robbins, 1972; Lindsley, 1971; Pennypacker, Koenig, and Lindsley, 1972). Precision teaching requires the recording of the child's specific behavioral actions. These actions (or "movement cycles") are reported in terms of their frequency, that is, the number of observations of the behavior over time. The benchmark of precision teaching is the standard behavior chart, a tool for efficient communications and for forecasting the course of behavioral frequencies into the future. Another feature of precision teaching is that it encourages continuous, daily recording of the "pinpointed" behavior, especially during the acquisition of proficiency in that behavior.

Indirect measurement of behavior occurs when we record one class of behavior in order to make inferences about another class, as in personality, intelligence, and aptitude tests. We have found that "tests" such as these serve the purposes of the resource teacher very poorly. But measurement can also be indirect when the *source* of the direct observation is once removed from the person doing the recording. The developmental assessment used in the ENCOR preschool project produced by Alpern and Boll (1972) is an example. This instrument for assessing a child's developmental level allows the use of the mother as the informant for determining what skills the child has acquired or not yet acquired. When the teacher assesses development based on the mother's report, the measurement is indirect. Overall, we found this type of recording to be useful, but in individual situations there are serious questions of reliability. Later in the chapter, we discuss data from the integrated preschool project that reflect both direct and indirect measurement systems. We find that a project's use of both a good developmental assessment, such as the Alpern-Boll, and the individualized, direct measurement produced through precision teaching, creates a rich, balanced data base. Whatever data system is selected, however, it must go beyond simply meeting the needs of project administrators; it must be functional for making planning decisions for each unique child. In other words, it must be useful for teachers.

The tactical questions discussed above represent some of the broader issues that were confronted. Many other issues dealt with are of limited interest here, particularly in the area of administrative control and funding.

Need for Variation in Service Models

The model of early integration we originally envisioned relied on the placement of full-time resource teachers in regular educational settings to serve the retarded young children there. Through time these setting arrangements increased to include nine regular centers across the service region. In the process of expansion, we discovered that the basic model was not going to serve the needs of all young children who are retarded. We were confronted with the need for more variation in service model types.

Infant Programs   Handicapped infants and their parents in Nebraska, and the Omaha area in particular, are well served by the Meyer Children's Rehabilitation Institute (MCRI), a component of the University of Nebraska Medical Center. MCRI offers an infant stimulation program under the direction of Dr. Cordelia Robinson. This program provides excellent evaluation of early development and weekly sessions for parents who can come to MCRI for guidance in assisting their children develop.

Because of their own constraints, however, the MCRI program was not able to offer two other services needed by many parents of handicapped infants: infant/parent home training and developmental day care services. ENCOR had the administrative flexibility and available resources to fill these service gaps. A truly functional collaboration between the Infant Stimulation program at MCRI and the ENCOR early educational services was developed to provide parents of handicapped infants a broad array of service options from which to choose.

The ENCOR home training program was based, in large part, on the Portage Project model. The Portage Project was developed by David and Marsha Shearer and their co-workers (see Shearer and Shearer, 1976) in Wisconsin to demonstrate the efficacy of home-based early intervention. The ENCOR program benefited from the Portage Project through in-service training and personal guidance for home training teachers as well as through materials sharing.

In addition, ENCOR staff received continuous training in evaluation and teaching from Dr. Robinson and her staff at MCRI. This training involvement was unique because both groups were serving the same children, although in different ways.

The stated purpose of the ENCOR component of infant services was to prepare the handicapped infant and his or her parents for successful involvement in an integrated early education program when the child reached the appropriate age. This preparation takes the form of helping the parent plan and take responsibility for the child's learning experiences. Short- and long-term planning is a process we wanted parents to incorporate into their thinking as early as possible.

Infant daycare, it turns out, is a service many parents of nonhandicapped children find difficult to obtain. It is doubly more difficult for parents whose infants already show significant developmental delays or physical impairments. Rather than set up our own separate infant daycare services, however, ENCOR staff recruited and supported regular daycare home persons who agreed to provide their service to infants who were delayed. Without additional monetary compensation, these daycare "mothers" willingly accepted the training necessary to manage the care and development of infants who were handicapped. A version of the home training model was used to monitor and support the services provided the infants placed in the daycare homes.

Itinerant Resource Teacher Support The development of some of the children identified as mentally retarded could, in time, be maintained without the full-time presence of a resource teacher. In such cases, it was wasteful of limited funds to provide a child more support than was needed. The function of the itinerant, or "traveling," resource teacher was created to ensure that the retarded children's growth was being maintained in the regular early education settings and that the teachers there were receiving support in their planning for the children. The traveling resource teacher visits each of his or her centers once or twice a week to record behaviors of the children in the natural settings, to assess the need for additional materials and equipment, and to consult with the regular teaching staff. The decision to move a child from full-time to traveling resource services is made by consensus in the team planning process.

"Cooperative Classroom" At the other end of the spectrum are the children with severe and profound handicaps, whose training and management needs exceed what can presently be supported in most regular centers. Children who must have passive range of motion exercises daily, or whose seizures are uncontrolled to the extent that close monitoring is imperative, or who rely on bulky positioning equipment, all require highly modified environments for at least some part of the day.

Because we did not want to provide even these children with their necessary support in separate facilities, and because the centers with which we were affiliated did not have the capacity to accommodate the highly specialized services, a compromise was in order. Two of the centers with which we were collaborating had unused rooms in their facilities. After a planning process was completed with the operators of the centers, ENCOR rented the rooms, renovated them to allow therapists and teachers the space they needed, and installed the special equipment each child required. The classrooms are indeed set apart from the rest of the regular center, but the boundary between the two settings is permeable. That is, nonhandicapped students easily move into the cooperative classroom space and vice versa. The social integration is a little less natural, but is much more likely than it would be if the children were separated in different buildings.

The "cooperative classroom" is a workable compromise, one based on the architectural limitations inherent in most regular centers in our community rather than on the limitations inherent in the severely and profoundly handicapped children themselves. As generic early education involves increasing numbers of handicapped children, we can anticipate that more attention will be paid to designing space that can accommodate the child with severe handicaps.

Continuity Continuity of early education services for children whose development is delayed clearly must start when the child is first identified, and must take into account all ages, levels, and "types" of involvement. Figure 1 displays a schematic summary of the flow among the service variations described above. The variations and their sequences should in no way be interpreted as the best or final arrangement of services.

Special and Generic Services 277

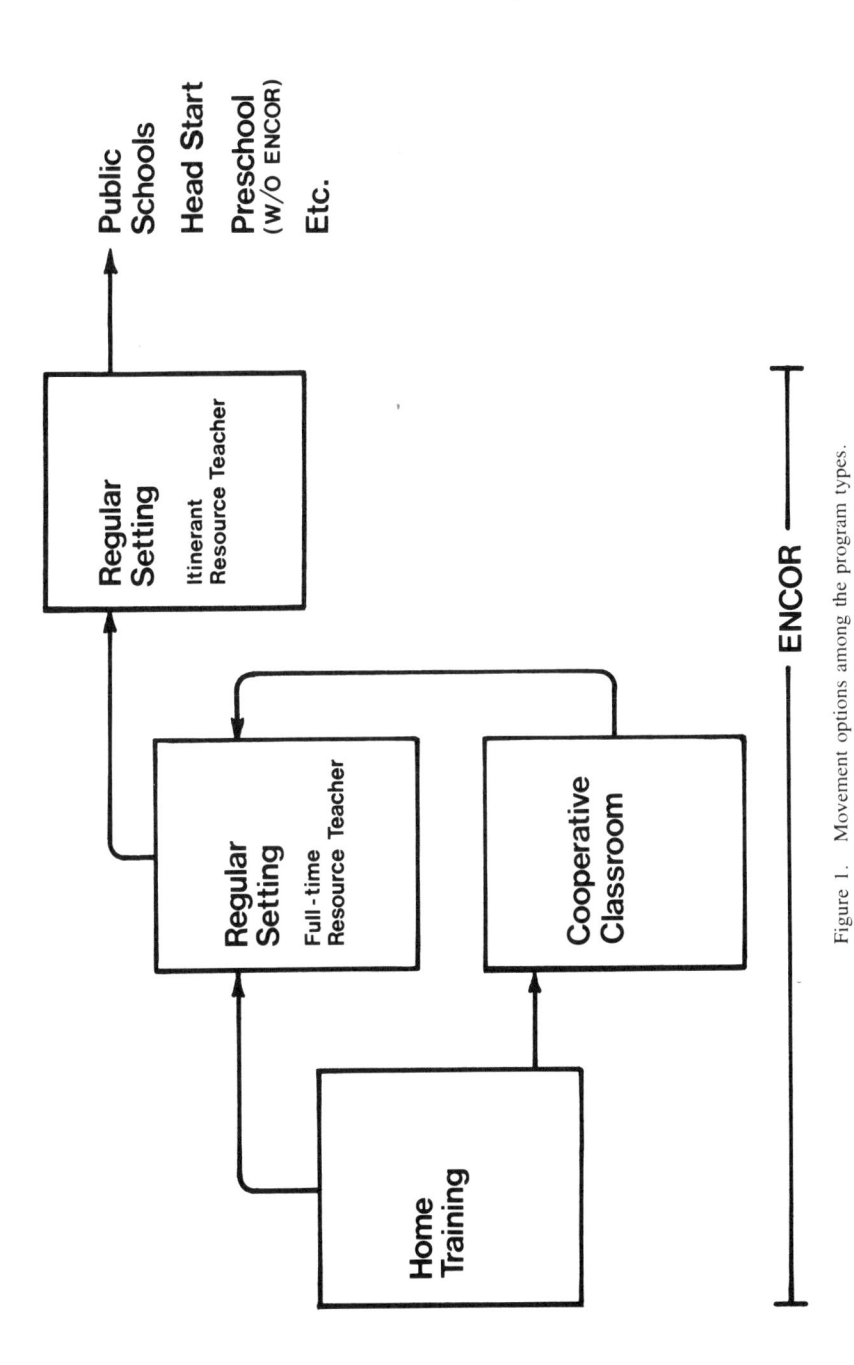

Figure 1. Movement options among the program types.

DEVELOPMENT OF CHILDREN IN INTEGRATED SETTINGS

It is important to note that the development of the ENCOR early education program was a service effort, not a research project. We employed no research assistants, no paid observers, and bought no automated recording equipment other than for videotape recording. To the extent that we expected behavioral data collection from the teaching staff, we did so only in order to plan and monitor better the children's developmental programs. The many teachers and assistant teachers who contributed so much to the program deserve immense credit for taking on behavioral measurement duties not typical of their professional colleagues. Attempts to ensure a sufficient degree of measurement reliability included periodic staff training in the administration of developmental profiles and the use of standard videotapes of children's behavior to improve commonality of recording across teacher-observers. Beyond this sort of training, attempts to assess reliability of measurement were sporadic and unsystematic.

Description of the Population

Table 1 summarizes some of the characteristics of the children served by ENCOR's early education program between March 1973 and January 1976, the dates when the first integrated preschool project was started and when the summary was last compiled. As the table shows, the project did not focus exclusively on mildly and moderately retarded young children; during the period summarized, almost a quarter of the children were classified as severely or profoundly retarded. In addition, about half the total population served qualified for the label "multihandicapped" (two or more educationally significant handicaps).

A summary of where the children moved to after formal termination from the program is also contained in Table 1. (As of January 1976, sixty-three of the one hundred sixty-seven reached an age where they moved from the program.) About one-third of the children "graduated" to nonsegregated educational services. As one would expect, these children were less handicapped than those who moved to typical, self-contained settings.

Analysis of Alpern-Boll Developmental Profile Data

As mentioned earlier, resource teachers administered the Alpern-Boll Developmental Profile periodically for each of the delayed children assigned to them. With certain exceptions, the profiles were reported about every six months that the child was in the program. The source of the information regarding skill attainment—mother or teacher—was left to the discretion of the teacher.

Table 1. Student count, characteristics, and movement

Student count	
Total students served through home training	37
Total students served through integrated preschool programs	146
Total number of students served by ENCOR early education programs (unduplicated count)	167
Handicapping conditions (home training and preschool: 167 children)	
Mental retardation	100%
Mild	49%
Moderate	27%
Severe	15%
Profound	9%
Multihandicapped	49%
(Of the current number of children, 57% are multihandicapped, showing the increasing participation of such children in home training and integrated preschools)	
Movement from program to:	
Public/private special education	23
Special programs (Meyer Children's Rehabilitation Institute, Omaha Hearing School)	6
Regular kindergarten	11
Regular preschool without ENCOR support (e.g., Head Start, public preschool, private preschool)	12
Other (e.g., left community, death, parents terminated involvement)	11
Total	63

Student profile records were included in the summary below on the basis of two criteria: (1) the student was enrolled in the integrated preschool program at the time of the file search; and (2) the child had on file at least two developmental profile records that were administrated while the child was participating in the preschool program (if a child had only two records, one administered while in the home training component, the file was set aside). Of the eighty-five children enrolled in the early education program at that time, fifty had files that met these two criteria. In terms of both percentage of multihandicapped children and distribution of levels of retardation, the "sample" of fifty children corresponds closely to the comparable percentages for all children served by the program to date. Of these fifty children, forty-six percent were classified as multihandicapped. The distribution by levels of retardation was: mild, fifty-two percent; moderate, twenty-four percent; severe, twenty percent; and profound, four percent. The median age of these children at the time of the administration of the first Alpern-Boll was three years, eight months.

The outcome of the full Alpern-Boll profile is an assignment, in addition to chronological age, of "developmental ages" in the following areas: physical age, self-help age, social age, academic age, and communication age. Using the two most recent reports, a change score in plus or minus months was calculated for each child for each developmental area, and for the number of months between the two administrations. These change scores were rank ordered, and the median and interquartile ranges were calculated. The same analysis was applied to the subgroups of three levels of retardation.

Figure 2 presents a picture of developmental age change reflected by the Alpern-Boll Developmental Profile. For the total group, the median time between administrations of the profile was six and a half months, with slight variations among the subgroups. Across the developmental areas, the mildly retarded children showed median gains of about one month's development for one month in the program, slightly lower in the "academic" area, and much better in the "self-help" area. The moderately retarded students showed average gains of two to five months across the developmental areas for the six months' participation in the program.

The summary data for the severely/profoundly retarded students were much less satisfying. The median change across all developmental areas was zero, with the exception of "social age," which showed an average of two months lost. In interpreting these results, at least two hypotheses can

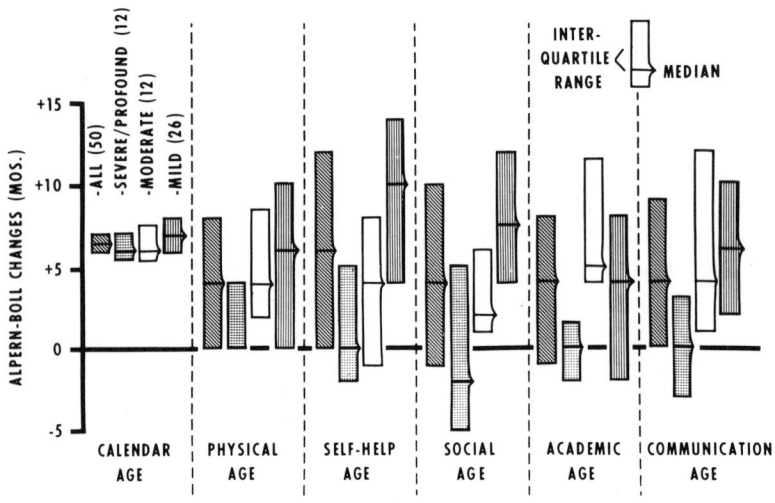

Figure 2. Developmental assessment changes across two administrations of the Alpern-Boll Developmental Profile.

be put forward: (1) the program provided to these children was not adequate to meet their educational needs; and (2) the developmental assessment used was not sensitive to behavioral growth at the first few months of "developmental age," the level at which these children were being evaluated. Our opinion is that the results stem from a little of both. The way that educational resources are allocated to this group of children needs to be carefully reevaluated, and a developmental assessment instrument with more discrete steps at the earliest months needs to be implemented in addition to the Alpern-Boll for comparison purposes. Until this work is completed, we will suspend judgment on the general effectiveness of the ENCOR early education programs for severely/profoundly retarded children.

Direct Observation of Child Behavior in Natural Settings

One of the routine responsibilities assigned to the resource teachers is to maintain direct observational records of the frequencies of a prescribed set of general behaviors:

1. Interacts with peers—The interaction was not assessed at this level of recording by way of quality nor were interactions with handicapped or nonhandicapped peers differentiated; the interactions included events such as toy exchange, touching, passing of food, hitting, etc.
2. Interacts with adults—Similarly, quality or source of initiation was not differentiated under this general class of activity; activities of attention getting, touching, and instructing are examples of these interactions.
3. Initiates interaction or activity—For this class to be counted, the child whose behavior was being observed had to instigate an interaction with either an adult or peer, or begin an activity without a direction to do so.
4. Says a nonword sound, a word, or a phrase—The routine in effect when the data were recorded called for the teacher to record each of these vocal behaviors for each target child during the observation period.

These routine records were made at least once a week for a thirty-minute period during a "free play" (nonstructured) part of the daily schedule. Normal frequency "aims" were determined for each of these classes of behavior by having the teachers make the same recordings of children who were of comparable chronological age but who were not identified as developmentally delayed.

There were three main purposes to this assignment. First, the recordings were made in free-play situations because there would be less direct adult coercion of behavior than during more formal activity periods. Second, these general behaviors put a child in a position in which natural consequences could act to refine the quality or "appropriateness" of the behavior. For example, for a child to learn how to interact well with another child or adult, the overall frequency of interactions, per se, must be sufficiently high to receive adequate corrective feedback from the natural audience. On the other hand, if the overall frequency of interactions was unusually high, we would have to deal with a different pattern of deviant behavior. Before the teacher could decide whether to work with a child to increase or decrease the frequency of interactions (or any other class of movements), the teacher would have to know the normal frequency range for that behavior. The best way to know the normal frequency range is to watch a group of normal children behave in comparable situations. This was the third purpose of the recording assignment; teachers were in a position to attend to both abnormal frequencies and features of these behaviors that would lead to the specification of individualized objectives and behavioral measurement for particular children. Summaries of these observations were reported for each child during each child's team meeting, and they were documented in the team report along with the individualized program data.

The files of the fifty children included in the Alpern-Boll analysis described above were reviewed for team reports that included the routine observational data. Children assigned to the "cooperative classroom" component do not participate in the center's free-play periods regularly enough to provide this information, and therefore they were excluded from the frequency summary. Thirty-two of the children had free-play observations contained in their team reports. For these students, two team reports were selected for comparison purposes: the most recent team report, and the team report for the closest preceding six months.

Figure 3 summarizes the observational data for three classes of behavior: interacts with peers, interacts with adults, and initiates interaction or activity. For each class of behavior, the "effect" of six months' involvement in the integrated setting was shown more on the total range of frequencies than on the median or average frequency (change from first to second display for each panel). The extreme frequencies were brought closer to the normal range ("aim") over the course of the six months.

The data on general vocal production contained in the team reports used in the analysis above proved to be inadequate for similar six-month comparisons. Too often over the six months, teachers stopped recording a more primitive class of vocal behavior (e.g., "nonword sounds") and started recording a more advanced class (e.g., "words") when the child demon-

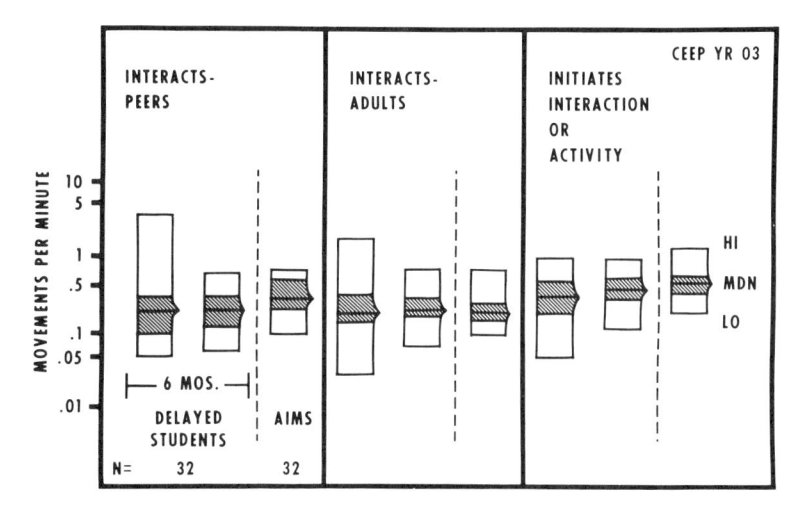

Figure 3. Median, full-range, and interquartile range (shaded area above and below median line) of behavioral frequencies for three classes of movements observed routinely for the children involved in the program. The "aim" frequencies reflect the behavior of normal classmates. These data were summarized at the end of the third year of the project.

strated growth in his or her linguistic production during the free-play situation. Fortunately, a similar analysis had been completed at the end of the first year of the project. However, we are now talking about a different group of children whose behavior was observed two years prior to those described in Figure 3. In addition, the data reported cover the period between the time the delayed child entered and the six months following entry. All the children included in the summary did not enter the program on the same date. Thus, more students are included in the "entry" group than in the "six months later" group. These vocal production comparisons are shown in Figure 4. Since we saw absolutely no tendency for more severely involved children to drop out of the integrated program after a few months, we are confident that the data presented in Figure 4 do not reflect a process of "selective attrition."

As Figure 4 shows, the median frequency of "nonword" sounds decreased for the delayed children over the six-month period, decreasing to almost exactly the level at which nondelayed children emit such utterances in free play. Over the same period, the delayed children's frequency of "words/phrases" (combined for presentation here) increased dramatically, though still below the level of the nondelayed peers. We must be cautious in drawing conclusions based on these data. Comparable "word/phrase" frequencies do not imply comparable linguistic sophistication. We can

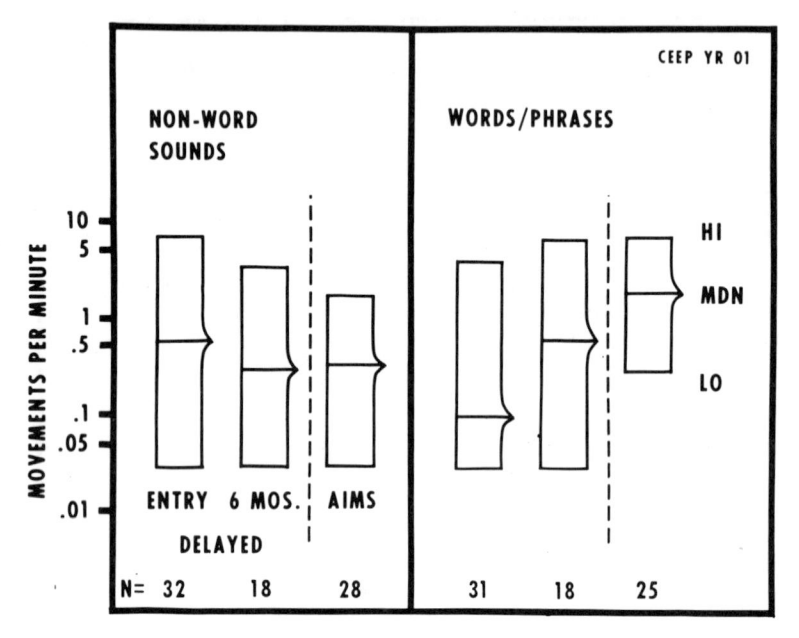

Figure 4. Frequencies of vocal production for delayed and nondelayed children involved in the integrated program. These data were summarized at the end of the first year of the project.

conclude, however, that the overall production of the class of behavior called "word/phrase" was becoming increasingly similar to that of the nondelayed students.

Perhaps the best that can be said about the data presented in this section is that they are suggestive. There are a wealth of untapped research possibilities contained in this new phenomenon called "integrated early education." As the quality of the research on the phenomenon continually improves, so will the quality of service delivery.

WHAT WE'VE LEARNED SO FAR

Integrated early education programs will be more likely to succeed if certain basic conditions are created and maintained.

Integration at All Levels

Integration naturally implies the physical and social co-mingling of children of wide-ranging competencies. It also requires the integration of all professional staff and the integration of the fundamental ideologies held by these essential persons.

Availability of Extraordinary but Complementary Resources

All of the usual special resource personnel available to handicapped children—the speech, physical, and occupational therapists, the psychologists, case managers, and specially trained teachers—can pursue their involvement with the children within the generic early education settings. The style of this involvement may have to be adjusted, however, to blend into a new environment. These extraordinary resource people must be even more sensitive to interactions and apparatus that may unnecessarily magnify the "differences" of the exceptional child. Externally worn hearing aids, braces, and helmets may be interpreted in strange ways by the child's normal mates. Simple demonstrations and explanations geared to the normal children's cognitive grasp can help them avoid stigmatizing interpretations. Minimizing the disruption of the regular center's schedule is also an important consideration for resource personnel.

Persons Responsible for the Growth of Developmentally Delayed Children

It may be nice to say that the child's developmental progress is the responsibility of all staff of the educational center, but it hardly ever works well that way. Although all persons can, indeed, support the child's progress, one person should be assigned responsibility for monitoring and planning each delayed child's development.

Quality of Early Education

Programs for young children can provide services ranging from only the bare essentials of custodial care to the highest level of support for development of the "total child." The quality of the program offered by an early childhood center enrolling handicapped children is a critical factor in their growth, since these children participate as fully as possible in the overall activities provided by the center. The same developmental limitations that more normal children may experience as a result of deficiencies in their day or preschool program will also affect the child who is handicapped. Conversely, a center that provides a variety of stimulating developmental experiences, and allows children to learn from these experiences according to their present level of competency, will be an appropriate educational setting for children with handicapping conditions. These variations in quality must be kept in mind when a center is being selected for the integration of developmentally delayed children. Put more simply, a program that is inadequate for "nondelayed" children will also be a poor choice for children whose development is delayed.

Perhaps the essential thing we have learned over the last several years is that to prepare handicapped children for the real world of adulthood, we must start by teaching them in and about the real world of childhood. And we expect that to prepare future nonhandicapped adults for a wider range of human diversity in their communities, a good place to start will be in a loving, co-supporting, early education environment where each child's own inevitable diversity is as much appreciated as it is in others.

REFERENCES CITED

Alpern, G. D., and Boll, T. J. 1972. Developmental Profile (manual). Aspen, Col.: Psychological Development Publications.

Barker, R. G., and Gump, P. 1964. Big School, Small School. Stanford: Stanford University Press.

Bell, P. B. 1977. A descriptive analysis of behaviors occurring between developmentally disabled and nondisabled preschoolers. Unpublished masters thesis, University of Nebraska at Omaha.

Bijou, S. W., and Baer, D. M. 1965. Child Development: Universal Stage of Infancy (Vol. 2). New York: Appleton-Century-Crofts.

Blatt, B. 1958. The physical, personality, and academic status of children who are mentally retarded attending special classes as compared with children who are mentally retarded attending regular classes. American Journal of Mental Deficiency, 62, 810-818.

Bricker, D., and Bricker, W. 1972. Toddler research and intervention project report: Year II. IMRID Behavioral Monograph 21, Institute on Mental Retardation and Intellectual Development, Nashville, George Peabody College.

Gardner, W. I. 1971. Behavior Modification in Mental Retardation. Chicago: Aldine-Atherton.

Gold, M. W. 1976. Task analysis: A statement and an example using acquisition and production of a complex assembly task by the retarded blind. Exceptional Children, 43, 78-84.

Guralnick, M. J. 1976. The value of integrating handicapped and nonhandicapped preschool children. American Journal of Orthopsychiatry, 46, 236-245.

Jordan, J. B., and Robbins, L. S. (Eds.). 1972. Let's Try Doing Something Else Kind of Thing: Behavioral Principles and the Exceptional Child. Arlington, Va: The Council for Exceptional Children.

Lesink, B. 1976. ENCOR, Nebraska. In R. B. Kugel and A. Shearer (Eds.), Changing Patterns in Residential Services for the Mentally Retarded (Rev. Ed.). President's Committee on Mental Retardation, Washington, D.C.: U.S. Government Printing Office.

Lindsley, O. R. 1964. Direct measurement and prosthesis of retarded behavior. Journal of Education, 147, 62-81.

Lindsley, O. R. 1971. Precision teaching in perspective. An interview with Ogden R. Lindsley. Teaching Exceptional Children, 3, 114-119.

Pennypacker, H. S., Koenig, C. H., and Lindsley, O. R. 1972. Handbook of the Standard Behavior Chart. Kansas City: Precision Media.

Peterson, C., Peterson, J., and Scriven, G. 1977. Peer imitation by nonhandicapped and handicapped preschoolers. Exceptional Children, 43, 223-224.

Richardson, S. A. 1970. Age and sex differences in values toward physical handicaps. Journal of Health and Social Behavior, 11, 207-214.

Robinson, C. C. 1976. Application of Piagetian sensorimotor concepts to assessment and curriculum for severely handicapped children. AAESPH Review, 1, 5-10.

Shearer, M., and Shearer, D. 1976. The Portage Project: A model for early childhood intervention. In T. D. Tjossem (Ed.), Intervention Strategies for High Risk Infants and Young Children. Baltimore: University Park Press.

Skarnulis, E. 1976. Less restrictive alternatives in residential service. AAESPH Review, 1, 40-84.

Snyder, L., Apolloni, T., and Cooke, T. P. 1977. Integrated settings at the early childhood level: The role of nonretarded peers. Exceptional Children, 43, 262-266.

Wolfensberger, W. 1972. The Principle of Normalization in Human Services. Toronto: National Institute on Mental Retardation.

AUTHOR INDEX

Abbott, M. S., 59, 69, 83
Abeson, A., 15, 24
Abt Associates, 234
Adams, J. A., 91, 95, 108
Akamatsu, T., 128, 137, 139
Alberto, P. A., 116, 142
Allen, K. E., 21, 24, 58, 59, 60, 68, 79, 120, 121, 140, 151, 160, 162
Allen, V. L., 34, 44, 45, 46, 48
Almy, M., 221, 235
Aloia, G. F., 9, 26
Alpern, G. D., 274, 286
Alrick, G., 195, 206
Altman, R., 43, 51
Amarel, M., 240, 259
Anastasiow, N. J., 94, 95, 97, 102, 108, 134, 140
Anderson, J. E., 53, 61, 79, 82
Apolloni, T., 6, 24, 55, 64, 65, 79, 83, 138, 144, 148, 150, 151, 152, 153, 154, 155, 161, 162, 163, 164, 165, 262, 287
Appleton, T., 97, 108
Arkans, J. R., 192, 206
Aronfreed, J., 44, 48
Auerbach, A. B., 224, 235
Ayers, D., 120, 142

Baer, D. M., 18, 25, 55, 56, 57, 58, 59, 60, 64, 66, 68, 69, 70, 79, 80, 81, 83, 87, 90, 97, 108, 121, 127, 135, 136, 137, 140, 142, 147, 160, 162, 273, 286
Bailey, J. S., 62, 80
Baldwin, C. P., 173, 189

Baldwin, A. L., 173, 189
Bandura, A., 18, 19, 24, 42, 43, 48, 87, 95, 96, 107, 108, 109, 121, 122, 125, 137, 140, 152, 162
Banet, B., 170, 187, 189
Barker, R. G., 34, 48, 266, 286
Barnes, K. E., 122, 140
Bartel, N. R., 5, 6, 24, 25
Barth, R., 240, 259
Baskin, A., 62, 81
Bates, E., 129, 140
Baumrind, D., 170, 189
Beaver, A. P., 53, 80
Bell, P. B., 261, 262, 286
Benning, P. M., 21, 24, 120, 140, 151, 162
Bereiter, C., 86, 89, 98, 109
Berger, M., 129, 142
Berkowitz, S., 152, 162
Berlund, R. M., 70, 84
Bierlein, M. W., 59, 66, 80
Bigner, J. J., 101, 109
Bijou, S. W., 55, 57, 80, 87, 147, 162, 273, 286
Billings, H. K., 174, 189
Birch, J., 116, 140, 218, 235
Blatt, B., 8, 24, 116, 140, 262, 286
Blesser, B., 216, 235
Bloom, L., 107, 109, 120, 140, 147, 162
Blott, J. P., 120, 143
Blumberg, L., 219, 235
Body, M. K., 66, 80
Bolick, N., 15, 24
Boll, T. J., 274, 286
Bond, J. T., 183, 189
Bowlby, J., 33, 48

289

Bowles, S., 88, 101, 109
Bradley, B., 60, 61, 69, 82, 121, 122, 143
Brawley, E. R., 57, 58, 81, 121, 142, 160, 163
Bricker, D. D., 7, 16, 17, 20, 24, 25, 105, 107, 109, 116, 136, 138, 140, 141, 148, 162, 163, 268, 286
Bricker, W. A., 3, 7, 16, 17, 20, 24, 25, 39, 50, 57, 61, 82, 105, 109, 116, 136, 138, 140, 141, 148, 162, 163, 268, 286
Brigham, T. A., 64, 80
Broen, P. A., 129, 130, 140
Bromley, D. B., 32, 50
Bronfenbrenner, U., 115, 140, 147, 163
Bronson, W. C., 29, 48
Broudy, H. S., 88, 109
Brown, R., 107, 109, 120, 140
Brownell, C. A., 37, 49
Bruininks, R. H., 174, 190, 213, 225, 230, 231, 236
Bruner, J. S., 32, 48, 106, 109, 122, 140, 219, 235
Budoff, M., 120, 140, 141
Buell, J. S., 59, 60, 61, 66, 68, 69, 79, 80, 121, 135, 140, 160, 163
Burgess, J. M., 64, 80
Burgess, R. L., 64, 80
Burke, M., 70, 77, 83
Burmeister, E., 59, 80
Bushell, D., 64, 83
Buss, W. G., 13, 14, 15, 26
Bussis, A. M., 240, 241, 259

Caldwell, B. M., 116, 141
Calvert, D. R., 213, 214, 235
Cane, V. A., 43, 51
Cantwell, D., 129, 142
Carlson, N. A., 108, 109
Carlson, P. M., 125, 137, 142
Carmichael, L., 53, 80
Carson, P. A., 216, 235
Carver, P. W., 221, 238
Cataldo, M. F., 55, 83, 121, 144
Charlesworth, R., 39, 48, 61, 80, 81, 137, 141

Chittenden, E. A., 240, 241, 259
Christy, P. R., 152, 163
Clark, B. S., 152, 163
Clifton, R., 97, 108
Coates, B., 41, 49, 59, 80, 152, 164
Coe, T. D., 70, 84
Cohen, J. S., 12, 25, 148, 163
Cohen, S. B., 88, 110
Conner, L. E., 207, 222, 235
Cooke, S. A., 64, 79, 153, 154, 155, 162, 163, 164
Cooke, T. P., 6, 24, 55, 64, 65, 79, 83, 138, 144, 148, 150, 151, 152, 153, 154, 155, 161, 162, 163, 164, 165, 262, 287
Cooper, B. P., 59, 69, 83
Cooper, M. L., 59, 66, 80
Coppersmith, G., 170, 189
Crawley, S., 152, 155, 157, 164
Cremin, L., 100, 103, 109
Cruikshank, W., 258, 259
Csapo, M., 152, 163

Dailey, R. F., 211, 236
Dakof, G., 148, 165, 173, 190, 234, 238
Dann, S., 28, 29, 49, 126, 141
Davis, H., 210, 213, 214, 225, 230, 235
Davis, J. E., 120, 141
Dawe, H. C., 53, 80
Debus, R. L., 43, 48
Deloria, D. J., 183, 190
Dennison, L., 17, 24
Derman, L., 247, 260
Des Jardins, C., 7, 25
Devalk, I., 192, 206
Devin-Sheehan, L. D., 44, 48
Devoney, C., 55, 64, 80, 122, 136, 141, 151, 152, 157, 163, 193, 206
DeWeerd, J., 109
Dewey, J., 87, 100, 103, 104
DeYoung, H., 12, 25, 148
Doke, L. A., 55, 80
Dollard, J., 43, 50, 152, 164
Doman, G., 97, 109
Doris, J., 5, 26

Author Index   291

Drummond, W. T., 21, 24, 120, 140, 151, 162
Dunn, L. M., 8, 25, 116, 141

Eckerman, C. O., 122, 136, 141, 151, 163
Edgerton, R. B., 9, 15, 25
Eisner, E. W., 240, 259
Elliott, L., 214, 235
Elliott, R., 43, 49
Engleman, S., 86, 89, 98, 99, 109
Epstein, A., 183, 189
Erber, N. P., 216, 235
Erikson, E. H., 96, 109
Ernst, M., 218, 238
Esveldt, K. C., 64, 80
Everett, P. M., 58, 59, 79, 160, 162
Evers-Pasquale, W., 118, 141
Ewing, A. W. G., 210, 235
Ewing, I. R., 210, 232
Eyman, R. K., 15, 25
Eysenck, H. J., 87, 109

Fagot, B. I., 39, 49
Feitelstein, D., 121, 141
Feldman, D. H., 90, 109
Feldman, R. S., 45, 46, 48
Ferguson, N., 34, 49
Filler, J. W., 20, 25, 116, 134, 141
Fouts, G. T., 19, 25
Foxwell, H. R., 59, 80
Fredericks, H. D. B., 195, 206
French, D., 37, 49
Freud, A., 28, 29, 49, 90, 96, 109, 126, 141
Freud, S., 92
Freyberg, J. T., 123, 141
Friedlander, B. Z., 240, 259
Furth, H. G., 103, 109

Gaeth, J. H., 215, 221, 235
Gage, M. A., 195, 206
Gagne, R. M., 87, 92, 97, 109
Gallagher, J. J., 94, 108
Garber, H., 147, 164
Gardner, W. I., 265, 286
Garner, R. T., 5, 25
Gartner, A., 138, 141

Gates, R. R., 215, 235
Gelman, R., 36, 51, 129, 130, 144
Gensley, J. T., 174, 190
Gesell, A., 101, 109
Geshuri, Y., 43, 49
Getz, S., 30, 49
Gewirtz, J. L., 19, 25, 54, 80
Giattino, J., 220, 235
Gibson, E. J., 94, 100, 107, 109
Ginsburg, H., 183, 189
Gintis, H., 88, 101, 109
Giolas, T., 221, 238
Glazer, J., 61, 81
Goetzinger, C. P., 215, 216, 235
Gold, H. A., 30, 49
Gold, M. W., 265, 286
Goldberg, S., 97, 108
Golden, M. M., 31, 50
Goldfein, M., 128, 145
Goldman, J. A., 36, 37, 49
Goldstein, S., 129, 143
Gomber, J., 157, 163
Gonso, J., 30, 49
Goodman, H., 120, 141
Goodman, L. V., 13, 25
Goodman, M. E., 174, 189
Gorelick, M. C., 221, 236
Gorham, K. A., 7, 25
Gottlieb, J., 120, 140, 141
Gottman, J., 30, 49
Graziano, W., 37, 49
Green, E. H., 53, 65, 81
Greenberg, P. 86, 109
Greenwood, C. R., 62, 81
Griffin, S., 153, 164
Gronlund, N. E., 231, 236
Grosser, D., 44, 49
Grossman, H. J., 130, 141, 193, 206
Grueneich, R., 36, 39, 50
Grusec, J., 18, 19, 24, 42, 48
Guess, D., 18, 25
Gump, P. V., 121, 141, 266, 286
Guralnick, M. J., 19, 21, 25, 43, 47, 49, 55, 64, 65, 80, 81, 107, 109, 115, 116, 118, 119, 120, 121, 122, 123, 124, 128, 130, 131, 132, 134, 136, 141, 148, 149, 150, 151, 152, 157, 163, 174, 189, 193, 206, 220, 236, 266, 286

Guskin, S. L., 5, 6, 24, 25

Hall, S. M., 43, 51
Hanners, B. A., 221, 236
Haring, N. G., 3, 25, 107, 109, 147, 164
Harlow, H. F., 30, 35, 49, 50, 51, 126, 144, 157, 165
Harris, F. R., 56, 57, 58, 59, 60, 61, 66, 68, 69, 79, 80, 81, 121, 135, 140, 160, 163
Harris, V. W., 62, 81
Harrison, R. H., 120, 141
Hart, B. M., 57, 58, 59, 60, 68, 79, 81, 121, 140, 160, 163
Hartley, R. E., 219, 236
Hartup, W. W., 6, 25, 36, 37, 38, 39, 41, 48, 49, 50, 61, 64, 80, 81, 83, 121, 122, 126, 136, 141, 151, 152, 159, 164
Harvey, O. J., 47, 51
Hass, K., 15, 24
Hawkins, D., 240, 259
Hayden, A., 107, 109, 147, 164
Hayes, L. A., 135, 142
Haynes, M. L., 102, 108
Hebb, D. O., 147, 164
Herber, R., 147, 164
Hegrenes, J. R., 129, 143
Held, M., 217, 136
Heller, H. B., 120, 142
Henker, B. A., 152, 165
Herbst, E. K., 66, 84, 160, 165
Hester, P., 135, 144, 160, 165
Hetherington, E. M., 53, 81
Hewitt, F. M., 94, 108
Hodges, W. L., 86, 102, 109
Hoffman, L. W., 53, 81
Hoffman, M. L., 53, 81
Hogan, J., 220, 233
Hogarty, P. S., 9, 26
Hohman, M., 170, 189
Hood, W. R., 47, 51
Hops, H., 135, 145
Hornung, M., 37, 39, 51
Horowitz, F., 61, 81
House, A. E., 78, 84
Howes, C., 136, 144, 174, 190
Howlin, P., 129, 142

Hunt, J. McV., 107, 111, 115, 138, 142, 147, 164
Hurlburt, N., 9, 26

Iaccobo, M., 152, 155, 157, 164
Iacino, R., 17, 24
Iano, R. P., 120, 142, 221, 238
Inhelder, B., 97, 103, 104, 110
Ironsmith, M., 128, 145
Isaacs, N., 219, 236
Ispa, J., 121, 138, 142
Jacobson, L., 9, 26
Jersild, A. T., 53, 65, 81
Johnson, C. A., 150, 164
Johnson, G. O., 249, 260
Johnson, M. W., 66, 81, 160, 164
Johnston, G. T., 63, 65, 68, 76, 81
Johnston, J. M., 63, 65, 68, 76, 81
Johnston, M. K., 59, 66, 81
Jolly, A., 32, 48
Jones, M. C., 125, 142
Jones, R. L., 9, 26, 116, 143, 174, 189
Jordan, J. B., 211, 236, 273, 286
Jordan, V., 195, 206
Joslin, N. H., 174, 190
Justen, J. E., 192, 206

Kallet, T., 240, 260
Kamii, C., 104, 110, 247, 260
Kanner, L., 116, 142
Karen, R. L., 41, 49
Karlan, G. R., 97, 111
Karnes, M. B., 86, 89, 93, 110, 115, 142, 147, 164
Katz, R. C., 150, 164
Kaufman, M. E., 116, 142
Kazdin, A. E., 128, 137, 142
Keasey, C. B., 31, 50
Keller, M. F., 125, 137, 142
Kelley, C. S., 59, 66, 81
Kennedy, P., 20, 21, 25, 174, 190, 213, 225, 230, 231, 236
Kent, R., 68, 82, 159, 164
Keogh, W. J., 122, 143
Kerr, M. M., 58, 83, 118, 144
Kirk, S. A., 147, 164
Kirkland, K. D., 44, 51

Author Index

Kirp, D. L., 13, 14, 15, 26
Klein, J. W., 85, 110, 219, 236
Knoblock, P., 249, 260
Kobasigawa, A., 42, 50
Koegel, R. L., 71, 81, 82, 121, 143
Koenig, C. H., 273, 287
Kohlberg, L., 247, 260
Kohler, M., 138, 141
Kohn, M., 61, 82
Konner, M., 34, 50
Kopfstein, D., 40, 50
Kozloff, M., 121, 143
Kupers, C. J., 152, 162
Kuriloff, P. J., 13, 14, 15, 26
Kutz, S. L., 122, 136, 141, 151, 163

Lavatelli, C. S., 101, 110
Lawrence, E. A., 174, 190
Lawser, S. A., 183, 190
Lawton, I., 247, 260
Lazar, A. L., 174, 190
Leblane, J. M., 59, 68, 83, 122, 143
Lee, L. C., 31, 38, 50, 59, 66, 80
Lesink, B., 267, 286
Leske, G., 70, 84
Leuba, C., 53, 82
Levak, L., 195, 206
Levin, H., 96, 110
Lewis, M., 33, 50, 53, 82
Liff, S., 213, 230, 236
Lilly, M. S., 8, 26
Lindsley, O. R., 95, 110, 264, 273, 286, 287
Ling, A. H., 220, 236
Ling, D., 220, 236
Lippitt, R., 44, 49
Lipsitt, L. P., 5, 26
Littman, R. A., 39, 50, 57, 61, 182
Livesley, W. J., 32, 50
Loevinger, J., 90, 94, 96, 102, 110
Long, J. S., 71, 82
Lord, F. E., 88, 110
Lortie, D. C., 87, 88, 110
Lougee, M. D., 36, 37, 39, 50
Lovaas, O. I., 71, 82
Lucas, T., 122, 143
Luper, H., 70, 84
Luterman, D. M., 213, 215, 230

Maccoby, E., 96, 110
MacDonald, J. D., 120, 143
MacMillan, D. L., 6, 9, 25, 26, 116, 143
Mahoney, G. J., 120, 127, 129, 133, 134, 143
Mahoney, M., 107, 110
Maioni, T. L., 37, 39, 51
Mansergh, G. P., 95, 97, 108, 134, 140
Marchant, R., 129, 142
Markey, F. V., 53, 65, 81, 82
Marshall, H. M., 43, 50
Marshall, H. R., 61, 82
Marshall, N. R., 129, 143
Martin, B., 101, 110
Martin, E. W., 9, 26, 116, 143, 208, 209, 236
Mason, M., 37, 50
Matthews, J., 94, 108
Matz, R. D., 183, 189
McCall, R. B., 9, 26, 122, 145
McCandless, B. R., 61, 82, 86, 102, 109
McCarthy, D., 183, 190
McCarty, T., 153, 164
McCauley, R., 20, 21, 25, 213, 225, 230, 231, 236
McConnel, F., 211, 213, 214, 230, 236, 237
McGettigan, J. F., 120, 142, 221, 238
McNeil, D., 127, 143
Meisels, S. J., 243, 246, 247, 260
Menlove F., 18, 19, 24, 42, 48
Mercer, J. R., 87, 108, 110, 116, 143
Meyer, E. L., 148, 164
Meyers, C. E., 116, 143
Michaeli, O., 121, 141
Miller, J. F., 16, 26, 120, 143
Miller, N. E., 43, 50, 152, 164
Miller, R. M., 122, 143
Miller, R. S., 43, 50
Mitchell, G., 157, 163
Mlodnosky, L. B., 101, 102, 110
Moerk, E. L., 129, 133, 143
Monroe, J. D., 174, 190
Moore, S. G., 27, 39, 49, 56, 82
Morehead, A., 104, 110

Author Index

Morehead, D. M., 104, 110
Morris, W. N., 43, 50
Mueller, E., 122, 143
Murphy, L. B., 53, 65, 66, 82
Mussen, P. H., 53, 82

Neisworth, J. T., 211, 237
Nix, G. W., 215, 237
Nordquist, V. M., 59, 60, 61, 69, 70, 71, 72, 74, 82, 84, 121, 122, 143
Northcott, W., 20, 25, 211, 213, 214, 215, 217, 218, 221, 223, 225, 226, 231, 232, 236, 237
Novack, M. A., 35, 50, 128, 145

O'Conner, E. F., 187, 190
O'Conner, R., 42, 50, 65, 82, 122, 125, 126, 135, 137, 143, 152, 164
O'Leary, K. D., 68, 82, 159, 164
Orpert, R. E., 174, 190

Page, R., 7, 25
Palmer, R., 248, 260
Parke, R. D., 43, 51
Parrish, V., 99, 111
Parten, M. B., 37, 39, 50, 53, 82, 122, 123, 143, 144, 175, 190, 194, 206
Parton, D. A., 18, 19, 26
Patterson, G. R., 39, 49, 50, 61, 82
Paul-Brown, D., 130, 131, 132, 134, 142
Pearl, A., 88, 110
Peck, C. A., 154, 155, 164
Peifer, M. R., 44, 50
Pennypacker, H. S., 273, 287
Peters, R. S., 240, 260
Peterson, C., 270, 287
Peterson, J., 270, 287
Peterson, R. F., 64, 82
Pettis, E., 7, 25
Phillips, E. L., 62, 80
Piaget, J., 30, 50, 87, 89, 96, 97, 103, 104, 106, 110, 219, 247, 248, 260

Pinkston, E. M., 59, 68, 83
Polansky, N., 44, 49
Pollack, D., 218, 230, 237, 238
Popham, W. E., 149, 164
Porter, R. H., 152, 155, 157, 164, 221, 238
President's Committee on Mental Retardation, 6, 26
Proud, G. O., 215, 216, 236

Quilitch, H. R., 55, 66, 83, 121, 122, 144, 160, 165

Ramsey, B., 152, 155, 157, 164
Rankhorn, B., 222, 238
Rappaport, D., 90, 110
Rasmussen, B., 30, 49
Ray, J. S., 121, 144, 152, 155, 157, 165
Read, K. H., 57, 83
Redd, W. H., 135, 144
Reese, H. W., 5, 26
Reese, N. M., 59, 68, 83
Reissman, F., 138, 141
Resnick, L. B., 240, 260
Reynolds, N. J., 57, 58, 81, 121, 142, 160, 163
Rhodes, W. C., 5, 26
Richardson, S. A., 262, 287
Ridgway, L., 247, 260
Rincover, A., 71, 81, 121, 143
Risley, T. R., 55, 63, 66, 79, 80, 83, 92, 108, 121, 122, 144, 160, 165
Rister, A., 213, 230, 238
Robbins, L. S., 273, 286
Robinson, C. C., 20, 25, 116, 141, 275, 287
Robinson, H. B., 8, 26
Robinson, N.M., 8, 26
Roff, M., 31, 50
Rogers, V. R., 240, 260
Rolf, J. E., 31, 50
Rondal, J. A., 129, 144
Rosekrans, M. A., 44, 50
Rosen, B., 5, 25
Rosenblum, L. A., 33, 50, 53, 82
Rosenthal, R., 9, 26
Rosenthal, T. L., 18, 26

Ross, A., 224, 238
Ross, D. M., 43, 48, 152, 165
Ross, M., 213, 214, 218, 220, 221, 235, 238
Ross, S. A., 43, 48, 152, 165
Rubenstein, J., 136, 144
Rubin, K. H., 37, 39, 51, 55, 64, 80, 122, 136, 141, 151, 152, 157, 163, 193, 206
Russell, D. H., 102, 110
Rutherford, G., 18, 25
Rutter, M., 129, 142

Sager, G. O., 39, 49
Sagor, M., 5, 26
Sailor, W., 18, 25
Sajwaj, T., 70, 77, 83, 135, 144
Sarason, S. B., 5, 26
Sattler, J. M., 183, 190
Scheiber, B., 7, 25
Schumacher, E. F., 218, 238
Scriven, M., 10, 11, 15, 26, 258, 260, 270, 287
Sears, R. R., 96, 110
Seely, P. B., 120, 127, 129, 133, 134, 143
Sells, S. B., 31, 50
Selman, R. L., 32, 51
Shatz, M., 36, 51, 129, 130, 144
Sheare, J. B., 6, 26
Shearer, D., 275, 287
Shearer, M., 275, 287
Sherif, C. W., 47, 51
Sherif, M., 47, 51
Sherman, J. A., 62, 64, 69, 79, 80, 81, 83
Sherman, M., 118, 141
Shores, R. E., 58, 83, 118, 135, 144, 153, 160
Shotel, J. R., 221, 238
Sibley, S. A., 59, 69, 83
Silverman, S. R., 213, 214, 235
Silverstein, A. B., 15, 25
Simmons, J. Q., 71, 82
Simmons-Martin, A. A., 216, 220, 238
Sisk, D. A., 174, 189
Skarnulis, E., 267, 287
Skinner, B. F., 55, 83, 95, 110
Sloane, H. N., 62, 81

Slobin, D. I., 122, 144
Smith, B. O., 88, 110
Smith, E., 95, 111
Smith, J. O., 192, 206
Smith, R. A., 20, 25, 116, 141
Snow, C. E., 129, 130, 144
Snyder, L., 55, 64, 65, 83, 148, 165, 262, 287
Solnit, A. J., 225, 238
Solomon, R. G., 41, 51
Solomon, R. W., 62, 83
Sontag, E., 8, 26
Sperling, K., 70, 84
Spock, B., 101, 111
Spradlin, J. E., 97, 111
Stanbaugh, E. E., 78, 84
Spicker, H. H., 86, 102, 107
Stark, M. J., 224, 238
Stern, V. W., 218, 238
Stingle, K. G., 19, 25
Stoddard, P., 59, 60, 61, 66, 69, 80, 121, 135, 140, 160
Strain, P. S., 58, 83, 118, 122, 135, 138, 144, 154, 160, 161, 165
Strichart, S. S., 19, 20, 26, 137, 144, 152, 165
Stuckless, E. R., 215, 238
Suomi, S. J., 35, 51, 126, 144, 157, 165
Swift, J. W., 54, 57, 83
Sylva, K., 32, 48

TADS (Technical Assistance Development System), 91, 98, 111
Talkington, L. W., 43, 51
Taylor, J., 245, 260
Taylor, K. W., 57, 83
Teeter, N., 70, 84
Teska, J. A., 147, 164
Thelen, M. H., 44, 51, 128, 137, 139
Thomas, M., 70, 84
Thompson, C. L., 59, 80
Thorndike, R. L., 9, 26
Tikten, S., 61, 83
Timbers, G. D., 62, 80
Timm, M. A., 58, 83, 160, 165
Tjossem, T. D., 115, 144
Tolman, E. C., 96, 111

Tremblay, A., 151, 152, 155, 157, 162, 164
Turner, K. I., 58, 59, 79, 160, 162
Twardosz, S., 55, 70, 77, 83, 121, 135, 144
Tyler, R., 95, 111

Ulfelder, L. S., 148, 165, 173, 190, 234, 238
Updegraff, R., 66, 84, 160, 165
Uzgiris, I. C., 107, 111

Valletutti, P., 221, 238
van Uden, A. A., 216, 219, 238
Vasta, R., 43, 49
Vergason, G. A., 148, 164
Vincent-Smith, L., 20, 26, 116, 141
Vygotsky, L. S., 94, 106

Wadlow, M., 195, 206
Wadsworth, B. J., 103, 111
Wahler, R. G., 40, 41, 51, 59, 62, 68, 70, 71, 78, 82, 83, 84, 121, 122, 123, 144
Waldner, D. N., 19, 25
Walker, H. M., 135, 145
Walker, V. S., 120, 142
Walters, R. H., 43, 51
Warfield, G. J., 148, 165, 211, 238
Watson, M. W., 19, 25
Watson, T. J., 217, 238
Weber, L., 105, 111, 240, 245, 260
Webster, C. D., 123, 145
Weikart, D., 86, 89, 94, 95, 99, 100, 115, 145, 167, 168, 170, 171, 183, 189
Weinstein, G. W., 218, 238
Weintraub, S., 121, 141
Weisler, A., 122, 145
Wetherby, B., 97, 111
Whalen, R. J., 148, 152, 165
Whatley, J. L., 122, 136, 141, 151, 163
White, B. J., 47, 51
White, R. W., 246, 260
Whitehurst, G. J., 64, 82, 128, 145
Whiting, B. B., 30, 51
Whiting, J. W. M., 30, 51
Wiegerink, R., 99, 111, 122, 144, 160, 165, 183, 190
Williams, S. M., 20, 21, 25, 213, 225, 231, 236
Winett, R. A., 249, 260
Winischel, J. F., 174, 190
Wintre, M. G., 123, 145
Wolf, M. M., 55, 56, 57, 59, 60, 62, 66, 68, 70, 79, 80, 81, 90, 97, 108, 121, 127, 136, 137, 140
Wolfensberger, W., 116, 145, 148, 192, 206, 263, 287
Wright, H. F., 34, 48
Wright, R. J., 240, 260
Wynne, S., 148, 165, 173, 190, 234, 238

Yoder, D. E., 16, 26, 120, 143

Zajonc, R. B., 138, 145
Zimmerman, B. J., 18, 26
Zook, E., 39, 49

SUBJECT INDEX

Achievement, academic, of hearing-impaired 3rd and 4th graders from integrated programs, 231
Age, chronological, and studies of peer interactions, 54
Aggression, peer, 57–59
Alpern-Boll developmental profile data, 278–281
Attitudes toward handicapped children
 effects on parents, 7
 effects of peer interaction on change of, 6
 and integration of handicapped and nonhandicapped preschoolers, 5–8
Audiologist, educational, for integrated nursery school, 220–221
Autistic child
 behavioral analysis of an, in integrated preschool program, 71–77
 producing behavioral changes, 71–74
 results of intervention, 74–76
Avoidance, severe, reducing, through peer contact, 126–127

Behavior
 child, direct observation of, in natural settings, 281–284
 self-directed, reducing, through peer contact, 126–127
 social and emotional analysis of, 178–180
 naturalistic observations of, in integrated classrooms, 173–183
 social play and language, promoting, 193–203
Behavior covariation and peer interaction, 69–71
Behavior modification program, 98–99
Behavioral analysis
 of an autistic child in integrated preschool program, 71–77
 of peer interactions, 53–84
Bitterness of parents of handicapped because of others' attitudes, 7

Child development
 implications of integration into regular nursery school, for hearing-impaired, 217–220
 and integrated early childhood intervention programs, 89–93
 in integrated settings, 278–284
 normal, as model in integrated early childhood intervention programs, 100–102
 opportunities for, in integrated settings, 136–138
 and peer relations, 29–31
Classroom structure in integrated early childhood intervention programs, 94
Cognitive development model of integrated early childhood intervention programs, 103–105

297

Cognitive learning model of integrated early childhood intervention programs, 105–107
Communication
  adaptive, in integrated preschool, 128–133
  by hearing-impaired in integrated nursery sschool, 219–220
Communication adjustments by peers, value of, 132–133
Competence, enhancement of, as goal of early education of handicapped, 264–265
Cost effectiveness of integrated nursery school, 229
Counseling, family, in integrated nursery school, 224–225
Court decision on integration of handicapped and nonhandicapped preschoolers, 12
Curriculum structure of cognitively oriented, integrated programs, 168–170

Day care setting, normal, integrating moderately and severely handicapped preschooler into, 191–206
Deaf, see Preschooler, hearing-impaired
Development, child, see Child development

Eastern Nebraska Community Office of Retardation, 267–277
Education
  early
    developmental approach to, 16–18
    elasticity of settings, 266–267
    marriage of generic and special services, 261–287
  open, see Open education

Education of All Handicapped Children Act, 13–15
Educators, recommendations to, on integrated programming, 159–161
Eliot-Pearson summary of tutorial work, 252–253
ENCOR, 267–277
Environment
  educational and therapeutic, integrated preschool as, 115–145
  heuristic, in open education, 243–248
Ethics, arguments based on, for integration of handicapped and nonhandicapped preschoolers, 4–11

Funding of integrated preschool project, 269

Grouping of children in integrated programs, 61
Guidance, family, in integrated nursery school, 224–225

Handicapped
  integration with nonhandicapped in preschool years, rationale for, 3–26
  normalization of early education, 263
  segregation of, 8–10
Hearing-impaired preschooler, see Preschooler, hearing-impaired

Imitation learning and integration of handicapped and nonhandicapped preschoolers, 18–20
Individualization
  experimental preschool as framework for, 117–118

Subject Index 299

and program objectives of open education, 242–243
Instructional strategies, alternative, in integrated preschool, 134–136
Integration
　at all levels, 284
　approaches to facilitate, in preschool, 120–121
　of children with special needs, and open education, 239–260
　educational effects, 157–158
　of handicapped preschool children within a cognitively oriented program, 167–190
　of handicapped and nonhandicapped preschoolers
　　legal-legislative arguments, 11–16
　　psychological-educational arguments, 16–22
　　rationale for, 3–26
　　social-ethical arguments, 4–11
　　some approaches tried in the past, 20–22
　of hearing-impaired preschooler, 207–238
　social, programming for, 151–156
Intervention, early educational, as cornerstone of individualized services, 209–210
Intervention programs, integrated early childhood
　behavioral model, 97–100
　strategies and models for, 85–111

Labeling and segregation of handicapped child, 8–9
Language of hearing-impaired preschooler, 214–215
Language interaction in integrated preschool, expectations from research on, 129–130

Language usage in integrated preschool, 127–128
Legislation on integration of handicapped and nonhandicapped preschoolers, 12–16

Mainstreaming
　dilemma of, 258–259
　the handicapped child, 208–209
　and open education, 249–257
Materials, use of, in integrated programs, 160
McCarthy Scales of Children's Abilities, 183
Models, peers as, 41–45
Moral development and peer interaction, 30–31
Motivation of hearing-impaired in integrated nursery school, 219

Nursery school
　integrated
　　example of, 222–229
　　research data on, 229–231
　　resources for, 220–222
　integration of hearing-impaired children into, 217–220
　parent/child, 227
　placement of hearing-impaired with nonhandicapped peers, 226
　prekindergarten, 227–228

Open education
　and education of children with special needs, 239–260
　grouping of children, 247–248
　individualization and program objectives, 242–243
　and mainstreaming, 249–257
　materials, 245–247
　model of teacher-child interaction, 240–242
　program elements, 249–252
　program in action, 250–257
　space, 244–245
　time, 245

300 Subject Index

Parents
    as components of integrated nursery school, 224—226
    deaf, of deaf child, 217
    form of participation in integrated preschool program, 271
    hearing, of deaf child, 216—217
    and integrated programs in Sonoma, Calif., 150—151
Peer aggression, 57—59
Peer imitation
    conditions affecting, 43—44
    by delayed toddlers and preschoolers, 153—156
    by nondelayed children, 158—159
    training, 152—156
Peer influence, mechanisms of, 38—46
Peer interaction
    the behavior covariation question, 69—71
    behavioral approach to analysis of, 53—84
    and change of attitudes toward handicapped, 6
    and child development, 29—31
    the durability question, 68
    and group tensions, 46—47
    peer attention procedures to develop and maintain, 61—63
    peer modeling procedures to develop and maintain, 63—65
    physical and spatial events to develop and maintain, 65—67
    and processes of socialization, 27—51
    reducing severe avoidance and self-directed behaviors through, 126—127
    same- and mixed-age, 33—38
    the setting generality question, 68—69
    social, generalization of, 135—136
    social play, in integrated preschool, 121—125
    teacher attention procedures to develop and maintain, 56—61
Peer modeling, 41—45
    of advanced speech in integrated preschool, 127—128
    procedures to develop and maintain peer interactions, 63—65
Peer rearing, example of, 28—29
Peer reinforcement, 38—41
Peers
    as socializing agents, 31—33
    as therapeutic agents in integrated preschool, 125—127
Peer tutoring, 45—46
Peer withdrawal, 59—61
Perception of the learner in integrated early childhood intervention programs, 95—96
Play
    of hearing-impaired in integrated nursery school, 219
    in integrated early childhood intervention programs, 94
Poverty programs, models of integrated early childhood intervention programs based on, 86—89
Preschool
    experimental, as framework for individualization and togetherness, 117—118
    integrated
        adaptive communication in, 128—133
        alternative instructional strategies, 134—136
        curriculum components, 119—120
        developmental opportunities in, 136—138
        as educational and therapeutic environment, 115—145

Subject Index

effects on nonhandicapped children, 138
evaluation of children's abilities in, 183–187
language usage in, 127–128
nonhandicapped peers as potential resources, 121–133
peers as therapeutic agents, 125–127
structural aspects, 118–120
Preschoolers
handicapped, integration within a cognitively oriented program, 167–190
hearing-impaired
categories and labels, 213–214
channel selection for primary reception of information, 215–216
deaf parents of, 217
first language of, 214–215
hearing parents of, 216–217
historical perspective, 210–211
integrating, 207–238
integration in regular nursery schools, 217–220
myths and stereotypes, 212–213
social status of, in regular classrooms, 230–231
integration of handicapped and nonhandicapped, rationale for, 3–26
moderately and severely handicapped, integrating into normal day care setting, 191–206
Preschool handicapped models, dimensions of, 89–96
Program, cognitively oriented classroom interactions, 175–178
curriculum structure, 168–170
daily evaluation and planning, 170
daily routine, 169–170
gains of handicapped children, 186–187
integration of handicapped preschoolers, within, 167–190
room arrangement, 168–169
Programming
individualized, barriers to, 211–212
integrated
implications and recommendations, 156–162
at infant, toddler, and preschool levels, 147–165
in Sonoma, Calif., 148–151
for social integration, 151–156
Public schools, closed structure of, 87–89

Rationale for integration of handicapped and nonhandicapped preschool children, 3–26
Reinforcement
in integrated early childhood intervention programs, 91–94
peer, 38–41
teacher, in integrated programs, 160
Research on integrated nursery schools, 229–231
Resources
efficient and effective allocation of, for both handicapped and nonhandicapped children, 10–11
for integrated nursery school, 220–222

Segregation of handicapped child, 8–10

Selection of children for integrated preschool program, 269
Self-attitude of handicapped child, effect of placement in regular vs. special class, 6
Service systems, human, assumptions and values, 262–267
Socialization, processes of, and peer interaction, 27–51
Social play interactions in integrated preschool, 121–125
Sonoma, Calif., integrated programs in, 148–151
Speech, advanced, peer modeling of, 127–128
Stigma, reduction of, as goal of early education of handicapped, 264–265

Teacher
  attention procedures to develop and maintain, 56–61
  of hearing-impaired children, 221–222
  for integrated nursery school, 221
  reinforcement from, in integrated programs, 160

Teaching session, individual parent/child, in integrated nursery school, 225–226
Tensions, group, and peer relations, 46–47
Togetherness, experimental preschool as framework for, 117–118
Training
  in-service
    in integrated early childhood intervention programs, 94–95
    for integrated nursery school teachers, 226–227
  peer imitation, 152–156
  of teachers for integrated nursery schools, 231–233
Tutoring by peers, 45–46

Verbal interactions among handicapped and nonhandicapped children in integrated preschool, 130–132

Withdrawal, peer, 59–61

MAY 14 1979
DISCHARGED 1979
JUN 27 1979
OCT 1979
DISCHARGED
JUL 16 1979
DISCHARGED
DISCHARGED 1981
MAY - 2 1980
DISCHARGED
APR 1980
DISCHARGED
DISCHARGED
MAR 1981
DISCHARGED
DISCHARGED
APR 24 1980
DISCHARGED 1982
DISCHARGED 1991
DISCHARGED
FEB 1985
JUL 4 1985
APR 17 1999
DISCHARGED
JUL 19 1998
AUG 10 1999
DEC 8 1998
DISCHARGED